MW00816781

Compact of the Republic

The League of States and the Constitution

Compact of the Republic

The League of States and the Constitution

David Benner

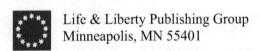 Life & Liberty Publishing Group
Minneapolis, MN 55401

www.davebenner.com

ISBN: 0692484264
ISBN-13: 978-0692484265

"*Resolved*, That the several States composing the United States of America, are not united on the principle of unlimited submission to their General Government; but that, by a compact under the style and title of a Constitution for the United States, and of amendments thereto, they constituted a General Government for special purposes – delegated to that government certain definite powers, reserving, each State to itself, the residuary mass of right to their own self-government; and that whensoever the General Government assumes undelegated powers, its acts are unauthoritative, void, and of no force."

-Thomas Jefferson, *Kentucky Resolutions of 1798*

Contents

Part I: The Genesis of the Compact

Part II: How the Compact Has Been Dismantled

Part I
The Genesis of the Compact

Chapter 1

The Compact:
An Outlawed Perspective

The states predated the federal government. This is an indisputable truth, but one that is often deemed irrelevant in the modern age. Even as many mischaracterize the federal government as a superlative entity that holds supremacy over the American states, the true genesis of the federal government reveals a strikingly different intention. To counter prevailing myths regarding the proper structure of the American union, this book asserts that the states created the federal government through a legal arrangement between multiple sovereign parties. Secondly, it refutes the common notion that United States government was formed by "one American people" in the aggregate. Instead, both the United States Constitution and the union it established were built by several independent, sovereign states.

A proper understanding of how our civil foundations came to be should be the paramount objective of all students of the founding era. Even so, modern Americans are rarely taught of the true origins of political authority in the United States. Though some casual observers possess a basic understanding of federalism – the division and balance of power between the central and local governments – many are unaware of the reasoning behind such partitions of authority.

History reveals the decentralized orientation of the American union, where the states were intended to play a greater political role in an average person's life than the central government. However, the average citizen behaves as if the inverse were true. Routinely looking to the federal government to address modern political ailments of all types, many perceive the United States as a unitary, centralized nation. As a result, nationalist inclinations that run antithetical to the intentions of the founders are unconsciously adopted by most Americans. To dispel the myths that have supported and prolonged this tendency, we must first look to the origins of the states and the union they created.

As this work aims to demonstrate, the antecedents that came before the Constitution add vital context to this matter, and provide a lasting memory of triumphs and failures in the pursuit of individual rights and public happiness. Historical circumstances that are relevant to this account will be covered with particular prominence. As Patrick Henry declared in a famous oratory, the candid scholar has only the "the lamp of experience" as a guide. Presciently, Henry admitted that humanity had "no way of judging of the future but by the past."[1] Accordingly, without the knowledge of history, no society can adequately understand their own political systems, or avoid the repetition of conditions that have endangered liberty.

The history of our republic recognizes an era that once properly accepted that the Constitution was a compact – a contract between sovereign entities. These states, the creators of the federal framework, transferred a small subset of powers to the federal government, retaining the remainder as independent bodies. In the Massachusetts ratification convention, Theophilus Parsons insisted that the Constitution established a government wherein "the people divest themselves of nothing," adding that "the government and powers which Congress can administer, are the mere result of a compact made by the people with each other."[2] Indeed, the Constitution was a sovereign agreement between the several states.

This reality has been continually distorted throughout American history, where various events were supposed to have "settled" the issue of nationalism over federalism forever. However, the original, unmolested, decentralized conception of the American union remains relevant despite post-ratification circumstances and unconstitutional precedents. Even as the Federalists implemented the national bank, Andrew Jackson threatened force against South Carolina, and the Whigs promised to deliver a host of unconstitutional programs, the originally ratified Constitution distinctly elevated federalism over nationalism.

Even though it is now sometimes considered unconventional or subversive to defend the original, decentralized vision of the federal republic, this propensity was once widely accepted. Regardless of modern political trends, the primacy of states was long considered an unmistakable political fact. In actuality, the very product of the Philadelphia Convention of 1787 considered the states as the foundations of the American political system. As Oliver Wolcott of Connecticut put it, the states were the "pillars which uphold the general system." According to Thomas Jefferson, they were the "surest bulwarks against antirepublican tendencies."[3]

In the contemporary, a proper comprehension of the Constitution is often hindered by an improper scope of research. A primary reason for this is that the words of those that drafted the Constitution in Philadelphia are generally overemphasized by academia and legal courses, whereas the way in which the states received the document are routinely minimized. Admittedly, the records kept during the Philadelphia Convention have concrete importance, but they do not exemplify the Constitution to its fullest extent. Truthfully, the explanations given in the state ratification conventions are more integral to the original understanding of the document. Moreover, the Constitution didn't become a legally binding document until it was ratified by nine states, so a candid student must look there to discover the framework's true meaning and purpose.

When the document was pending their endorsement, James Madison described the Constitution as a compact between states, where each polity considered membership in the federal union independently:

That it [the adoption of the Constitution] will be a federal and not a national act...the act of the people, as forming so many independent States, not as forming one aggregate Nation – is obvious from this single consideration: that it is to result neither from the decision of a majority of the people of the Union, nor from that of a majority of the States. It must result from the unanimous assent of the several States that are parties to it, differing no otherwise from their ordinary assent than in its being expressed, not by the legislative authority, but by that of the people themselves.[4]

Holding to this view in old age, the Virginian wrote that the document was ratified by the people "as embodied into the several States" and therefore was "made by the States." He called this notion an "undisputed fact."[5] The significance of Madison's observation cannot be overstated, because the identity of the union and the rightful balance of power between the states and federal government hinges upon it.

Divergent from this understanding of the union, an opposing view has achieved more legal prominence. This nationalist view contends that the states are largely subordinate to a central government with virtually unlimited power. It rests such a deduction on the argument that ratification was a national effort by a singular American populace as a whole, justifying a system in which the authority of the federal government supersedes that of the states. Some support this view by pointing out that some of the founders concocted plans to create a powerful national authority that had vested power over the states. In actuality, these proposals fundamentally failed to sway delegates at the Philadelphia Convention, and were never even considered by the states.

Hardly the product of a central entity, the true constitutional apparatus was born from rigorous debate and deliberation in the states. The states – as the architects of the union – formed a general government out of convenience, and remained as self-determining political units. This was the chief way the supporters of the Constitution explained the document, and the manner by which it was accepted by the state ratification conventions. Despite the current prominence of the orthodox nationalist view, there was no systematic nationalist theory until the 1833 commentaries of Supreme Court Justice Joseph Story emerged.[6] Because Story's account was written and published a full generation after the document was drafted and ratified, the perspective that the Constitution was a compact was the only way it was understood for decades.

Story's elaborate interpretation to the contrary was published in his most famous work, *Commentaries on the Constitution of the United States*. A pupil of John Marshall, the longest tenured and most influential Chief Justice of the Supreme Court, Story also made a significant impression upon American jurisprudence. Originally a Jeffersonian Republican, he was appointed to the high court by James Madison. Ironically, Madison had hoped the Story appointment would help restore a philosophical balance to the court and counteract the inclinations of Marshall, an unparalleled Federalist partisan. Once on the Supreme Court, however, Story embraced Marshall's nationalist understanding of the Constitution and built upon it.

Today, Story receives substantial praise from those of all political stripes. Ronald Reagan's Attorney General, Edwin Meese, once proclaimed that the jurist "personified the republican commitment to the rule of law and fundamental notions of natural law and justice."[7] One prominent law professor lauded Story's legal contributions as "tremendous achievements" that "entitled him to be ranked as a jurist of the first rank."[8] Story County, Iowa, is named in his honor. At the prestigious Harvard University, where he studied and eventually taught law, a dormitory bears his name. Story's construal of the Constitution introduced millions to the nationalist narrative, and was wholly accepted by prominent antebellum politicians such as Henry Clay and Daniel Webster. It would be hard to dispute that today's political culture in Washington, D.C., draws heavily from Story's conclusions.

Story's seminal work asserts that the Constitution was written by and adopted for a singular group of American people, and was therefore the product of a nationalist design. He contended that the states voluntarily relinquished their sovereign powers to create a national government that stood in stark contrast with that of the Articles of Confederation. Story claimed that "none of its advocates [in the ratification conventions] pretended to deny, that its design was to establish a national government, as contradistinguished from a mere league or treaty, however they might oppose the suggestions, that it was a consolidation of the states." He cited the preamble's usage of "We the People" as demonstrative proof of this idea, and posited that there was "nowhere found upon the face of the constitution any clause, intimating it to be a compact, or in anywise providing for its interpretation, as such."[9] Additionally, Story disputed that those who ratified the Constitution opposed the presence of "implied" powers, which would permit authority not explicitly granted in the document:

And this leads us to remark, in the next place, that in the interpretation of the constitution there is no solid objection to implied powers. Had the faculties of man been competent to the framing of a system of government, which would leave nothing to implication, it cannot be doubted, that the effort would have been made by the framers of our constitution. The fact, however, is otherwise.[10]

Pointing to the omission of the word "expressly" in the text of the Tenth Amendment, Story attested that implied powers could be utilized at the behest of Congress.

On each of these points, Story was mistaken. Many representatives within the state ratification conventions denied that the Constitution meant to establish a national, consolidated government, and their explanations will be explored in this work. Even the Federalist advocates of the Constitution, who favored a more powerful central government, dismissed such claims during the ratification struggle. In opposition to Story's contention, the Constitution was commonly referred to as a compact by many in the founding generation, including James Madison, who is often given the most credit for the document. The preamble's text was originally written as "We the States," after which was an itemized list of the several states. This format was modified to its eventual form because it was deemed impossible to determine, with certainty, which states would ratify. Doing otherwise would have appeared presumptive to the states considering adoption, perhaps leading such governments to believe the delegates in Philadelphia had taken their approval for granted.[11] By "We the People" – the document clearly meant the people of the several states that chose to ratify it.

In like fashion, Story incorrectly postulated that the Constitution contained no objection to implied powers. Conversely, the document was exhaustively described as a model through which the general government could exercise only the powers listed, reserving all others to the states. This was clarified overtly in the Tenth Amendment, despite Story's erroneous conclusion that the amendment's lack of the word "expressly" proved otherwise. Furthermore, the Supremacy Clause refutes Story's assertion by making clear that only laws made "in pursuance" of the

Constitution are to be considered "the supreme law of the land" – eliminating the mere possibility of unlisted, unenumerated powers.

A significant portion of this text is devoted to contradicting Story's claims, and dedicated to the historical proceedings that were overlooked in his *Commentaries*. These brief refutations will be given greater context, with the help of primary sources, to illustrate my case. In its conclusion, this work will also suggest a method to bring power seized by the federal government back to the states and the people – one that Thomas Jefferson described as the "rightful remedy" to federal encroachment and usurpation.

In contrast to Story, James Madison promoted an entirely different understanding of the Constitution. Speaking at his state's ratification convention in Richmond, the Virginian claimed that thirteen independent entities entered into a league of states on mutual footing:

Who are parties to it [the Constitution]? The people—but not the people as composing one great body; but the people as composing thirteen sovereignties: were it as the gentleman asserts, a consolidated government, the assent of a majority of the people would be sufficient for its establishment, and a majority, have adopted it already, the remaining states would be bound by the act of the majority, even if they unanimously reprobated it: were it such a government as it is suggested, it would be now binding on the people of this state, without having had the privilege of deliberating upon it; but sir, no state is bound by it, as it is, without its consent. Should all the states adopt it, it will be then a government established by the thirteen states of America, not through the intervention of the legislatures, but by the people at large.[12]

According to Madison's explanation, the Constitution is of a very different design than Story's account holds. By nearly all measures, the American states of the 1780s had vastly different political, cultural, and religious identities – which had developed and grown autonomously for over a century before the Declaration of Independence. The people of one state had little connection to those in other states, and the only notable similarity that the colonies shared, prior to independence, was an allegiance to the

British crown. Even then, each colonial association with Britain originated through different conditions and colonial charters.

In addition to Madison, famous antebellum figures such as Thomas Jefferson and John Calhoun contradicted Story's nationalist inclinations with their trademark eloquence. Even those of less prominence, such as John Taylor of Caroline and Abel Upshur, persuasively refuted his notions and described the Constitution as a compact – where the states were the masters of their own creation. Though some of these individuals are nearly forgotten today, this work aspires to rectify that, if only to inspire new appreciation for such characters and to provide a more sincere examination of the republic's original structure and purpose.

Today we reap the benefits of a founding generation that largely understood the recurring nature of tyranny and oppression. Indeed, those who wrote the Constitution realized that when the government violated the document, the parchment would not simply produce fangs or a scorpion's tail to bite or sting the offender. Surely, they recognized that the document would not enforce itself, and required public virtue and propriety to uphold. Tellingly, the parties involved in the creation of the Constitution believed in providing some form of recourse to hold the federal government – the primary entity that could misconstrue or violate it – within its confines. To protect this vision, this work stresses that decentralized government depends upon pushing back upon the offender when constitutional wrongdoing is perpetrated.

The history of the early republic demonstrates that the Constitution's restrictions on federal power would have to be continually reasserted when they go ignored by civil officials. Consequently, policing national abnegations was intended to be the obligatory duty of the states. To effectively accomplish this, the founders recognized that it would take a tireless, vigilant, and educated populace to prevent constitutional desecrations. This book will show that state resistance against federal usurpation was once a fruitful undertaking – and still remains possible today – even if the tradition has become obscured, ignored, or overridden through time.

Nonetheless, contemporary political sensibilities are highly critical of such a perception, and it is now considered inflammatory to perceive the states as the supreme, sovereign creators of the federal system. Public school history classes are usually predicated on the nationalist tale, and children commonly learn of the grandeur of powerful executives such as Franklin Roosevelt and Abraham Lincoln. In contrast, presidents who exercised constitutional restraint on the pressing matters of their day are considered weak, cold-hearted, and ineffectual. In the same way, Congressmen that endeavored to exert undelegated authority are celebrated, while those who recognized constitutional constraints are condemned. In most cases, constitutional transgressions are either justified on the basis of precedent or ignored altogether.

In a contrarian spirit, this work explains how two presidents who consistently rank at the bottom of best president polls were among the strictest adherents to the Constitution, recognizing the document as a compact between states rather than a mechanism for political centralization. Acting in the manner required by Article II, they denied that the Constitution was a nationalist fabrication and worked to keep the general government within its intended constitutional boundaries. In addition, this account explores the deeds of other figures who emerged as true devotees of federalism and the Jeffersonian cause.

In the present day, the political merits of decentralized government are rarely explored in a serious way. Even though many realize that different states have varying laws on any given topic, few question why this is so. Some don't find it relevant, or claim that a decentralized political system without uniform laws necessarily creates a chaotic or hectic environment. Some think the states benefit from the guidance of a powerful central government, or espouse the idea that the phrases "state powers" or "states' rights" simply represent the thinly-veiled support of deplorable causes. None of these assertions are historically accurate, and this work asserts an alternative view. It also exposes the many historical attempts to homogenize law and seize power from the localities to embolden the authority of the central government.

Nonetheless, this work does not aim to portray the state governments as infallible entities. Undoubtedly, the same tendencies to consolidate power and constrain liberty often arise within the state governments as well. Instead, the narrative aims to reveal that the state governments were designed to remain politically relevant despite the modern tendency of political centralization. In a world of federal mandates, constitutional usurpations, and erroneous court decisions, it also aspires to demonstrate the benefits of a system wherein the states arduously protect the sovereign powers that inherently belong to them. It seeks, above all, to prove that federalism was once the chief bedrock of America's constitutional system.

Besides making a historical case for the true structure and purpose of the federal system, this work also contends that decentralized government is also defensible on practical grounds, and argues that liberty is most likely to exist and thrive in areas of regionalized power, where local societies can develop their own civil order and push back against national intrusion.

Though it now appears otherwise, the tradition of opposing national supremacy is deeply rooted in American history, going all the way back to the establishment of the colonies themselves. The independent nature of each society remained apparent through the colonial disputes with Britain, and continued after the colonies became republican states. In fact, the colonies perceived their struggle for independence as a constitutional crisis, one that was predicated on the denial of English rights and local government. On that account, this work will clarify how the states developed varying societies and actualized distinct traditions in their struggle for liberty.

The formation of the union under the Constitution was one of voluntary association, where the existence of the federal system depended on the will of the states. Highlighting this case were North Carolina and Rhode Island, both of which withheld their assent to ratification until long after the new Congress convened and George Washington was inaugurated. During this time, the two states were independent republics, and both maintained a cordial, well-mannered relationship with the United States. Had the American founders truly devised a different system, where membership was compulsory, one may rightfully wonder why the same individuals spearheaded efforts within their states to leave the British system in the first place. As it turns out, many of the same dedicated their lives, fortunes, and sacred honors to the cause of governmental autonomy.

Under the ratification process, no grand overseer was given the overarching power to compel the states to adopt the document, nor was any type of national ratification referendum suggested. No central state threatened invasion against states that did not ratify, nor was such a prospect entertained in any fashion. Under such designs, the states simply would not have chosen to ratify the Constitution when its legal existence depended upon them. Instead, the states were free to choose for themselves whether to enter into the constitutional union – and they did so upon the same footing as all other states.

The states functioned in almost every capacity as independent units throughout the War of Independence, under the Articles of Confederation that followed, and in the early republic under the Constitution. In Connecticut's ratification convention, for instance, Samuel Huntington noted that "among the American states there is such a difference in sentiments, habits, and customs, that a government which might be very suitable for one might not be agreeable to the other."[13] Indeed, states had their own governors with varying degrees of executive authority. They maintained their own legislatures, all with the independent power to tax and administer their own regions. They had their own currencies, official religions, and courts to adjudicate disputes. Above all, these dynamics disprove the notion that the union was created by a single society. Instead, the union brought about by the Constitution respected a collection of societies, with independent interests in mind. This league of states – solidified by a compact between them – was the unambiguous cornerstone of the Constitution.

Unfortunately, prevailing trends in the modern legal community and an incremental shift toward national authority has worked to undermine this view. Melancton Smith, a key figure of the contentious ratification struggle in New York, argued to the contrary of these modern trends. During his state's ratification contest, he contended that each party to the constitutional compact – the states – had the right to judge its ramifications. "On this momentous question, every state has an indubitable right to judge for itself," he avowed. This right, declared Smith, was secured to each state "by solemn compact." Joining him was prominent Federalist from Virginia, George Nicholas, who wholeheartedly echoed these views. Nicholas declared that through ratification the states were "thirteen individuals" entering into a contract with each other, and that no supplementary conditions could be imposed upon any state. The states, Nicholas said, would be exonerated from this arrangement whenever any circumvention of this principle was attempted. "The Constitution cannot be binding on Virginia, but with these conditions," Nicholas insisted.[14] Accordingly, since the states initially held all political authority themselves, then delegated powers afterward to the general government, the states maintained the ultimate sovereign trump over the new government.

Calling the general government "the breath of the nostrils of the States," prominent statesman John Randolph of Roanoke insisted that the Constitution was "not the work of the amalgamated population" of the people generally, but the progeny of the states.[15] The states were the foundation, and the general government was unable to stand without the support of its building blocks. This concept was uncontroversial at the time, and emerged as the original theory of constitutional understanding.

Even figures who disliked the idea of a federal union explained the Constitution in such a way. In *The Federalist* No. 15, for instance, Alexander Hamilton professed that the document created a framework of that exact form:

> There is nothing absurd or impracticable in the idea of a **league or alliance between independent nations for certain defined purposes** precisely stated in a treaty regulating all the details of time, place, circumstance, and quantity; leaving nothing to future discretion; and depending for its execution on the good faith of the parties. Compacts of this kind exist among all civilized nations, subject to the usual vicissitudes of peace and war, of observance and non-observance, as the interests or passions of the contracting powers dictate.[emphasis added][16]

During the ratification struggle, this was the only way the union was described by its advocates – as the distinct league of independent states that entered into a compact for defined purposes.

Prior to an effort by some inquisitive historians to return to primary sources and constitutional proceedings, the perception that Constitution is a compact has been largely brushed over, ignored, or misconstrued by popular academia. In its place are public schools, law school curricula, and politicians that generally promote the nationalist view. Mainstream histories typically cite the post-1789 accounts and doings of Alexander Hamilton, John Marshall, and Joseph Story as the definitive ones, neglecting the assessments of those that persuasively contested their viewpoints. Due to these institutionalized affinities, many have been made unaware that the Constitution was a contractual agreement among multiple parties to provide framework for government. This narrative will reveal how the original compact between states has been dismantled over time, to the detriment of liberty and republicanism. Surely, any earnest attempt to restore the states to their rightful place in the constitutional system relies upon learning from and overcoming those transgressions.

Chapter 2

The War of Independence as a Constitutional Crisis

Campaigns to solidify political centralization in America have not always been widely popular. In fact, many of the most prominent figures of the founding period championed decentralized rule as a preferable system that acknowledged 18th century political realities. Because the American colonies developed unique and often divergent cultural traditions, governmental structures, and laws, many took for granted that federalism was the defining characteristic of the colonial system. British Parliament's drive to meddle in the internal affairs of the colonies in the 1760s and 1770s, therefore, provoked widespread outcry and riled accusations that the crown had violated its own constitutional apparatus. In this way, the American War of Independence was very much a constitutional crisis.

The British Constitution is an unwritten instrument. Accordingly, the British identify their constitutional system as a series of traditions, customs, court decisions, written documents, and historical circumstances. Significant documents such as the Magna Carta, Petition of Right, and English Bill of Rights play a role in the conceptualization of this constitution, but so do governmental actions and precedents. In this way, the British constitution is the polar opposite of counterparts in the United States, where written constitutions of the states were intended to have a fixed meaning and were alterable only through predefined amendment processes. It was only after the century-spanning history of the colonies and the termination of the War of Independence that written constitutions, fully divergent from the British model, were produced.

By the time of the American struggle for independence, the British constitutional system was widely regarded as one of the most revered forms of government in human history. To the Whig politicians that would rise up to confront their government, its preservation was undoubtedly the focal point of their objective. Charles de Montesquieu, whose work profoundly influenced them, opined that the British constitution was "a beautiful system" that served the purposes of its subjects against their rulers, and produced a country where "every man who is supposed a free agent ought to be his own governor." A young John Adams wrote that searching "into the spirit of the British constitution" was necessary to defend "the inherent rights of mankind against foreign and domestic tyrants and usurpers." Along these lines, his famous cousin Samuel Adams wrote that its charter secured the natural rights of all inhabitants under the dominion of Britain.[17]

In the struggle against the British, the resistance of the American states relied upon an earnest effort to preserve the constitutional system they lived under. On the eve of war, James Wilson asserted that "both the letter and the spirit of the British constitution" justified the resistance of the colonies. The year prior, he wrote that "the principles, on which we have founded our opposition" were "the principles of justice and freedom, and of the British constitution." Rather than uproot and revolutionize their constitutional system, the American states hoped to fortify it. As historian Gordon Wood put it, the American patriots "revolted not against the English constitution, but on behalf of it."[18]

JAMES OTIS AND THE WRITS OF ASSISTANCE

In the early 1760s, one of the most explosive matters that drove a wedge between the American colonies and the British government was the implementation of the writs of assistance. Viewed as an intrusive tool of oppressors, British enactment of the general writs in the colonies allowed the government to violate the solitude of the people it alleged to protect. Under the writs, British officials received blanket authority to search property, seize assets, and invade the general privacy of citizens without probable cause. Ships, boats, vessels, vaults, cellars, warehouses, shops, and other property could be searched without a search warrant, and such an evasive scheme was completely sanctioned by binding law. Consequently, the controversy over the writs represented what many deemed to be the first constitutional crisis in the American colonies.

Unlike genuine search warrants, which required a much higher level of scrutiny and had to be approved by a judge, the writs of assistance did not expire and did not require an itemized list of items to be seized. Under the general writs, customs officials were given virtual *carte blanche* – complete discretionary freedom – to enter and search private property.[19] These two factors made the writs especially contemptible, rousing the indignation of those who believed that traditional liberty was rooted in the inviolability of property rights.

Most often, the writs were utilized to impede smuggling and to assure compliance toward provocative policies that inspired colonial resentment. The mercantilist system of the day was premised upon trade privileges that Parliament bestowed to particular companies. These protectionist policies effectively established corporate monopolies, tying the financial interests of the companies to the government. The primary method the crown used to enforce their monopolies was to allow for such extensive search mechanisms to be utilized. Americans may have wished to trade with other nations, but they could not do so legally unless the practice was first sanctioned by the Parliament of Great Britain. The ability to search and confirm acts of smuggling was principle to the execution of British policy. By design, the acts served to confirm illegal acts of free trade while they violated the sanctity of private property. Eminent patriot lawyer in Boston, James Otis Jr., therefore declared the writs of assistance "the worst instrument of arbitrary power."[20]

Aligning himself most staunchly against the writs of assistance, Otis fought diligently against the contentious policy. Once an agent of the crown, Otis later resigned from his position and argued vigorously against the search practices of the British, exposing the writs of assistance as oppressive measures that violated individual rights. Representing a large group of Massachusetts merchants in 1761, he argued for hours against legality of the writs at the Old State House in Boston. Otis directly admonished the British on the basis that the writs were an existential threat to the British constitution:

> These principles and these rights were wrought into the English constitution as fundamental laws. And under this head he went back to the old Saxon laws and to Magna Carta and the fifty confirmations of it in Parliament and the executions ordained against the violators of it and the national vengeance which had been taken on them from time to time, down to the Jameses and Charleses, and to the position of rights and the Bill of Rights and the revolution.[21]

Believing that the crown had entirely abandoned constitutional principles by implanting the writs, Otis contended that their enforcement must be voided by the civil authority. Stubbornly defending the people's liberties during this trying ordeal, he maintained that the writs brought forth irreconcilable conflict between Massachusetts and the British government. In a pamphlet dedicated to the subject, *The Rights of the British Colonies Asserted and Proved*, Otis wrote that the "authority of the parliament of Great Britain is circumscribed by certain bounds." If exceeded, he remarked, "their acts become those of meer power without right." Undertakings that contradicted the fundamental precepts of the British constitution, wrote Otis, "are void."[22]

As a central theme of his opposition, Otis argued that life, liberty, and property were the most essential values upon which the British tradition rested. The writs would undermine these maxims, he thought, and guarantee despotic behavior. "Every one with this writ may be a tyrant," Otis professed. If the legality of the writs was affirmed, "a tyrant in a legal manner, also, may control, imprison, or murder any one within the realm." Under the continuation of the writs, he warned that no agent of the government would be accountable for his actions. According to Otis, the mere existence of the writs encouraged perpetual tyranny.[23]

Otis' speech won the attention of many enthusiasts. Although most of his contributions are understated and underappreciated in the contemporary, his famous oratory against the writs has been compared to Patrick Henry's "Liberty or Death" speech for its stirring impact. Despite the gradual diminishment of his prominence in the American consciousness, Otis' words convinced the colonies that the British government undermined the confines of its constitution through haphazard rule. Most importantly, he persuaded many that these egregious measures could only be counteracted if they were forcefully opposed outright by a tireless and agitated population.

In contrast to the British position, Otis stated that "one of the most essential branches of English liberty is the freedom of one's house." The writs, he cautioned, "totally annihilate this privilege." The young John Adams wrote that Otis "asserted that the security of these rights to life, liberty, and property had been the object of all those struggles against arbitrary power...in every age." All British subjects and their descendants, he claimed, were entitled to all individual rights held by Englishmen. These blessings, he professed, were secured "by the British constitution as well as by the law of nature and our provincial character."[24] Defining the crisis before him in constitutional terms, Otis helped solidify the catalyst of independence by revealing the constitutional destabilization.

His vocal opposition to the writs inspired other peers, such as John Dickinson, a well-respected lawyer who became known as one of the most important figures of his era, to take an equally rigid stance on the issue. In accordance with Otis' arguments, he wrote that the writs would be "dangerous to freedom, and expressly contrary to the common law." Dickinson contended that the British constitution "ever regarded a man's house as his castle, or a place of perfect security."[25]

While five judges decided to uphold the constitutionality of the writs and Otis lost the case in question, he made a potent impression on compatriots that sympathized with his unyielding and radical stance. A young John Adams was so moved by the persuasive power of Otis' words, he wrote that "American independence was then and there born." Counting himself among an immense crowd that witnessed his famous oratory, Adams declared that Otis' oration against the writs "breathed into this nation the breath of life." One biographer considered the speech as "the living voice which called [the colonies] to resistance, first Boston, then Massachusetts, then New England and then the world!" Another historian described the oratory as "the first log of the pile which afterward made the great blaze of the Revolution."[26]

The umbrage of British loyalists paralleled Otis' rising popularity as a defender of traditional liberty and a guardian of private property. According to one detractor, it was Otis who "first broke down the barriers of government to let in the Hydra of rebellion."[27] Undeniably, his persuasive eloquence and inspiring message had made him a public enemy. Conversely, as Otis inspired the American colonies to grow more and more resistant toward British policies in the 1770s, prominent American Whigs lauded his efforts and praised his character. One account held that his history would "enroll his name among the most distinguished patriots who have ever expired on the blood-stained theater of human action." History would therefore remember "his humanity was conspicuous, his sincerity acknowledged, his integrity unimpeached, his honor unblemished, and his patriotism marked with the disinterestedness of the Spartan."[28]

John Adams wrote that Otis was "extraordinary in death as in life," remarking that "he has left a character that will never die while the memory of American revolution remains; whose foundation he laid with an energy, and with those masterly abilities, which no other man possessed."[29] By 1791, his memory helped inspire the Fourth Amendment of the United States Constitution, emphatically and unambiguously limiting the government's ability to intrude upon the privacy of the individual. Rather than a mere subject, he was an unwavering patriot stalwart.

THE STAMP ACT CRISIS

After Britain emerged triumphant in the French and Indian War – the North American theatre of the Seven Years War – British patriotic sentiment within the American colonies was at its absolute height. The war had secured safety and prosperity in what was then the western frontier, as France ceded all of its territory east of the Mississippi River to the British government. The conclusion to the struggle also had the tangible effect of lessening the continuance of Indian raids in North America, creating a new continental safeguard.

These circumstances led Parliament to view the colonies as the sole beneficiaries of the victory, believe that they should be obligated to bear some of the burden that came from the expensive conflict. The first true product of this idea was the 1765 Stamp Act, which would tax all legal documents, published works, newspapers, and even playing cards in North America. To signify compliance with the tax, a piece of paper with the image of King George III would adorn each taxed item. The impact of the policy would also be amplified in comparison to internal colonial taxes, as Parliament required the stamp tax to be paid in British currency rather than the inflationary paper money of the colonies. As history would witness, the colonies viewed the act as the most oppressive and callous of Britain's schemes of taxation.

From the outset, the Stamp Act inspired widespread boycotts against British goods and heated vitriol. However, lacking representation in Parliament, the colonies had few legislative remedies against the egregious law. Rather than attempt to call for an honest repeal of the policy and resign themselves to petition for a redress of grievances, colonial activists sought to nullify the policy. Through a fervent effort to thwart its enforcement, the colonies fought the Stamp Act head on.

When unease toward the law was at its height in Virginia, a set of sweeping resolutions was introduced within the House of Burgesses that aimed to oppose the law directly and assert Virginia's unilateral authority over internal affairs. Authored and introduced by the young and then-unknown lawyer Patrick Henry, the resolutions were considered by some within the assembly to be radical and inflammatory. His opinion undisturbed, Henry defended his proposals on the grounds that the Stamp Act was a uniquely appalling law that disrupted the bounds of the British constitution.

One of the most contentious resolutions asserted that Virginia's General Assembly had "the only and exclusive Right and Power to lay Taxes and Impositions upon the inhabitants of this Colony."[30] Henry claimed the only legitimate authority over the colonies were the colonial governments, and that Parliament had no supremacy over Virginia's legislative assembly. In doing so, he recognized that Virginians desired that political matters be addressed in Williamsburg rather than London. If Britain intruded upon Virginia's local government, he argued, the crown would necessarily eschew Virginia's "ancient constitution" that was recognized for centuries. This idea, thought Henry, stretched all the way back to the original charter of Virginia, and even before that to the Magna Carta, a harbinger of British liberty.

Another resolution, which would have legally blocked any enforcement of the Stamp Act, declared that Virginians were "not bound to yield Obedience to any Law or Ordinance" of taxation that originated outside of their own colonial assembly. While this resolution was defeated, and a conservative faction in Virginia managed to strike another from the official record, four of Henry's resolutions were adopted. The spirit behind them undoubtedly influenced the other colonies to pursue a similar course in the face of the belligerent law. Indeed, historian Murray Rothbard wrote that the Virginia Resolves "spread like wildfire through the colonies, providing the needed spark that aroused them from their solid resignation to active resistance to the hated Stamp Act."[31]

When word of the Virginia Resolves spread to Massachusetts, Samuel Adams and his political allies embraced the same method in an attempt to thwart the Stamp Act within their own state. Adams and his closest associates, the "Loyal Nine," spent several weeks organizing groups of merchants and other citizens to take binding oaths in opposition to the law. Over time, massive crowds began to gather and intimidate those connected with enforcement of the law. As the throng of Bostonian radicals migrated from place to place, they chanted "liberty, property, and no stamps!" An effigy of Andrew Oliver, the man tasked with distribution of the stamp paper in Boston, was hung from a liberty tree. Later, a huge crowd beheaded the effigy in front of Oliver's home, conducted a mock funeral, stamped the corpse, and burned it in a bonfire. The next day, Oliver was pressured to resign, thereby eliminating any possibility the law would be enforced. Afterward, the agitators vowed that any replacement officer tasked with enforcing the Stamp Act would be treated in the same fashion.[32]

Jared Ingersoll, British agent assigned to enforce the Stamp Act in Connecticut, was also forced to resign after the diligent insistence of public dissent. "This cause is not worth dying for," he admitted. As he relented, those who opposed the law in Wethersfield forced him to yell "liberty and property!" Upon the crowd's insistence, he threw his hat into the air in surrender and traveled to Hartford to read his resignation to the colonial assembly. Elsewhere, Patriot demagogue Christopher Gadsden – who receives fame today for designing the Gadsden Flag – was instrumental in the stamp resistance movement in South Carolina. There, his efforts motivated South Carolinians to burn stamp paper distributed in Charleston, and his supporters persuaded two stamp distributors within the colony to flee for their lives.[33]

These tactics were adopted and employed by many of the other colonies, including Pennsylvania, New York, Rhode Island, North Carolina, and Georgia. Therein, hostile groups seized stamp paper, pressured officers to delay the law's enforcement, urged local representatives to pass noncompliance resolutions, and forced stamp distributors out of commission.[34] The acts of the patriots made it virtually impossible to distribute any of the stamped paper, and the law became effectively unenforceable.

Several seminal works on the period portray this ordeal as America's first nullification campaign. For instance, Edmund and Helen Morgan's great work, *The Stamp Act Crisis: Prologue to Revolution*, relies upon this interpretation. Sons of Liberty groups and sympathetic representatives in every colony, they wrote, "had no hesitation in planning the nullification of the Stamp Act." In like fashion, Murray Rothbard's groundbreaking history of the colonies, *Conceived in Liberty*, portrayed the campaign against the law as "the people's nullification of the Stamp Act."[35]

The strategy of resistance against the Stamp Act was executed on the premise that the law's passage had been a direct violation of the British constitutional system. While not always acquainted with the legal precepts of such an argument, tireless factions of colonists were incredibly receptive and empathetic to the idea that the contentious law deserved a bold response. The Parliamentary power of taxation was denied by the colonies, the masses threatened those sent by the British government to enforce the law, and none of the paper to implement the policy was actually utilized.

After these events, delegates from nine colonies joined together in late 1765 to form a Stamp Act Congress, aiming to adopt a concerted response to the burdensome law. The ultimate product of the gathering was the Stamp Act Resolves, an array of resolutions that solidified colonial opposition to the law. While affirming the colonists' status as loyal subjects to the king, the resolutions also insisted that the colonists, by virtue of their birth, were afforded all of the same rights and privileges of Englishmen. Among those rights, they explained, was the right to be taxed only by the representatives of the people. Since the colonies viewed their colonial representatives as their only legitimate representatives, Parliamentary taxation was deemed unlawful.

Both houses of Parliament rejected the petition on the basis that the Stamp Act Congress was an illegitimate and unconstitutional assembly, and because the resolutions denied Parliament's right to levy taxes on the colonies. However, while the gripes of the colonies fell on deaf ears in Britain, the pleadings of the British merchants who traded with the American colonies did not. The pervasive boycotts of British goods ate into the prosperity of the merchant class, who dreaded the Stamp Act because the law acted as a crippling tax on their own profit. Edmund Burke, a Parliamentarian who sympathized with the colonists, consequently organized various factions within London to call for the repeal of the law.[36]

After hearing the outcry of the desperate merchants, and in recognition that the Stamp Act became impossible for the British government to enforce in the American colonies, Parliament repealed the controversial law in early 1766. The repeal act received royal assent shortly thereafter. With the stroke of a pen, this episode could have concluded uneventfully and the Imperial Crisis could have been a footnote in American history. However, the Parliament's next move guaranteed that there would be no immediate end to acrimony between the American colonies and Britain.

Parliament immediately followed the repeal of the Stamp Act with the Declaratory Act, a law that reiterated the Tory position that Parliament wielded "full power and authority" to impose laws upon the American colonies. This power, according the law, bound the colonial governments "in all cases whatsoever." Though Parliament yielded on the Stamp Act, it was hardly willing to concede its rigid stance on the British constitutional system and its implications for North America.

Celebrations broke out in many American cities, and in the sudden merriment, the New York General Assembly even ordered a statute of King George III to be built and placed upon the southern tip of Manhattan. Still, some believed the adoption of the Declaratory Act negated any sense of ease in the colonies. Patriot firebrand Thomas Paine, for example, deemed the act "the loftiest stretch of arbitrary power that ever one set of men or one country claimed over another." Taxation, he wrote, "was nothing more than putting the declared right into practice."[37] In Paine's mind, Parliament's stubborn position that it could make policy binding upon the colonies made the repeal of the Stamp Act irrelevant. After all, the continuance of the Declaratory Act prolonged the explosive dispute and guaranteed conflict in the years to come.

While the repeal appeared at first to resolve the Stamp Act controversy, no such palpable resolution took place. The next year, Parliament enacted the Townshend Acts, a new set of taxes on paper, paint, lead, glass, and tea. The architect of the policies, Charles Townshend, believed that the laws would prove less provocative because they enacted duties on trade rather than create direct schemes of taxation. Unsurprisingly, the new acts drew the same objections and indignation that fueled the Stamp Act Crisis. The coming years proved instead that the Declaratory Act was everything the American colonies had protested against in 1765 – an encroachment upon the American understanding of the British constitutional system.

THE BATTLE OVER PARLIAMENTARY SUPREMACY

In contradiction to the American Whig perspective that the British government embodied something of a federal system, the crown adopted the divergent position that all laws of Parliament were invariably binding upon the colonies. The culmination of the Glorious Revolution, Tories argued, elevated the status of Parliament to that of a supreme legislature for the entire empire. The principle of parliamentary sovereignty – now the defining feature of the British constitution – meant that Parliament could impose compulsory obligations upon the American colonies through legislation. As such, the body was to be regarded as a superlative council, where the legitimate passage of Parliamentary law superseded regional power in the hands of Britain's colonial assemblies.

Making the most persuasive case against the theory of parliamentary sovereignty was a young lawyer from North Carolina, James Iredell, who penned *To the Inhabitants of Great Britain* just prior to the American War of Independence. Iredell reasoned that the colonial charters were bestowed upon the colonies long before the principle of parliamentary sovereignty was instituted and accepted in England. "By the severe labor and virtue of their ancestors," he wrote, colonial forefathers had arrived "with the utmost difficulty, expense, and hazard, and for many years almost entirely at their own risk...by their own and their children's labor."[38] This

argument was echoed the same year by Thomas Jefferson in his own famous pamphlet, *A Summary View of the Rights of British America*. Both
men insisted that the toils, struggles, and risks their ancestors took to establish and preserve the colonies superseded the later adoption of parliamentary sovereignty. Because the colonies developed separate identities,
with local legislatures and autonomous governments, both Iredell and Jefferson considered them federalized entities with autonomous authority.
The common attachment the colonies shared with other parts of British
Empire was to the king, they argued, not to a singular overarching legislature.

Iredell also insisted that the paramount responsibility of any government was to provide happiness for its people, a proverb that outweighed
all other political considerations. Ignoring this precept, Iredell reasoned,
would invalidate its legitimacy entirely. "A free government can only sub-
sist by the general confidence of the people," he wrote.[39] Whenever and
wherever policy is formulated, Iredell argued that all parts should play a
role in its foundation:

Where an empire is divided into several different and distinct states, the
aggregated good of all these ought to be consulted. For where would
be the justice to regard only one or two of these as worthy of the care
and tender provision of laws, and expose the rest to chance, or the very
uncertain, whimsical caprice, or mean rapacity of the others?[40]

Denying such a guideline, he wrote, would bring about public unrest and
societal convulsion. Policy that was broadly unpopular – whether or not
constitutional - would be "totally destructive of this universal right." As-
sociating such a view with the lack of colonial representation in Parliament, Iredell revealed the British position to be fully negligent of American happiness.[41]

As to whether the acts of Parliament were binding upon the American
colonies, Iredell made his opinion unmistakable. "This is not the condition
of freemen, but of slaves," he declared, and was "the very definition of
slavery." Refuting the argument that Parliament and the colonial legislatures, as independent entities, would clash on every issue, he mentioned
that each legislature was established on "a separate scale" that pertained

to "different objects." Parliament could therefore legislate for the empire, but should not interfere in the local, confined matters of the colonies. In subjects of great controversy, Iredell hoped the king – as the common executive of the British Empire – would veto of all contentious laws that oppressed the colonies. "His negative can prevent the actual injury to the whole of any positive law in any part of the empire," he wrote.[42] At this point, many clung to the hope that the king would intervene to placate the flaring tensions between Parliament and the American colonies.

Iredell's widely read pamphlet catapulted his popularity within North Carolina, and afforded him an avenue into local politics. Remarkably, he was only 23 years old when the tract was published. Despite his youth, the lucid constitutional arguments he promoted were consequently assumed by others in the colonial struggle against the British. Framing the scuffle with Britain as a contest between local and national interests, Iredell's attitudes prompted many to perceive the divisive conflict as a constitutional crisis, where the merits of each inflammatory policy were relatively insignificant in comparison to the more pressing question of whether the law of the colonies or the Parliament were supreme.

Another popular challenge to parliamentary sovereignty denied that such a principle could be reconciled with an honest appreciation of natural rights. John Dickinson, a well-respected lawyer who became known as one of the most important figures of his era, wrote that the negation of natural law through the exertion of the British authority would be an intolerable injustice. "A parliamentary assertion of the supreme authority of the British legislature over these colonies," he wrote, was insufficient grounds to demand automatic compliance.[43] Similarly, James Otis contended that every British subject born on the continent or any other dominion was, "by the law of God and nature," entitled to "all the natural, essential, inherent, and inseparable rights of our fellow subjects in Great-Britain." Any repudiation of this notion, he remarked, would violate the most sacred palladium of Britain's constitutional tradition.[44]

Samuel Adams, Boston's chief agitator against the acrimonious laws, argued that natural rights were "to be free from any superior power on earth, and not to be under the will or legislative authority of man, but only to have the law of nature for his rule." Government authorities, he said, "have no right to seek and take what they please" in violation of such rights. Otherwise, he declared, "they would soon become absolute masters, despots, and tyrants." In Adams' estimation, the mere idea of parliamentary sovereignty was "utterly irreconcilable to these principles and to many other fundamental maxims of the common law, common sense, and reason." Adams asserted instead that Parliament had no more power to violate natural rights than it did to choose the Emperor of China.[45]

The same year, Virginia's colonial assembly also made a strong push to reject Britain's assumption of absolute parliamentary sovereignty over the American colonies. Through the Fairfax Resolves – a set of resolutions written and introduced by George Mason – the colony expressed a radically incompatible viewpoint. Far from merely specifying the particulars of a boycott of British goods, the purpose of the Fairfax Resolves was much broader, and every idea expressed therein was a direct extension of America's antithetical position on the British constitution.

The first resolution conveyed that the colony of Virginia, unlike a conquered country, was established peacefully through a charter that expressed constitutional prerogatives. The second resolution iterated that the "most important and valuable Part of the British Constitution, upon which it's very Existence depends," was that the people could be governed by no laws "to which they have not given their Consent, by Representatives freely chosen by themselves." On the same grounds, the third resolution made clear that the colony was unrepresented in Parliament, and could not feasibly be due to logistical constraints. Accordingly, the provision maintained that all legislative power over Virginia must be exercised by its own colonial assembly. The fifth resolution explicitly rejected the notion of parliamentary supremacy, calling such an idea "diametrically contrary to the first Principles of the Constitution, and the original Compacts by which we are dependant upon the British Crown and Government."[46] This position directly challenged Britain's assertion that the Parliament – as the supreme legislature of the British Empire – overrode the colonial charters and the dictums of local assemblies.

THE DESTRUCTION OF THE TEA

American Whigs, who valued traditional British liberties above all other axioms, also thought commercial rights to be utterly germane to public tranquility. In accordance with this outlook, the emerging resentment toward the British found another focal point of strife in the defilement of trade rights. To ensure a regular influx of commerce to support government-sponsored monopolies, Parliament forced firms that attempted to compete with their hand-picked favorites out of the market. This was done through the implementation of law that established trade privileges, which push competition out of the market and compelled citizens to buy products from a particular firm.

The most famous and incendiary of these policies came in the form of the Tea Act of 1773. Prior to the law's enactment, a famous British corporation, the British East India Company, struggled to maintain itself in the face of economic turmoil. Tea had long been sold by the company, but the profitability of the product was dwindling, mostly as a result of foreign competition. In addition, the company was forced to pay the British government a large sum of 400,000 pounds in taxes per year, which was made exponentially more difficult to sustain in light of the company's severe financial woes. Consequently, Parliament made a series of concessions aimed at saving the company from financial collapse. Parliament looked to North America to bail the struggling company out, and the new legislation forced the American colonies to purchase tea exclusively from the British East India Company. Britain hoped that this enactment would also set a precedent to legitimize Parliament's ability to tax the colonies, since it would require the colonists to pay Townshend duties on the tea.

A concerted spirit of organized resistance against these measures in Massachusetts culminated with the Boston Tea Party in December of 1773. New Englanders understood the implications of a government that could force its populace to buy product from a particular firm, and rebelled accordingly. The colonists were not particularly disturbed by the rate of taxation on the tea – as the 1773 act actually lowered taxes on the tea – but instead for the fact that the policy was coercively imposed by that which was viewed as a foreign legislature. After all, the colony had elected its own representatives to serve in a colonial assembly, which the inhabitants considered the legitimate government of Massachusetts.

Massachusetts was not alone in its defiance of the law. The 1773 Tea Act sparked controversy in several other colonies, where numerous organized acts of resistance toward the policy materialized. In Charleston, tea brought into the colony was left to rot on the docks. In New York and Philadelphia, the product that was shipped was rejected and returned to Britain. In Boston, most famously, a group of patriots donned the garb of Mohawk Indians, boarded a ship carrying tons of the company's tea, and dumped it into Boston Harbor over the course of several hours. In so doing, those who engaged in the "Destruction of the Tea" – as the event was then called – established oaths with each other to conceal the identities of those who participated.[47]

Almost immediately, Britain retaliated through the Intolerable Acts – a new set of laws designed to harshly punish Massachusetts. The Boston Port Act resulted in closure of Boston's port until the East India Company had been repaid for the destroyed tea. Parliament sought to guarantee favorable verdicts of British officials through the Administration of Justice Act, which allowed the governor to place trials of accused officials in other geographic locations. A new Quartering Act controversially required Bostonians to arrange housing for British soldiers, viewed as an abject affront to private property. Through the Massachusetts Government Act, Parliament also sought to alter the composition of the Massachusetts colonial assembly by requiring virtually all civil positions to be appointed by agents of the crown. In addition, the law prohibited town meetings and abrogated Massachusetts' colonial charter, which had been respected since 1691.[48]

To the radicals in Massachusetts, Parliament's dissolution of the colonial legislature was eerily reminiscent of the actions of Charles Stuart, the infamous king who steered England into a series of catastrophic civil wars in the 17th century. The colony's elected assembly responded to the Government Act by leaving Boston and forming a shadow government – the Massachusetts Provincial Congress – which nullified the law in practice. As a result, the provincial government maintained de facto power over the state during the course of the coming war.

THE MUSE OF THE REVOLUTION

While some in Boston inspired civil resistance against the British through their actions, Mercy Otis Warren encouraged the patriot cause with her words. A famous historian, pamphlet writer, and friend of many of the founding fathers, Warren was a sister to James Otis, Jr. She was also the wife of James Warren, an elected member of the Massachusetts colonial assembly, which closely connected her to many other patriot leaders in Boston. A true firebrand, Warren developed a grasp of the time exceeded others, and set out to create a chronicle of events that framed the conflict. In time, Warren published one of the first and most detailed histories of the War of Independence, *History of the Rise, Progress, and Termination of the American Revolution*.

Like others who supported the patriot cause, Warren also realized that the cause for independence was a constitutional crisis, where the hallowed liberties of Englishmen were threatened by government overreach. In doing so, she celebrated those that stood most ardently against the British crown. Although their actions would be considered treasonous, Warren thought that the same individuals pursued noble ends by making costly sacrifices for the cause of liberty. The rights they fought for, she wrote, were "conferred on all by the God of nature," and the privileges of Englishmen were "claimed by Americans from the sacred sanctions of compact."[49]

Reflecting upon the Stamp Act Crisis, Warren wrote that "the vigilant guardians of the rights of the people directly called upon him to relinquish the unconstitutional stipend, and to accept the free grants of the general assembly for his subsistence, as usually practiced." According to Warren, the controversial mandate affirmed that "the barriers of the British constitution" were "broken over" by the government. Warren fiercely rebuked the law, making the observation that the British constitution provides that no funds could be raised on for such a policy without consent from the people's representatives.[50] Most importantly, she realized that political power can only be derived from the people; it is not assumed at will by kings or Parliaments.

Warren derided the droves of armed British forces under the British occupation of Boston, writing that the British constitution "admits not armed force within this realm, but for the purpose of offensive and defensive war." Sending troops into the heart of British America, she asserted, was "a breach of privilege, an infraction on the natural rights of the people, and manifestly subversive of that happy form of government they had hitherto enjoyed." Warren explained that the presence of a standing army within the colony was nothing more than a dereliction of the privileges guaranteed to the colonists by virtue of their status as British subjects.[51]

Detesting Britain's establishment of a standing army in Boston, Warren celebrated the colony's moral fortitude nonetheless by commending its opposition the overt campaign of military intimidation. When the British Governor of Massachusetts requested requisition from General Gage to quarter additional troops within the town of Boston, she wrote that the assembly courageously responded by censuring both the governor and General Gage for "wantonly acting against the constitution."[52]

Warren's abhorrence of Britain's military occupation of Boston was bolstered by historical precedent. Less than a century prior, Parliament charged King James II with "raising and keeping a standing army within this kingdom in time of peace without consent of Parliament, and quartering soldiers contrary to law."[53] This unambiguous rebuke made clear that English subjects were to be free from such a condition. Britain's actions in Massachusetts seemed disturbingly similar, and appeared to be a direct violation of the country's constitution. Warren recalled that the British engaged in the "arbitrary designs of government" through the introduction of a standing army. Beyond this, the king had permitted "encroachments on civil liberty."[54]

Warren also attacked the Quebec Act, which denied the principles of the British constitution and eliminated the right of trial by jury. This law also drastically expanded the territory of Quebec, conflicting with many colonial land grants. New York, Pennsylvania, and Virginia protested most strongly because the law seized lands that had been granted by royal charters. In essence, the law also alienated large groups of loyalists with land claims, expanding the base of antagonism against the British government. Warren considered this plan offensive to both the French and English inhabitants of the continent, because they now found their divergent interests inseparably connected. Despotically, the British mercantilist system afforded assistance to some individuals which were "employed by the crown" at the expense of all others.[55]

Warren's outlook was closely matched by other inspiring minds of the period, such as Patrick Henry, Thomas Jefferson, and Samuel Adams. Nevertheless, she possessed a unique form of eloquence that allowed her to connect with patriot readers, and recognized the serious and volatile nature of British policy in the colonies. In Warren's estimation, the British government had no respect for the constitutional limitations intentionally placed upon it by the vigilant patriots that preceded her.

After the war, Jefferson befriended Warren, and paid homage to her by ordering subscriptions of her work for himself and his cabinet. Both sharing a similar republican vision, the two became friends. Jefferson raved that Warren's writings "furnish a more instructive lesson to mankind than any equal period known in history." Biographer Nancy Stuart wrote that Warren had a strong command of her abilities, understanding that words could be "as explosive as gunpowder."[56] In every way, Warren's praiseworthy chronicle revealed the constitutional nature of the conflict with Britain.

THE CONSTITUTIONAL BOUNDS OF TAXATION

The constitutional crisis of the 1770s was also evident in a clash of opinions in regard to taxation. According to the patriots, the crown had endeavored to force illegitimate taxation schemes upon the colonies, breaking one of the oldest limitations on Parliamentary prerogative. Even though many American agitators readily admitted that Parliament possessed the power to impose indirect taxes upon the colonies to regulate trade, the position that denied the crown's power to levy direct taxes became a widespread rallying cry. Such internal, direct taxers, they said, could only be imposed by the colonial legislatures.

In Rhode Island, Stephen Hopkins professed that Parliamentary confines in regard to taxation were restricted to "things of a more general nature, quite out of the reach of these particular legislatures," he wrote. As a direct tax, the Stamp Act had acted as a clear violation of this precept. Benjamin Franklin, who gave a three-hour testimony before the House of Commons, repeated such a mantra when he declared that the difference between external and internal taxation was "very great." While acknowledging Parliament's authority to lay duties to regulate commerce for the colonies, Franklin argued that the imposition of internal taxes was "unconstitutional and unjust." In his own writings, John Dickinson assumed the same stance.[57]

Rather than accept Britain's newfound strategy of taxation, the colonial governments adopted an adversative position. Constitutionally, the predominant viewpoint of the American patriots was that taxation could only be levied by the people's elected representatives, organized in their local assemblies. One of Virginia's Fairfax Resolves, passed in 1774, tackled this issue explicitly:

> Resolved that Taxation and Representation are in their Nature inseperable; that the Right of withholding, or of giving and granting their own Money is the only effectual Security to a free People, against the Incroachments of Despotism and Tyranny; and that whenever they yield the One, they must quickly fall a Prey to the other.[58]

The resolutions also acknowledged that the interests of Parliament often fundamentally conflicted with those of the American colonies. This truism, claimed another resolution, provided Britain with a "defective and often false" sense of American interests. In like fashion, the colonial assembly in Pennsylvania adopted a resolution affirming "the inherent Birthright and indubitable Privilege of every British Subject to be taxed only by his own Consent or that of his legal Representatives." An analogous resolution in Massachusetts held that the right to taxation only by local assemblies was "one of the main pillars of the British constitution."[59]

The same general perspective caught fire elsewhere. In 1765, Patrick Henry declared that Virginia had the "only and exclusive right and power to lay taxes and impositions upon the inhabitants of this colony, and that every attempt to vest such a power in any person or persons has a manifest tendency to destroy British as well as American freedom." George Washington affirmed that taxes not levied by the people's representatives would be universally viewed as a "direful attack" upon the liberties of the people. He considered such a ploy to be an "unconstitutional method of Taxation." Making the same case, John Adams warned that if the British position that Parliament could directly tax the colonies was to be acknowledged, and established, "the Ruin of America will become inevitable."[60] While the political landscape of each colony differed drastically, opposition toward the Parliamentary taxation was virtually unanimous.

Thomas Jefferson added to the amalgam of constitutional arguments against Britain by contending that the crown had systematically denied the natural right of free enterprise. In his widely publicized 1774 pamphlet, *A Summary View of the Rights of British America*, Jefferson wrote that the recent transgressions against the American colonists had proved that "bodies of men, as well as individuals, are susceptible of the spirit of tyranny." The young Virginian accused Parliament of hiding behind the guise of commercial regulatory power as an excuse to tax the colonies without their consent.[61] This approach, he thought, was simply a crafty gambit to avoid constitutional obligations.

THE HAND OF FORCE

Taking another angle against British coercion over the colonies, Jefferson chastised the government for dissolving the colonial legislatures. Since the Glorious Revolution of 1688, he wrote, such a power had never been exercised in Britain. According to Jefferson, the "united voice of his people" contended that "his majesty possessed no such power by the constitution." Britain's will to dissolve the American colonies was thus viewed as a hypocritical act. "But your majesty, or your governors, have carried this power beyond every limit known," he warned.[62]

Jefferson also stressed the British monarch's authority to refuse royal assent, which would effectively veto any unscrupulous and unconstitutional law. Viewing this mechanism as a substantive check on the power of Parliament, he urged the king to "resume the exercise of his negative power, and to prevent the passage of laws by any one legislature of the empire, which might bear injuriously on the rights and interests of another." Conversely, Jefferson also criticized the royal tendency to leave colonial laws in a state of neglect, whereby popular acts of pressing importance would sit in limbo for long lengths of time, without being confirmed or annulled by the king.[63]

Noting the prevalence of Britain's constitutional violations, Jefferson added that "these exercises of usurped power have not been confined to instances alone, in which themselves were interested, but they have also intermeddled with the regulation of the internal affairs of the colonies." In his mind, regular exploitation of the American colonies was a commonplace practice, not just an exception to normalcy. "Single acts of tyranny may be ascribed to the accidental opinion of a day," Jefferson wrote, "but a series of oppressions" that continued "unalterably through every change of ministers," plainly demonstrated "a deliberate and systematical plan of reducing us to slavery."[64]

Defying the Tory narrative, Jefferson asserted that natural rights could not be eradicated by acts of government. His reasoning, he was explained, was that individuals were imbued – by virtue of their birth – with certain rights that could not be debased by government. "The God who gave us life gave us liberty at the same time; the hand of force may destroy, but cannot disjoin them," he wrote.[65]

COMMON SENSE AND THE RIGHTS OF MAN

While the zeal of the most diligent agitators successfully thwarted the implementation of some abhorrent policies, Britain continued to maintain its stranglehold over its colonies. The schism reached its boiling point at Lexington and Concord in 1775, prompting Thomas Paine to write *Common Sense*, a pamphlet that successfully brought the appeal of independence to the masses.

Published in early 1776, *Common Sense* arrived at a time when loyalist sentiment was strong and American independence had yet to be declared. Still, the pervasiveness of patriot fervor was also nearing its height, and the masses were hungry for a well-written summation of the American position. By the end of 1776, Paine's most famous writing entered firmly into the American consciousness. In summary, Paine argued that monarchy itself was immoral, that Britain's government had violated its constitutional bounds, that the colonies could not be feasibly represented in Parliament, that the principle of parliamentary supremacy violated the most basic elements of optimal government, and that it was logistically impracticable to be ruled by a power so far away. A master of history, Paine remembered Britain's past as a time of deceitful rulers, cyclical tyranny, and recurring oppression that appeared to be playing out once again.

In his famous tract, Paine argued that bending to the will of magistrate that ruled from so far away would effectually lead to the enslavement of the American colonies:

And is there any inhabitants in America so ignorant, as not to know, that according to what is called the present constitution, that this continent can make no laws but what the king gives leave to; and is there any man so unwise, as not to see, that (considering what has happened) he will suffer no Law to be made here, but such as suit his purpose? We may be as effectually enslaved by the want of laws in America, as by submitting to laws made for us in England.[66]

According to Paine, Parliament had abandoned its duty to safeguard public happiness by discounting the independent nature of the colonial governments. In his eyes, the obligation to submit to laws made in England without representational interests of the people in mind was a callous and revolting prospect.

An accurate recognition of the arbitrary rule of Britain was not Paine's only poignant observation. After emigrating from England to Philadelphia in 1774, Paine came to realize the glaring contrast between the British Isles and the American colonies. Americans were not a singular collective, but instead a collection of inhabitants with variable cultural traits and customs:

And by a just parity of reasoning, all Europeans meeting in America, or any other quarter of the globe, are countrymen; for England, Holland, Germany, or Sweden, when compared with the whole, stand in the same places on the larger scale, which the divisions of street, town, and county do on the smaller ones; distinctions too limited for continental minds. Not one third of the inhabitants, even of this province, are of English descent. Wherefore, I reprobate the phrase of parent or mother country applied to England only, as being false, selfish, narrow and ungenerous.[67]

As Paine witnessed, the American colonies hardly formed a homogeneous, unitary society in the aggregate. On the contrary, the differences between the colonies were easily observed by honest spectators. To claim that the entire British Empire constituted "one people" that could be dictated to by a singular legislature, he thought, was a fallible proposition.

While Paine professed that the aims of the British constitutional system had been good, the substance was easily disturbed throughout the ages by various oppressors:

I offer a few remarks on the so much boasted constitution of England. That it was noble for the dark and slavish times in which it was erected is granted. When the world was overrun with tyranny the least there-from was a glorious rescue. But that it is imperfect, subject to convulsions, and incapable of producing what it seems to promise, is easily demonstrated.[68]

Because he believed the British constitutional system to be historically "subject to convulsions," Paine apprehended the nature of such an arrangement. He considered such a "living constitution" to be unable to cope with the enactment of whimsical, unpopular law that encroached upon liberty and violated the maxims of rule by the consent of the governed. Arguing that the British constitutional model relied upon a series of precedents that gradually expanded the government's reach, Paine viewed such as a shift as an encroachment upon natural precepts. A framework that was so easily alterable by government, he thought, was the chief defect of the British constitution.

As the future would demonstrate, this was the same "living" constitutional system the founding generation rebelled against. In practice, a malleable model that was so easily changeable by temporary rulers would always produce undesirable results over time. James Madison, eminent statesmen from Virginia, concurred with Paine's assessment of such a constitutional model:

And what has been the progress and event of the feudal Constitutions? In all of them a continual struggle between the head and the inferior members, until a final victory has been gained in some instances by one, in others, by the other of them.[69]

Both men observed that government would never voluntarily concede that it is embarking on an unconstitutional path or treading upon unlawful ground. A constitution that was limited only by the good will of its operators, they believed, was no constitution at all. As an alternative, American Whigs championed government only as an arrangement between individuals, based on the consent of the governed, where there governing authority was held down by specific limitations through written constitutions.

Ironically enough, it was the talents of an English penman that resonated most with the American colonies. Although most of the themes Paine enunciated had already been expressed by others in the same era, his genius was displayed in the ability to captivate a common audience that was hardly aristocratic or learned on legal matters. Historian Sidney Hook considered Paine a "remarkable popularizer whose gift for bold and graphic expression made him a natural pamphleteer."[70]

Years after establishing himself as the penman that drove commoners to resist the British and support independence, Paine expounded upon his conception of ideal government. In a deeper analysis of republicanism, he viewed government on its smallest level as a compact between individuals. In *The Rights of Man*, Paine professed that individuals in a state of nature predated and morally superseded governing constructs that came afterward:

> The fact therefore must be, that the individuals themselves, each in his own personal and sovereign right, entered into a compact with each other to produce a government; and this is the only mode in which governments have a right to arise, and the only principle on which they have a right to exist.[71]

Paine understood that individuals pre-exist government, and as it followed, maintained the ultimate power to control or subvert said institutions. As the basic units upon which governments lay their foundation, the individual thereby has a moral obligation to thwart injustice and oppression. Republics composed of representatives of a state's inhabitants were therefore built from the individual to the authority, not from the authority to the individual. Drawing much of his understanding from John Locke, Paine understood that government was only just when its structure was supported by the units that built it.

Paine also recognized that the source of constraint on government is a firm, grounded constitution, fully unassailable by impulsive governmental modification. Without a restrictive baseline, governments would be able to mold themselves into any design they wished, whether or not the rights of the people were affected or violated. In a more preferable arrangement, Paine believed that government should be forcibly prohibited from assuming its own authority:

A government on the principles on which constitutional governments arising out of society are established, cannot have the right of altering itself. If it had, it would be arbitrary. It might make itself what it pleased; and wherever such a right is set up, it shows there is no constitution.[72]

Rigid constitutions of such form would necessarily prevent the enlargement and oppression of government, as long as the people were virtuous enough to hold officials to such strict limitations. Conversely, a government that could define size, scope, and extent of its own powers would render any constitution irrelevant.

REVOLT, HOSTILITY, AND REBELLION

Just before shots were exchanged at Lexington and Concord, the colonies were forced to make a pressing choice – whether to provide material support to those suffering at the hands of the redcoats terrorizing Massachusetts, or to abstain with the hope of preferential treatment by the British authorities. In early 1775, after all, many viewed the occupation of Boston as an isolated matter that called for calculated disregard. Providing overt military support to the beleaguered New Englanders, some thought, would only invite a new set of Intolerable Acts to punish the abetting colony.

In the midst of the pressing conundrum, one Virginian endeavored to convince his state that devoting direct military support against the British – to rectify constitutional injustice – was a moral obligation. As the most popular figure in his state, and possibly the most skilled orator of his generation, Patrick Henry pleaded his fellow Virginians to commit military support to the beleaguered Bostonians at the Second Virginia Convention of 1775:

They tell us, sir, that we are weak; unable to cope with so formidable an adversary. But when shall we be stronger? Will it be the next week, or the next year? Will it be when we are totally disarmed, and when a British guard shall be stationed in every house? Shall we gather strength by irresolution and inaction? Shall we acquire the means of effectual resistance by lying supinely on our backs and hugging the delusive phantom of hope, until our enemies shall have bound us hand and foot?[73]

Despite the sheer might of the British, Henry urged Virginia to join the cause for independence. He proposed that each measure of constitutional usurpation should be confronted it directly, regardless of the hardships his country would face. Decrying indecision, Henry realized that the destruction of liberty would never be reversed unless a vigilant body of citizens opposed each exertion of subjugation.

Henry's most novel assertion was that the legitimate authority over the colonies were the colonial governments, not Parliament. His countrymen in Virginia, he reasoned, expected internal political matters to be addressed in Williamsburg rather than London. If Britain violated these ties to local government, it would necessarily reveal contempt for Virginia's "ancient constitution" that was recognized for centuries.

Repeated calls for peace had run their course, thought Henry, and the outbreak of bloodshed in Massachusetts necessitated an immediate choice between freedom and despotism:

It is in vain, sir, to extenuate the matter. Gentlemen may cry, Peace, Peace – but there is no peace. The war is actually begun! The next gale that sweeps from the north will bring to our ears the clash of resounding arms! Our brethren are already in the field! Why stand we here idle? What is it that gentlemen wish? What would they have? Is life so dear, or peace so sweet, as to be purchased at the price of chains and slavery? Forbid it, Almighty God! I know not what course others may take; but as for me, give me liberty or give me death![74]

Much of the Virginia General Assembly was stunned by the provocative nature of Henry's comments. Those still hoping to avoid independence strongly believed that such words would cause additional strain between Virginia and the mother country, and Henry was even accused of treason for his oratory.[75] Despite the objections of some, Henry's resolutions passed by the narrowest of margins, with popular figures such as George Washington and Richard Henry Lee voting in favor. In a prelude to political independence, Virginia joined the military cause against the British.

Despite Virginia's palpable commitment of military support, some delegates in the Continental Congress believed hostilities between the colonies and Britain could be settled by a concerted act of reconciliation between feuding parties. Chief among them was the distinguished Pennsylvanian lawyer John Dickinson, ardent opponent of British taxation. Unlike some of his more radical peers, Dickinson believed that seeking out the king's favor in good will was most advantageous way to end the enmity between the colonies and crown. By convincing the king to use his authority to challenge Parliament on the controversial policy, he thought, would provide a remedy to the suitability of both the colonies and Britain.

With such an earnest desire for peace in mind, Congress adopted the Olive Branch Petition – primarily the work of Dickinson. Addressed to the king, the article protested that the colonial assemblies had been "repeatedly and injuriously dissolved" and that "commerce has been burdened with many useless oppressive restrictions." Nonetheless, the petition urged peace, clarifying that such sentiments "are extorted from the hearts that much more willingly would bleed in your majesty's service." The document reiterated that the colonies remained hopeful for "peace, liberty, and safety," and emphasized reconciliation. As a compromise, the Olive Branch Petition recommended a trade settlement that made taxes more equitable with rates that were paid by native Britons. Promising to preserve the king's "royal authority" and the "connection with Great Britain," the colonies pledged to "carefully and zealously endeavor to support and maintain" their association to the motherland.[76]

At this point, Dickinson's faction of peacemakers truly believed that the king would understand the misgivings of the colonies, and intervene on their behalf. With the guidance of the king, this group thought, arbitration would occur and the years of strife would be over. With the power of Parliament subdued, the colonies could continue as they were and the crown could raise revenue to support its financial anguishes. Additionally, the Declaration of the Causes and Necessity of Taking Up Arms – an explanation of reasons for which the British were confronted in Massachusetts - was also sent to London. As such, both documents represented a candid attempt to avert war, even after bloodshed had transpired in Lexington and Concord.

King George III rejected the American overtures of peace almost immediately, and denounced Congress as an illegitimate assembly. Also jeopardizing the prospect of peace was the British interception of a letter written by John Adams. Within the communication, Adams revealed his opinion that the petition would be frivolous and that war with Britain was inevitable. In August of 1775, the king formally declared the colonies to be in "open and avowed rebellion," and suggested that the conflict with the American colonies had been "promoted and encouraged by the traitorous correspondence, counsels and comfort of divers wicked and desperate persons within this realm."[77]

That October, Britain's king expounded upon his position in regard to the American colonies in his Speech from the Throne, a customary address to Parliament:

Those who have long too successfully laboured to inflame my people in America by gross misrepresentations, and to infuse into their minds a system of opinions, repugnant to the true constitution of the colonies, and to their subordinate relation to Great-Britain, now openly avow their revolt, hostility and rebellion. They have raised troops, and are collecting a naval force; they have seized the public revenue, and assumed to themselves legislative, executive and judicial powers, which they already exercise in the most arbitrary manner, over the persons and property of their fellow-subjects.[78]

Despite the numerous constitutional usurpations cited by the colonies, and the grievances made on their behalf, the king claimed that the actions of the British government were lawful and binding. Deeming the petition illegitimate, the king refused to act as an intermediary between Parliament and the colonies. Fearing that rebellion would quickly spread to the other colonies, the monarch instead demanded a "speedy end to these disorders by the most decisive exertions."[79] Any lingering uncertainty in regard to the king's sensibilities was now dispatched.

By mid-1776, American support for independence was pervasive. The Continental Congress – through the individual votes of state quorums – aptly responded by severing all political ties to Britain through a resolution introduced by Richard Henry Lee of Virginia. The resolution, which recognized the colonies as "free and independent States," professed that all political connection between them and Britain was to be "totally dissolved." Adopted on July 2, 1776, the resolution also called for Congress to seek out foreign alliances to recognize the new governments and secure financial and military support.

The Declaration of Independence, which was approved two days later, pronounced that the colonies were "Absolved from all Allegiance to the British Crown," and therefore "Free and Independence States." As such, they now had the power to "levy War, conclude Peace, contract Alliances, establish Commerce, and do all other Acts and Things which Independent States may of right do." According to the document, the new states were now autonomous polities with sovereign powers, no different from "the State of Great Britain."

In the Declaration of Independence, Jefferson portrayed the king as a tyrant who trampled upon Britain's constitutional system. "He has combined with others to subject us to a Jurisdiction foreign to our Constitution and unacknowledged by our Laws; giving his Assent to their Acts of pretended Legislation," he wrote.[80] Among the other listed grievances, Jefferson condemned the seizure of the colonial charters, which affirmed the traditional rights of the colonists. By "taking away our charters, abolishing our most valuable laws, and altering fundamentally the form of governments," he alleged the king was responsible for destabilizing the same constitutional system the colonies sought to uphold.

Jefferson's famous treatise also attacked the king for dissolving the colonial legislatures, and for sending "swarms of Officers" to harass the colonists and "eat out their substance." The crown's propensity to cut off foreign trade, impose taxes without the consent of the colonies, and deprive subjects of due process was also likened to abject despotism. The document suggested that the king's transgressions were part of a grand scheme – a "long train of abuses and usurpations" – which endangered the rights of the colonists. In observation these abuses, Jefferson declared the king's deeds had made him unfit to rule over the colonies. "A prince whose character is thus marked by every act which may define a Tyrant, is unfit to be the ruler of a free people," he affirmed.[81]

In such a trying time, both Henry and Jefferson shared a unique affinity for political decentralization. The marked embrace of such a maxim, both men felt, was the key to securing individual liberty and domestic tranquility. To reach such an end, confrontation against their unreceptive and domineering central government was a necessary aspiration. This form of recourse – where localities asserted their rightful sovereignty – had long been appreciated by generations of Englishmen. It was only the neglect of Britain's constitutional antecedents, therefore, that allowed government power to gain ground and actualize the treacherous whims of arbitrary authority. The common crusade of Jefferson and Henry, which defied such a trajectory, demonstrates that both men had drawn inspiration from a historical series of constitutional settlements, long held as axioms from Britain's tumultuous past.

Chapter 3

Essential Constitutional Antecedents

American's founding generation perceived the imperial quarrel with Great Britain as a constitutional crisis that threatened the foundation of the colonial framework. Of course, this could not have been the case if Britain had no constitutional system at all. Without any such arrangement, government was simply a fully arbitrary edifice, and the unpredictable nature of overreaching government could never be controlled. After recollecting the past, and weighing the merits of the British constitutional system, Americans ultimately favored written constitutions over unwritten alternatives. Nevertheless, the founding generation drew great influence from Britain's constitutional history. These constitutional antecedents, where the treacherous acts of tyrants clashed with counteracting interests of patriots, became an important focal point of American's own constitutional tradition.

Indeed, "Penman of the Revolution" John Dickinson wrote that English history was full with examples in which individuals had reclaimed their liberty in the face of oppression:

The English history abounds with instances, proving that this is the proper and successful way to obtain redress of greviances. How often have kings and ministers endeavoured to throw off this legal curb upon them, by attempting to raise money by a variety of inventions, under pretence of law, without having recourse to parliament?[82]

Countless times, Dickinson wrote, had Englishmen "reaped the benefit of this authority lodged in their assemblies." As Dickson figured, the application of a local check against the central authority restored the desired constitutional equilibrium. While not everyone that played a role in American independence shared the same political vision, all believed that safeguarding English liberty required an industrious populace to defend their own rights. Alexander Hamilton wrote that this was the type of remedy "obtained by the barons, sword in hand, from King John" in 1215.[83]

THE MAGNA CARTA

Few individuals throughout history hold such a cruel and tyrannical reputation as King John of England. Brutal and cunning, his abuses of power expanded the king's arbitrary power to centralize England's kingdom under a system of direct rule. In time, his exploits riled his subjects to action, encouraged an infamous series of 13th century restraints upon the king's prerogative.

The youngest surviving son of King Henry II, John was crowned in 1199. His most prominent 19th biographer wrote of the king's notorious streak of oppression:

In his inner soul John was the worst outcome of the Angevins...His punishments were refinements of cruelty, the starvation of children, the crushing of old men under copes of lead. His court was a brothel where no woman was safe from the royal lust, and where his cynicism loved to publish the news of his victim's shame. He was as craven in his superstitions as he was daring in his impiety. He scoffed at priests and turned his backs on the mass, even amidst the solemnities of his coronation, but he never stirred on a journey without hanging relics round his neck.[84]

Outside of these vicious excesses, John regularly killed political dissidents that challenged his rule, had his own nephew strangled and drowned, deliberately starved the wife and son of his former friend, and hanged other adversaries. He regularly engaged in adulterous affairs with noblewomen, a highly scorned practice which was considered detestable. He routinely "thirsted for revenge and crowed at the humbling of his rivals," and was charged with having the "inclinations of a petty tyrant."[85] Today, he serves as the example of a tormentor who ruled in a most spiteful manner, grasping all power for himself while recognizing no limits to his own authority. History now recognizes John in terms of the means taken to oppose him and limit his aptitude for despotism.

Restrictive shackles were eventually placed upon John's rule by the Magna Carta – or "Great Charter" – which was written and sealed during his reign. The limitations enumerated in document were intended as direct impediments to the arbitrary rule of the crown, and the document has since served as a cornerstone of the British constitutional tradition. The common rights bestowed upon the English and recognized in the Magna Carta became likened to a shield that guarded individuals from overwhelming and authoritative power. Hardly an impulsive political reaction confined to the 13th century, the array impositions on the king's royal authority have been viewed as constitutional maxims for over 800 years.

The document was the outgrowth of controversy and bloodshed, suffered by generations long past, created for the cause of preserving liberty through vigilance. Its influence on western civilization has been incomparable, and it has served as a noteworthy precursor to the United States Constitution. The conditions that arose in England as preludes to the Magna Carta have revealed why such a cause was championed by the rebel barons. Beyond this, a true study of this momentous agreement serves to illustrate why such reverence is now given to the document, and how it unmistakably changed the world forever.

Early in his reign, King John forcefully pursued costly wars in continental Europe to reclaim Normandy, which invariably depleted the English treasury. Upon this realization, he became troubled that the taxing tools at his disposal would not allow him to raise the funds necessary to continue his European conquests. Prior to implementing new methods of taxation to address this issue, John raised money through the scutage system, which forced citizens to pay the government to avoid military conscription. Furthermore, he applied court fees, taxed charter sales, initiated short-term dues on land sales, subjected the merchant classes to custom duties, and even levied taxes on wine to generate government revenue. In the continual discovery of new ways to fleece his subjects, the king refused to acknowledge any barrier to his revenue schemes. Biographer Frank McLynn therefore criticized him as "avaricious, miserly, extortionate, and moneyminded."[86] Hoping to uproot opposition against him, John even used greater enforcement power to collect taxes from political enemies.

Of all his treacherous policies, John's most controversial was the imposition of a widespread income tax – or "thirteenth tax" – in 1207. Unprecedented at the time, the scheme cruelly deprived the populace of their property and productive capital in order to support the king's pet endeavors. Lands of the barons who refused to pay the tax were summarily confiscated by the crown, amplifying resentment toward the policy. This tax was the first of its kind in England, and it was soundly detested. Reflecting on the potential of an income tax in 1758, Benjamin Franklin wrote that "it would be thought a hard Government that should tax its people one-tenth part of their time."[87] Surely Franklin based his observation upon the example of John's reign, or was at least aware of the hardships faced as a result of his most ill-reputed ploy.

John's income tax was collected meticulously by a growing base of government officials, who were deployed across England as agents. The barons saw this collection project as a means to restrict their livelihood, and viewed the policy as a malevolent attempt to seize their property in the name of perpetual war. Historian Ralph Turner wrote that John's desire for money drove him to arbitrary rule, and his dangerous personality traits impelled the king toward tyranny. His constant effort to exhaust every possible means of taxing England made the people consider the growing corps of officials as parasites, not public servants.[88]

John engaged in another act of duplicity by meddling with England's religious apparatus. By the selection of John de Gray as Archduke of Canterbury – the most powerful religious figure in the kingdom – the king challenged the preference of the barons and sparked a civil conflict. The head of the Catholic Church, Pope Innocent III, also found John's choice distrustful and believed de Gray would only serve as a political pawn of the king.

Stephen Langton, the cardinal favored by the barons, was eventually consecrated by Innocent in defiance of John's selection. As a kindred opponent of John's rule, the barons perceived Langton as a fair-minded official that would help temper Jon's wicked compulsions and act as an independent director of the country's religious affairs. Recognizing Langton as "archbishop of Canterbury, primate of all England and cardinal of the holy Roman Church," the Magna Carta made clear that the king was restricted from enacting policy without the consent of the council of barons and the Archduke:

All fines made with us unjustly and against the law of the land, and all amercements, imposed unjustly and against the law of the land, shall be entirely remitted, or else it shall be done concerning them according to the decision of the five and twenty barons whom mention is made below in the clause for securing the pease, or according to the judgment of the majority of the same, along with the aforesaid Stephen, archbishop of Canterbury, if he can be present.[89]

The new council of barons – an important precursor to all representative assemblies in the western world – was an unprecedented institution that influenced the direction of the British constitutional system. While the barons were not representatives of the people, they were regional feudal landholders that sought to protect the seizure of their property and the desecration of their respective regions. With their assent necessary to carry the king's decrees forward, the new assembly served as an institutional forerunner to Parliament in London – and eventually to Congress under the United States Constitution. In the latter case, such a novel breakthrough influenced the requirement for treaties, laws, and appointments to be made with the consent of a representative council.

Furious over the rejection of his desired candidate for Archduke, John worked to rebuke his electors and undermine the "rebel" barons. The king maintained that Stephen Langton was personally unacceptable to him, and that he had been denied his traditional right to patronage.[90] The conflict over the Archduke led to the Catholic excommunication of John, and a vast campaign of retributions against Catholics in England. As John seized attempted to stop Langton from entering England, the Pope sent a commission in attempt to stifle the policy. When this failed, Innocent went so far as to place an exclusionary order to prevent Catholic services from taking place in England. This injunction enraged John, who forcibly seized lands of the clerics that opposed him, as well as the Pope's English property. After John's belligerent response, Innocent finally excommunicated the king in 1209.

The Magna Carta importantly asserts another principle that is widely accepted in the British constitutional tradition – the assertion that only the people's representatives can levy taxes. This is an ideal that remains noticeable in the United States Constitution, as Congress is the only body that can "lay and collect" taxes. This maxim became an essential part of Britain's underlying political system, where the principle was invoked on several notable occasions. Similarly, the Magna Carta asserted that "no 'scutage' or 'aid' may be levied in our kingdom without its general consent." In direct contravention of John's illicit taxes, the document binds the taxation power to specific activities. This provision now serves as the direct ancestor of the United States Constitution's requirements for indirect taxes. Article I, Section 8 of the same framework also places other limitations on taxes, such as the requirement that indirect taxes must remain at a uniform rate throughout the states.[91]

The Magna Carta also specifically inhibits any type of military tax to be levied except that by "common counsel of [the] realm." This is a reference toward the "common counsel," another forerunner to Parliament that acted as a representative body of regional aristocrats. Under the new charter, any form of taxation would have to be agreed upon by the counsel rather than forced by the prerogative of the king.

In addition to his other scandals, John also toppled England's legal system by absolving individuals of criminal offenses in return for bribes for the king. Discarding this system, the Magna Carta reversed such a course, declaring that "we will sell to no man, we will not deny or defer to any man either Justice or Right."[92] This stipulation was clear rejection of the system that John implemented, which fraudulently allowed abusers to sidestep the judicial process and escape criminal punishment.

The barons also disposed of the scutage system, which allowed John to collect funds even in the absence of military campaigns. In the run-up to such a decision, the king had declared the kingdom in a constant state of war to justify his collection of the funds. With no end to such a condition in sight, the barons viewed the scheme as a pernicious violation of liberty and property, and ended the king's archaic means to expand his own taxing prerogative.

The Magna Carta also challenged the legality of standing armies by restricting foreign soldiers during peacetime:

As soon as peace is restored, we will banish from the kingdom all foreign born knights, crossbowmen, serjeants, and mercenary soldiers who have come with horses and arms to the kingdom's hurt.[93]

This historic provision was the first real limitation against peacetime military presence in England. Influencing the course of the country's constitutional history for centuries, the passage set the first of many precedents that established that England would disband its military during peacetime. From that point, the king could only raise armies under a set of preconditions that included a declaration of war and appropriations funding. Based on similar trepidations of extended military presence, the United States Constitution limits appropriation for military activity to two years.[94]

As students of history and observers of the British constitutional tradition, many of the American founders emphasized the dangers of standing armies, and rigidly sought to prohibit them entirely. For instance, Thomas Jefferson cautioned that standing armies would endanger the liberty of individuals and subvert the will of the civil authority:

There are instruments so dangerous to the rights of the nation and which place them so totally at the mercy of their governors that those governors, whether legislative or executive, should be restrained from keeping such instruments on foot but in well-defined cases. Such an instrument is a standing army.[95]

In support of Jefferson's outlook, esteemed statesman Elbridge Gerry called standing armies "the bane of liberty." Warning that "a standing military force" had always been "the instruments of tyranny at home," James Madison expressed similar anxieties. During the Massachusetts ratification convention, Theodore Sedgwick figured individuals would enslave "themselves and their brethren" by allowing a standing army to rule over the states.[96] The concerted disdain for standing armies, then, was the direct byproduct of John's attempt to maintain a perpetual force in the 13th century.

Outside of his preoccupation with taxation, John took many indiscriminate measures to jail political dissidents. Compounding this problem, England had no independent judiciary and the country's system of law was directed by the king's arbitrary discretion. To counter this, the Magna Carta imposed the following stipulation against the king:

No freeman is to be taken or imprisoned or disseised [or robbed of property] of his free tenement or of his liberties or free customs, or outlawed or exiled or in any way ruined, nor will we go against such a man or send against him save by lawful judgement of his peers or by the law of the land. To no-one will we sell or deny of delay right or justice.[97]

This text – sometimes called "Chapter 39" – is now viewed as western civilization's foundation for due process rights. Largely because of this passage, Americans now recognize the constitutional guarantee of due process in the Fifth Amendment of the United States Constitution. The Seventh Amendment – which necessitates a representative cross-section of citizens to serve as jurors in criminal cases – is also influenced by this text. In America's case, both amendments were intended to prohibit government from detaining individuals indefinitely.

Because of John's subversions of the legal process, many generations of Britons remained suspicious of selective jurisprudence that was held by the hand of the king. Consequently, the Constitution forbids bills of attainder – decrees that declared persons guilty of a crime without any form of due process. The same clause eliminated ex post facto law, restraining the government from criminalizing legal activities that took place prior to their illegality.[98]

The Magna Carta represented the first clear denunciation of the idea that the king is entitled to govern by his own personal prerogative, and countered the notion that the only limitations to his rule are those of his own choosing. In the fields of Runnymede, the king was forced by the barons, at sword point, to place his royal seal upon the document in 1215. While John temporarily acquiesced to the stipulations of the barons, it was soon clear that he would not voluntarily yield to the restrictions the document placed upon him. The same year, he disregarded the specifics of the document, and plunged England into a new war against the barons. Ultimately, he died the next year while trying to cling to his authoritarian tendencies, stubbornly refusing to abide by the candid attempt to inhibit his power.

Above all, the Magna Carta proved that subjects of government could oppose a central government even when it seemed particularly strong and immutable. In the end, the local authorities emerged triumphant over John, creating a tradition that still lives on today in the annals of American constitutionalism. The document thus remains a significant refutation of the crown's power, plainly asserting that a single monarch could not be trusted with absolute authority over a kingdom.

Under the recollections of future Pennsylvanian statesmen John Dickinson, the people did not "acquire powers" or "receive privileges" through the Magna Carta. Instead, "they only ascertained and fixed those they were entitled to as Englishmen."[99] Viewing the occasion in this way, the document was an agreement between the governed to hold the central authority to a limited subset of powers. Henceforth, the king's defilements would be openly condemned as bellicose violations of individual liberty and English rights.

THE PROVISIONS OF OXFORD

Another defining moment of Britain's constitutional heritage was the adoption of the Provisions of Oxford, a set of constitutional reforms that created another 13th century forerunner to the United States Constitution. These refinements, codified in 1258 by another group of barons, created a system under which the consent of a new council of representatives would be required to oversee additional governmental decisions, make civil appointments, and even investigate abuses by government officials. The new codicils had the immediate effect of forcing King Henry III, the son of King John, to accept new limitations to his rule. Without submitting to the boundaries set forth by the barons, Henry fell prey to another baron revolt, similar to the one that led to his father's death. Following the groundwork of the Magna Carta, the new council was a direct response to impulsive royal privileges, and inhibited the king's ability to create his own like-minded panel of advisors.

This United States Constitution, which requires the president to secure the approval of two-thirds of the Senate in order to make treaties or civil appointments, had resulted from the same style of legal discernment as that which produced the Provisions of Oxford.[100] Moreover, the American president's veto power was subject to override with the popular support of representatives, further solidifying the doctrine that a singular executive head could not unilaterally command a free society of people. Beginning these foundations in the 13th century, the barons began chipping away at the royal prerogative of the monarch.

BRITISH FEDERALISM

Even before adoption of the Declaration of Independence, Thomas Jefferson argued that the British colonies fit into a federalized system. From the inception of the colonies, Jefferson argued, the original inhabitants of North America had successfully differentiated their own societies from others. In his influential 1774 pamphlet, *A Summary View of the Rights of British America*, Jefferson considered the economic structure, legal system, and social conditions of each part of the British Empire to be the remarkably distinct:

Our ancestors, before their emigration to America, were the free inhabitants of the British dominions in Europe, and possessed a right which nature has given to all men, of departing from the country in which chance, not choice, has placed them, of going in quest of new habitations, and of there establishing new societies, under such laws and regulations as to them shall seem most likely to promote public happiness. That their Saxon ancestors had, under this universal law, in like manner left their native wilds and woods in the north of Europe, had possessed themselves of the island of Britain, then less charged with inhabitants, and had established there that system of laws which has so long been the glory and protection of that country.[101]

With the observation that the ancestors of the colonists endured much risk, hardship, and adversity to create each colonial society, Jefferson remarked that they sought not to emulate England entirely but to carved out new, improved communities with English tradition in mind. Indeed, the colonists' "own blood was spilt in acquiring lands for their settlement, their own fortunes expended in making that settlement effectual; for themselves they fought, for themselves they conquered, for themselves alone they have the right to hold."[102]

By the act of forging their own governmental path, and through the grant of the original colonial characters, Jefferson reasoned that Britain could not claim legitimate possession of the colonial polities. Conversely, he argued that the societies created by the inhabitants thereof had naturally divested themselves of the crown's will. Through the passage of time, he contended, the colonies became disassociated entities, with their only common tie to Britain in their political attachment to the same monarch.

As *A Summary View* revealed, Jefferson's enduring penchant for federalism was built upon the noteworthy lessons of the past. Therein, the famous penman reflected upon the villainous actions of another British monarch from the past, one who attempted to suppress commercial endeavors, expand war powers, seize property, and establish corporate favoritism. Paralleling such hardships, he believed, were the circumstances of his own time:

That the exercise of a free trade with all parts of the world, possessed by the American colonists, as of natural right, and which no law of their own had taken away or abridged, was next the object of unjust encroachment...But that, upon the restoration of his majesty king Charles the second, their rights of free commerce fell once more a victim to arbitrary power; and by several acts of his reign, as well as of some of his successors, the trade of the colonies was laid under such restrictions...History has informed us that bodies of men, as well as individuals, are susceptible of the spirit of tyranny.[103]

Refusing to concede that the right to trade could be legally taken from Englishmen, Jefferson castigated the same type of "arbitrary power" that had riled masses of languishing people to indignation. He therefore lamented the cyclical potential for liberty to fall victim to repressive kings, and likened the duplicitous deeds of Charles to the 18th century struggle between the American states and British crown.

CHARLES I AND THE ELEVEN YEAR TYRANNY

As the 17th century demonstrated, the seeds of economic control were planted long before Jefferson's time. At that juncture, King Charles I became known throughout the world for his adamant devotion to the divine right of kings, his outlandish taxation schemes, and his crafty maneuvers to eschew and undermine the will of Parliament. He granted legal monopolies to certain firms, capriciously taxed land grants, and fined subjects who failed to attend his coronation. The most egregious of the taxes Charles initiated was for ship money – a duty imposed upon coastal towns to furnish ships during wartime – without the consent of Parliament. Under the scheme, the king required towns to provide a certain quota of ships. If they could not do so, they were forced to pay a sum of money to cover the cost.

Charles' ship money program was a radical departure from the traditional bounds the power's previous usage, and served as a serious source of public vexation. The ship money tax was never before levied during peacetime, and many denied the presence of any wartime emergency necessitate its application. In addition, Charles expanded ship money's impact by subjecting the policy to all counties in England, including inland regions that were nowhere near the coast. Due to the resulting unrest, the ship money policy faced several legal battles. In a famous court case that concentrated on the king's usage of the tax, a collection of 12 judges – all appointed by Charles – predictably sided with the king and declared that the monarch had not violated any part of his royal prerogative in its enactment.

During this timeframe, Charles also adopted several forms of corporate favoritism that contravened Parliamentary law. The king's duplicity in this regard violated the country's 1624 Statute of Monopolies, which established the first English statutory law and prevented such government-backed monopolies from being awarded by the crown. Nonetheless, Charles believed the new monopolies would generate revenue to fund his pet endeavors. Furthermore, without the need to seek the approval of Parliament, their creation would not require the favor of England's merchant class. By all accounts, the king's unprecedented economic intervention had sweeping ramifications. For instance, one wildly unpopular monopoly was awarded on soap, where a lackluster product was broadly mocked.

In response to Charles' deceitful acts, English Parliament set out to draft an enumerated a list of subjects the king could not infringe upon. This document the body produced became known as the Petition of Right of 1628, which reasserted principles held sacred from centuries prior. The indenture condemned Charles' methods of taxation, noting that his heinous taxes "imprisoned, confined," and in other ways "molested and disquieted" the people. Additionally, the document reproved the king's proclivity to inflict severe punishments upon religious dissidents and other political opponents. It was for these reasons that the founding generation in America adamantly opposed unjust taxes and monopolies, and objected to cruel and unusual punishments. The latter was prohibited explicitly in the Eighth Amendment of the United States Constitution.[104]

To the contrary of Charles' rule, the Petition of Right also declared "that no man, of what estate or condition that he be, should be put out of his land or tenements, nor taken, nor imprisoned, nor disinherited nor put to death without being brought to answer by due process of law."[105] This clause serves today as a parent of America's Fifth Amendment acknowledgment of due process, which reiterated axioms as old as the Magna Carta. The Petition of Right asserted another grievance that attacked billeting – the practice of forcing subjects to provide housing to soldiers:

Soldiers and mariners have been dispersed into divers counties of the realm, and the inhabitants against their wills have been compelled to receive them into their houses, and there to suffer them to sojourn against the laws and customs of this realm, and to the great grievance and vexation of the people.[106]

In the United States Constitution, the Third Amendment injunction against the forced quartering of soldiers was derived from this predecessor.

The Petition of Right also denounced the enactment of martial law, proclaiming that "no commissions of like nature may issue forth to any person or persons whatsoever to be executed as aforesaid." Article I, Section 9 of the United States Constitution specifically affirms the existence of habeas corpus – a judicial writ to prevent indiscriminate detention by the government. Scolding the king's disregarding for the Magna Carta in general, the document affirmed that "no man shall be forejudged of life or limb against the form of the Great Charter and the law of the land."[107]

In need of financial support for his wars, Charles reluctantly accepted the Petition of Right. In a royal address to the kingdom, Charles discordantly claimed that he only wished to use his authority to protect his subjects, and professed that Parliament stood in the way of such an aim:

And I assure you that my maxim is that the people's liberties strengthen the King's prerogative and that the King's prerogative is to defend the people's liberties...I have done my part, wherefore if the Parliament have not a happy conclusion the sin is yours. I am free from it.[108]

Like King John before him, Charles was forced to accept a charter that affirmed the people's liberties. As in John's case, he intensely resisted its precepts, and the next years demonstrated that Charles' words were idle platitudes.

Even after accepting the Petition of Right in 1628, Charles' actions continued to fuel Parliamentary resistance. Mere months after the adoption of the document, Charles demanded the imposition of tonnage and poundage – a collection of duties from the sale of imported wine. When the assembly responded with harsh opposition, Charles decided to dissolve Parliament in order to eliminate further impediments to his reign. He also took advantage of his period of "Personal Rule" by granting a new series of contentious monopolies, and imprisoning nine Parliamentarians that had opposed his program. As it turned out, the period in which Charles ruled alone was soon called the "Eleven Years' Tyranny."

With the intention of raising new taxes, Charles finally summoned Parliament again in 1640. When he did so, the assembly refused to endorse the king's financial bills. Instead, the Long Parliament prepared a list of grievances called the Grand Remonstrance of 1641. The document – a striking forebear to the Declaration of Independence – described the "various distempers and disorders which had not only assaulted, but even overwhelmed and extinguished the liberty, peace and prosperity of this kingdom." The document articulated Parliament's claim that the king had pursued "a malignant and pernicious design of subverting the fundamental laws and principles of government."[109] Primarily written by John Pym, its issuance was a key precursor to the English Civil Wars.

The Grand Remonstrance documented 204 separate points of opposition to the reign of Charles. One of the reprimands upon the king's actions included creating "monopolies of soap, salt, wine, leather, sea-coal, and in a manner of all things of most common and necessary use." With the acknowledgement that life, liberty, and property had fallen prey to the outlandish policies, Parliament rebuked Charles for "the restraint of the liberties of the subjects in their habitation, trades and other interests."

Another point alleged that the king had stolen from the coffers of the people. "Public faith" had been broken, read the charge, through the seizure "of the money and bullion in the mint." Consequently, the "whole kingdom" had been "robbed at once in that abominable project of brass money." The king's notorious effort to replace England's hard money with worthless brass artfully bypassed Parliamentary opposition to his taxes, and greatly depreciated the value of the currency. In addition to his inflationary project, Charles simultaneously ventured to collect the controversial taxes. "Tonnage and poundage hath been received without colour or pretence of law," the Grand Remonstrance stated, and "many other heavy impositions continued against law." The document also challenged the king's creation of new courts without any legal basis, opposing the array of "new judicatories erected without law."[110]

The Grand Remonstrance also admonished the enlargement of England's royal forests, contrary to a pre-existing statute granting private usage of such lands as sources of fuel for heating and cooking.[111] The

Parliament plainly saw this as a scheme to deprive people of private property, and bolster the king's financial standing. The House of Commons also scolded the king for dissolving the previous Parliament and suppressing political dissidence:

> Upon the dissolution of both these Parliaments, untrue and scandalous declarations were published to asperse their proceedings, and some of their members unjustly; to make them odious, and colour the violence which was used against them; proclamations set out to the same purpose; and to the great dejecting of the hearts of the people, forbidding them even to speak of Parliaments.[112]

As Charles' reputation suffered, his frustrations led him to initiate drastic action against his political rivals. Ultimately, these harsh ripostes harmed the king's reputation even more.

In contemporary consideration, the intrusions of liberty listed in the Grand Remonstrance are truly eerie. Today, the United States federal government has taken legalized monopolies in industries such as automobile manufacturing, transportation, health care, and postage. It has established national banks that arbitrarily manipulate interest rates and inflate the currency through the elimination of hard money. It has raised arguments for creating "sustainable land developments" in the interests of seizing property and taxing owners. Rather than nominal excises and tariffs, the federal government now imposes income taxes, gas taxes, capital gains taxes, gift taxes, and others. It has asserted that its legislative decrees and proceedings are dominant over state law, and that due process does not apply to certain activities that appear seditious to the government. It has created military tribunals and FISA courts to try offenders in shadowed secrecy, and assumed the power to indefinitely detain American citizens. Rather than typical and benign exertions of governmental authority, in 17th century England such maneuvers were considered serious infringements of liberty that called for immediate confrontation. In due time, Charles would eventually lose his head for his role in their enactment.

In the run-up to war, the founders of the United States believed that Parliament under George III employed similar measures of despotism. To that generation, the usurpations and villainous actions that occurred in mid-17th century England were not reminiscent of a time long gone, but a living reality. It is no coincidence, then, that the Declaration of Independence of 1776 similarly enumerated a list of indictments against George, as some of the same practices of governmental misconduct surfaced.

Charles officially responded to the Grand Remonstrance by denying that he had overstepped his constitutional bounds, and suggested that England's problems were not the result of his policies. Despite this, he set out to dismiss several government officials and replaced them with more pliable alternatives, and took firm action against mobs that protested his rule.[113] Charles ordered the arrest of a key government official, Lord Mandeville, who was a leading agitator of the claims against him.

England's monarch took his most extreme step to rout out the dissent against him by invading Parliament. In early 1642, he entered the House of Commons to arrest five of the most influential Parliamentarians. An unprecedented deed, Charles defilement of Parliament's proceedings represented a grave and desperate retort against the growing opposition to his rule. John Pym, who had drafted the Grand Remonstrance, was among those the king attempted to arrest. Along with four others, Pym had already fled from the House by the time Charles entered.

Charles charged the figures with sedition, alleging that they had endeavored to subvert the fundamental laws of England. In the process, the king alienated several previous allies and galvanized oppositional factions against him. The House of Commons responded with concerted indignation, refusing to surrender the men to royal prosecution. Outraged, the king responded that "no privilege can protect a traitor from legal trial."[114] At this point, Charles was the actual traitor to England in the eyes of Parliament.

These five men would become known as the "Five Members," and their defiance is still recognized in modern England. To this day, at Britain's State Opening of Parliament, a customary commemoration takes place each year where the king approaches the House. As he gets there, the doors of the Commons Chamber are slammed in his face. This is a traditional rebuke of the king and a way to honor those in Parliament who acted against Charles' despotic tendencies. In addition, the event represents an official denunciation of absolute monarchy.

When Parliament proposed statutes that would deprive Charles of his executive powers for his perfidious actions, the king's defiance set the course for a period of great carnage in England. The House of Commons stood vigilant against Charles' arbitrary tyranny, defending the tenets of liberty laid out for them by the bloodshed of generations prior. Like the conflict between John and the barons, the country was thrust into a new series of conflicts – the tragic consequence of a malevolent king.

As a result of dissonance between Parliament and the king, the English Civil Wars consumed the country for the next decade. The wars, like those in the states of North America many years later, were viewed as a constitutional crisis where the rights of Englishmen were endangered by a broad and powerful government under a superlative monarch. Refusing to abide by the precepts clearly laid out in the Magna Carta and Petition of Right, Parliament and the king both began raises armies to do battle. Plunged into a series of clashes with each other, the crisis was extraordinarily bloody, with a total of 618,000 deaths attributed to the English Civil Wars in sum.[115] Beyond taking lives of the participants, these struggles were particularly destructive to civilians. Plague, famine, and disease spread throughout England.

After the culmination of the First England Civil War, Charles was placed into the custody of Parliament. It looked for a time as if peace would be made, and Charles would return to the throne under a constitutional settlement that restricted his power in minor ways. However, he quickly squandered such an opportunity in 1647. At that point, Charles signed a secret agreement with the Scots that would ensure Presbyterianism was established in England for a period of three years. In return, the Scots promised to invade England on Charles' behalf and restore him to the throne. After catching wind of such duplicity, the leadership of senior officers in the English Army – known as Grandees – affirmed their duty "to call Charles Stuart, that man of blood, to an account for that blood he had shed, and mischief he had done."

In 1648, the Second English Civil War began as the Scots invaded at the behest of Charles. Considering the bloody losses that had already transpired, the Parliamentary army now had no reservations about their aim to remove the king from power entirely. While once expressing indifference to the institution of the crown, the introduction of foreign troops into

England caused New Model Army commander Oliver Cromwell to view Charles' actions as unforgivable. Cromwell declared that "we will cut off the King's head with the crown on it."[116]

The Second English Civil War resulted in the victory for the Parliamentarians, and the assembly indicted Charles on counts of high treason and "other high crimes." The head of the court, John Bradshaw, referred to Charles' actions as "great calamities that have been brought upon this nation." Cromwell spared no wrath against the king, calling him "a man against whom the Lord [had] witnessed." When John Cook, the Solicitor General, described Charles as a "tyrant, traitor, and murderer," the king responded by laughing at the accusation.[117] When forced to reply, the king protested that the court had no right to try him, argued that it lacked authority to make him answer for his crimes. The king, like so many tyrants after him, believed he was above the law. Following the trial, the king was declared guilty and sentenced to death. At the behest of Cromwell, 59 commissioners – or regicides – signed his death warrant. Charles was executed in 1649, and England soon established a republic called the Commonwealth of England.

Reflecting upon Charles' downfall, John Dickinson recalled that "nothing less than the utter destruction of the monarchy could satisfy those who had suffered and thought they had reason to believe they always should suffer under it." The consequences of the king's reign, he wrote, were "well known," and his tyrannous inclinations had built "a system of oppression." Dickinson declared that there was no time in which the people had "been so constantly watchful of their liberty, and so successful in their struggles for it."[118]

Indeed, the commissioners who signed Charles' death warrant realized that their actions would be considered treasonous to royalists who still believed in the legitimacy of the crown. Like those who signed the Declaration of Independence over a century later, the Parliamentary regicides pledged their lives, fortunes, and sacred honors, knowing that retribution would ensue if Charles' bloodline was restored. When Charles II took the throne upon the English Restoration of 1660, that exact scenario came to fruition when the crown brought about a campaign of retribution against the living signers of Charles' death warrant. Some escaped, but ten were hung, and nineteen others were imprisoned for life.

OLIVER CROMWELL

Oliver Cromwell's constitutional influence extended beyond the English Civil Wars and his role in the king's beheading, and the years that followed Charles' death that defined his legacy. Once an admired, vigilant, painstaking defender of liberty, Cromwell eventually betrayed the republican principles he once championed. By adopting some of the same tendencies that led to the demise of Charles, Cromwell inspired the end to the English republic that he helped create.

Cromwell's fall from republican virtue was most apparent in 1653, when he expressed hostility toward what he perceived to be legislative inaction. Against his wishes, the Rump Parliament had not yet passed laws to establish a tolerant national church and bring local regions under the English centralized authority, and Cromwell viewed the assembly's posture as indecisive and agitating. In response, he barged into a sitting session of Parliament. He announced, "I will put an end to your prating. You are no Parliament. I say you are no Parliament. I will put an end to your sitting." Cromwell then called the military into the House and dissolved the assembly by force. Former friend Henry Vane decried Cromwell's exploit, and professed that his former friend had acted "against morality and common honesty." Enraged, Cromwell reprimanded Vane, approached the front of the room, and snatched up Parliament's bauble – a symbol of the body's authority.[119] The bauble was taken away by force, sharing the same fate as the new Commonwealth.

John Bradshaw, an ardent republican that had also once been warm to Cromwell, also rebuked his deed. "All of England will hear" of such a deceitful operation, he declared. Because "no power under heaven" could dissolve Parliament, he demanded that Cromwell take notice of his usurpation of authority."[120] Over a century later, the colonists in British North America observed that George III's coercive dissolution of their local assemblies, much like that which had transpired under Cromwell's malfeasance, had repeated one of the grimmest offenses of constitutional abnegation in the British tradition.

Once respected as a prominent republican leader, Cromwell gradually favored power and control over republican virtue. Even after ensuring republicanism, he proved that respected figures could become tarnished by authority and prestige. Taking note of this, the founding generation in the United States grew extremely distrustful of the mass concentration of power in a single, central executive. This propensity undoubtedly influenced the near-universal opinion that the ideal republican executive had to be checked and limited by specific powers, competing power centers, and the local representatives of the people.

THE GLORIOUS REVOLUTION OF 1688

Virginia statesman George Mason, a self-described "man of 1688," often cited the historical tradition of British liberty in justification of his own work.[121] Like his philosophical predecessors, Mason believed that all free people were entitled to a declaration of rights – a set of guaranteed protections against the unpredictable power of government. His sensibilities led him to draft the Virginia Declaration of Rights in 1776, a precursor to other American bills of rights. This perceived necessity was consistent with the traditions of the Magna Carta, Petition of Right, Grand Remonstrance, and English Bill of Rights before it, all of which limited the authority of the central power.

Mason's belief in such a bill of rights was so strong that he left the Philadelphia Convention of 1787 in resenting that the new Constitution lacked such an instrument. Refusing to attach his name to such a framework, the eminent Virginian professed that his fellow delegates had made a serious mistake by doubting the necessity of such an addendum, and by extension, had failed to account for the tribulations of the past. One of such events, one could reason, was the English political crisis of 1688.

A pivotal year in the history of England, 1688 saw yet another English king deposed. After the culmination of the Glorious Revolution of 1688, as it was called, Parliament was declared the ultimate sovereign power of the country, with a general authority to legislate on all matters pertinent to the British Empire. When the American founders were writing the Constitution in Philadelphia, they were less than 100 years removed from such events. Truly, the crisis epitomized the historical tradition of resistance against an overreaching central authority. It was a direct result of the treacherous acts of King James II, who provoked a civil struggle that eventually removed the king from power. The result of the Glorious Revolution would again prove that the king did not wield plenary authority in England, and that the people's representatives could impede, alter, and even abolish the executive's right to rule.

The 17th century was an epoch of great tumult in Britain. Many of those who lived during the Glorious Revolution also witnessed the English Civil Wars and consequential transformation of the English kingdom into a republic. Temporary tranquility was achieved after the Cavaliers were vanquished and Charles was beheaded, but this would soon change as liberty was threatened once again by yet another notorious king. After Cromwell's death and a short reign of his son as Lord Protector, Charles' son became king in 1660, reclaiming the throne and reinstating the monarchy in the English Restoration. Naturally, England's political power was once again consolidated into a centralized structure. As the years passed, Charles II became embroiled in his own scuffles with Parliament, and the groundwork was laid for the reign of the next king. When Charles died in 1685, his brother, James II, took the throne. The next three years proved that the reign of James was one of England's most boisterous and consequential periods.

The most controversial enactment of James' short reign was a pair of royal proclamations known as the Declaration of Indulgence. These pronouncements – intended to be read by clergy in all British and Scottish churches – articulated the king's views on religious matters in an attempt to liberalize religious freedom. This campaign came to be seen by the Anglican religious majority in Britain as a harshly interventionist measure that compromised their own religious practices. The edicts backfired on James, as the Declaration of Indulgence came to be seen as an invasion of religious liberty.

In terms of religious reforms, James was most interested in removing the Test Acts, oaths that were taken to proclaim allegiance to the Anglican Church as a pre-requisite to public office. Ironically, the pronouncements aimed to secure religious tolerance toward the Catholics, but most Englishmen rejected the idea that the Anglican pulpit should be used to carry out the king's political policy. Putting himself in direct conflict with the Anglican religious identity, James used his dispensing authority – the monarch's prerogative to obstruct the enforcement of laws – to suspend England's penal laws, made by the people's representatives.[122] While

James hoped to advance a program of religious toleration, his deeds provoked a fiery opposition that condemned him for meddling in the Protestant churches.

The controversy was exacerbated when England's royal courts affirmed the king's "sovereign power and prerogative" for the king's use of the dispensing powers. Emboldened, king continued to use the dispensing authority to suspend statutes that he personally disliked. This inflamed tensions further, reinforced by the fact that James had already ousted judges that stood against his viewpoints. A second court case culminated with an opinion that James overstepped his authority through the usage of the dispensing authority, and Justice John Powell pontificated that the king's use of this power had gone far beyond the bounds of traditional use. If James' use of this power continued to be tolerated, he warned, "there will be no Parliament; all the legislature will be in the king."[123]

When seven bishops refused to read the Declaration of Indulgence in their respective congregations, the king charged them with seditious libel and sent them to the Tower of London. After rampant outcry and a public trial, the seven men were acquitted, and their freedom was welcomed with a wave of rejoicing which the government could neither prevent nor punish.[124] The liberation of the bishops was seen as a legal mandate against James' reign, and a rallying cry for the English Whigs that opposed him.

On top of the dispensing scandal and its aftereffects, James also engaged in an extraordinary scheme of interference in England's elections in order to coerce regional electors to support his rule. Historian John Miller notes that such manipulation was backed up by broad campaigns of "canvassing and propaganda" that embodied a calculated political purge. An invasive arrangement that was micromanaged by the king, James' interference in the elections caused his reputation to suffer dramatically. Going beyond his Anglican intrusions, James also interfered in Catholic practices by encouraging forcible Catholic conversions. In sum, James used this royal prerogative in ways that were legally dubious and outright unconstitutional, provoking fears of kingly absolutism.[125]

Despite James' push to exempt Catholics from the Test Acts, it became clear that he had tried to silence and intimidate the Anglican clergy in the process. The king's attempt to undercut the laws also raised apprehensions that the dispensing precedent would result in the effective end of all laws made by the people's representatives. "If he did [have the authority]," wrote Miller, "nobody's person or property would be safe." In desperation, James' political opponents desperately considered foreign military assistance to overthrow his government, and English subjects in general experienced a complete breakdown in government.[126]

Another factor working against James was that he was considered far too politically connected to the French. This fear was not misplaced, as James grew up in France and served in the French military. His French cousin, Louis XIV – one of the most powerful monarchs in European history – ruled over the Bourbon Dynasty. A strict adherent to the divine right of kings, Louis contended that a king's reign is derived from God's will alone rather than the consent of the governed. James' provocative undertakings during his short reign appeared to the Whigs to confirm that he shared a similar philosophy, as the king exuded a lofty view of his own authority and expected his subjects to comply with his mandates. As tensions amplified, James and Louis came to be viewed as potential allies, craftily working behind the scenes to build a system of universal monarchy in Europe.[127]

English subjects grew disdainful of the king's invasive attitude toward Anglican practices, and apprehended the prospect of a new Catholic-headed hereditary monarchy. Until 1687, James' crown was expected to be passed to Mary, his Protestant daughter. At this time, the prospect of a son being born to James and Mary of Modena became a reality. When James' wife produced a male Catholic heir, anxieties grew to new heights. At the time, Catholicism was a minority sect in England, and English subjects lived in fear of rulers who persecuted their Anglican traditions. This apprehension was not unfounded, as the last centuries witnessed numerous Catholic monarchs who persecuted their Protestant subjects with implacable cruelty.[128] With the roots of their unease stretching as far back as far as King John's time, the Anglican majority was now fearful that the Church of England would be toppled by a new Catholic dynasty.

At the time of his reign, England was also deeply concerned that James would bring other aspects of French culture to the country, such as a French-oriented legal system. The British respected a distinct British system of law that had its foundations in the 11th and 12th centuries. Common law, as it came to be known, was the system of legal code favored in

England and asserted in the constitutional documents of the 17th century. In yet another threat to Protestants, James raised a huge standing army in 1687, repeating the classic constitutional abnegation of his predecessors. His plan employed many soldiers, each to be placed into positions of power strictly by measure of their adherence to Catholicism. Meanwhile, James purged and disarmed his Irish army of Protestants completely.

James' opponents in Parliament considered this behavior highly capricious, and responded by articulating a significant irony. A king who was in favor of abolishing the Test Acts, they suggested, would be hypocritical to restrict army appointments to Catholics. When leaders in Parliament threatened James directly, Louis XIV of France offered to intervene militarily to preserve his cousin's reign. James ultimately declined this offer of assistance, believing that the acceptance of military support from France would cause all remaining factions in England to align against him. Still, the upcoming clash against James' power was partly sparked by English antipathy toward French absolutism and the French political system.

In early 1688, several statesmen in Parliament engaged in corresponded with William, Prince of Orange, and eventually provided him invitation to invade England at their behest to remove James from the throne. A Protestant, William disavowed the actions of his father-in law. While James corresponded with William at the same time, he remained ignorant of the looming political incursion against him.[129] Meanwhile, William assembled a huge invasion force with plans to land on the English coast, raising an army of 20,000 soldiers for the purpose of deposing James.

After a last attempt to subdue the opposition against him, James abandoned the throne and fled from England. He left for France, never to return to London again. Overwhelmed by the insurmountable situation, he threw England's Great Seal into the Thames River, a symbol of abdication.[130] James' rule was past the point of no return, as the Parliament-backed revolutionary coup successfully sealed the king's fate for all time.

THE ENGLISH BILL OF RIGHTS

After the Glorious Revolution, England experienced the unique condition of a dual kingship that would share executive authority. Serving as a cooperative monarchy, William and Mary were required to take a pledge that deferred supremacy to the Parliament. By doing so, the two new monarchs recognized Parliamentary entitlement as authoritative, and accepted a notable diminishment to their own executive standing. William and Mary generally respected British law, and found themselves unequivocally opposed to France in the following years. Under the new arrangement, they reigned as relatively popular monarchs.

Almost 100 years later, Patrick Henry reminded his peers of these incidents at Virginia's ratification convention. In Henry's mind, as in fellow Virginian George Mason's, a document that explicitly spelled out the liberties of the people was paramount to the preservation of a republic, and equally necessary in both England and the United States. With the English Bill of Rights in mind, Henry recalled:

> The rights of the people continued to be violated till the Stuart family was banished, in the year 1688. The people of England magnanimously defended their rights, banished the tyrant, and prescribed to William, Prince of Orange, by the bill of rights, on what terms he should reign; and this bill of rights put an end to all construction and implication. Before this, sir, the situation of the public liberty of England was dreadful. For upwards of a century, the nation was involved in every kind of calamity, till the bill of rights put an end to all, by defining the rights of the people, and limiting the king's prerogative.[131]

In Henry's estimation, only a bill of rights would provide a necessary set of safeguards against centralized power, and act to preserve the liberty of the people.

The byproduct of the Glorious Revolution, the English Bill of Rights of 1689 set a new course for English constitutionalism. The direct result of the overthrow of James, the document was born from a rich tradition of liberty that built upon the heritage of the Magna Carta, Petition of Right, and Grand Remonstrance. Consequently, the English Bill of Rights became the newest mechanism to guarantee a host of liberties that applied to all ages – including those of political uncertainty and domestic upheaval. The document also repeated that rights that could not be infringed upon by the central authority; they existed regardless of government action.

Paramount in importance, the English Bill of Rights assured the unfettered right to bear arms. This prose is now recognized as a parent of the Second Amendment to the Constitution of the United States. Made to arm the populace with the ability to throw off their government and establish a new one, the colonies understood this guarantee quite well after their successful War of Independence. Since an armed populace played a crucial role in freeing England from the king's rule, and because James adamantly intended to disarm his subjects, the English hoped to guard against such villainous tendencies for all time.

Excessive fines and "illegal and cruel punishments" were also prohibited in the document, a noteworthy precursor to the Eighth Amendment in the United States. In another obvious forerunner to the liberties affirmed in the American First Amendment, the "right of the subject to petition the king" and the "freedom of speech" were also affirmed by Parliament. In addition to these correlations, The English Bill of Rights also intended to prevent any misuse of the legal system after it was abused by James, undeniably influencing the Fifth and Sixth Amendments to the United States Constitution.

As the direct result of James' behavior in the runup to the crisis, many Englishmen became skeptical of governmental overreach in religious matters. A century later, the American Whigs could only conclude that such schemes were unambiguous affronts to religious liberty. The subsequent policy of religious non-intervention – which took root in several of the fledgling states – was therefore inspired in part by the Glorious Revolution and the deposition of James.

By the time of the Philadelphia Convention, several American sovereignties had adopted measures guaranteeing the free practice of religion. Virginia incorporated the Virginia Statute for Religious Freedom, which abolished the state's Anglican association and instituted a policy of religious non-intervention. Other states – such as Pennsylvania, New Jersey, and Delaware – never adopted any established church, while the remainder maintained official churches. Through the ratification of the United States Constitution, the states restrained the central government from impeding the free exercise of religion, and prohibited the usage of religious tests to qualify civil officeholders.

Regardless of the age in question, human nature and the experience of government has always been the same. Through hundreds of years of turmoil, Britons recognized the need to stand up for innate, inviolable, individual rights. Despite all of these striking motifs, very little in the English Bill of Rights was considered new. Instead, the document mostly served as a strong reaffirmation of British rights that had simply been violated by another king. Even still, the constitutional settlement following the Glorious Revolution served as a critical constitutional metamorphosis. In the 17th century alone, England radically transformed its monarchy.[132]

These concepts and events became such a part of the English spirit that their immeasurable influence became woven into the fabric of the western world – and to American political theory by extension. Even though English hardships were often characterized by social disorder and the tumult of war, liberty cyclically triumphed over despotism. In each case, the people endeavored to enter into agreements with each other to restrain their rulers. Without question, these precursors greatly influenced the American founders and shaped the world they occupied. Nevertheless, the young United States built a constitutional model that fundamentally differed from the British system. In its written form, it was distinctly American.

Chapter 4

The Philadelphia Convention and State Ratification Conventions

The Continental Congress, formed by the representatives of thirteen states, had no legal authority. Historian and judicial scholar Andrew Napolitano recalled that the "real political power that existed in 1776 was in the governorship and the legislature of each of the thirteen states." Without the power to enact laws, the body could only pass resolutions which would not override the exertion of authority by the state governments. Far from a national legislature, the assembly could do little more than direct General George Washington as he waged war upon the British on behalf of the states.[133]

By extension, the sovereign and independent states, each with their own identities, norms, and customs, did not embody a homogeneous collective. They instead represented distinct and autonomous regions with vastly different societies. In this framework, Congress was represented by state delegations, with each state holding equal suffrage and standing with all other states. The Articles of Confederation, ratified by the states in 1781 to give legal credence to the arrangement, explicitly recognized that "each state retains its sovereignty, freedom, and independence, and every power,

jurisdiction, and right, which is not by this Confederation expressly delegated to the United States, in Congress assembled." Without question,
America's political system was defined by its league of states.

FAILED UNIFICATION ATTEMPTS

In the 18th century, there were several notable attempts to create a unified American government of the colonies, all of which failed. The most
prominent effort in this vein came through Benjamin Franklin's Albany
Plan of 1754. At that time, the wildly popular Pennsylvanian recommended uniting the colonies under the crown to produce a concerted system of defense to repel invasions. While these concerns of defense proved
to be legitimate – the French and Indian War was just breaking out in North
America – the proposal was defeated for several reasons. Chief among
them was the fact that colonial sensibilities were far too divergent, with
each colony possessing different cultures, economic interests, and even
governmental structures. While Franklin's project failed, these colonial
distinctions were the cornerstones of the future compact that would nomi-
nally associate the states with each other. Viewing the failure of the Albany Plan in a positive light, Franklin wrote later that if his plan had succeeded "the subsequent Separation of the Colonies from the Mother Country might not so soon have happened."[134]

Another undertaking to bring about a greater sense of colonial unification took place in Annapolis, Maryland, in 1785. The convention was in
part inspired by an agreement between Virginia and Maryland in 1785 regarding navigation of the Potomac River. With five states in attendance of
the Annapolis Convention, the organizers hoped to formulate a strategy to
amend the Articles of Confederation. By that time, the Articles were seen
as a governmental framework that had several weaknesses, even among
those that supported the constitutional system overall. Ultimately, the Annapolis Convention failed to produce any type of national government or
change the political conditions in the United States.

As the result of the convention's failure, those with compulsions to create a more stringent American union intensified their efforts. A young Alexander Hamilton voiced sincere displeasure in a summary of the Annapolis Convention's proceedings, and called for an additional general convention of all the states to meet in Philadelphia the next May. In so doing,

Hamilton revealed his concern that the convention in Annapolis did not alleviate the problems it convened to solve, but expressed hope that a broader meeting of parties would produce a more desirable result. The future convention he called for would ultimately become known as the "Constitutional Convention," or more properly the Philadelphia Convention of 1787.

THE PHILADELPHIA CONVENTION OF 1787

From 1786-1787, James Madison devoted most of his time to an enormous research project. He studied ancient political systems, compared governmental structures, and made inferences about what characteristics were associated with governments that endured for long periods of time. After his thorough scholarship, Madison committed himself to the creation of a plan that would address the perceived flaws in the American political system. Understanding the timing of the upcoming convention, Madison intended to finalize the proposal prior to any of the debates. He reasoned that if he was the first to act, his blueprint would become the focal point for deliberation. Madison's general outline for government evolved into "The Virginia Plan," a pitch that would be debated vigorously in the Philadelphia summer of 1787. Madison's aims in this endeavor were also shared by his friend and Governor of Virginia, Edmund Randolph.

Among the most recognizable and unique aspects of both the Virginia Plan and eventual Constitution was the noticeable emphasis on the separation of powers doctrine. Separation of powers was a political theory that was famously espoused by Baron Charles de Montesquieu of France in his seminal 1748 work, *The Spirit of the Laws*. Montesquieu famously wrote that "when the legislative and executive powers are united in the same person, or in the same body of magistrates, there can be no liberty."[135] This theory held that liberty was much more likely to thrive when political powers were divided into separate governmental entities. Because authority would be dispersed into separate branches of government, attempts to usurp power would likely be constrained by the other branches. Montesquieu's theory ingeniously held that legislative, executive, and judicial duties should be allocated to different bodies, and that too much power in an oligarchy of few individuals was a dangerous prospect for any government.

Montesquieu's ideas were mentioned to several times during the Philadelphia Convention debates, and were cited by Madison and Randolph while explaining how the Virginia Plan was intended to function. Both men surmised that without this principle, the republic would trend toward a monarchy. "According to the observation of Montesquieu," Madison declared, it would be "dangerous to suffer a union" of powers in a single branch, for "tyrannical laws may be made that they may be executed in a tyrannical manner."[136] Montesquieu's principles were highly influential to the delegates in Philadelphia, many of whom had studied Montesquieu and were familiar with his views. The Constitution therefore affirmed an explicit distribution of power into three separate branches, and the text of the document is structured in a way to show plainly that this division of power exists.

A topic of much contention in Philadelphia, and perhaps the most controversial among the states, was the subject of representational apportionment in the general government. A provocative matter from the outset, representation became one of the hardest issues to solve to the satisfaction of all regions. While the powerful and populous states wanted to assert their influence in a greater way, the smaller states were inherently fearful that a national conglomeration of powerful states would eliminate their standing completely. Because of these seemingly incompatible attitudes, intense deliberation was necessary to strike a compromise.

The most controversial plans for apportionment in the legislature either gave too much power to the larger and more powerful states, or too much power to the weaker states. As part of the Virginia Plan, Randolph and Madison advocated for two legislative houses, both of which were to be apportioned by populace. This system would have retained the political stature of states such as New York, Pennsylvania, and Virginia, but this concept was not ideal to the smaller states. In comparison, The New Jersey Plan, promoted by William Paterson, called for one house of Congress that would have been represented equally. This idea would generally replicate the Confederation Congress under the Articles of Confederation, which respected each state as an equal federated entity.

Regardless of the various proposals, each state shared the belief that this was an enormously important question. Apportionment sparked many inquiries concerning how this would affect the executive authority, civil appointments, and a potential taxing power – all pressing matters that provoked sectional tensions and political rivalries. Both plans produced intense debate, and the New Jersey Plan was rejected outright on June 19. Discussions that centered upon the Virginia Plan were long-winded, but no less contentious. Indeed, many delegates viewed Madison and Randolph's plan as an undesirable nationalist framework that would siphon away too power from the states.

The convention eventually decided upon a bicameral legislature that would be apportioned by state populace in the lower house, and a delegation of two individuals for each state in the upper house. In a sense, the Connecticut plan that offered such a concession blended the aims of the New Jersey and Virginia Plan into one platform. Being less controversial and agreeable to all parties, Congress could be constructed in a fashion that pleased all of the states – those that were large and influential as well as those that were small and less powerful. This settlement would become known as the "Connecticut Compromise" because its architects, Roger Sherman and Oliver Wolcott, were from Connecticut.

Another important negotiation that was struck to resolve a combative issue was embodied in the Three-Fifths Compromise, which was the product of an argument over how much apportioned power the southern states should have. Northern delegates who sought to undermine the political strength of the South – where slavery was more widespread – proposed that only free inhabitants of all the states were counted, while the representatives from the southern states pushed for enslaved inhabitants to be counted fully for representative purposes. With the relative power of the states in Congress the most pressing source of debate at the Philadelphia Convention, a bargain was reached to count slaves as three-fifths of their actual numbers for the purposes of legislative apportionment. This concession reduced the representation of slave states relative to southern aspirations, but satisfied the northern delegates because enslaved peoples would not be counted in full.

In the contemporary, some have been apt to misrepresent Constitution by purporting that slaves were made into "three-fifths of a person" through this clause. On the contrary, the disputed ratio was only an argument over relative power of the states and their sway in the Electoral College and relative representation in the House of Representatives. Contentious as it was, the product of the compromise was not an indictment upon black people in any physical or biological sense, and the clause did not endorse slavery or insinuate that slaves were subhuman.[137]

Another noteworthy invention of the Philadelphia Convention the systematic rejection of a plan to require members of the state legislatures to take oaths to observe laws passed by the general government. Roger Sherman particularly opposed a proposal which would force them to do so, for reasons of "unnecessarily intruding into the State jurisdictions." Elbridge Gerry of Massachusetts also protested such a notion, arguing that there was "as much reason for requiring an oath of fidelity to the States" as there was to the general government. Furthermore, Luther Martin of Maryland moved to strike out the oath requirements and observed that such commitments may be contrary to oaths already taken by officials of a sovereign state.[138] As a result of the antagonism toward such a prospect, there is no measure within the Constitution that requires elected state officials to swear allegiance to laws passed by the general government.

One aspect of the Constitution that exposes the federal orientation of the new model is present in Article I, Section 7. Confining bills for raising revenue to the House of Representatives, the "origination" provision made localities into safeguards against financial exploitation by the general government. In support of this idea, James Madison wrote:

The House of Representatives cannot only refuse, but they alone can propose, the supplies requisite for the support of government. They, in a word, hold the purse that powerful instrument by which we behold, in the history of the British Constitution, an infant and humble representation of the people gradually enlarging the sphere of its activity and importance, and finally reducing, as far as it seems to have wished, all the overgrown prerogatives of the other branches of the government.[139]

Since the people's coffers had been continually exploited by the central authority throughout British history, it was considered imperative that such abuse was prevented in the new American republic. To avoid "gradually enlarging the sphere," therefore, it was necessary to attach the purse strings of the general government to the most representative house. Certain that unscrupulous individuals would eventually attempt to implement broad, costly, unconstitutional expenditures, the writers of the Constitution sought to undermine such a situation through this feature.

Permitting the Senate to initiate spending bills would have been improper, thought Madison, because the House of Representatives more closely reflected the direct interests of the people. The architect of the Virginia Plan claimed this was because those in "the more permanent and conspicuous the station" were more likely to forget their attachments to their constituencies and propose erratic expenditures.[140]

Realizing the new taxing power was the basis of great dispute, Madison championed the origination clause as the operational solution. Alexander Hamilton of New York concurred with Madison's rumination, arguing that the confinement of the spending power to a single council would inhibit spending abuses and discourage perpetual militarism:

> Will any man who entertains a wish for the safety of his country trust the sword and the purse with a single Assembly, organized on principles so defective? Though we might give to such a government certain powers with safety, yet to give them the full and unlimited powers of taxation and the national forces would be to establish a despotism, the definition of which is, a government in which all power is concentrated in a single body.[141]

Granting ultimate authority over the republic's purse to a small number of people, remarked Hamilton, would be "despotism." In support of his case, the young lawyer declared that "where the purse is lodged in one branch, and the sword in another, there can be no danger."[142]

Another matter to be decided in Philadelphia was the process through which the Constitution could be amended. The founders wisely understood that the inclusion of a change mechanism was crucial, but came to the realization that the process should not be easy, or the document would be rendered irrelevant by shifting political whims. George Mason, delegate from Virginia and future opponent of the Constitution, fought arduously to allow the states themselves to propose and ratify new amendments, thereby bypassing the general government entirely. Mason believed that the potential national assembly would never voluntarily yield to modifications that deprived it of its authority. Whenever the federal government resisted popular constitutional alterations, he concluded, the states needed a mode of recourse. Mason consequently introduced the following provision:

> Amendments therefore will be necessary, and it will be better to provide for them, in any easy, regular, and Constitutional way than to trust the chance and violence. It would be improper to require the consent of the Natl. Legislature, because they may abuse their power, and refuse their consent on that very account.[143]

Madison and Hamilton, who favored a strong national government, disagreed with the plan and alleged that the federal legislature would adequately represent the states.

Roger Sherman of Connecticut, who "never said a foolish thing in his life" according to Thomas Jefferson, suggested a course of action that would satisfy the concerns of Mason and others. Sherman moved to add an additional procedure that would authorize Congress to propose amendments, but stipulated that "no amendments shall be binding until consented to by the several States." Pennsylvanian James Wilson recommended the addition of "three fourths of" before "the several States," which was agreed upon by the convention at large.[144] By addressing the concerns of Mason and others who feared the prospect an unchangeable national government, Sherman and Wilson acquiesced to the notion that the states, as parties to the compact, should have the most power over the Constitution's alteration device.

In the end, two approaches to propose amendments were implemented into the finalized document. The first process allowed for such proposals to originate in the general government, and if approved by two-thirds of Congress, the amendment would be sent to the states to ratify. If three-fourths of the states ratified the amendment, it would then be added to the Constitution. The second method allowed the states to call a convention with the application of two-thirds of the states, where new amendments could be proposed. If the recommendations were approved by three-fourths of the states, the amendment also became part of the framework. The latter process would transpire whether or not the amendment was proposed, discussed, or mentioned in the general government at all.

In today's age, most Americans are unaware of the state-initiated amendment process, and it has never been utilized. Even though this provision is rarely acknowledged, Article V allows the states to retain significant power to alter the Constitution. This is demonstrative proof that the document's change mechanism echoed the orientation of the federal union, and the compact that created it. The philosophy behind the measure relied upon the idea that since the states built the Constitution, only the states can change it. It makes such a case even stronger by asserting that the states alone hold the ability to alter the compact – even if it irritates or hinders the general government.

Economic considerations also guided many of the debates in Philadelphia, and the convention took place at a time of great commercial turmoil in North America. As the result of the legal embrace of paper money over hard currency, a severe financial crisis broke out in the 1780s. During the War of Independence, the Continental Congress rapidly printed "Continentals," a paper currency that was distributed throughout the states. The Continentals depreciated in value so rapidly during the war that they were essentially worthless by 1781. At the same time, the state governments emitted bills of credit, paper fiat that functioned as hidden taxes against wealth holders. As a severe economic impairment to debt owners, the paper money policies were extremely controversial. James Madison was particularly disturbed by the rampant emissions of paper money in the states, and commented that "restraints against paper emissions and violations of contracts are not sufficient" in the Confederation system.[145]

In a stubborn attempt to reduce the inflationary practices of government, Roger Sherman also attached his reputation to the cause of opposing paper money. A rigid hard money warrior, he fought vigorously to insert language that would prohibit the government from printing of paper money at all. Though some delegates continued to argue for the retention of paper money in times of political crisis, Sherman also attracted a share of supporters that recognized the tragedy that came with the abandonment of hard currency.

In North Carolina's state ratifying convention, for instance, William Davie observed that "it is essential to the interests of agriculture and commerce, that the hands of the states should be bound from making paper money, installment laws, or pine-barren acts." By "such iniquitous laws," he continued, "the merchant or farmer may be defrauded of a considerable part of his just claims." Even Alexander Hamilton, a fierce proponent of national banking, posited that "the emitting of paper money by the authority of Government is wisely prohibited to the individual States, by the National Constitution." Beyond this, he professed that "the spirit of that prohibition ought not to be disregarded, by the Government of the United States."[146]

In concurrence, Thomas McKean of Pennsylvania pointed out the inherent defects of the standing system, which shunned hard currency and encouraged the massive devaluation of wealth:

> Sir, some security will be offered for the discharge of honest contracts, and an end put on the pernicious speculation upon paper emissions – a medium which has undermined the morals, and relaxed the industry of the people, and from which one-half of the controversies in our courts of justice has arisen.[147]

Lending his hand to the same cause, James Wilson joined Sherman in the proposal forbid the general government to emit bills of paper. In addition, he recommended the addition of a clause that would prevent the states from making anything other than gold and silver a legal payment for the discharge of debts. A complete departure from The Articles of Confederation, the two changes made the ban on bills of credit absolute, safeguarded lenders from financial ruin, and reasserted the necessity of hard money. As Madison's notes reflect, Sherman believed the economic doldrums were "a favorable crisis for crushing paper money" – and he acted upon such an inclination in earnest. He noted that without such constraint, the friends of paper money would make "every exertion to get into the Legislature in order to license it." The prohibition on the emission of bills of credit was adopted by the convention, and the finalized Constitution barred both the general government and the states from printing paper money.[148]

In addition to the paper money crisis, economic conditions worsened when several states enacted protective tariffs against each other. These taxes produced obstacles against free trade, and no state was prepared to defend them by the time of the Philadelphia Convention. With inflation plaguing the states, barriers to trade served to depress the state economies even further. Madison explained this was a source of "dissatisfaction was the peculiar situation of some of the States, which having no convenient ports for foreign commerce, were subject to be taxed by their neighbors, thro whose ports, their commerce carried on." Much to his discontent, Madison lamented that "the Articles of Confederation provided no remedy for the complaint." After debate on the wording of a trade article, the representatives passed a motion that prevented the states from placing imposts or duties on goods. Massachusetts representative Rufus King declared that the provision was added "so as to prohibit the states from taxing either."[149]

Of pressing importance was the matter of how executive power should be vested and utilized. In his own pitch to the convention, Alexander Hamilton, who promoted a powerful, kingly executive that would serve for life. Drawing upon the British model for influence, Robert Yates' account of the convention shows that Hamilton also proposed a legislative body that would be "constituted during good behavior or life." Influenced by the British House of Lords, its members would be appointed by the national executive. In addition, Hamilton proposed that the executive would also appoint the state governors. Under this model, state sovereignty would be effectively done away with, essentially incorporating all of the states into a single nation. A steadfast supporter of both the British governmental structure and mercantilist economic system, Hamilton at one point stated that "the British government forms the best model the world has ever produced." By the end of the convention, the nationalist from New York realized his proposals were not popular ones, and admitted that his plan was "very remote from the idea of the people."[150]

Hamilton's notes shed even more light on his proposal for a de facto monarchy for the United States. He referred to the chief executive as a "monarch," noted that this individual's role should be hereditary instead of elected, and should have so much power that "it will not be his interest to risk much to acquire more." Hamilton's notes added the absurd proclamation that "he is above corruption," and "must always intend, in respect

to foreign nations, the true interest and glory of the people." While republican forms of government were defined by the rule of law, Hamilton's
ideal model would be characterized by the rule of men. His design for
government was never seriously entertained at the Philadelphia Convention, and after hearing his pitch the delegates focused only on the other
proposals.[151]

Other plans for the executive office were considered, including a proposal that would split the executive power into the hands of multiple individuals. Departing from this suggestion and the Hamiltonian vision, the
final Constitution produced a single executive office with very few and
defined powers. Of the authority granted to the executive, nearly every
action could be checked in some way by the legislature. His advisors, treaties, and court appointees all had to be made with the advice and consent
of the Senate, Congress was required to declare war before he could direct
it, and his veto power could be overridden by the same body. In many
ways, the original vision for the presidential office provided its occupant
with less power than a state governor.[152]

After laying plans for a new central judiciary – which did not exist in
the Confederation system – debates took place in regard to how the new
judges should be elected. Several delegates, such as James Madison, contended that members of the federal judiciary should be appointed by the
legislature. His Virginia Plan, after all, would have created an especially
strong national judiciary that had jurisdiction over almost any controversy.
Despite these inclinations, many feared that a powerful court system, populated with judges that served for life, would invest too much power into
too few hands. In the end, the Supreme Court could only exercise original
jurisdiction in three types of cases, and the state courts retained the power
to adjudicate most internal disputes.

Of all Madison's objectives for a more unified government, his most
prized nationalist goal was to provide the new national legislature the ability to override state laws it considered improper or contradictory. In collaboration with Charles Pinckney of South Carolina, Madison ridiculed
the "constant tendency in the States" to encroach upon the authority of
Congress, and insisted that his proposed federal veto over state law was
the "mildest expedient that could be devised for preventing these mis-
chiefs." Though he insisted the states would retain the "support of their

own powers" under such an instrument, a huge debate swirled around this proposal. Hugh Williamson of North Carolina denied that the veto should apply to all state laws, but supported vesting the national legislature with "the power of negativing such laws" that encroached upon the constitutional authority of the national government. Gunning Bedford of Delaware lashed out at Madison and Pinckney's proposal, arguing that it would disproportionately grant influence to the larger, more populated states. Observing that "this mode of government so strongly advocated by the members of the great States," Bedford suspected sinister motives upon the realization that Virginia and Massachusetts had so overwhelmingly supported the measure. Even Bostonian Elbridge Gerry, a tireless advocate of decentralized power, supported Madison's veto proposal.[153]

The legislative veto over the state laws was defeated handily, much to the irritation of Madison. In the end, only three states voted for it, with seven against. Roger Sherman observed that "such a power involves a wrong principle," and even quintessential archnationalist Gouverneur Morris remarked that such an undertaking would "disgust all of the states."[154] Undeniably, the majority of states perceived the federal negative on state law as a catastrophic impediment to their sovereign standing – an antithesis of the compact between states.

Several months later, Madison expressed his frustration over the defeat of the veto proposal in a letter to Thomas Jefferson. Complaining that a "constitutional negative on the laws of the States seems equally necessary to secure individuals against their rights," Madison believed that contradictory state laws produced the climate in which the delegates were called to the Philadelphia Convention to fix. "The evils issuing from these sources contributed more to that uneasiness which produced the Convention," he continued to assert.[155]

The vast majority proposals made by the nationalists in the Philadelphia Convention were soundly defeated, and Madison lamented their failure. Calls for a powerful executive, a strong judiciary with authority over all disputes, and the national legislative veto over state laws did not make it into the finalized Constitution. In totality, he counted this as a significant political loss:

I hazard an opinion nevertheless that the plan should it be adopted will
neither effectually answer the national object nor prevent the local mis-
chiefs which every where excite disgust against the state governments.[156]

Despite the defeat, Madison still maintained a persistent defense of his
initial aims, including the national veto proposal. "A power of negativing
the improper laws of the States," he declared, "is at once the most mild &
certain means of preserving the harmony of the system."[157]

Even though he is today considered the "Father of the Constitution,"
Madison was largely dissatisfied with the final document because it lacked
the nationalist traits he favored. He preferred a political model where both
houses of the legislature would be apportioned by state population, though
the end result featured only one assembly of such a kind. He wanted a
federal judiciary that could take up any case of perceived importance, but
the Constitution ensured that the federal courts could only adjudicate specific types of disputes, mostly involving state quarrels and cases in which
the United States was a party. He hoped for the legislative veto over state
law, and was overruled decisively. He reasoned that the Constitution
should only be amendable with consent of the general legislature, but Article V negated such a prospect. In so many ways, he was defeated in Philadelphia.

In so many ways, Madison's interests were defeated by his peers in
1787. While the Virginian made some lasting contributions to the Constitution, his influence has been more subdued than has often been portrayed
by historians, and his reputation as a great trailblazer in Philadelphia has
been greatly exaggerated. The inherent irony of Madison's aforemen-
tioned objections to the document, however, is that he soon found favor
with decentralized federalism, and took the position that states could exercise a veto on law created by the general government – the inverse of his
push for a federal veto over state law. In the coming years, Madison tran-
sitioned into a tireless advocate of states against the federal government,
and aligned his political interests with those of Thomas Jefferson.

Shortly after the Philadelphia Convention, and while Jefferson served
as a diplomat in France, Madison explained the proposed Constitution in
a written letter. He elaborated upon its various aspects in one his longest

known letters, and made Jefferson privy to its controversies. Jefferson's intrigue was piqued when Madison pointed out that a line of demarcation had been drawn by the framework that gave "the general government every power requisite for general purposes," but left "to the States every power which might be most beneficially administered by them." Expounding upon this claim, he added that "in the American Constitution The general authority will be derived entirely from the subordinate authorities."[158]

While most societies featured a government that was oriented from the top down, the general government of the United States was assembled by peripheral units. All authority first originated in the people, who vested some power in the states to protected liberty and property. From there, the states transferred an array of specific powers to a federal government. This authority was built upon the premise that these powers, held by a general body, would be more convenient for the states. In observance of this truth, Madison recognized that a compact had been constructed between states despite his instincts for political centralization. Historian Thomas Woods noted that while Madison favored a national government, he "acknowledged that such a thing was neither what had been drafted in Philadelphia nor what the people ratified in the conventions that followed." A leading proponent of the Constitution and contributor to *The Federalist*, Madison "defended not what he wished had been ratified, but what had actually been ratified."[159]

In addition to the explanation in regard to the Constitution's key features, Madison also provided Jefferson with a list of common arguments the document's opponent had raised in the states. Among these misgivings included the impression that the federal judiciary was too powerful, the omission of a bill of rights, and the allegation that the Senate was too powerful. Madison's letter reveals that he could foresee the controversy that would erupt during the upcoming state ratification debates, and prepared him for his next task. Preparing himself to defend the document and refute the assertions of its adversaries, he turned his focus to Virginia. There, he faced some of the most popular and persuasive critics imaginable.

Differences in opinion in regard to the Constitution caused a political rift that divided delegates into two general factions. The "Federalists" – sometimes called friends of the Constitution – favored its ratification. In general, Federalists believed the defects within the Articles of

Confederation were too numerous for modest amendments. During the rat-ification conventions, they were typically called upon to explain the doc-ument to skeptical observers who had not shared in the proceedings or contributed to its prose.

Opposite the Federalists were the "Anti-Federalists," sometimes re-ferred to as opponents or enemies of the document. However, the name was hardly self-given, and most of this ilk preferred to be called republi-cans. The Anti-Federalists overwhelmingly apprehended the consolidation of national political power, and claimed the Constitution's text practically guaranteed the usurpation of state authority. True believers in decentral-ized government, they insisted the document must be rejected, and acted as a thorn in the side of the Federalists.

Early in the ratification struggle, a series of oppositional essays written by "Brutus" started to materialize in New York publications. The essays contained some of the most persuasive arguments against the Constitution, and many advocates of the document dedicated a considerable amount of time to refuting the assertions that were made within them. The series was almost certainly the work of Robert Yates, a man from the New York del-egation that left the Philadelphia Convention in protest prior to its conclu-sion. Yates felt that the representatives had gone beyond their authority to create a new form of government rather than making candid attempts to amend the Articles of Confederation. He took extensive notes in Philadel-phia, leaving him with an excellent record of the subjects covered and the opinions of the delegates. Decades later, his notes would be the first to be published from the convention, giving people the first glimpse of the pro-ceedings.

Among other charges, Brutus claimed that the state governments would essentially be destroyed if the Constitution was ratified:

This government is to possess absolute and uncontrollable powers, leg-islative, executive and judicial, with respect to every object to which it extends...all that is reserved for the individual States must very soon be annihilated.[160]

Convinced that a nationalist plot to destroy the state governments was in motion, Brutus cautioned that "posterity will execrate your memory" if the new plan was adopted. Certainly, he was not alone. "It is beyond a doubt that the new federal constitution," another opponent wrote, "will in a great measure destroy, if it do not totally annihilate, the separate governments of the several states."[161] The writings of Brutus and his kindred opponents of the Constitution left an impression neutral observers, and convinced the supporters of the Constitution to expend considerable energy in the quest of refuting their claims.

The Constitution that was adopted and signed at the Philadelphia Convention was not legally binding until nine states ratified it.[162] Lacking the distinction of legal force, the document was sent to the individual states for consideration shortly after the delegates left Independence Hall. In response to the momentous decision that lay before them, the states then conducted republican elections for special conventions that would decide the momentous question before them.

Echoing the independent nature of each of the states, the elections were conducted in different manners and produced representatives with vastly differing opinions on the question of ratification. As sovereign bodies, the states themselves – not the people of the states in the aggregate – had plenary authority to determine whether or not to enter into the compact through ratification. The act of ratification, wrote Madison, would therefore "not be a national, but a federal act." Until the framework achieved the acceptance of the states, claimed Archibald Maclaine in North Carolina's ratification convention, the Constitution was "only a mere proposal."[163]

DELAWARE

In Delaware, the ratification of the Constitution was all but a foregone conclusion. The 30 delegates elected to the state's ratification convention were all committed Federalists, and the document received the assent of the assembly after only three days of consideration. Accurately projected to be a state that would ratify quickly, Delaware considered the model to be consistent with its sovereign interests. Giving the state an equal footing with the powerful states in the Senate, Delaware ratified the Constitution on December 7, 1787.

PENNSYLVANIA

Pennsylvania was the first true test for the Constitution. One of the most influential arguments in support of the document came in the form of James Wilson's "State House Yard Speech," a prelude to the Pennsylvania's ratification convention. Before the delegates assembled, Wilson was asked to explain basic facets of the document and respond to some of the criticisms against it on the lawn of Independence Hall. Before the convention met, there were already rumblings of opposition to the document, and antagonists had begun a campaign to portray the new constitutional model as an instrument that would subvert state authority and permit the new Congress to wield an oppressive array of new powers. Others attacked the Constitution because it lacked a bill of rights, which they suggested was necessary to limit the new general government and provide safeguards for traditional rights.

Like many Federalists at the time, Wilson opposed adding a bill of rights to the Constitution because he believed it would be unnecessary and redundant. "It would have been superfluous and absurd," he claimed, "to have stipulated with a federal body of our own creation, that we should enjoy those privileges of which we are not divested, either by the intention or the act that has brought the body into existence." In other words, since the general government wasn't given constitutional license to violate such liberties, a bill of rights would be superfluous. This train of logic was repeated by Alexander Hamilton in *The Federalist* No. 84. Under the proposed Constitution, he wrote, "the people surrender nothing; and as they retain every thing they have no need of particular reservations."[164] The addition of a bill of rights, Hamilton warned, may even prove destructive to the liberties of the people:

> I go further, and affirm that bills of rights, in the sense and to the extent in which they are contended for, are not only unnecessary in the proposed Constitution, but would even be dangerous. They would contain various exceptions to powers not granted; and, on this very account, would afford a colorable pretext to claim more than were granted. For why declare that things shall not be done which there is no power to do?[165]

Federalists generally agreed with the sentiments of Wilson and Hamilton, denying the necessity of a bill of rights. Their stance on the matter contrasted strongly with eminent figures such as John Hancock, George Mason, Patrick Henry, and Luther Martin – all of which insisted that a bill of rights was a necessary factor to ensure the longevity of the new government and the happiness of the American people.

In his speech, Wilson also ventured to refute some of the common allegations about the Constitution, such as the fear that it would disallow citizens from receiving a trial by jury in civil cases:

> Let it be remembered then, that the business of the Federal Convention was not local, but general – not limited to the views and establishments of a single State, but co-extensive with the continent, and comprehending the views and establishments of thirteen independent sovereignties...The cases open to a trial by jury differed in the different States. It was therefore impracticable, on that ground, to have made a general rule.[166]

Here we have corroboration of the notion that the Constitution was a compact made by "thirteen independent sovereignties" that had their own state-level courts to try offenders. "Since there has never existed any federal system of jurisprudence, to which the declaration could relate," Wilson iterated, it was unnecessary to add additional prose in regard to civil cases.[167]

To the accusation that the Constitution gave the general government powers which were not explicitly stated, Wilson responded that "everything which is not given is reserved." He clarified that power in the Constitution was not granted by "tacit implication, but from the positive grant expressed in the instrument of the union."[168] Therefore, a power had to be enumerated in the Constitution if it was to be utilized by the general government. This understanding was made explicit by proponents of the Constitution well before the Tenth Amendment reiterated the same.

Several other trepidations were raised by opponents of the document in Pennsylvania, including an assertion by "Philadelphiensis" that the new framework would produce a military government:

Before martial law is declared to be the supreme law of the land, and
your character of free citizens be changed to that of the subjects of a
military king-which are necessary consequences of the adoption of the
proposed constitution - let me admonish you in the name of sacred liberty, to make a solemn pause...A conspiracy against the freedom of
America, both deep and dangerous, has been formed by an infernal
junto of demagogues. Our thirteen free commonwealths are to be consolidated into one despotic monarchy. Is not this position obvious? Its
evidence is intuitive...Who can deny but the president general will be
a king to all intents and purposes, and one of the most dangerous kind
too-a king elected to command a standing army.[169]

Philadelphiensis warned of an American king who would institute martial
law, wage war with a standing army, and reign as a monarch. He reinforced
this sentiment by noting that Luther Martin, an esteemed republican from
Maryland, also raised the same anxieties after leaving the Philadelphia
Convention.[170] Joining a host of others, Philadelphiensis feared the new
government model would emulate the British system – a terrifying prospect for fervent republicans.

In response to Brutus' implication that the Constitution would eradicate
the state governments, Wilson answered that "the existing union of the
States, and even this projected system is nothing more than a formal act of
incorporation." To the claim that the Constitution authorized a standing
military presence in times of peace, Wilson assured naysayers that "the
government must declare war, before they are prepared to carry it on."[171]

Wilson also actively worked to refute the statements of "An Old Whig,"
an opponent of the Constitution in Pennsylvania that warned Pennsylvania's delegates not to adopt the new model:

It is beyond a doubt that the new federal constitution, if adopted, will
in a great measure destroy, if it do not totally annihilate, the separate
governments of the several states. Every measure of importance, will
be Continental.[172]

After the loss of state sovereignty, An Old Whig alleged, the Constitution
would give Congress the impetus to "steadily pursue the acquisition of

more and more power to themselves and their adherents." Foreseeing imminent doom upon ratification, the writer bemoaned that "the cause of liberty, if it be now forgotten, will be forgotten forever."[173] Despite An Old Whig's arguments, Wilson's repudiation of the allegations resonated with the delegates, and there is evidence that he swayed some divergent minds in favor of the model. Beyond its ramifications in Pennsylvania, his narrative was adopted by Federalists in the other states, who used his general arguments in their own state conventions.

Wilson's arguments provoked several responses, including those made by an opponent using the pseudonym "Centinel." Centinel warned that the general government would quickly devolve into tyranny, and regulate the individual liberty of the people. The general government would "restrain the printers, and put them under regulation," he cautioned. Centinel also complained that every local decision would be subject to the power of Congress, and denied that the Constitution denied the "sovereignty, freedom, and independence" of the states as guaranteed by Article II of the Articles of Confederation.[174]

In the western counties of Pennsylvania, political tides were strongly opposed to the Constitution. Despite the widespread hesitation, Federalists in the state legislature worked to reorganize districts to ensure a favorable outcome in the ratification convention, and the reformed regions effectively destroy much of the palpable dissent. This factor, combined with the dedication of prominent Pennsylvanians like Benjamin Franklin, James Wilson, Gouverneur Morris, and Robert Morris, helped secure the ratification of the document. Ultimately, the combined efforts of An Old Whig, Centinel, and opponents in the convention were not enough to thwart the model, and the Constitution was approved in Pennsylvania by a margin of 46 to 23. With Pennsylvania's approbation, the Constitution had passed its first tangible hurdle.

NORTH CAROLINA (PART 1)

When the North Carolina ratification convention first met in Hillsborough, most representatives were opposed to the Constitution. Timothy Bloodworth argued that the document appeared "to sweep off all the constitutions of the states." Calling the system "a total repeal of every act and constitution of the states," he cautioned that the plan would "produce an abolition of the state governments." Its sovereignty absolutely annihilates them," he claimed.[175] James Iredell, an esteemed advocate of the document, largely echoed the sentiments expressed by the Federalist friends of the Constitution, and refuted the allegations of Bloodworth.

Countering the charges against the document, Iredell insisted that the Constitution would grant no powers outside of those enumerated:

> The powers of the government are particularly enumerated and defined: they can claim no others but such as are so enumerated. In my opinion, they are excluded as much from the exercise of any other authority as they could be by the strongest negative clause that could be framed.[176]

Furthermore, Iredell clarified that the Supremacy Clause would not permit the general government to encroach upon issues outside of the jurisdiction of the general government. "If Congress, under pretense of executing one power, should, in fact, usurp another," Iredell remarked, "they will violate the Constitution." William Davie responded in concurrence with Iredell, affirming that federal law "can be supreme only in cases consistent with the powers specifically granted, and not in usurpations."[177]

Cynics in North Carolina purported that under the Constitution, the state's judicial system would be displaced and overridden by the courts under the new general government. Nevertheless, Samuel Spencer dispelled this notion through the explanation that "the two jurisdictions and the two governments, that is, the general and the state governments may go hand in hand, and that there may be no interference, but that every thing may be rightly conducted."[178] While Spencer opposed the Constitution, he admitted that the state authority and general government could exist alongside each other with separate domains of power. This left the states, in his eyes, in command to handle the majority of matters that affected American citizens. Still, the assurances of the Federalists failed to sway the state in favor of the model.

With minimal support for the Constitution in North Carolina, the plan failed to secure ratification in the summer of 1788. The representatives decided "neither to ratify nor reject the Constitution proposed for the government of the United States," but entertained the possibility for the future.

While the state left the door open to reconsider ratification at a later time, the convention also recommended a list of proposed amendments to the Constitution. These alterations, if adopted, would put the representatives more at ease with ratification. Under a patient approach, North Carolina remained an independent republic for over a year.

NEW JERSEY

As in Delaware, the Constitution was not particularly controversial in New Jersey. The state's 38 electors were all Federalist supporters of the framework, selected just prior to the state convention. After the Connecticut Compromise destroyed Virginia's hopes of a bicameral Congress in which both houses would be apportioned by state population, and a federal veto over state law, New Jersey's delegation believed that the resultant framework would be satisfy the interests of its people.

Though the New Jersey Plan failed to sway delegates to the Philadelphia Convention, some measures to protect smaller states were preserved under the proposed document. Most appealing of these to the state was the Senate, which would allow New Jersey to retain equal suffrage in that body with larger, populous, more powerful states. Although the notes from state's ratification convention do not survive, the Constitution received overwhelming support within the state. After nine days, the document was ratified by New Jersey on December 18, 1787.

GEORGIA

There was virtually no opposition to the Constitution's ratification in Georgia, and there are very few detailed records of the state's ratification proceedings. The official convention journal lists only attendance and the topics covered. However, the records that do exist illustrate that while the Constitution was read fully to the convention, the representatives had assumed the document would be adopted outright.

Georgia's representatives likely found the new system advantageous because it the new general government would provide support against Indian raids that the state was vulnerable to. Like Delaware and New Jersey, it would also profit greatly from equal representation in the

Senate. Joseph Habersham, one of 26 men selected to the convention, wrote that the Constitution would "be adopted in the course of a few days."[179] By a unanimous margin, Georgia became the fourth state to ratify on January 2, 1788.

CONNECTICUT

Connecticut's chief proponents of the Constitution were Roger Sherman and Oliver Ellsworth, who had exercised considerable influence on the Constitution in Philadelphia. At the opening of the state's ratification convention in Hartford, Ellsworth's remarked that a new union was necessary "for the purposes of a national defence," and proclaimed that the problems under the Articles of Confederation would be corrected under the new model. Appealing to the interests of Connecticut, Ellsworth asked, "If divided, what is to prevent the large states from oppressing the small?" Believing that the new framework would elevate his state's position in the new union, Ellsworth postulated that remaining outside of the new union would only cause a greater hinder to smaller states such as his own. Referring to New York, he asked: "Do we not already see in her the seeds of an overbearing ambition?" Ellsworth believed that Connecticut's ratification could successfully challenge the expansionary tendencies of neighboring states, while also giving credence to the state's influence in the general government. Emphasizing the decentralized orientation of the new plan, he cited Germany and the Dutch Republic as examples of federal republics that thrived while preserving local political autonomy.[180]

In the same convention, Oliver Wolcott claimed that the Constitution "effectually secures the states in their several rights." As an extension of this principle, he added, the states were "the pillars which uphold the general system." Wolcott recognized that the general government derived its few powers from the states, and thus the states were the "pillars" that hoisted the general government into being. In concordance with the same theme, Richard Law described both the legislature and the executive office as the offspring of the people of the states:

Our president is not a king, nor our senate a house of lords. They do not claim an independent heredity authority. But the whole is elective;

all dependent on the people. The president, the senate, the representatives, are all creatures of the people. Therefore the people will be secure from oppression.[181]

Law's viewpoint was consistent with the traditional republican perspective that governments derive all authority from the people of their respective societies. Lacking the people's consent, a government's rule was considered illegitimate by those who adhered to the classical liberal tradition of John Locke and Algernon Sidney.

Sherman, writing under the pseudonym "A Countryman," worked to dispel some of the other allegations against the Constitution. The common attacks against the Constitution, he wrote, were tantamount to "nonsense and alarm." Like several other leading Federalists, Sherman did not believe a bill of rights was necessary because fundamental rights were not alterable under the unamended constitutional model. After all, no provision of the document gave the government the power to deny individuals the right to assemble, worship, or possess firearms. In addition, Sherman pointed out that Connecticut already had its own bill of rights that affirmed the liberties of its citizens. Furthermore, Sherman assured his peers that the Congress could "take no improper step" to assume powers not granted, and that skeptics "need not apprehend that they will usurp authorities not given them to injure that society of which they are a part."[182]

The Constitution was described in Connecticut as a compact that preserved state power and recognized the states as the building blocks of the republic. Wolcott reiterated this concept by assuring disbelievers that the general government secures the rights "of the several states." Reverberating this sentiment, Governor Samuel Huntington proclaimed that the state governments "will not be endangered by the powers vested by this constitution in the general government." Because few powers were divested, Huntington commented that the general government "will not have the disposition to encroach upon the states." On one of the final days of the convention, Ellsworth declared that in times of disagreement with the general government, the states could forcibly reject repugnant law through their own independent means. "If the United States and the individual states will quarrel, if they want to fight," Ellsworth said, "they may do it, and no frame of government can possibly prevent it."[183]

Sherman and Ellsworth's joint letter to the governor of Connecticut also highlighted one of their several achievements at the Philadelphia Convention – the text in Article I, Section 10 that forbid states to emit bills of credit. The two noted that the clause – which Sherman spearheaded – was added in Philadelphia in order to "secure the rights of the particular states, and the liberties and properties of the citizens."[184] Above all other accomplishments, this adjustment was deemed the most crucial political victory of the Connecticut delegation.

In Connecticut, ratification was a largely popular cause. Some writers and delegates within the state were hostile toward the Constitution, but their influence was far less notable in comparison to those that supported the document. Many of the contentious issues were not debated in Hartford, as the floor was dominated by supporters of the new plan. The most important members of the assembly in favor of the document, such as Sherman and Ellsworth, were at the Philadelphia Convention and contributed greatly to crafting its prose. The active roles these men played in the convention proceedings undoubtedly helped secure the document's acceptance. After only five days, Connecticut adopted the Constitution by a margin of 120 to 48.

MASSACHUSETTS

Massachusetts, which did much to instigate the War of Independence in its earliest days, held a very argumentative and divisive convention. Some of the state's most famous representatives – including Samuel Adams and John Hancock – opposed the model from the beginning. Another rigid opponent, Elbridge Gerry, left the Philadelphia Convention without signing the document, citing the lack of a bill of rights and trepidations of central power.

Within Boston's convention, much debate hinged upon the length of senatorial terms and the enumerated powers of Congress. Future Governor of Massachusetts John Brooks supposed that the power of the Senate would be checked by the attachments of the senators to their home states. "Their political existence depends upon their good behavior," he claimed. With this in mind, William Jones expressed anxiety regarding six-year terms for senators. As these fears emerged, Fisher Ames professed that the senators would remain under the "control of the people" because they depended on the state legislatures for their instruction. Ames stated that "the state governments are essential parts of the system, and the defence of this article is drawn from its tendency to their preservation." The senators, he said, "represent the sovereignty of the states."[185]

William Bodman raised another concern that the general government would act as an imposing, supervisory body that would suppress commerce in Massachusetts, and asked if the listed powers would give Congress the ability to "do harm" to the state economy. This unease seemed extremely relevant, after all, considering that the economy of Massachusetts was highly dependent upon trade and shipping. Bodman's inquiry was answered by Theodore Sedgwick, who said that if the Constitution would have such an affect, he would be the last to vote for it. When some opponents of the plan pointed to taxing power as source of potential abuse, Christopher Gore advised that the power to tax was not unlimited because the states would only "vest the Congress with the powers described in" Article I, Section 8. The power to tax, then, would not confer the power to do so for any purpose. He therefore concluded that the new assembly would have only the "authority alluded to," not untold or implied powers.[186]

Perhaps the most persuasive opponent of the Constitution in the convention, Charles Thompson, recommended a bill of rights. Echoing the concerns of Gerry, he described the instrument as a crucial and obligatory safeguard of the people's liberties. A bill of rights "shall check the power of congress, which shall say, thus far shall ye come and no farther," he averred. Aiming to ensure that the general government could not trample over the rights of individuals or interfere with state powers, Thompson declared that "the safety of the people depends on a bill of rights."[187] As in other states, some disagreed with the necessity of such an addition, such as former state governor James Bowdoin:

With regard to rights, the whole constitution is a declaration of rights, which primarily and principally respect the general government intended to be formed by it. The rights of particular states, or private citizens, not being the object or subject of the constitution, they are only incidentally mentioned. In regard to the former, it would require a volume to describe them, as they extend to every subject of legislation, not included in the powers vested in Congress.[188]

Believing that Congress never had the power to legislate on subjects of individual liberty or deprive states of their authority, Bowdoin thought a bill of rights was unnecessary and redundant. Nevertheless, the renowned statesman worked hard to convince the most ardent skeptics in his state to support the framework.

At the end of the convention, Samuel Adams and John Hancock dropped their opposition to the Constitution under a settlement that guaranteed a bill of rights would be drafted by the First Congress. In a long-winded speech, Hancock expressed the belief that such a device would prevent the miscarriage of power by the general government. Under this assurance, the popular figure now declared his support of the Constitution. Hancock's sentiment was highly persuasive, as a subset of representatives changed their stances to match Hancock's outlook. With a dramatic conclusion to the convention, ratification was secured in Massachusetts by the narrow margin of 187 to 168.

MARYLAND

The most devout opponents of the Constitution in Maryland, Luther Martin and John Mercer, had attended the Philadelphia Convention. Like Robert Yates and John Lansing of New York, both men left the Philadelphia Convention before proceedings ended, and concluded that the body had violated its original purpose to recommend amendments to the Articles of Confederation. The attendees, they suggested, had violated their legal authority and duties as delegates from the states. Considering the new framework as little more than a nationalist power grab, both Martin and Mercer began a formidable campaign to obstruct the document. However, three Maryland delegates – James McHenry, Daniel of St. Thomas Jenifer, and Daniel Carroll – stayed in Philadelphia and endorsed the Constitution.

Long before Maryland's ratification convention took place, Luther Martin unleashed his own case for opposition in *Letter on the Federal Convention of 1787*, a pamphlet written shortly after his departure from

Philadelphia. Within the work, Martin summed up his reasons for leaving the convention:

I considered [the Constitution] not only injurious to the interest and rights of this state, but also incompatible with political happiness and freedom of the states in general; from that time until my business compelled me to leave the convention, I gave it every possible opposition in every stage of its progression. I opposed the system there with the same explicit frankness with which I have here given you a history of our proceedings, an account of my own conduct, which in a particular manner I consider you as having a right to know.[189]

Federalists within Maryland took note of Martins' letter, and viewed the cause of ratification contest in the state as an uphill slog.

From the outset, many in Maryland prepared to reject the Constitution unless a bill of rights was added. William Paca, a signer of the Declaration of Independence, announced that he would only support the document "under the firm persuasion, and full confidence, that such amendments would be peaceably obtained, as to enable the people to live happy under the government." Despite his objections, leading proponents of the framework responded that the Constitution should be ratified "as speedily as possible, and do no other act," and argued that their convention to consider ratification was not inherently authorized by their constituencies to debate the merits of constitutional amendments.[190]

While some resisted the Constitution until the end of the convention, Paca secured a deal with the Federalists. Under the agreement, he would drop his opposition to the Constitution in exchange for the inclusion of a list of popular constitutional amendments in state's the ratification ordinance. A committee of thirteen representatives was formed for such a purpose, and its report articulated the imperative need for such alterations:

We consider the proposed form of national government as very defective, and that the liberty and happiness of the people will be endangered if the system not be greatly changed and altered. The amendments agreed to by the committee, and those proposed by the minority are now laid before you for consideration, that you may express your sense

as such alterations as you may think proper to make in the new constitution.[191]

The report noted that the proposed amendments were "calculated to preserve public liberty, by those checks on power, which the experience of
ages has rendered venerable."[192] With the understanding that amendments
were necessary, the Constitution was ratified in Maryland by a margin of
47 to 27.

SOUTH CAROLINA

Charleston's leading supporter of the Constitution, Charles Pinckney,
complained that the Confederation system provided inadequate power to
counteract against the economic tragedy of the Critical Period.[193] While
his own plan for government was mostly ignored in the Philadelphia Convention, he found favor with the new Constitution and sought to convince
his state to support it. In his pitch for ratification, he promoted the new
constitutional model as a remedy for the ailments of the Confederation.

Charles Cotesworth Pinckney, not to be confused with his cousin, addressed the claim that powerful oppressors would take control of the new
government and deprive individuals of their liberty. He countered this supposition by explaining the Constitution's impeachment power, and clarified that the process could be used to remove not only the president and
vice president, but also civil officers.[194] If the executive office was abused,
Cotesworth Pinckney explained that he could be summarily removed from
office.

Patrick Dollard raised the suspicion that the general government had
too many powers under the new constitutional proposal. Likening the new
system to a "box of Pandora" that was "particularly calculated for the me-
ridian of despotic aristocracy," he warned the Constitution would "promote the ambitious views of a few able and designing men, and enslave
the rest." In like fashion, James Lincoln claimed that ratification of the
Constitution would place its sovereign powers "into the hands of a set of
men who live one thousand miles distant from you." In response to both
critics, Pinckney asserted that the general government had no right to "exercise powers not expressly delegated to it." By extension, he insisted that

South Carolina "certainly reserve to ourselves every power and right not mentioned in the Constitution."[195]

Just as in the other states, the anxieties of apprehensive Carolinians were addressed by the unwavering rebuttal that the general government simply did not possess the degree of power naysayers warned of. Assured of this by leading Federalists, marked unease within the state was reduced, and South Carolina endorsed the compact by a margin of 149 to 73.

NEW HAMPSHIRE

In a close contest, Federalists in New Hampshire successfully convinced its convention that ratification was necessary in order for the state to maintain power and relevance. Most notes from the debates were not preserved, but records indicate that the state was strongly split in its will to adopt the Constitution. Ratification was ultimately secured in June of 1788 by a vote of 57 to 47. Like Virginia, New Hampshire proclaimed "that all powers not expressly and particularly delegated by the aforesaid Constitution are reserved to the several states, to be by them exercised."[196]

VIRGINIA

Virginia's political elite was completely divided on the issue of ratification, producing a convention that was among the most contentious of all the states. The records of the proceedings were also very well chronicled, making the state one of the most studied in the ratification struggle. A proud state built upon a sovereign political tradition, the "Old Dominion" appeared unwilling to break this streak without the guarantee that its own sovereign authority would remain undisturbed.

Several very well-known and famous Virginians held great reservations about the Constitution, two of the Philadelphia Convention's most active participants refused to sign the document. Both Governor Edmund Randolph and George Mason – the writer of Virginia's first republican constitution – were concerned about various aspects of the plan and its lack of a bill of rights. Mason also lambasted the Constitution for prohibiting Congress from eradicating the importation of foreign slaves for twenty years. This practice, complained Mason, was a "nefarious trade."[197]

Randolph cited other motives for opposing the document, including his view that the House of Representatives would be too small, the lack of limitation on a standing military, and a belief that the power to tax commerce should be restrained.

Though under the impression that the Articles of Confederation should amended to an extent, Patrick Henry refused even to venture to the Philadelphia Convention. Fearing the proposal would be too destructive to the states, he detected sinister motives even before the convention began. While chosen to represent his state in Philadelphia, Henry refused the invitation and famously said that he "smelt a rat."[198]

In Henry's estimation, there was no reason to cede additional power to a central authority, and Virginia's sovereign tradition recognized the self-sufficiency of the Old Dominion. The esteemed spokesman also believed that liberty was more likely to thrive in localities, and deeply dreaded the prospect of a nationally-oriented government that proactively intruded upon the affairs of Virginians. Under the impression that the Philadelphia Convention had effectively discarded the Articles of Confederation rather than pursue the process to amend it, Henry threw all his political energies behind the defeat of the new framework. Joining him and Mason were other prominent figures such as William Grayson and future president James Monroe.

One of the most common refrains of opposition in Virginia was the accusation that the newly-created central judiciary – the first of its kind in North America – would function as an aloof and overbearing body that would inevitably encroach upon the state court systems. A new assembly of judicial appointees, these foes warned, would act as something of a national oligarchy that contravened laws passed by the states. Accordingly, the negative ramifications of such a judiciary would be amplified by the judges' unfamiliarity with the laws of the individual states. Many remained doubtful that a new central court system, existing many miles away from most states, could make accurate judgments on pressing controversies without violating the sovereignty of the states.

In the Virginia ratification convention, this outlook was brought forward most vociferously by Mason. Ideologically opposed to a powerful federal judiciary, Mason feared that the federal courts would come into conflict with the state courts. "There is no limitation" to the federal court system, he complained. "The inferior courts are to be as numerous as Congress may think proper," he added, and would "be of whatever nature they please." Mason protested that the variety of the cases that would be taken up by the federal judiciary would be virtually unlimited. Their power of arbitration over so many different cases, he suggested, would allow the new court system to expand its power beyond constitutional confines through judicial precedent. The "effect and operation" of the federal courts, Mason asserted, "will be utterly to destroy the state governments."[199]

Beyond the vast array of cases the federal courts would oversee, Mason also projected that the same system would possess unlimited power. To give the federal courts jurisdiction in cases between a state and citizens thereof, he claimed, was "utterly inconsistent with reason or good policy." After hearing this, the convention minutes reflect that George Nicholas stood and refuted Mason's understanding of the federal court apparatus. Echoing Nicholas' answer the next day, John Marshall retorted that "the objection, which was made by the Honorable member who was first up yesterday has been so fully refuted, that it is not worth while to notice it."[200] Mason was told that this assertion was unwarranted.

Marshall, a Federalist whose actions would later expand the power of the federal judiciary greatly as Chief Justice, disavowed Mason's suggestion and countered that such authority could not be wielded by the new courts: "How disgraceful is it that the State Courts cannot be trusted, says the Honorable Gentleman! What is the language of the Constitution? Does it take away their jurisdiction?" Marshall boldly maintained that such judicial confiscation would not transpire, promising that "the State Courts will not lose the jurisdiction of the causes they now decide."[201] While quashing some of the apprehensions at his convention, Marshall's future actions on the Supreme Court would betray these words.

After Mason warned that the federal judiciary would attempt to supplant Virginia's state judicial authority, he was told his concerns were unwarranted. Unfortunately, the Supreme Court succeeded in doing just that in the years after the Constitution's ratification. Mason's prophetic arguments at Virginia's ratifying convention foreshadowed *Marbury v. Madison*, *Fletcher v. Peck*, *McCulloch v. Maryland*, and other cases that propelled the federal judiciary toward rapid expansion. Considering modern trends, he could not have been more perceptive in regard to the evolution of the federal courts. In contemporary consideration, Mason's fears appear to be especially prophetic.

In the run-up to the debates in Richmond, Governor Randolph made an abrupt shift, joining forces with the Federalists to promote the Constitution. The transition was the result of the news that eight states had by that time ratified the document, forcing Virginia to choose between disunion and significant standing the general government. Choosing the latter, Randolph now deemed the new model worthy of patronage. A talented speaker that was not as prone to physical illness as Madison, he quickly emerged as the state's chief advocate of the document.

Federalists in Virginia responded to the various complaints by pointing to the representative nature of the new government. When opponents expressed the trepidation that ratification would deprive Virginia of its stature as a powerful and influential body, the supporters of the Constitution pointed out the representational advantage Virginia would have over other states in the House of Representatives. Additionally, they echoed the position that all unlisted powers were reserved to Virginia. After being pressed by detractors, Randolph guaranteed that all authority was "completely vested in the people, unless expressly given away." Furthermore, Randolph declared that the government under the Constitution be a "body arising from a compact, and with certain delineated powers."[202]

In the end, two important elements led to Virginia's narrow acceptance of the document. First, Edmund Randolph's assurance that the framework was one of expressly delegated powers carried weight and successfully allayed concerns that the Constitution would bring about a leviathan government of unlimited power. Secondly, George Nicholas assured the assembly that if the general government exploited the terms of the compact, Virginia was released from its commitment to the union. After these two promises, Virginia's representatives voted to ratify the Constitution by a margin of 89 to 79. By their state's self-determining act of ratification, historian Kevin Gutzman observed that "Virginians understood themselves to be entering into a compact/contract with the other parties: the other states. The states were primary, the federal relationship a convenience."[203]

NEW YORK

New York's ratification struggle, much like Virginia, was characterized by a divisive political landscape. The state's political and economic
influence made the controversy of the day ever more salient, and factions
developed on all sides. In one of the most the dramatic moments in Poughkeepsie, John Lansing embarrassed Alexander Hamilton by revealing that
Hamilton had championed a nationalist government at the Philadelphia
Convention. Referencing the records of the convention, Lansing professed
that Hamilton supported a system through which "the state governments
ought to be subverted, at least, so far as to leave them only corporate
rights." Despite the presence of the notes – which Lansing must have received from Robert Yates – Hamilton patently denied the allegation. An
"altercation" transpired between Lansing and Hamilton, with the latter insisting that he had been misrepresented. This quarrel lasted for the remainder of the day and occupied a "considerable" part of a second.[204]

In addition to the attempt to undermine his ideological foe, Lansing
worked with Melancton Smith, Thomas Tredwell, George Clinton, Abraham Yates, and other opponents to attack the Constitution. Their best strategic recourse seemed to rely upon the route taken by other states – the
suggestion of a written bill of rights. Lansing took the lead in such a project, and painstakingly worked to craft a set of restrictions against the
power of the general government. If his political allies could not defeat the
document in convention, he thought, they could at least temper its potential for misuse.

Writing under the pseudonym "Cato," one constitutional nemesis
quickly made use of the New York presses to expose the defects of the
new system. Most likely the secret identity of New York Governor George
Clinton, Cato raised particular suspicion in regard to executive authority.
His power under the Constitution, the writer argued, would "lead to oppression and ruin." He would be surrounded by "favorites and flatterers"
that would lead him to wrongdoing, and his lust for power would inspire
the creation of "an arbitrary and odious aristocracy or monarchy." The office was likely to spawn a tyrant reminiscent of a Caligula, Nero, or Do-
mitian – all notorious Roman villains. Though the "frame of government"
would be different, Cato admitted, the presidential office would differ

"very immaterially from the establishment of monarchy in Britain."[205] To devout republicans that called for public virtue, a passive government of limited powers, and the legal embrace of individual rights, the British mode of government was a dreadful prospect.

Cato also disapproved of the relatively small size of Congress, believing such a number would be "too few to resist the influence of corruption, and the temptation to treachery." He also supposed that the legislature would be inclined to regulate the powers of the states and push for permanent taxes on property. Inside the convention proceedings, delegates adopted the same mantra. The mere notion that the general government would stay out of the affairs of the states, stated Thomas Tredwell, was an "absurdity."[206] Those that rejected the Federalist effort overwhelmingly suspected the new Constitution would establish a colossal central authority and diminish the relative power of New York.

Denying these pessimistic visions, Hamilton explained that the laws of the federal government would only be supreme if they were valid, enumerated, and constitutional:

But the **laws of congress are restricted to a certain sphere**, and when they depart from this sphere, they are no longer supreme or binding. In the same manner **the states have certain independent powers, in which their laws are supreme**: for example, in making and executing laws concerning the punishment of certain crimes.[emphasis added][207]

Under the new plan, Hamilton added, "the states cannot be controlled." Instead of federal supremacy, the powers of the state and general government would coincide without overlapping. According to the young Federalist lawyer, the "two governments are concurrent, and yet supreme."[208]

Addressing the crowd of detractors, Robert Livingston assured the assembly that the Constitution model was a republic "formed by a league of states." Scrupulously refuting those who denied this, he claimed that those making false accusations about the model "have either misunderstood or perverted" the explanation he and his like-minded supporters had provided. Livingston also countered the attacks on the power of the president by clarifying that almost all powers resided in Congress, including authority over war, peace, and taxation. Therefore, the government – including its executive – could not make unlimited demands upon the states.[209] According to Livingston, the structure and purpose of the government limited its potential to challenge or overtake the states.

Despite these pledges, and a convention that brought over a month of clarification and debate, antipathy toward the Constitution was overwhelming in New York. At one point, frustrated Federalists planned for New York City to secede from the state and ratify the document as an independent entity if the convention refused to do so as a whole.[210] Under such a scenario, the new polity would become the crucial ninth "state" to ratify the Constitution – the requisite number for the Constitution to go into legal effect.

Facing the enormous obstacle of the Constitution's shrewd foes, Hamilton believed it was necessary to broaden the audience of the debate. Prior to the convention, he devised a method to persuade the citizens of New York as a whole rather than challenging his political rivals directly. Since the state was seen as a hostile battleground for the Constitution, it was a considerable task to sway the public in favor of the plan. This was partially due to the plethora of compelling writings that were hurled against it, and also because the Constitution's supporters vastly outnumbered the opposition – New York City was the only real Federalist stronghold in the state. With these factors in mind, Hamilton concluded that his aims could only be accomplished through the press. He therefore endeavored to gather the most persuasive writers in favor of the model, and use their colorful narratives to garner support for the Constitution. Thus, *The Federalist* project was born.

The Federalist essays occupy a unique place in the modern understanding of the Constitution, principally because they are the most popularly referenced series of writings that explain the document. By the end of the ratification contest, the series contained 85 distinct articles – all written by nationalists who strongly favored the constitutional model. After seeking help from several friends, John Jay and James Madison were recruited to assist Hamilton with the venture. Writing under the pseudonym "Publius," these Federalists intended to prove that the Constitution would exemplify a superior republican framework, protect individual liberty, fix the defects of the Articles of Confederation, and counteract the common arguments of the model's opponents.

In modern times, *The Federalist* is continually cited in Supreme Court opinions, and the series is considered a uniquely pure accurate interpretation of the Constitution. However, its actual effect on New York's ratification was minimal. Many of the topics written about in *The Federalist* were covered at length during the Poughkeepsie Convention, but the series itself did not sway the convention in favor of the document. Far from a universal source of reference, its influence on the ratification of the other states was also limited. Eight other states had ratified the document by the time the final essay was published, and the publication of the essays did not have significant reach outside of New York.[211]

By the end of New York's proceedings, some of the Constitution's most vocal opponents changed their minds. After a series of guarantees, and the persuasive refutation of adversarial claims, many were willing to reverse their position. Even some of the state's lead adversaries, such as Melancton Smith, decided to vote in favor. In his address to New York's citizens, Smith said that the addition of proposed amendments would address most of his anxieties. If there were written boundaries that eliminated federal powers, he reasoned that the general government would not be able to trample upon the states or individuals.

New York's ratification instrument articulated the state's act of ratification was contingent upon the addition of a bill of rights:

> Resolved, As the opinion of this committee, that the constitution under considering ought to be ratified by this convention: Upon condition, nevertheless, That until a convention shall be called and convened for proposing amendments to the said constitution.[212]

As in Virginia, the Federalists in New York were also able to alleviate concerns regarding the potential loss of state authority by accepting a clause which guaranteed that the state could "reassume" its sovereign powers if they were seized by the general government.[213] If New York didn't desire to remain in the union, it was absolved from the compact. Based on the prospect of New York City's secession from the state, the assurance that a bill of rights would be added, and the guarantee that the state could leave the union whenever it wished, New York ratified by an extremely narrow margin of 30 to 27.

NORTH CAROLINA (PART 2)

North Carolina withheld its assent to the new constitutional proposal for some time. The state's original 1788 ratification convention in Hillsborough concluded without adopting the Constitution, but a new convention was set to meet in Fayetteville the next year to reconsider the same question. Months after the first session of Congress, the inauguration of George Washington, and after eleven other states had joined the federal union, the state finally decided to ratify the Constitution on November 21, 1789. During its interregnum, North Carolina remained an independent republic, with Hugh Williamson serving as a foreign diplomat to the United States.

While the state abstained from adopting the new model, North Carolina was not coerced by the other states to ratify, and was never threatened by military force. As in all states, the act of ratification was the a strictly voluntary decision, and North Carolina's political trajectory served as the prime example of this fact. Ratification was ultimately accomplished in part because the circumstances had changed enough to satisfy Anti-Federalist concerns. The First Congress had recently proposed a bill of rights, and George Washington had been elected president of the new government.

As in other parts of the union, those within North Carolina considered the sitting president uniquely deserving of trust, a man that would not overstep his authority or betray the common interests of the states. Beyond these dynamics, political dynamics suggest that North Carolina politicians found ratification desirable because it would prevent the state from being treated as a foreign power for the purposes of trade. While tariffs could be imposed upon goods from foreign countries, within the union no such tax could be levied upon a particular region or state.

Like New York, North Carolina made its acceptance of the Constitution conditional. On the contrary, Archibald Maclaine announced that the state would disregard unconstitutional laws and rebuke the general government for passing them:

If Congress should make a law beyond the powers and spirit of the Constitution, should we not say to Congress, 'You have no authority to make this law. There are limits beyond which you cannot go. You cannot exceed the power prescribed by the Constitution. You are amenable to us for your conduct. This act is unconstitutional. We will disregard it, and punish you for the attempt.[214]

Maclaine's pledge was an unmistakably stern warning that asserted how unconstitutional transgressions by the federal government would be treated. As a constitutional maxim, it provided a blueprint for all states to follow.

RHODE ISLAND

Rhode Island, often an outlier in North American politics, protested the Philadelphia Convention and refused to send delegates. Believing that the convention would work against its interests, and would likely produce undesirable amendments to the Articles of Confederation, the state invoked its independent streak and remained an independent republic as during the entirety of Washington's first year in office. Contesting the need for any change to the federal structure, Rhode Island did not ratify until May 29, 1790. Like numerous other states, Rhode Island's newly-adopted position was largely inspired by the prospect of a bill of rights. By ratifying the document, Rhode Island also hoped to avoid the implementation of tariffs that would discourage American trade with the state's inhabitants.

THE RESUMPTION CLAUSES

Among the states that ratified the Constitution, three states placed "resumption clauses" within the text of their ratification decrees. These passages were definitive, explicit declarations that the states would take back powers they delegated to the federal government if the new government overstepped its authority. Virginia, Rhode Island, and New York all made such guarantees. By helping to secure ratification in the most contentious states and underscoring the Constitution as noncompulsory compact, the resumption clauses demonstrated that the states did not view their act of ratification as a perpetual or unending obligation.

The Constitution's most popular and ardent enemies in Virginia, such as Patrick Henry and George Mason, were particularly worried that federal officials would use stealthy tactics to steal reserved powers from the states. For many, a bill of rights was the proper remedy to this malady. Still, Virginia adopted an even stronger guarantee of its sovereign capacity. The state incorporated a clause that declared the right of its inhabitants to take back the powers it delegated to the federal government if the central authority oversteps its constitutional bounds. It was an unmistakable warning to the general government that Virginia would abandon the compact – withdrawing from the union entirely – if such a scenario unfolded:

> We, the delegates of the people of Virginia…Do, in the name and in behalf of the people of Virginia, declare and make known, that **the powers granted under the Constitution, being derived from the people of the United States, be resumed by them whensoever the same shall be perverted to their injury or oppression,** and that every power, not granted thereby, remains with them, and at their will; that, therefore, no right, of any denomination, can be cancelled, abridged, restrained, or modified, by the Congress, by the Senate or House of Representatives, acting in any capacity, by the President, or any department or officer of the United States, except in those instances in which power is given by the Constitution for those purposes.[emphasis added][215]

Since Edmund Randolph described Virginia as one of thirteen parties to the compact, the clause would placate archetypal fears and Virginia's sovereign interests would be protected. In Richmond, the Federalists repeatedly vowed that their state would remain sovereign over the new general government, which would hold very few, defined powers.

Near the conclusion of Virginia's ratification convention, Edmund Randolph proclaimed that his state would "confederate with the twelve other governments" under an act of ratification. Virginians were expecting a system in which they could resume their sovereign power after usurpations, and came to believe that the state's interpretation of the Constitution was binding on the other parties. George Nicholas, another Federalist, referred to the ratification as thirteen "individuals" that were about to make a contract:

> [If] one [state] agrees to it, but at the same time declares that he under-
> stands its meaning, signification, and intent, to be, what the words of
> the contract plainly and obviously denote, that it is not to be construed
> so as to impose any supplementary condition upon him and that he is
> to be exonerated from it, whenever such imposition shall be at-
> tempted—I ask whether in this case these conditions on which he as-
> sented to, would not be binding on another twelve? In like manner these
> conditions will be binding on congress. They can exercise no power
> that is not expressly granted them.[216]

Virginia immediately took its ratification vote after Nicholas's calculated assurance. By adopting this text, Virginia made its stance clear – the Constitution was to be respected only as an instrument which did what Virginia understood it to. It also asserted that Virginia's understanding of the document was binding on the other states. Despite his cynicism, Patrick Henry declared that his state would never surrender its sovereign authority.[217] In Virginia's conception, delegating powers to a general authority was not considered an act of unending attachment.

Rhode Island, which crafted a resumption declaration with similar ver-biage, included a provision iterating that "the powers of government may be reassumed by the people, whensoever it shall become necessary to their happiness."[218] As the most slothful adopter of the Constitution, Rhode Island reactively implemented the open-ended clause to protect its own sovereignty. Like Virginia, Rhode Island's convention specified that the Constitution was to be an instrument of limited authority, where the residuary powers were retained by the state government. Most importantly, the state reserved the ability to reclaim the powers it delegated.

New York, which ratified the Constitution in July of 1788 by an extremely narrow margin, also recognized the utility of a power resumption clause. The chief Federalist advocates within the state, who at one point threatened to have New York secede from the rest of the state and ratify the document independently, eventually acquiesced to this guarantee in order to make ratification a realistic possibility.[219] The language unequivocally proclaimed that all powers originating in New York could be retaken by the state whenever it was deemed conducive to the happiness of the people within it.

Consenting to the Constitution did not mean that the states had authorized an unlimited and permanent surrender of all delegated powers. Since the Constitution was an agreement among various parties, violations would not be tolerated and the states reserved the right to rescind their ratification and reclaim their inherent authority. All three of these states made clear that when the federal government violates the compact, the states have the right of recourse – they could obstruct, they could resist its usurpations, and they could leave.

RESPONDING TO THE CONSTITUTION'S OPPONENTS

The writings that opposed the Constitution far outnumbered those in support of the document, but the oppositional pieces have never achieved the widespread notoriety of *The Federalist*. Nonetheless, the arguments they raised framed the debates and predicted the future. The most enthusiastic adversaries of the document – An Old Whig, Brutus, Cato, Centinel, and others – contributed greatly to the ideological foundations of the founding era. Despite their marginal position in the contemporary, the influence they had in their own era was tangible. While they are almost never cited by federal officials or judges, these individuals genuinely predicted many shortcomings that would materialize in the new federal government. Today, some of their forecasts seem especially prescient.

Even though history indicates that the Constitution should be understood as a product of the states, this aspect of constitutional ratification has been ignored or understated. A candid audience should thus emphasize the defenses made on its behalf by Federalists who sold the document to the state ratifying conventions. These friends of the Constitution insisted that the framework would not create an overwhelming juggernaut of centralized authority. Moreover, they claimed the apprehensions of the Constitution's enemies were misguided by persistently reiterating that the general government would only have the powers it was "expressly" delegated.[220] With the assurance that the federal judiciary would only adjudicate a small number of specific types of cases, Federalists professed that state courts would maintain authority over local disputes. To assuage the most zealous critics, they denied that the new presidential office would produce a malevolent king. Perhaps most importantly, they acquiesced to early concerns about the lack of a bill of rights.

Reflecting on the proper manner to interpret the Constitution, Thomas Jefferson wrote that the document should be understood "according to the true sense in which it was adopted by the States, that in which it was advocated by its friends, and not that which its enemies apprehended."[221] Concurring with this understanding of the constitutional interpretation, James Madison espoused the same opinion in *The Federalist* No. 39:

> Each State, in ratifying the Constitution, is considered as a sovereign body, independent of all others, and only to be bound by its own voluntary act. In this relation, then, the new Constitution will, if established, be a federal, and not a national constitution.[222]

Both men claimed that the plentiful notes, debates, speeches, and proceedings left by the ratification struggle should be cited to determine the objective constitutional truth. The plan's opponents, they believed, should not tarnish the proper understanding because the suspicions that they raised were not that which was ratified. Nevertheless, this theory of constitutional interpretation has largely faded from the limelight. The reasoning for this, in large part, is that early federal precedents, Joseph Story's commentaries, and the rulings of the Marshall Court have effectively brushed aside the plain truth, filling the gaps with faulty narratives to justify modern interpretations of the Constitution.

The Constitution produced a government of enumerated powers, where only the specified powers could be exercised – and this was the only way in which the Constitution was explained. Soon after the First Congress was seated, representative Richard Bland Lee reiterated this by noting that the government "is invested with powers for enumerated purposes only." The federal government, he declared, "cannot exercise any others whatsoever." Massachusetts representative Fisher Ames condemned the implementation of additional powers, saying "we are sworn as much to exercise constitutional authority, for the general good, as to refrain from assuming powers that are not given to us." James Iredell of North Carolina reiterated that any law made, if not warranted by the Constitution, was a "barefaced usur-pation."[223]

Legislative limitations were not the only ones observed and docu-mented. Virginia representative Alexander White, for instance, criticized the mere suggestion that the president could unilaterally enact law himself. Viewing any circumvention of the legislature as a clear constitutional vi-olation, he stated categorically that the president doesn't have powers be-longing to other branches. Roger Sherman concurred, recommending "that we avoid making this declaration, especially in favor of the president, as I do not believe the constitution vests the authority in him alone." White remarked that if the president did in fact possess the power to make law, he did not know how there could be a more "arbitrary government."[224]

White compared the holder of such unconstitutional power to a ruler with "the powers of the most absolute monarch." A Congress that usurped expansive authority beyond the boundaries of the Constitution, he added, would violate the instrument that "has defined their limits."[225] These hy-potheticals, he said, negated the form of government prescribed by the document:

This is a government constituted for particular purposes only; and the powers granted to carry it into effect, are specifically enumerated, and disposed among the various branches. If these powers are insufficient, or if they are improperly distributed, it is not our fault, nor within our power to remedy...We can neither enlarge nor modify them.[226]

White's words show that this interpretation of the Constitution was the same as that which had been established at the state ratification conven-tions. Far from an erroneous deviation, his perception was universally acknowledged and extensively documented. Remaining consistent with their ratification pledges, honest representatives respected the guidelines adopted by the states that ratified the document.

If the Constitution is to be understood in the sense by which it was "advocated by its friends," it had to be viewed as a document that did what the Federalists explained it did. If the document is not to be understood by "that which its enemies apprehended," it didn't have the treacherous func-tion its opponents claimed. James Madison, despite having inclinations toward a nationalist model for government, realized this to be the case. Although his political proclivities lost out in Philadelphia, he recognized that the ratified Constitution was a federated model. For a time, even arch-nationalist Alexander Hamilton and his political allies purported to subscribe to such an understanding.

Chapter 5

The Jeffersonian Tradition

Thomas Jefferson's conception of the relationship between the states and the general government was the cornerstone of his political philosophy. Believing decentralized government was necessary to protect individual liberty, the principles Jefferson espoused were a continuance of Virginia's political tradition and its ratification process. To his chagrin, the federal government soon worked to dismantle his ideals, even during the course of his own lifetime. Nevertheless, his political philosophy lived on throughout many decades. Never meant to wither away at the behest of a leviathan federal government, they remain a significant part of the American political psyche.

JEFFERSON AND STATE INDEPENDENCE

The political achievement that is most commonly attributed to Jefferson is his authorship of the Declaration of Independence. The famed writing was first conceived when a committee of five delegates was formed during the Second Continental Congress. Along with the committee chairman, John Adams, delegates Benjamin Franklin, Roger Sherman, and Robert Livingston joined Jefferson in the great task of summarizing the patriot position and justifying the severance of the American states from the British Empire. While some states had already declared independence, in June of 1776 each delegation had been sent to their home states to receive instructions in regard to the matter at hand. At this point, Jefferson's home state of Virginia had already forced its royal governor to flee, adopted a declaration of rights, and ratified its first republican constitution.

According to Adams, Jefferson was the only appropriate choice to write the document. First, he came from the most influential state, and Adams strongly believed Virginia's support was vital to the cause of independence. Secondly, Adams also had a great deal of respect for the eloquence of Jefferson's pen, and was familiar with *A Summary View of the Rights of British America*. A third and most telling reason that Jefferson should write the document, thought Adams, was that Jefferson was popular and trustworthy, while Adams was disliked by the other delegates. "I am obnoxious, suspected, and unpopular," wrote Adams, and Jefferson was "very much otherwise."[227] Staying behind in Philadelphia, Jefferson completed the first draft in a matter of days.

The introduction of the final document made clear that there are certain times when it becomes necessary to dissolve the bands that tie one people with another. This is a direct reference to the dissolution of the connection between the colonies and the British crown. Separation was necessary at times, Jefferson wrote, to obtain the "separate and equal station to which the Laws of Nature and of Nature's God entitle them." At the time, friends of independence such as Jefferson recognized that liberty could not be held by the peoples of the states while still in submission to the powerful authority of Britain. He also indicated that the reasons for the severance – "the causes which impel them to the separation" – should be explained and elaborated upon. The remainder of the American creed, therefore, fulfilled such a purpose.

The Declaration of Independence, first and foremost, justifies the people's natural right to overthrow their government. Jefferson wrote that "whenever any form of government becomes destructive to these ends, it is the right of the people to alter or abolish it, and to institute new Government, laying its foundation on such principles and organizing its powers in such form, as to them shall seem most likely to effect their Safety and Happiness." Expounding upon this notion, the document indicated that the citizenry has the moral obligation to discard their government in the face of tyranny. "It is their right, it is their duty, to throw off such Government, and to provide new Guards for their future security," Jefferson wrote.[228] Accordingly, the people could rightfully depart from or abolish their government and replace it with a new one.

The Declaration of Independence was strongly influenced by the writings and philosophy of John Locke, the famed English political philosopher that contributed greatly to natural law and social compact theory. Some of the wording of the document is lifted almost directly from Locke's writings, including the assertion that the king had engaged in a "long train of abuses." To the founding generation, Locke's influence was extensive. American historian Carl Becker asserted that "most Americans had absorbed Locke's works as a kind of political gospel." Religious leaders understood, sympathized, and preached the fundamentals of Locke's political theory, especially in the New England colonies. Historian Clinton Rossiter wrote that "Locke rode into New England on the backs of Moses and the Prophets." Patriot lawyer James Otis wrote that "the authority of Mr. Locke has been preferred to all others." Benjamin Franklin said that Locke was one of the "best English authors" in the fields of history, rhetoric, logic, moral and natural philosophy. Richard Henry Lee went as far as to describe the Declaration of Independence as a copy of Locke's work. Jefferson himself called Locke one of the three greatest men who ever lived, without exception.[229]

In its quintessence, the Declaration was truly a proclamation of secession that conveyed the reasons for which the states decided to cut all ties with the mother country. The signers were aware that the deed would be considered treasonous, and the British penalty for such an was death by hanging. Facing a momentous choice, the delegates knew what became of those who abolished the English monarchy and signed the death warrant of Charles I. Knowing their actions would be deemed seditious, the representatives remained steadfast in their quest to establish independence. In this ordeal, the representatives of the several states mutually pledged their "lives," "fortunes," and "sacred honor" to a declaration of secession. The gesture was considered paramount in order to overcome tyranny, though the patriots knew of the potential for harsh ramifications to come from their actions. The act of disassociation, as it turned out, was at the heart of the Jeffersonian legacy.

Perhaps the most understated and important aspect of the Declaration was its explicit acknowledgement of state sovereignty in the final paragraph. This section explained that the states were free and independent, and had all of the powers and abilities that characterized nations throughout the world. In clarification of this, Jefferson wrote that the former colonies were now "Free and Independent States" that were "Absolved from all Allegiance to the British Crown." By the extension of this status, "all political connection between them and the State of Great Britain, is and ought to be totally dissolved." The Virginian characterized the states as the ultimate wardens of their own authority, and masters of their own sovereign destinies. The states were no longer subservient to the will of George III or Parliament, which declared that they were bound by Parliamentary law "in all cases whatsoever."[230]

Jefferson wrote that the new "Free and Independent States" had "full Power to levy War, conclude Peace, contract Alliances, establish Commerce, and to do all other Acts and Things which Independent States may of right do." The words made it definitively known that the states are not only independent of Great Britain, but independent of each other. All of them, per the document, had the same powers as autonomous countries. Indeed, these functions were actualized by the individual states during the drafting of the document and in the following years. For example, various states fitted and deployed their own military vessels, engaged in independent military excursions, and used such authority to issue letters of marque and reprisal.[231]

While often called a "founding document," the Declaration was not an act of political unification, and founded no government. Instead, the text referred to the states in the plural, recognizing their sovereign and independent stature. In addition to its philosophical underpinnings, the Declaration merely justified the passage of the Richard Henry Lee Resolution. This act, accepted on July 2, 1776, declared that all ties with Britain were "totally dissolved." To consider the document to be a proclamation of secession rather than a founding document is not to say the writing has no worth – on the contrary, it was the masterful work of a deft hand.

The effort to convince those all the state delegations to support independence was an uphill battle. Some representatives, such as John Dickinson and Robert Morris of Pennsylvania, abstained from the vote on independence entirely. As Pennsylvania's leading conservative politician, Dickinson believed that foreign alliances should be established prior to such a decision. If the radical step of independence was embraced too hastily, he thought, the potent might of the world's most powerful military quickly undermine the entire patriot cause. Ultimately, both men agreed to abstain from swaying their state delegation on the matter, allowing the rest of the Pennsylvania delegation to vote in favor of the motion.

For its part, South Carolina opposed independence in the days prior to the official vote. Edward Rutledge, just 26 years old at the time of the crucial decision, made clear that his state desired unanimity among the delegations before casting a vote in favor. When Adams diligently worked to secure an undivided result, and it became clear that such a scenario would come to fruition, Rutledge changed his position and South Carolina voted in favor.

New York abstained from voting on independence completely, and Delaware's delegation remained divided on the subject on the eve of the vote.[232] Since each state had a single vote in all matters, and a quorum was required, only Caesar Rodney's arrival allowed Delaware's position of support to be carried. Tied to their localities, representatives were prohibited from voting in favor of this severance until receiving direct instructions to do so from their home states. Each state's representatives in the Continental Congress therefore acted as the physical manifestation of their own state's sovereignty, a model that inspired the future United States Senate. This understanding of the states is needed to appreciate the manner in which the states emerged as independent powers.

While some states had already declared independence individually, their delegations crucially decided to establish the principle as the common cause of the states. On July 2nd, the resolution on independence was adopted with twelve votes in the affirmative, with New York abstaining. A week after the resolution passed, New York received instructions from its Provincial Congress to vote in favor of independence. By this time, the Declaration of Independence was adopted by the Continental Congress and widely publicized.

Tellingly, the Declaration refers to "the State of Great Britain" in the same way in which the American states are conceptualized. This fact is especially noteworthy because it reflects the intended relationship between the American states. At the time, a "state" was defined as a sovereign body not unlike an independent country. The Declaration sustains the idea that the states were on the same sovereign level as all countries, as Jefferson used the term "state" indiscriminately to refer to all thirteen former colonies and to Britain. By announcing that they were independent entities, the states had entered the world stage as autonomous bodies.

Reflecting on the event many years later, John Taylor of Caroline affirmed that a state was "a political community." What other word, he asked, "was more proper to describe the communities recognized by the Declaration of Independence, the Union of 1777, and the Union of 1787?" Luther Martin recognized the same definition during the Philadelphia Convention. "When the States threw off their allegiance on Great Britain," he noted, "they became independent of her, and each other." The polities then "confederated for mutual defence, and this was done on principles of perfect reciprocity-they will now again meet on the same ground."[233] Rather than an establishment of national will, these men realized that independence meant political autonomy.

JEFFERSON AND HAMILTON

Jefferson's feud with his political arch-nemesis, Alexander Hamilton, brought attention to his hallmark, career-spanning defense of decentralized political authority. While the two served in the same presidential cabinet, their political inclinations could not have been more divergent. At the same time Jefferson favored yeomen landholding, federal nonintervention, and state control over most matters, Hamilton became the flagbearer of northern industry, political consolidation, and central economic planning. George Washington held both men in high esteem, but in the end favored Hamilton's impulses over Jefferson's penchants. The latter eventually ended his tenure in Washington's cabinet as a troubled man, sincerely dejected by the extent to which Hamilton was able to steer Washington in matters of policy.

Jefferson's opposition to Hamilton took the form of many political clashes, most of which centered upon the relative power of the states and the general government. While Jefferson adamantly believed that centralized banking economic mercantilism were destructive forces that would undermine republican government, Hamilton thought his economic system was necessary to establish national credit and impose financial order. Although Jefferson thought perpetual debt was a tool to enslave future generations and leave them in bondage, Hamilton lobbied for the accumulation of debt under the belief that it would make the states subordinate to the will of the central government, and establish a system of public credit.

Before his selection to Washington's cabinet, though, Jefferson achieved one of his greatest political accomplishments while serving as a diplomat to France. As it turned out, the battle over religious freedom in Virginia revealed the plausibility of confronting and overtaking political challenges at a local level. In contrast to Alexander Hamilton's sensibilities, Jefferson's perception was that wrongheaded policy could be uprooted at the local level, satisfy the needs of a state's citizens, and leave the other states to manage most matters of policy for themselves.

JEFFERSON AND RELIGIOUS FREEDOM

At Monticello, Jefferson's headstone still recognizes authorship of the Virginia Statute for Religious Freedom, one of the cornerstones of Virginia's early republic. Jefferson first introduced his radical religious bill to the Virginia General Assembly in 1779, but it was summarily disregarded. By the 1780s, the bill had become a dead letter. However, as the debate over religious freedom raged again in the mid-1780s, representative James Madison emerged as a tireless promoter of the same cause. Debates concerning religious funding produced a significant political squabble in Virginia, and two influential political factions clashed with one another.

Before Jefferson and Madison's work, the Church of England was the official established religion of the Commonwealth of Virginia. By 1784, some representatives suggested that the conclusion of the war had resulted in a general loss of morality. The best way to cure this, some thought, was to implement a new system of taxation to support religious causes. A chief proponent of this proposition was Patrick Henry, the most famous Virginian of the era. Henry proposed a system where Virginia's taxpayers would engage in a "religious assessment" to designate contributions to a religious assembly of their discretion. Another famous Virginian, Richard Henry Lee, also favored Henry's plan. Under Henry's plan, the Virginian government would distribute the funds to local churches under the terms of the assessment.[234]

In Madison's perspective, this was a troublesome prospect because it put the government in the position of deciding contentious religious matters. Primarily, he felt that it would be impossible for courts of law to decide what "Christianity" was from a neutral standpoint. Madison asked which translation of the Bible was to be preferred, wondered whether Protestant, Catholic, or Lutheran traditions would be accepted, and questioned if one's view of the holy trinity could disqualify them from the distinction. Moreover, he doubted that any judge could objectively decide who was a Christian and who was not. Henry's plan, according to Madison, would allow such judgments to be made by the government on the basis of an arbitrary assessment.[235]

Madison's position spurred political confrontation. Through secret authorship, he penned the *Memorial and Remonstrance Against Religious Assessments*, a succinct pamphlet that outlined his objections to Henry's plan. He was persuaded to pursue this undertaking by George Nicholas, who believed Madison's ideas should be distributed throughout the Commonwealth. Ultimately, the plan was successful. Henry's "bill establishing a provision for the teachers of the Christian religion" was never again revisited.[236] This rejection served as a forerunner to Madison's alternative, The Virginia Statute for Religious Freedom, which was supported by George Mason.

The Virginia Statute for Religious Freedom contained a philosophical preamble that articulated Jefferson's sensibilities in regard to government's role in religious affairs. It declared that "God hath created the mind free, and manifested his supreme will that free it shall remain by making it altogether insusceptible of restraint."[237] Because the creator made man's mind free, Jefferson believed that any governmental restraint upon religious expression contravened natural law:

The impious presumption of legislators and rulers, civil as well as ecclesiastical, who being themselves but fallible and uninspired men, have assumed domination over the faith of others, setting up their own opinions and modes of thinking as the only true and infallible.[238]

The law also attacked the government propensity to create compulsory religious oaths on the basis that they violated inherent religious liberty:

Therefore the proscribing any citizen as unworthy the public confidence by laying upon him an incapacity of being called to offices of trust and emolument, unless he profess or renounce this or that religious opinion, is depriving him injuriously of those privileges and advantages to which, in common with his fellow citizens, he has a natural right.[239]

Several years later, Jefferson conceptualized his views on religious matters by writing that he was "for freedom of religion & against all maneuvers to bring about a legal ascendancy of one sect over another."[240] One method by which governments attempted to do exactly that was through religious oaths – governmental barriers that hindered religious dissenters from obtaining civil office. To Jefferson, such hurdles were moral wrongdoings that abnegated freedom of conscience.

Like Jefferson, Madison believed God needed no manmade institution to support his cause, and favored governmental impartiality in religious matters. Madison biographer Kevin Gutzman considers the passage of the Virginia Statute for Religious Freedom to be Madison's greatest political accomplishment.[241] Where Madison deserves credit for his tenacious promotion of the act, Jefferson should receive credit for its conceptualization. The law was also an important precursor to the First Amendment to the United States Constitution.

The functional portion of the law freed all men from the dictates of religious oaths, and established a system of free exercise in Virginia:

We the General Assembly of Virginia do enact that no man shall be compelled to frequent or support any religious worship, place, or ministry whatsoever, nor shall be enforced, restrained, molested, or burthened in his body or goods, nor shall otherwise suffer, on account of his religious opinions or belief; but that all men shall be free to profess, and by argument to maintain, their opinions in matters of religion, and that the same shall in no wise diminish, enlarge, or affect their civil capacities.[242]

According to the resolution's premises, all religious inclinations were personal matters for which there should be no governmental interpolation or interference. In an era that generally accepted taxes for religious establishments as a societal norm, the provision was a radical proposal.

While Jefferson was overseas, Madison assiduously defended the bill's merits. Alongside him was an avid coalition of philosophical advocates of religious freedom, various factions of religious minorities, and those who merely found Henry's proposal unnecessarily intrusive.[243] If not for Madison's diligent campaign to push the issue forward, the bill would certainly have withered into the shadows of history as a forgotten memory. Because he worked instead to perpetuate the Jeffersonian tradition, passage of the groundbreaking act was secured when Madison was only 34 years old. By all accounts, it was a groundbreaking model for the preservation of religious liberty.

Passage of the Virginia Statute for Religious Freedom continued the time-honored tradition of resistance against governmental attempts to meddle in religious affairs. From the days of King John onward, British history bore witness to the punishment of religious dissidents, enactments of religious favoritism, and prohibitions of certain religious practices. Even the American states, in many cases, continued these practices until Virginia's crucial model was established. In a world less than 100 removed from the Glorious Revolution of 1688 – waged over similar precepts – Jefferson and Madison's act successfully averted cyclical oppression and preserved individual liberty by removing government from the realm of religion altogether.

NULLIFICATION AND THE PRINCIPLES OF '98

Jefferson's political philosophy encompassed more than his fervent devotion to independence and religious freedom. His desire for federalism over nationalism colored his perception of the Constitution, clearly influencing his stance on all other political circumstances. As vice president, one of such conditions manifested as a constitutional calamity that threatened the young republic. Aspiring to correct the evil and set American republicanism back on its proper course, Jefferson adopted a strategy of resistance that became known as the "Principles of '98."

Within eight years of the formation of the republic, a specific set of laws – the Alien and Sedition Acts – challenged the sustainability of the union and brought about a new constitutional crisis. Under the 1798 laws, many came to believe that all American political dissent would be squashed by ruthless tyranny, that free elections could never take place again, and that the intended structure of the federal government was lost forever. In tandem, the policies seemed to undermine idea that republican governments could long survive without trending toward tyranny. In the heart of the crisis, the bounds of the Constitution were put to the ultimate test, and Jefferson was greatly disheartened.

To Jefferson, the implementation of the contentious acts brought about a tear in the fabric of the republic, a political calamity he likened to a "reign of witches." Certainly, the acts seemed to violate some of the Constitution's most basic precepts, and as such, appeared more befitting a monarchy than a republic. The significance of this crisis is unparalleled in the annals of Jeffersonian political philosophy, because it precipitated a theory of recourse that the states could utilize to rebuke and override unconstitutional action. In recognition of the compact view of the union, the Jeffersonian response to these heinous acts cannot be understated.

The Alien and Sedition Acts were a set of four distinct pieces of legislation passed during the John Adams administration, including An Act to Establish an Uniform Rule of Naturalization, An Act Concerning Aliens, An Act Respecting Alien Enemies, and An Act for the Punishment of Certain Crimes against the United States – also called "The Sedition Act." When the Alien and Sedition Acts were passed by the Federalist Congress, tensions between Federalists and Republicans exploded. Political detractors insisted that the laws had disastrous ramifications, and were fully inconsistent with republican government. Most controversial was the Sedition Act, which criminalized individuals for voicing minor criticisms against the President of the United States or members of Congress. The laws were signed by John Adams on July 14, 1798, on the same day Bastille Day was celebrated in France. The timing of the law's approval was undoubtedly a calculated move by Adams and the Federalists, as Republicans celebrated the date as the birth of the French Republic.[244]

In his disdain toward the laws, Jefferson was not alone. John Taylor of Caroline, another prominent Republican who maintained regular correspondence with Jefferson, expressed the same qualms. In his seminal work *Tyranny Unmasked*, Taylor portrayed the time as a quandary that threatened America's constitutional system. The right of free expression, he wrote, had been "assailed" by the Sedition Act, which sought "the establishment of a supreme consolidated government." Rather than serve the interests of the people, the law was merely a targeted campaign "by the will of a geographical majority" to uproot political dissent. The effort, Taylor professed, would produce a climate of "excessive corruption and the keenest resentment."[245] With of the guise of protecting the fledgling American government from destruction, Taylor believed the despicable law would subvert liberty and christen a despotic government.

Indeed, the Alien and Sedition Acts brought about serious political upheaval in the states. In his correspondence with Jefferson, Taylor went as far as to recommended that Virginia secede from the union in order to evade the severe ramifications of the unconstitutional legislation. In light of the circumstances, Jefferson found himself in an intermediary position. His response to Taylor on June 4, 1798 revealed his sympathy for his friend's prognosis. In plain terms, Jefferson agreed with Taylor's claim that the Federalists had gradually seized power over the course of a decade and weakened the state authorities:

> It was the irresistible influence & popularity of Gen. Washington, played off by the cunning of Hamilton, which turned the government over to anti-republican hands, or turned the republican members, chosen by the people, into anti-republicans.[246]

Jefferson recognized the problems the country faced, citing "the public and authentic avowal of sentiments hostile to the leading principles of our Constitution," the new "prospect of a war in which we shall stand alone," and a host of new condemnable taxes.[247] However, the ideological figurehead of the Republican Party developed a method of recourse that differed from Taylor's proposition.

Though he agreed with Taylor on the dire nature of the controversy, Jefferson reasoned that Virginia's secession from the union would not provide a cure for the problem because regional motivations remained the same:

If to rid ourselves of the present rule of Massachusetts & Connecticut we break the Union, will the evil stop there? Suppose the N. England States alone cut off, will our natures be changed? Are we not men still to the south of that, & with all the passions of men?[248]

Having authored the Declaration of Independence, Jefferson viewed secession as the inherent prerogative of a free state, but he believed it was not yet time to tread such a path. Instead, he believed the entities that built the general government should assert their position in regard to whether the abominable laws were "pursuant" to the Constitution. Building upon this notion, Jefferson rallied support among Republicans to support state-level nullification of the laws. In so doing, each state would unilaterally declare the acts void and non-binding within their respective territories, and utilize state resources to actively obstruct their enforcement. Valuing Jefferson's advice, Taylor soon became a local crusader for James Madison's Virginia Resolutions of 1798. As a member of Virginia House of Delegates, he labored to push the legislature to adopt the obstructive resolves.

Nullification is usually considered extreme and subversive in the contemporary, but to Jefferson it was the moderate middle-ground between boundless submission to unconstitutional law on one hand, and separation from government on the other. Jefferson told Taylor to hold firm in his principles, but to allow the measures of state resistance to play out. "A little patience," Jefferson wrote, "and we shall see the reign of witches pass over, their spells dissolve, and the people, recovering their true sight, restore their government to its true principles."[249] Having faith that his fellow citizens would resist the laws and restore the proper relationship between the states and general government, Jefferson shared Taylor's sensibilities but leaned more heavily on Virginians to correct the infraction without the need for desperate measures. Never challenging the permissibility of secession, and while respecting Taylor as his ideological equal, Jefferson merely recommended a different approach.

In Jefferson's mind, the Constitution was a compact, an agreement to which the states were mutual parties. As such, each state had the ability to decide whether or not act of the general government were constitutional. In addition, the states would have the applicable power to render federal laws null and unenforceable within their own jurisdictions. Certainly, the states had to have some kind of recourse when the government acted in a manner which was never conceived of during the ratification of the Constitution. If they couldn't, thought Jefferson, the original structure of the government be lost forever, trampled under the crushing foot of repeated federal expansion.

Any contract, or compact, between individuals, would be considered illegitimate if only one party to that contract had exclusive authority over interpreting it. Consider this allegory: Person A makes an agreement with Person B, in which Person B agrees to cook dinner every weekday for Person A for a specific payment. The two parties draft and sign a contract describing the arrangement, and both parties are satisfied. At some point, the two parties decide on the variety of foods that will be cooked without feeling the need to specify such selections in the contract. As a result of circumstances unforeseen by Person A, Person B claims sole power to interpret the original contract. Person B starts to please Person A with their cooking skills, making an array of dishes that are to the liking of Person A. As time goes on, however, Person B starts to denigrate the process, cooking cheaper foods that were not agreed upon. Additionally, Person B makes the determination that meals do not have to be prepared on holidays, even if they happen to fall on a weekday. Person A starts to complain that the food and preparation no longer warrant the amount of money being paid, and argues that cooking is required on weekday holidays in order to fulfill the terms of the contract. Person A understandably requests some kind of resolution in the form of a compromise. However, Person B is hardly inclined to consider these arguments in earnest, being the sole arbiter of the contract, and benefitting from the powers that come with a monopoly on the interpretation of the agreement.

The end result of such a situation is that new stipulations and conditions are created by Person B to take advantage of the contract, and Person A is left with no recourse. This arrangement would seem to reek of corruptibility, and allows Person B to exploit Person A. This occurred primarily because Person B assumed the sole ability to interpret the agreement, which will inevitably denigrate Person A to an inferior condition. Although both parties created the original agreement, the argument of Person A was ignored and circumvented. In the same way, our Constitution is the product of a compact, whereby multiple sovereign parties made a pact to delegate certain powers to a general authority. The states agreed to this compact through rigorous debate and explanation in their own state ratification conventions. These states, as we observed earlier, largely adopted the compact on the condition that the general government could not assume powers not granted by the contract. After basing their action on this reasoning, the states even enacted resolutions warning that power would be taken back by the states if the terms of the original contract were violated.

Over time, the general government started to behave like Person B. It first assumed implied powers as a justification to create a national bank by the design of Alexander Hamilton's specifications. Next, the government decided to enforce its excise taxes with military force, invading a state without the constitutional authority to do so.[250] Finally, the general government enacted a series of laws that would penalize citizens for benign criticisms of the president and members of Congress. After all of these transgressions, the Supreme Court did not intercede on behalf of the Constitution and the states that formed the agreement. Meanwhile, the general government claimed sole right to determine the extent of its own powers.

In the hypothetical scenario, it seems quite certain that Jefferson would have empathized with Person A. He realized, after all, that the federal courts were a part of the federal government – hardly an impartial arbiter or independent council. "The idea that the general government is the exclusive judge of the extent of the powers delegated to it" was "nothing short of despotism," declared Jefferson. Rather than seeking "the discretion of those who administer the government," he reasoned, the Constitution itself should be the true guide in regard to the extent of federal power.[251]

James Madison, Jefferson's lifelong friend and political ally, also echoed these sentiments:

> If the decision of the judiciary be raised above the authority of the sovereign parties to the Constitution, the decisions of the other departments, not carried by the forms of the Constitution before the judiciary, must be equally authoritative and final with the decisions of that department...The resolution supposes that dangerous powers, not delegated, may not only be usurped and executed by the other departments,

but that the judicial department also may exercise or sanction dangerous powers beyond the grant of the Constitution; and, consequently,
that the ultimate right of the parties to the Constitution, to judge
whether the compact has been dangerously violated, must extend to violations by one delegated authority, as well as by another; by the judiciary, as well as by the executive, or the legislature.[252]

Both Jefferson and Madison agreed – the supposition that the general government is the exclusive judge of its own power was "nothing short of
despotism," and that the right of the states to determine "violations by the
one delegated authority" must be realized. This opinion was directly in
line with that established Virginia tradition that grew from the state's original colonial charter, and perpetuated by the state's ratification of the Constitution. According to Madison, allowing the general government to overstep its clearly defined authority would sanction "dangerous powers" worthy of rejection. Even Federalist disciples in Virginia, such as Edmund
Randolph and George Nicholas, strongly insisted that powers reserved to
the states could not intruded upon.

The Alien and Sedition Acts were passed at a time where there was a
notable fear of French camaraderie. With France at war with Britain and
Austria, Federalists dreaded that the Republican affinity for France would
allow the bloody excesses of the French Revolution to spill into the young
country. At the root of fear was a partisan feud. Several years prior, France
had requested financial assistance from the George Washington administration, arguing that the Franco-American alliance during the War of Independence was a binding agreement that justified reciprocal support.
However, Washington famously decided upon a policy of neutrality. Both
he and Hamilton argued that the treaties with France were made with the
Bourbon monarch Louis XVI, who had been beheaded by that time, and
were thus rendered void.

The Federalists considered French influence to be a negative prospect.
French migrants to the United States were generally inclined to support
the revolutionary tendencies of Jefferson and Madison's Republican Party,
which had defined itself by the time of the Adams administration. The
Federalists generally believed that European wars, which had plagued the
continent for centuries, would inspire political upheaval in the United

States and threaten the general government. Additionally, after the Jay Treaty reestablished trading relations with the British and following the XYZ Affair, dealings with the French were noticeably strained.

Shortly after the Alien and Sedition Acts were passed, the United States became involved in an undeclared series of naval clashes with the French, known as the Quasi-War. As the on-again, off-again conflict raged, Federalists promoted the Sedition Act as a necessary expedient to protect the repute of the president and members of Congress during the wartime footing. Conversely, Jefferson's Republican Party viewed the law as the embodiment of evil, and likened it to ancient monarchical laws that suppressed political dissent.

The Sedition Act explicitly declared that any published or spoken criticism toward the president, or members of Congress, carried a harsh punishment:

That if any person shall write, print, utter or publish, or shall cause or procure to be written, printed, uttered or published, or shall knowingly and willingly assist or aid in writings, printing, uttering, or publishing any false, scandalous or malicious writing or writings against the government of the United States, or either house of the Congress of the United States, or the President of the United States, with intent to defame the said government, or either house of the said Congress, or the Said President, or to bring them, or either or any of them, the hatred of the good people of the United States, or to stir up sedition with the United States, or to excite any unlawful combinations therein, for opposing or resisting any law of the United States, or any act of the President of the United States, done in pursuance of any such law, or of the powers in him vested by the constitution of the United States, or to resist, oppose, or defeat any such law or act, or to aid, encourage, or abet any hostile designs of any foreign nation against the United States, their people or government, then such person, being thereof convicted before any court of the United States having jurisdiction therefore, shall be punished by a fine not exceeding two thousand dollars, and by imprisonment not exceeding two years.[253]

The Sedition Act provided no leniency to critics of the president and Congress. The wording of the law was shrewdly constructed to cover almost any type of response that could be considered subversive or seditious in the eyes of the ruling government. Conspicuously, the vice president is omitted from the list of parties that could not be criticized under the act. This struck as a sardonic gesture because Jefferson was the elected vice president at the time, making him the only elected official that Americans were lawfully allowed to criticize. Though he had once befriended John Adams during the Continental Convention, Jefferson believed this act to be a betrayal that ruptured the United States Constitution and displaced the federal orientation of the union. Beyond that, the law seemed to be a calculated attack against Jefferson and his party.

Many individuals were indicted, charged, and convicted under The Sedition Act. Federal judges energetically enforced the laws, committed to the notion that the incendiary law provided needed security in the midst of conflict with France. In one instance, a man named Luther Baldwin was arrested at a Newark, New Jersey welcoming ceremony for John Adams. As part of his procession, several cannons were fired in the sky to greet the president. Baldwin remarked, "I wish they'd fire the cannons through John Adam's ass." There were many Federalists in a nearby crowd, and hearing this remark, Baldwin was arrested for his comments. While the man was considered a nonthreatening town drunkard, the Federalists who sought to punish him made every effort apply the new law to his aside. Because his words were considered a seditious threat to the president, he was tried, fined, and jailed.[254]

In Massachusetts, a man named David Brown raised a sign that read: "No Stamp Act, No Sedition Act, No Alien Bills, No Land Tax, downfall to the Tyrants of America; peace and retirement to the President; Long Live the Vice President." Brown's sign was posted in Dedham, which was the home of Fisher Ames, former Congressman and one of the most partisan Federalists. "The liberty-pole is down," Ames observed, "but the devil of sedition is mortal, and we, the saints, [have] an endless struggle to maintain with him." Ultimately, Brown was jailed with a $4,000 bail. At the time of this writing, the amount carries the contemporary value of about $77,000, a serious penalty for anyone to endure. After his conviction, Brown was jailed for 18 months with a $450 fee. At his trial, Supreme

Court Justice Samuel Chase demanded that Brown identify those who helped him erect the sign, with the apparent hope of punishing others. When Jefferson took the presidential oath of office in 1801, Brown was still languishing in jail because he could not pay his fine. His petitions to the Adams administration for release went unanswered, and he would not be freed after Jefferson took the oath of office and pardoned those still confined under the treacherous act.[255]

In another case, a world traveler named William Duane was charged under the Sedition Act for activity that took place while he was editor of the *Aurora*, a Philadelphia newspaper. After printing material that was highly critical of the Adams administration, he gained the immediate adoration of local Republicans. In 1799, authorities in Philadelphia indicted Duane on charges that he "willfully and maliciously stirred up a seditious riot" because he advocated the repeal of the Alien Friends Act. He was acquitted at trial, but Federalists were so enraged that 30 members of Philadelphia's volunteer cavalry dragged Duane from the *Aurora's* office, beating and whipping the man until he was unconscious.[256]

Plantation operator Samuel Cabell was indicted because he criticized President Adams in letter addressed to the constituents of his home state of Virginia. Jefferson responded by creating a petition to call for the impeachment and trial for the members of the grand jury that indicted Cabell, on the grounds that Virginia did not grant the government the ability to restrict the correspondence of elected officials with their constituents. This incident caused Republicans in Virginia to consider several methods of resistance against the Federalists.[257]

The most scathing conviction under The Sedition Act affected a sitting Congressman from Vermont named Matthew Lyon. Lyon was charged, convicted, sentenced, and imprisoned for violating the law because he wrote that the president had "unbounded thirst for ridiculous pomp, foolish adulation, and selfish avarice."[258] Lyon wrote the critique in a letter to a Vermont newspaper in July of 1798, where he also suggested that the president had absurdly invoked religious precepts to expand his authority to wage war. Lyon defiantly used the perceived unconstitutionality of the acts as his primary means of defense, but it was to no avail. For an act that would today be viewed as a standard criticism of a sitting president, Lyon was sentenced to four months in jail and ordered to pay $1,000 in fines.

The Judge presiding over his case actually lamented that he could not hand a harsher punishment to Lyon.[259] This event stirred the movement of resistance to the acts by exposing their brutality, and this event was highly publicized. Lyon materialized as a political martyr to the Republicans, who strongly promoted his case. Humorously, Lyon was re-elected to his seat in the Congress while in jail, winning his race while confined. Most poignantly, when the House of Representatives was forced to decide who would become the next president, Lyon cast the deciding ballot for Jefferson in 1800.

All in all, there were 25 arrests, 11 trials, and 10 convictions brought about by the enforcement of the Sedition Act. It is almost unfathomable to consider such a situation taking place today, with long jail sentences and hefty fines for typical political discourse. However, the Federalists applied the law vigorously, regardless of the constitutional barriers that stood against it.

Enormous unease swept through Virginia. In addition to John Taylor of Caroline, future governor William Branch Giles began openly advocating for secession. A new armory was soon built in Richmond, and the state made arrangements to strengthen their militia. The forces began drilling energetically, preparing for a possible armed confrontation with the general government. An ominous atmosphere enveloped the state, where the controversial acts were detested and the Federalists were reviled. Nevertheless, Jefferson prepared a strategy to negate the unjust policy, such that the Constitution's inherent constraints could save Virginia from the bowels of tyranny. The remedy Jefferson had in mind was a specific set of resolutions he and Madison would write.

Despite the heightened political turmoil, the actions of many prominent Republicans during this general period are a mystery. This was because many believed that open communication would be met with government retribution under the new laws. Even so, evidence suggests that a group of prominent Republicans met to discuss the matter at Jefferson's home of Monticello in the summer of 1798. It can be surmised that Jefferson explained his strategy there, and introduced the blueprint for what ultimately became the Kentucky and Virginia Resolutions of 1798. Among Republicans, the sincere dedication to secrecy was particularly apparent, and very few written records from this period remain. Jefferson left the world with over thirty thousand documents, but saved very few letters from this year. Madison's known correspondence for 1798 is also sparse.[260]

Instead of trembling in fear and suffering the law's most egregious repercussions, Jefferson and Madison hoisted themselves into the forefront of opposition. Rather than wait fruitlessly, clinging to the hope that the Federalist courts would negate the laws for lack of constitutionality, the prepared a list of resolutions that would be introduced in Virginia and Kentucky. A genuine reflection of the Jeffersonian political philosophy, the resolutions articulated the compact view of the states and challenged the legitimacy of the laws in a direct way. They also drafted a plan of resistance that all of the states could utilize to oppose and invalidate the unconstitutional laws.

The Kentucky and Virginia Resolutions were crafted in secret by Jefferson and Madison, and their authorship was only disclosed several years later. Though it has sometimes been alleged that this was because two men knowingly figured their actions to be considered treasonous, Jefferson and Madison merely sought to avoid reprisal through enforcement of the Sedition Act. After all, the text of the law affirmed that the government may well be inclined to view their deeds as "opposing or resisting any law of the United States," or engaging in plans of a "hostile design." Both measures were introduced and eventually adopted by the legislatures of Kentucky and Virginia. The resolutions stated categorically that the Alien and Sedition Acts were null and unenforceable within the respective states.

Decorated by the penmanship of Jefferson, the Kentucky Resolutions of 1798 are one of the most powerful enunciations of the view that the Constitution was a compact between states. One prominent historian wrote that "the Kentucky Resolutions are, first and foremost, an acknowledgement of the irreplaceable role played by the states in safeguarding the constitutional balance against the risk of consolidation of federal power."[261] The greatest written contribution Jefferson made to the pronouncement of state authority, the resolutions were a manifesto that summarized Jefferson's perception of the American union.

Jefferson began the first resolution with a bold defense of the intended structure of the federal government. "The several States composing the United States of America, are not united on the principle of unlimited submission to their General Government," he insisted. Instead, the

Constitution was a compact that "constituted a General Government for special purposes." In so doing, the states "delegated to that government certain definite powers, reserving, each State to itself, the residuary mass of right to their own self-government."[262]

In the first point of his case against the constitutionality of the recent acts, Jefferson averred that the very structure of the federal government disallowed it. The statement was reminiscent of former secretary of state's position in the 1791 debate over the First National Bank. In that case, Jefferson argued that the rigidity of enumerated, specified powers was the "foundation" of the federal Constitution, and that diversion from that view was "to take possession of a boundless field of power, no longer susceptible of any definition."[263]

If the government was to overstep such inflexible restrictions, Jefferson wrote that "its acts are unauthoritative, void, and of no force."[264] Because the Alien and Sedition Acts had ventured outside of the acknowledged confines of the general government's predefined power, he considered the laws wholly illegitimate. Without binding force of constitutional authority, the acts were to Jefferson no laws at all. Because the 10th Amendment strictly carved out an explicit line of demarcation between the authority of the states and the federal government, and because Congress was delegated no authority to pass laws restricting or regulating migrations of peoples, freedom of the press, or the ability to criticize federal officials, Kentucky did not have to yield to the dictates of the provocative laws.

In the fourth resolution, Jefferson alleged that the Alien Enemies Act unduly interfered with state authority over immigration:

That alien friends are under the jurisdiction and protection of the laws of the State wherein they are: that no power over them has been delegated to the United States, nor prohibited to the individual States, distinct from their power over citizens.[265]

By granting the power to displace migrants to the executive, Jefferson believed that Congress had overstepped its bounds and assumed more power than the Constitution allowed. As such, the Alien Enemies Act had ruptured the intended structure of the federal system, making the law patently unconstitutional.

In direct opposition to the eventual position of the Federalists, Jefferson asserted that the states could unilaterally come to the conclusion that laws were unconstitutional, fully independent of the perspective reached by the federal courts. He considered this as an obvious observation based on the existing tenets of contract law – "as in all other cases of compact among powers having no common judge, each party has an equal right to judge for itself, as well of infractions as of the mode and measure of redress."[266]

The Constitution, Jefferson wrote, "has accordingly fixed the limits to which, and no further, our confidence may go." In the interests of avoiding the destruction of "those limits," he recommended that the free people of each state deliberately bind the general government "down from mischief by the chains of the Constitution." Whenever "powers are assumed which have not been delegated," Jefferson declared that "a nullification of the act is the rightful remedy." He concluded that "every State has a natural right in cases not within the compact…to nullify of their own authority all assumptions of power by others within their limits."[267]

Taking issue with the notion that only the federal courts could determine whether or not a particular law was constitutional, Jefferson maintained that "the government created by this compact was not made the exclusive or final judge of the extent of the powers delegated to itself." This was because, wrote Jefferson, such a power "would have made its discretion, and not the Constitution, the measure of its powers."[268] In his mind, no constitutional provision gave the federal judiciary, as part of the general government, the ability to determine the extent of the general government's power. If the Constitution truly intended to do so, Jefferson thought the federal courts would inevitably expand the power and prerogative of the general government. Such a tendency would make the entire document purposeless and irrelevant, he postulated.

The eighth resolution created "a committee of conference and correspondence" to "communicate the preceding resolutions to the Legislatures of the several States." In addition to Kentucky's proclamation, Jefferson hoped to establish a synchronized coalition of states that opposed the laws. The resolution also promised that the state of Kentucky remained "sincerely anxious" for the preservation of the union, despite the political conundrum created by the Alien and Sedition Acts. The peace and happiness of the citizens of the states, however, depended on the propensity of the state governments to maintain the boundaries of their own authority. Therefore, "to take from the States all the powers of self-government and transfer them to a general and consolidated government" was an abominable offense against the compact – a violation that should entice the sympathy of other states. Kentucky and all other "co-States" that joined in the effort would be unwilling "to submit to undelegated, and consequently unlimited powers in no man, or body of men on earth." The last resolution allowed Virginia to communicate with those that signed onto a similar effort in the other states.[269]

In adopting the resolutions, Kentucky's legislature made minor tweaks to some of the verbiage in Jefferson's original draft, but almost all of the text – and certainly the essence of the resolutions – remained fully intact. In so doing, Kentucky had accepted the position that the general government had circumvented its intended confines, that the Constitution was a compact between states, that unconstitutional laws were void, that the states could independently determine whether or not the compact was violated, and that the states could utilize their own inherent power to thwart illegitimate exertions of authority from the general government. All of these stances amounted to legal acceptance of the Jeffersonian position.

At the heart of Jefferson's argument was the sheer importance of the intended structure of the federal government, an imperative that he believed the Alien and Sedition Acts obliterated. The demagogic laws had unjustifiably diminished the primacy of the states, the building blocks of the federal framework. Viewing the matter as a constitutional crisis that called the longevity of the union into question, Jefferson thought that no truly free political election could take place under the Sedition Act. While Jefferson undoubtedly sympathized with those terrorized by the enforcement of the acts, the general government's dismantling of the ratified federal structure was his primary grievance.

Summarizing the strategy of opposition against the Alien and Sedition Acts, famous biographer Dumas Malone wrote the following of Jefferson's devotion to the cause of political decentralization and its propensity to safeguard individual rights:

He resolutely opposed the Alien and Sedition Acts as a sincere champion of the highest practicable degree of human liberty in all fields.

And, in seeking a weapon against them, he turned to state arsenals –
seeing no other recourse and believing the states to be the best guardians of the human rights that were unquestionably imperiled.[270]

When the states embraced the "Principles of '98" and actualized their own
inherent powers, no unconstitutional deed would go unnoticed. As long as
states proactively determined that the federal government had engaged in
overreach, nullification could be used as a shield.

Despite Jefferson's candid attempt to roll back the oppressive expansion of power by the general government, most of the states controlled by
Federalists denounced the resolutions. Many believed that the Alien and
Sedition Acts were constitutional and just, and thought the law was desperately needed. Rhode Island's legislature, for instance, declared that the
acts were "well within the powers delegated to Congress, and promotive
of the welfare of the United States." In a similar manner, the Massachusetts Senate explicitly claimed that they were not only constitutional but
"expedient and necessary."[271]

In Virginia, James Madison's style of resistance mirrored Jefferson's.
Madison's Virginia Resolutions of 1798 – introduced in his home state –
also contained several provisions that would render the inflammatory acts
unenforceable therein. However, Madison emphasized that the resolutions
should not be misconstrued as to advocate for severance from the union.
According to the resolutions, Virginia would "support the government of
the United States in all measures warranted by [the Constitution]."[272]
However, the cunning implication within this clarification was that the
resolutions were written to address deeds that were not permitted by the
document.

From the outset of the work, Madison echoed Jefferson's assertion that
the Constitution was a compact between sovereign parties, which had entered into agreement with each other for specific, predefined purposes. The
resolutions stressed that Virginia "views the powers of the federal government, as resulting from the compact, to which the states are parties; as
limited by the plain sense and intention of the instrument constituting the
compact." The general government, Madison suggested, was limited to the
powers "authorized by the grants enumerated in that compact."[273]

In the "case of a deliberate, palpable, and dangerous exercise of other powers, not granted by the said compact," Madison insisted that the states "who are parties thereto" had "the right, and are in duty bound, to interpose for arresting the progress of the evil, and for maintaining within their respective limits, the authorities, rights and liberties appertaining to them."[274] Implying that it wasn't enough to condemn the treachery of unconstitutional laws, the resolution suggested that Virginia should also use its authority to actively thwart them.

The general government, wrote Madison, had endeavored to "enlarge its powers by forced constructions of the constitutional charter that defined them," – justifying a swift response by the states. By attempting to pass laws that violated the document, Congress had acted "to destroy the meaning and effect, of the particular enumeration which necessarily explains and limits the general phrases." In an even more stirring charge, he added that the laws endeavored to "consolidate the states by degrees, into one sovereignty," which would "transform the present republican system of the United States" into "an absolute, or at best a mixed monarchy."[275]

The Alien and Sedition Acts, wrote Madison, were the very incarnation of powers "no where delegated to the federal government," and therefore had subverted "the general principles" and "positive provisions of the federal constitution." As in Jefferson's case, Madison pointed to the predominant importance of the 10th Amendment and its essential principle that possession of all powers not enumerated was unwarranted. The inability to comply with such a clear dictate, he felt, was an unmistakable usurpation. All powers "not delegated by the constitution," and "positively forbidden by one of the amendments thereto," should rile Virginians. As Madison put it, the circumstances "ought to produce universal alarm."[276]

Like the Kentucky counterpart, the Virginia resolutions warned that the Alien and Sedition Acts had obviously undermined the constitutional guarantee that "Liberty of Conscience and of the Press cannot be abridged, restrained, or modified by any authority of the United States." The text reiterated that Congress and the states had even gone so far as to propose and ratify a specific constitutional amendment with the intention of making those principles categorical.[277]

Having "the most sincere affection for [Virginia's] brethren of the other states," the resolutions vowed "the most scrupulous fidelity to that constitution, which is the pledge of mutual friendship" between the states. As in Kentucky's case, the resolutions permitted Virginia's governor to transmit a copy of the text to the executive of each of the other states. Madison concluded with the earnest hope that "proper measures will be taken by each" state to maintain "the Authorities, Rights, and Liberties, referred to the States respectively, or to the people."[278]

After a series of discussions, Madison's resolutions were adopted by the Virginia General Assembly on December 24, 1798. After their passage through the legislature, Governor James Wood complied with the responsibility of transmitting the resolutions to other states. Alongside them was a candid request to adopt the same general strategy in concord with Kentucky and Virginia. Hoping to establish a firm league of friendship between like-minded states, Virginia had made its position unmistakable.

Some historians have viewed the Virginia Resolutions of 1798 as less imposing and forceful than their Kentucky counterparts.[279] However, this supposition is not consistent with the historical record, which can be plainly ascertained from the Virginia legislature that considered and passed the resolutions. The reason for such confusion seems to stem from the fact that the words "not law, but utterly null, void, and of no force or effect" were removed from the Virginia version, leading some to conclude that this was done simply to make the act into a declaration of criticism rather than one that obstructed enforcement of the laws in Virginia. From a semantic approach, one can easily discern that simple repudiation of the Alien and Sedition Acts would do nothing to torpor the "progress of evil." Moreover, organized objection to laws does not render them inane. The records of the Virginia Assembly show that the real reasoning for which the terminology was dropped was for its redundancy, not because the function of the resolutions was materially different.

According to the notes of the Virginia General Assembly, debates on the topic centered upon, first, whether the Alien and Sedition Acts were unconstitutional, and second, what should be done about the crisis if they in fact were. Jefferson's close friend John Taylor of Caroline, the chief sponsor of the resolutions in the Virginia House of Delegates, set the tone by likening laws to Charles Stuart's issuance of unconstitutional imposition of the ship money tax on the eve of the English Civil Wars. "If the king at any time overleaped his boundaries," Taylor explained, "it was always certainly opposed, and met with correction." He compared this situation to the current political quandary, justifying his sponsorship by insisting that the resolutions would "remove oppression." Taylor bolstered his case by opining that the powers reserved to the states should never been surrendered to the "arts of sophistry and ambition."[280] Virginia should take an unambiguous corrective action, he argued, rather than engaging in mere criticism against the general government.

Corroborating this account are the recorded comments from other members of the Virginia House of Delegates. Representative George Taylor noted that the passage of the Virginia Resolutions would create a political landscape of open resistance, professing that the resolutions "made it the duty of the people to defend themselves against them." He stated definitively that the consequence of pursuing the resolutions would be "insurrection."[281] Despite his opinion that the Alien and Sedition Acts were actually constitutional, Taylor understood the pending resolutions would obstruct the implementation of the laws.

John Mercer, another member of the House of Delegates and future governor of Maryland, described the resolutions as acts which would maintain "entire independence" for Virginia. In reference to Mercer's oratory, the notes reflect that the "right of the state government to interfere in the manner proposed by the resolutions was clear to his mind." In a similar manner, delegate Charles Magill noted that "the resolutions declare those laws null and void." Popular General "Light-Horse Harry" Lee observed that the resolutions "recommended resistance" and nullified the unpopular laws in question. In addition, he contended that the resolutions would produce civil disobedience and open insurrection in Virginia. Such a condition goes beyond the tenets of nullification, but proves this was not merely a controversy over whether or not to codify the state's disapproval to the Alien and Sedition Acts.[282]

Madison biographer Kevin Gutzman also rejected the popular notion that the Virginia Resolutions created a less extreme form of resistance than the Kentucky equivalent. Gutzman noted that when the resolutions were introduced, they called the offending federal acts "not law, but utterly null, void, and of no force or effect." This language was dropped in the final wording of the resolutions, but the debates from the House of Delegates show that Taylor agreed to the deletion only because the other proponents of the resolutions understood "unconstitutional" to include "not law, but utterly null, void, and of no force or effect." This was a reference to a portion of text that declared the acts "aforesaid" to be "unconstitutional." Taylor stated that through the passage of the resolutions, the state authorities would comply with measures of resistance, ensure that the laws were of no force or effect, and protect the rights reserved to the people. Being this the case, this text in question was removed not to change the purpose of the resolutions, but because it was considered superfluous. Furthermore, there is no tangible difference between "null, void, and of no force or effect" and "invalidity," or between "nullifying" a statute and "interposing" to prevent its enforcement.[283]

Despite his painstaking efforts to reverse the expansion of the general government, Jefferson's spirits were at a low point by 1799. If their cause ultimately failed to mollify the effects of the malignant laws, he lamented to Madison, it would be better "to sever ourselves from that union we so much value, rather than give up the rights of self-government which we have reserved, & in which alone we see liberty, safety & happiness."[284] To the vice president, secession was less detestable than to suffer the ramifications of unconstitutional law. The plans the two had crafted to oppose tyranny, and their articulation thereof, became so paramount in importance that the two were willing to risk everything to maintain "the Principles of '98."

The Federalists devoted a significant amount of energy and resources to undermine the arguments expressed in the Kentucky and Virginia Resolutions. One of the most grandiose refutations came from a pamphlet penned by "Plain Truth," the pseudonym of a citizen of Westmoreland County, Virginia. The writer disputed that the Constitution was a compact, and made the fallacious claim that the state governments "were not parties in any greater degree than the general government itself."[285]

Plain Truth also purported that the Constitution was "proposed, not to the different state governments, but to the people for their consideration and adoption." On the contrary this claim, the states were certainly the entities that considered and ratified the Constitution through independent, state-based ratification conventions. No singular body of people ratified the document, and the Philadelphia Convention used state-based quorums to vote on all matters. Plain Truth also argued that the Constitution "derives no portion of its obligations from the state governments."[286] Such a statement is also without merit, because the powers delegated to the general government by the Constitution were previously held and executed independently by the governments of the states themselves.

Almost all of the Federalist repudiations of the resolutions were based upon the notion that the Republicans sought to dissolve the union.[287] Conversely, inherent to the principles of nullification is the desire to render pernicious laws unenforceable, not to leave the union. Ironically, both Jefferson and Madison had argued that nullification would placate attempts to leave the union or to dissolve it. As such, nullification was actually the judicious middle ground between suffering through unconstitutional action and secession.

It has sometimes been alleged that nullification was simply an opportunistic political reaction against Federalist policy, constructed by Jefferson and Madison on a whim to impede the aims of their political rivals. However, this can be disproven by recognizing how the Constitution was described to the states. Additionally, Madison already laid the groundwork for such a mechanism in *The Federalist* No. 46, where he wrote that the state governments would "still have the advantage in the means of defeating such encroachments" by way of their own authority. Madison recommended that a "refusal to co-operate with officers of the Union," bolstered by "legislative devices," would obstruct treacherous federal policy and "present obstructions which the federal government would hardly be willing to endure."[288]

As we can see, Madison had already envisioned scenarios in which the federal government would be tempted to extend its power beyond the bounds of the Constitution. In doing so, he confirmed that the state governments had the constitutional means to defeat federal acts of overreach. Even those of a nationalist persuasion confirmed the same principles during the ratification struggle. For instance, Alexander Hamilton wrote that "we may safely rely on the disposition of the State legislatures to erect barriers against the encroachments of the national authority."[289]

To add clarification to the function of the Virginia Resolutions, Madison wrote a lengthy dissertation for the Virginia General Assembly in January of 1800. The Virginia Report of 1800, as the writing was called, explained the philosophical underpinnings of the resolutions and provided ample justification for their passage. It was yet another extension and defense of Jefferson and Madison's contention that the Constitution was a compact between sovereign polities.

Madison immediately pointed out that Virginia understood that the style of the United States Constitution was that of a compact, "to which the states are parties." The report considered such an observation to be "free from objection." Although Madison recognized that the term "state" often held different meanings, in the case used by the resolutions it meant the political societies within the states that ratified the document. As he wrote, "the Constitution was submitted to the "states," in that sense the "states" ratified it; and, in that sense of the term "states," they are consequently parties to the compact, from which the powers of the federal government result." His assessment that the sovereign people of the states ratified the Constitution separately, as independent entities, was an indisputable fact.[290] Indeed, the general government was the creature of the states, as were the powers deposited within the scope of its authority.

Yet again, Madison averred that the powers of the general government were limited to the "grants therein enumerated." This was so clear a proposition, he wrote, that no "just objection can lie against" the claim. The central idea was simple – "if the powers granted, be valid, it is solely because they are granted: and, if the granted powers are valid, because granted, all other powers not granted, must not be valid."[291] Because the Alien and Sedition laws enacted powers not granted, Virginia had embraced its position to render them null.

Perhaps the most important part of Madison's elucidation was its answer to what was meant by Virginia's decision to "interpose for arresting the progress of the evil, and for maintaining within them their respective limits, the authorities, rights, and liberties appertaining to them." In response to such a question, Madison made the compelling and unyielding claim that "there can be no tribunal above" the authority of the states, to "decide in the last resort, whether the compact made by them be violated." After all, the Constitution "was formed by the sanction of the states, given by each in its sovereign capacity." Echoing Jefferson's counterpart, Madison wrote that this idea was "essential to the nature of compacts." As it followed, the states – as parties to the compact – "must be the rightful judges in the last resort," persistently determining "whether the bargain made has been pursued or violated." Offering this form of rejoinder, he asserted, rested upon "legitimate and solid foundation." All things considered, Virginia's interposition against unconstitutional law added "stability and dignity" to the Constitution.[292]

Madison also used a portion of the report to support the claim that the federal judiciary – as the offspring of the states – did not hold the sole power to judge the constitutionality of federal acts:

> If the decision of the judiciary be raised above the authority of the sovereign parties to the Constitution, the decisions of the other departments, not carried by the forms of the Constitution before the judiciary, must be equally authoritative and final with the decisions of that department.[293]

As the building blocks of the union, Madison contended that the states – not the federal courts – were the final arbiters over constitutional matters. Accordingly, only they could determine whether the general government had exceeded its authority. Although he conceded that the federal judiciary had a duty to void laws contrary to the Constitution, Madison indicated that the states were superlative over such determinations. As he reasoned, the states should resist the idea that the child should control and override the parents.

Not only were the states to decide whether laws passed by the general government were unconstitutional, the severity and approach of their responses were to be independently decided as well. In support of his case, Madison suggested that the states should "themselves decide, in the last resort, such questions as may be of sufficient magnitude to require their interposition." This meant that it was up to each state to implement a strategic response after having come to the conclusion that an act was unconstitutional. As seen here, Madison fully expected that there would be a wide range of retorts among the states in respect to any given transgression. Indeed, this was a theme he touched upon during the ratification struggle.[294]

The report also conveyed that the Virginia Resolutions were more than a mere censure of federal policy. "The resolution has done more than guard against misconstruction," he wrote. The utilization of state resources to interpose against the law, he continued, would thwart the malevolence of the act, "preserve the constitution itself," and "provide for the safety of the parties to it."[295] Failure to embrace the path of resistance the resolutions built the foundation for, warned Madison, would result in political calamity:

> There would be an end to all relief from usurped power, and a direct subversion of the rights specified or recognised under all the state constitutions, as well as a plain denial of the fundamental principle on which our independence itself was declared.[296]

Here Madison compared the crisis to that which swayed the American states to break free from the British system. The "fundamental principle" he referred to was that of Parliamentary sovereignty, or the notion that the central government's power is absolute. Such a delusion, he argued, was irreconcilable with the American arrangement under the Constitution. In his eyes, the impetus for the independence of the states extended naturally to contemporaneous political circumstances. Confirming Madison's impression that the federal courts could not provide adequate reprieve, none of the appeals of those convicted under the Sedition Act were heard.

Madison did not expect interposition to be utilized in a hasty or indiscriminate manner. On the contrary, he wrote that it should not be applied to cases "of a light and transient nature, but of a nature dangerous to the great purposes for which the Constitution was established." Accordingly, interposition should be invoked in situations "not obscure or doubtful in its construction, but plain and palpable." Because Madison believed the laws in question amounted to the latter – as blatant constitutional violations – he advised a direct response from the states. Sternly defending the purpose of the resolutions, Madison wrote that Virginia had "accordingly guarded against any misapprehension of its object, by expressly requiring for such an interposition."[297]

The report's most striking assertion may have been its unwavering defense of the decentralized structure of the federal union. "So far is the political system of the United States distinguishable from that of other countries," Madison wrote, that "the caution with which powers are delegated and defined" are of paramount importance.[298] This aspect, to Madison, was an exclusive facet of the American system. Hardly an insignificant piece of minutia, the federal orientation of the union was paramount to both Jefferson and Madison – it colored every avenue of their political sensibilities.

Dreading that the United States might soon degenerate into a monarchy, Madison warned that complying with the acts would be a tragic mistake that invited dire consequences. If such laws went unchallenged, he feared, the states would be reverted into subjugated colonies, not unlike circumstances that existed prior to the departure of the states from Britain's royal system:

> Had "sedition-acts," forbidding every publication that might bring the constituted agents into contempt or disrepute, or that might excite the hatred of the people against the authors of unjust or pernicious measures, been uniformly enforced against the press, might not the United States have been languishing at this day, under the infirmities of a sickly confederation? Might they not possibly be miserable colonies, groaning under a foreign yoke?[299]

Madison felt the Alien and Sedition Acts had abhorrent and destructive potential that had not yet been seen in the early republic. Their "certain tendency to pave the way to monarchy," he wrote, "seems not to have been contested."[300]

Shattering the idea that the Constitution allowed for "implied powers" not expressly enumerated, a theory originated by Alexander Hamilton and widely accepted by the Federalists, Madison cited the litmus adopted by the states in their endorsement of ratification:

> Whenever, therefore, a question arises concerning the constitutionality of a particular power, the first question is, whether the power be expressed in the Constitution. If it be, the question is decided. If it be not expressed, the next inquiry must be, whether it is properly an incident to an express power, and necessary to its execution. If it be, it may be exercised by Congress. If it be not. Congress cannot exercise it.[301]

Denying Madison's opinion, Federalists had cited the Necessary and Proper Clause of the Constitution – which allowed for incidental laws to support "carrying into Execution the foregoing Powers" – as the source of unlisted and unspecified authority. On this basis, Hamilton contended that the creation of the First National Bank was constitutionally permissible.[302]

Carving a wide gulf between the Federalist and Republican positions on nullification and the Alien and Sedition Acts, the Report of 1800 framed the Jeffersonian doctrine. The future president admired the tract so much that he secured a copy from fellow Virginian James Monroe, and quickly worked to distribute the text to leading Republicans throughout the country. Rather than attempt to persuade adamant Federalists to agree with their outlook, Jefferson and Madison hoped to influence the American population at large.[303]

TENNESSEE AND GEORGIA RESPOND

While some of the Federalist-controlled states admonished the constitutional positions of Kentucky and Virginia, the same cannot be said for other states. Recent studies have revealed that both Tennessee and Georgia also passed similar resolutions that opposed the pernicious Alien and Sedition Acts. One of Tennessee's resolutions declared that the Alien and Sedition Acts were "in several parts opposed to the constitution, and are impolitic, oppressive, and unnecessary." Acting as requested by Kentucky and Virginia, the state similarly communicated its frank disapproval of the laws and called for them to be openly rejected.[304]

Georgia also called for a repeal of the acts, suggesting that the "people's allegiance and fidelity" depended on doing so. Furthermore, the state assumed the position that it would not act to interfere with the enforcement of the federal acts. Georgia's resolution instead expressed the belief that the Alien and Sedition Acts should be "repealed without the interposition of the state legislature."[305] This position showed, as Virginia's proceedings demonstrated also, that "interpose" had a more potent meaning than a simple, inane criticism of federal law.

In addition to Tennessee and Georgia's resolutions in opposition to the Alien and Sedition Acts, a similar set of resolutions passed one house of North Carolina's assembly, the governor of South Carolina denounced the

Sedition Act, a grand jury in Tennessee censured the controversial laws, New Jersey and Pennsylvania refused to explicitly rebuke the actions of Kentucky and Virginia as many of their northern counterparts had, and Georgia's governor fiercely condemned an arrest under the acts.[306]

The magnitude of hostility toward the Alien of Sedition Acts was much more widespread than originally imagined. Prior to these revelations, the standard academic narrative held that Kentucky and Virginia were generally isolated in their attitudes toward the laws.[307] Moreover, the supposed unpopularity of their stance has long been used to rationalize northern criticism of the Kentucky and Virginia Resolutions of 1798. With the gifts of recent scholarship, however, this view no longer withstands honest scrutiny.

THE REVOLUTION OF 1800

As one of the biggest issues of the 1800 presidential campaign, Jefferson and his political allies capitalized on its vindictive affects, and the Federalists endured considerable political fallout. After a tied result in the Electoral College, the House of Representatives ultimately selected Thomas Jefferson to the presidency over fellow Republican Aaron Burr. As the architect of the Kentucky Resolutions of 1798 prepared to ascend to the executive office, the Sedition Act expired on the last day of the Adams administration. After taking the oath of office, Jefferson used his constitutional authority to pardon those convicted and still serving sentences under the egregious law, and the divisive policy suffered a natural death. Jefferson's conception of nullification nevertheless became an important part of American political heritage, and would be invoked again.

THE NULLIFICATION CRISIS

More than 30 years after the Kentucky and Virginia Resolutions, the issue of nullification first raised the forceful might of the general government. Although the principle had been utilized by the New England states in the interim to resist the Embargo Act of 1807 and conscription during the War of 1812, on this occasion the central authority first responded to nullification with the threat of military force against a state.

During Andrew Jackson's presidency, a momentous dispute emerged after many southerners, especially those in South Carolina, perceived the Tariff of 1828 as a severe threat to the southern economy. This was because the law acted as a barrier to free trade, and made northerners the sole beneficiaries of the protectionist arrangement. The legislation aimed to encourage the South to buy goods from the North rather than from European powers, which would be accomplished by a punitive tax on foreign goods. South Carolinians saw this as a scheme to restrict their choices in the market and enact regional favoritism.

The Constitution allowed tariffs to be passed, but many argued that such taxes were intended only to raise revenue rather than to protect domestic industry. Since the 1828 Tariff had a protectionist function, South Carolina viewed the plan as impermissible and excessively harmful. However, this was not the first political stir caused by federal tariff policy. Widespread concern over protective tariffs emerged as early as the George Washington administration, when the government passed a federal carriage tax. While northern states possessed relatively few carriages, a huge number of southern carriages were affected – causing an outpour of unrest from the southern states. In characteristic fashion, John Taylor asserted that the carriage tax reduced Virginians to slavery by depriving them of their own property.[308] Protesting the policy, he professed that the carriage tax was a direct tax that had to be apportioned among the states. Even so, the United States Supreme Court determined otherwise in the 1796 case of *Hylton v. United States*.

South Carolinian John C. Calhoun perceived the 1828 "Tariff of Abominations," as the law would be called, as an unmistakable act of federal overreach that would penalize southern production and disproportionally benefit northern industrialists. In the public, lengthy and persuasive redresses of grievances were hurled at the general government, but none produced a cure to the problem. As Andrew Jackson's vice president, the policy widened an existing political rift between Calhoun and the president. Nonetheless, the southern aristocrat hoped to do what he could to temper the extreme effects of the plan.

As vice president, Calhoun articulated his case against the federal tariff in an anonymous and influential writing known as the *South Carolina Exposition and Protest*. Within the tract, he echoed Jefferson and Madison's view that "the General Government is one of specific powers, and it can rightfully exercise only the powers expressly granted...all others being reserved expressly to the States, or to the people."[309] The esteemed South Carolinian first defined the scope of the defilement:

> The violation, then, consists in using a power granted for one object to advance another, and that by the sacrifice of the original object. It is, in a word, a violation by perversion, the most dangerous of all because the most insidious and difficult to resist. Others cannot be perpetrated without the aid of the judiciary; this may be by the Executive and Legislative departments alone. The courts cannot look into the motives of legislators.[310]

Calhoun described the tariff as "unconstitutional, unequal, oppressive, and calculated to corrupt the public morals, and to destroy the liberty of the country." Condemning its disproportionately negative effect on the South, he mourned that the law had made southerners into "serfs of the system."[311]

According to Calhoun, the general government "is one of specific powers" that "can only rightfully exercise only the powers expressly granted." Admitting that the Constitution did allow for the passage of tariffs, the writing reasoned that such taxes could only be levied for the purpose of generating revenue for the general government. Revenue tariffs, he wrote, were by their nature "essentially different from that of imposing protective or prohibitory duties." This power, he claimed, had been "abused by being converted into an instrument for rearing up the industry of one section of the country on the ruins of another." Revenue and protective tariffs, Calhoun wrote, were "incompatible" – the latter being a "violation of the spirit" of the Constitution. The exposition articulated that the radical tariff violated the United States Constitution's revenue clause in Article I, Section 8, because the high rates deter importation at the expense of revenue collection – thereby making them constitutionally illegitimate. Calhoun argued that fundamentally protective tariffs, such as the inflammatory 1828 model, had been a "perversion" of the document. In his eyes, this enlargement of the federal government's power was an "insidious" scheme.[312]

Rather than suffer the tariff's harsh impact, Calhoun believed his state should fiercely admonish the law. In this, he felt South Carolina was wholly justified. "It would be impossible to deny to the States the right of deciding the infractions of their powers, and the proper remedy to be applied for their correction," he wrote. Without such a check, he continued, the general government "would exercise unlimited and unrestrained power" over the states.[313]

In his quest to disseminate the Jeffersonian political creed, Calhoun contended that the courts were impotent to assist South Carolina in its struggle with the general government because they could not determine legislative motive. Calhoun called the Constitution "a constitutional compact" and appropriately noted that the general government could not venture outside of its "proper sphere" of power. He ended his attack on the tariff by citing Madison's language from the Virginia Resolution of 1798, openly declaring that South Carolina's act was necessary to "arrest the progress" of unconstitutional action. If it did not, he declared, the law's consequences would "corrupt the public morals and destroy the liberty of the country."[314]

While southerners continued to deride the 1828 tariff, Calhoun hoped that the rampant bitterness would persuade the federal government to temper its ramifications. Several years later, Congress passed the Tariff of 1832, a second protective act. While lessening the average rate, the policy retained high duties on woolen goods, iron, and other items of demand in the South.[315] In response, Calhoun resigned from the vice presidency. Shortly thereafter, he was elected to the Senate by his state. In so doing, he abandoned his political standing in favor of his philosophical opposition to the radical tariff.

Firmly persuaded by Calhoun's stance, South Carolina invoked the "Principles of '98" and held a special convention that nullified both the Tariff of 1828 and the Tariff of 1832. Like Jefferson and Madison before him, Calhoun reminded naysayers that the union existed for the sole convenience of states, and argued that the general government had violated the compact through the passage of the protective tariff. When the South Carolina Ordinance of Nullification was enacted in November of 1832, it declared that the acts "shall be held utterly null and void" within its borders. The act also referenced language from the Declaration of

Independence, calling its nullification a power "which sovereign and independent States may of right do."[316] The state had drawn upon the true quintessence of the union – a compact among the states. In doing so, it categorically refused to yield to the deplorable dictate of a nationalist, supreme government.

South Carolina's brand of nullification differed from that of Jefferson and Madison's. This was because Calhoun argued that a state's enactment of nullification held full legal bearing unless overturned by a supermajority of three-fourths of all states in the union.[317] In contrast, Jefferson and Madison promoted nullification as a unilateral action that did not involve the other states at all. In some quarters, Calhoun's divergent conception has therefore been construed as a bastardization of nullification. Nonetheless, South Carolina's action was a strong statement against federal overreach.

Furious at the gesture, Andrew Jackson deemed the actions of South Carolina as unambiguously subversive. The citizens of South Carolina had been "seduced," wrote the president, by the injurious "theories and misrepresentation of ambitious, deluded & designing men." The nullification effort, sneered Jackson, was an endeavor perpetrated "by those who abuse your confidence and falsify your hopes." Nullification was "treason" that subjected its offenders to "all the pains and penalties that are provided for the highest offense against" the United States.[318] According to the president, South Carolina's effort threatened the stability of the union, and implied the that the state's actions inspired the prospect of bloodshed. "Woe to those nullifiers who shed the first blood," he declared.[319]

Ironically, it was Jackson and the federal government that had postured for armed warfare. In early 1833, Congress passed the "Force Bill," a law that permitted the president to deploy the United States military to South Carolina to enforce the tariff. In addition, Jackson ordered a naval blockade of the state, sent warships to Charleston harbor, and threatened to hang supporters of the nullification in the state. In response, South Carolina began to organize its own militia for a possible armed invasion, and Calhoun condemned the Force Bill as an overt declaration of war against his state.[320]

Eventually, a settlement between the federal government and South Carolina was struck in the form of the Tariff of 1833, which reduced the impact of the tariff gradually over the next ten years. Nevertheless, seeds of disdain toward coercive federal policy were planted in the minds of those who recognized the general government's attempt to consolidate power in Washington, D.C. South Carolina's nullification convention convened again in March of 1833, where the assembly rescinded its nullification of the federal tariffs. Before adjourning, however, the convention comically nullified the Force Bill that would have sanctioned Jackson's foray into South Carolina.

The culmination of the Nullification Crisis revealed that South Carolina's steadfast to resistance to the tariff provided a favorable result for both parties. Trade continued, no war transpired, and South Carolina continued to pay the tariff at the reduced rate. The usage of nullification – as the middle ground between leaving the union and suffering the law's acute consequences – resulted in a compromise that satisfied the concerns of both South Carolina and the federal government. Simply put, nullification worked.

Despite this result, most contemporary historians have sided with Jackson in regard to the constitutionally and efficacy of nullification. For example, biographer Jon Meacham called South Carolina's nullification campaign "The Mad Project of Disunion," asserting that the real issue at the heart of the conflict was "power, and ultimately about slavery." This was despite the fact that Jackson was himself a slaveholder, and the controversy involved taxation and federal overreach rather than slavery. The proposition that two factional figureheads, both slaveholders, were embroiled in a dispute over slavery is unsubstantiated and unrelated to the context of the nullification. Additionally, it was the federal government – not South Carolina – that threatened to use military force in what would be more appropriately described as a "mad project." Moreover, Famous Jackson biographer Robert Remini stated that "nullification declares that a state has a right to nullify any federal law within its borders that it feels violates its rights and interests." On the contrary, in the conception of Jefferson, Madison, and Calhoun, laws could be nullified only when they contravened the Constitution, not whenever a state disapproved of the law in question. Remini also concluded that Jackson pursued a "states' rights policy."[321] However, this claim is contrary to the president's efforts to suppress nullification, the ultimate expression of state sovereignty. Jackson's abstraction of the union simply didn't mesh with Jeffersonian doctrine.

HISTORICAL USES OF NULLIFICATION

Today, the principles of nullification are sometimes written off as an outdated philosophical product of the southern states, which always sought to interfere with the will of the general government. Opponents of nullification have also been quick to associate such principles with appalling causes such as slavery. Since 1798, however, nullification has been used to resist federal attempts to conscript underage soldiers without parental consent, to prevent the suppression of free trade with other nations, and to dispose of the notion that slaves could be turned over to slaveholders on the basis of hearsay.

One noteworthy exertion of nullification followed the Jefferson administration's decision to enact the Embargo Act of 1807. At that time, France and Britain, as constant wartime rivals, were engaged in military conflict yet again. Jefferson hoped the embargo would avert war with two major powers, and ultimately and keep the United States out of the Napoleonic Wars that had swept through Europe. Instead, the embargo completely destroyed the maritime economy of New England, which had thrived on shipping and trade. Stirring the resent of those who benefitted from commerce in New England, it was the absolute low point of Jefferson's presidential administration. To make the issue even more contentious, the president planned to enforce the embargo with the full vigor of the general government. In retaliation, Jefferson's political opponents in the New England states passed ordinances of nullification against the architect of the principle.[322]

In another episode, various northern states found reason to apprehend and oppose the federal government during the War of 1812. At such a time, the states were largely unprepared to fight Britain. Lacking resources and relying solely on the militia of the states for defense, the James Madison administration proposed a conscription plan that would draw soldiers from the American states. In 1815, Connecticut took preventative action by nullifying these plans, announcing that the mandatory enlistment of minors was "grievously oppressive" and "repugnant to the spirit of the constitution."[323]

The same year, a group of five New England states gathered in Connecticut to organize a series of meetings known as the Hartford Convention. At the conference, the states hoped to adopt a concerted plan of response, fearing that the conscript plan threatened to tread upon the sovereign interests of the northern states. A report produced by the convention proclaimed that "such an interference with the municipal laws and rights of the several States, could never have been contemplated by the framers of the Constitution."[324] As such, the report continued, the states must determine when Congress abnegated the document:

That acts of Congress in violation of the Constitution are absolutely void, is an undeniable position...When emergencies occur which are either beyond the reach of judicial tribunals, or too pressing to admit the delay incident to their forms, States, which have no common umpire, must be their own judges, and execute their own decisions.[325]

Even Daniel Webster, the ardent nationalist senator of Massachusetts, explained in 1814 that it was "the solemn duty of the State Governments to protect their own authority over their own militia, and to interpose between their citizens and arbitrary power." In light of the protests, the Massachusetts denounced and nullified the conscription plan as an unconstitutional scheme. Connecticut followed suit, passing a law that restricted the governor from ordering the state militia to aid in the war against the British.[326]

Shattering traditional narratives, the use of nullification also assisted fugitive slaves. As part of the Compromise of 1850 – a settlement that attempted to resolve various disputes between northern and southern states – a new law to facilitate the return of runaway slaves was passed. The Fugitive Slave Act of 1850, as it was called, controversially required citizens in all states to assist with the capture and return of slaves that had fled from their masters, and penalties were imposed upon those who evaded this duty. Through the enforcement of the law, slaves were often deprived of due process and held indefinitely in northern jails. Beyond this, they were prohibited from testifying on their own behalf in court, and were often captured as the result of hearsay. The federal government also imposed

penalties upon marshals who refused to enforce the law, and federal commissioners stood to profit more from their responsibilities when slaves
were returned to their owners.[327]

Tensions exploded in 1854, when a slave named Joshua Glover was
captured after escaping to Wisconsin. After his arrest, the public outcry
against the law was so strong that an armed mob defied the law by breaking into a Milwaukee jail and freeing Glover. Furthermore, Wisconsin's
highest court ruled the federal law unconstitutional and authorized
Glover's release. In *Ableman v. Booth*, the United States Supreme Court
opined that Wisconsin was in the wrong, and Glover should not have been
freed. In response, Wisconsin's legislature passed a set of resolutions
which nullified the 1850 Fugitive Slave Act:

> Resolved, That this assumption of jurisdiction by the federal judiciary,
> in the said case, and without process, **is an act of undelegated power,
> and therefore without authority, void, and of no force**…That the
> government formed by the Constitution of the United States was not
> the exclusive final judge of the extent of the powers delegated to itself;
> but that, as in all other cases of compact among parties having no com-
> mon judge, each party has an equal right to judge for itself, as well as
> infractions as of the mode and measures of redress.[emphasis added][328]

Wisconsin invoked the Principles of '98 by referring to the compact model
of the union. The resolution also used Thomas Jefferson's verbatim language to declare the law void. Now galvanized against the treacherous
policy, several northern states passed similar legislation that effectively
undermined the law by making it unenforceable in various ways. Collec-
tively, the state barriers against the Fugitive Slave Act of 1850 became
known as the "personal liberty laws."

In 1850, Vermont passed an act requiring law enforcement to provide
assistance to captured fugitive slaves and to hinder the federal law. The
"Habeas Corpus Law" rendered the entirety of the Fugitive Slave Act of
1850 unenforceable within the state. Vermont's act even went as far as to
fine individuals who transferred slaves into the custody of a civil official
other than that of the Vermont authorities.[329] President Millard Fillmore,
like Andrew Jackson before him, even threatened military reprisal against

the state for their refusal to abide by the federal mandate. Due to the escalating measures of resistance in the other states, however, these threats never materialized. While the federal government attempted to coerce the states and bend them to its will, the acts of state nullification and obstruction became too consequential for the federal government to deal with effectively.

Michigan prohibited the federal government from using its jails to hold fugitive slaves in 1855. In the same act, the state iterated that fugitive slaves had all the benefits of habeas corpus and due process. Similarly, a Massachusetts law called for the removal of any state official that assisted in the return of runaway slaves, and authorized the impeachment of state judges who allowed federal commissioners to enforce the law. After its passage, there is no record of a fugitive slave ever being returned from Massachusetts. In 1857, "forcibly or carrying off" a free black person in Ohio was punishable by three to eight years of hard labor.[330] In all of these states, nullification was used to thwart slave power.

SLAVERY AND NULLIFICATION: A MISTAKEN ASSOCIATION

To the contrary of the idea that nullification protected slavery, by the time of the Civil War there were no federal laws that prohibited slavery in the states. In fact, the federal government often made itself complicit with the expansion of slavery through the enactment of the popular sovereignty doctrine, which held that all peoples within a territory could determine whether to permit slavery or not. Avowed supporters of this principle, such as Stephen Douglas, successfully implemented this concept through various federal enactments. Its application was demonstrated in the case of the 1854 Kansas-Nebraska Act, which permitted the inhabitants of both territories to determine whether or not to allow slavery within each region.

Many recalled the northern struggle against the Fugitive Slave Act of 1850, and one state cited northern acts of nullification as justification for seceding from the union. In South Carolina's 1860 declaration of secession, the state defended is departure by citing these northern campaigns to guarantee the liberty of fugitive slaves:

But an increasing hostility on the part of the non-slaveholding States to the institution of slavery, has led to a disregard of their obligations, and the laws of the General Government have ceased to effect the objects of the Constitution. The States of Maine, New Hampshire, Vermont, Massachusetts, Connecticut, Rhode Island, New York, Pennsylvania, Illinois, Indiana, Michigan, Wisconsin and Iowa, **have enacted laws which either nullify the Acts of Congress or render useless any attempt to execute them**. In many of these States the fugitive is discharged from service or labor claimed, and in none of them has the State Government complied with the stipulation made in the Constitution...Thus the constituted compact has been deliberately broken and disregarded by the non-slaveholding States, and the consequence follows that South Carolina is released from her obligation.[emphasis added][331]

The nullification of federal laws that withheld the return of slaves to their owners was a troublesome situation for the slaveholding South. Many within the region, including South Carolina's secession convention, rejected the principle of nullification since it became a northern method to impede the capture and return of fugitive slaves.

Jefferson Davis, who became the only President of the Confederate States of America, was similarly despondent over the usage of nullification by the northern states. His speeches and writings indicate that he was deeply troubled about the impact of nullification upon his native South. In 1861, Davis made a farewell address to the United States Senate when he learned that his home state of Mississippi had seceded from the union. In the speech, Davis explicitly affirmed his disdain toward nullification:

Nullification and secession, so often confounded, are, indeed, antagonistic principles. Nullification is a remedy which it is sought to apply within the Union, against the agent of the States. It is only to be justified when the agent has violated his constitutional obligations, and a State, assuming to judge for itself, denies the right of the agent thus to act, and appeals to the other states of the Union for a decision; but, when the States themselves and when the people of the States have so acted as to convince us that they will not regard our constitutional rights, then, and then for the first time, arises the doctrine of secession in its practical application.[332]

As we can see, Davis attacked nullification in a fashion reminiscent of South Carolina's ordinance. These leanings were hardly consistent with someone who believed in the constitutional fortitude of the principle or the legitimacy of its usage. Instead, Davis believed that nullification was improper and unconstitutional because it exempted northern citizens from abiding by what he considered to be a constitutional obligation.

Vice President of the Confederate States of America, Alexander Stephens, expressed similar views concerning nullification in 1858. On the contrary of those defending the Principles of '98, Stephens explained that he "did not believe in the doctrine of nullification." Instead, he firmly categorized himself as "no nullifier" during a debate about South Carolina's usage of nullification during the Jackson administration."[333] As we can see, Davis' stance was not unique. On the contrary, much of the southern aristocracy rejected the principles of nullification. Instead of appreciating its merits or utilizing its potential, they held disdain toward it.

JEFFERSON AND THE FEDERAL COURTS

Shortly after Jefferson became president, the federal courts attempted to erode his conception of the union as a league of states. This stood as an extraordinary affront to Jefferson, who strongly believed that those who wrote and explained the Constitution intended for the federal judiciary to have relatively less power than the other branches of government. If the federal courts could successfully subvert the other branches and undermine the reserved powers of the states, the general government's power would expand to an unimaginable degree. Jefferson's marked trepidation toward such a prospect, then, became a distinct part of his political philosophy.

During his presidency, Jefferson found himself completely at odds with the Federalist courts and the judicial appointees of John Adams, his presidential predecessor. In response, the Virginian did whatever he could to diminish the power of the federal judiciary, believing that judicial restraint and an emphasis on the state courts was consistent with the ratified Constitution. Indeed, Jefferson realized that a powerful, expansive court system was unnecessary, because there were only a few types of cases that the courts had the constitutional authority to decide.[334]

Jefferson regularly criticized the federal judiciary throughout his life, and believed that small numbers of people in high federal courts could not adequately settle all constitutional matters. Jefferson's mistrust of the federal courts was rooted in the history's confirmation that powerful central courts often served as the proxies of corrupt kings. Such as dastardly apparatus, he thought, was an aspersion to the American republic. Under English kings, the appointed royal court judges served as perceived lackeys that would naturally rubber stamp the monarch's policies. Jefferson realized this, and did what he could to dispel the consolidation of unconstitutional judicial authority in a repeat of the past.

As part of his plan to dismantle the Federalist judicial stronghold, the Republican controlled Congress repealed the Judiciary Act of 1801 shortly after Jefferson's inauguration. The law had allowed the creation of multiple lower courts that would be packed with partisan, Federalist justices, and Adams worked diligently in his last days in office to sign commissions for the "midnight judges." By all accounts, the act legalized Adams' desire to prolong the influence of the Federalist Party beyond its widespread electoral losses in 1800.

Despite his political battles with Adams, Jefferson and Adams' wife, Abigail, remained on good terms. Reflecting on this circumstance, Jefferson later admitted to Abigail that the court-stacking plan was the one act of his predecessor's life that gave him "a moment's personal displeasure." As a gesture that was "personally unkind," Adams had appointed Jefferson's "most ardent political enemies" to the courts."[335] The scheme, he thought, was merely an underhanded scheme to apply political power without the endorsement of the people of the states.

When Jefferson's party emerged victorious in the elections of 1800, he perceived the occasion as a bold statement that vindicated the states as the rightful masters over the general government and Adams' irrational policies. The Jeffersonian Republicans used their newfound political capital to repeal the Judiciary Act of 1801, end the excise taxes on distilled spirts, and eliminate other "unnecessary offices" that had been created by the

Federalists.[336] As a result of the 1800 elections, the Federalists lost power in the government and never regained it. Certainly, Jefferson perceived this development as revolutionary change in favor of his own inclinations.

An enormous controversy erupted over the Marshall Court's usage of judicial review in its 1803 *Marbury v. Madison* opinion, which now stands as the most influential Supreme Court case in United States history. In his written opinion, Chief Justice John Marshall determined that a portion of the Judiciary Act of 1789 that had allowed William Marbury to bring up his suit was unconstitutional, setting a precedent for all time. No mechanism for judicial review was written expressly into the Constitution's text, although several Federalists announced that the power would be used during the ratification struggle.[337] The biggest controversy erupted when Marshall took the opportunity to scold the Jefferson administration, and Madison in particular, for not delivering the judicial commission to Marbury. To Jeffersonians, Marshall's rant was viewed as a form of political theater and legal browbeating the presumptuously elevated the judiciary above the presidency.

In addition, the *Marbury v. Madison* opinion led to a widespread belief that Marshall had carved out a pivotal role for the federal judiciary – the sole power to judge the constitutionality of the acts of the other branches. Jefferson was repulsed by the suggestion, and countered that such a proposition would create a despotic organization:

You seem…to consider the judges as the ultimate arbiters of all constitutional questions; a very dangerous doctrine indeed, and one which would place us under the despotism of an oligarchy. Our judges are as honest as other men, and not more so. They have, with others, the same passions for party, for power, and the privilege of their corps... Their power the more dangerous as they are in office for life, and not responsible, as the other functionaries are, to the elective control. The Constitution has erected no such single tribunal, knowing that to whatever hands confided, with the corruptions of time and party, its members would become despots. It has more wisely made all the departments co-equal and co-sovereign within themselves.[338]

Jefferson referred to the philosophy of these judges as having a maxim of "boni judicis est ampliare jurisdictionem," a Latin phrase that means "it is the part of a good judge to extend his jurisdiction." The Virginian resented this development because it greatly expanded the power of the federal courts, and allowed the judiciary to negate and criticize the constitutional actions of the other branches. It has been alleged that Marshall, in one grand stroke, promoted the Supreme Court to the highest of the government's three branches through the *Marbury v. Madison* opinion.[339]

During his presidency, Jefferson defended a philosophical alternative to judicial review – concurrent review. His candid assertion was that each branch, in the exercise of its own responsibilities, had the independent authority to determine the constitutionality of its actions:

But nothing in the Constitution has given them a right to decide for the executive, more than to the executive to decide for them. **Both magistrates are equally independent in the sphere of action assigned to them**. The judges, believing the law constitutional, had a right to pass a sentence of fine and imprisonment, because that power was placed in their hands by the constitution. But the Executive [Jefferson], believing the law to be unconstitutional, was bound to remit the execution of it; because that power has been confided to him by the constitution. **That instrument meant that its co-ordinate branches should be checks on each other**. But the opinion [of the Marshall Court in *Marbury v. Madison*] which gives to the judges the right to decide what laws are constitutional, and what not, not only for themselves in their own sphere of action, but for the legislative and executive also in their spheres, **would make the judiciary a despotic branch**.[emphasis added][340]

While the judiciary may render an opinion on constitutional matters, it cannot bind the other branches of government – or the states – to its own views on the matter. For instance, the president may decide that an existing law was unconstitutional, and refuse to enforce it on that account. In the same way, the Senate can reject treaties created by the president's ambassadors for reason of their perceived usurpation of Congressional authority. At no point, Jefferson thought, did the Constitution establish that the judiciary could override the constitutional behavior of all actors in all branches.

The Constitution specifies that federal judges can serve during "good Behaviour." Despite the typical inclination to view judicial positions as life terms, this prerequisite was to Jefferson a strict limitation on judicial tenure. His resolve on this subject became relevant in regard to Samuel Chase, a sitting judge on the United States Supreme Court who had also signed the Declaration of Independence. As an ardent Federalist, Chase was a particularly partisan judge that gleefully secured the convictions of Republicans charged with violating the Sedition Act. Passions were ignited when Chase presided over the trial of James Callender, a Republican pamphleteer.

Callender published a fiercely anti-Federalist pamphlet called *The Prospect Before Us*, which harshly criticized Adams as a "tempest of malignant passions." After he was charged for this offense under the Sedition Act, Chase conducted his trial in a grossly unfair manner. At one point, the judge insulted both the Commonwealth of Virginia and Callender's attorneys. Passions were ignited when Chase continued to berate Jefferson and his Republican supporters in the midst of the trials, and Callender was convicted of sedition. Calling the Jefferson administration, a "mobocracy," he later told a Baltimore grand jury that the Republican repeal of the Judiciary Act of 1801 would deprive "all security for property and personal liberty." This allegation came even though the Constitution clearly grants Congress the authority to constitute and control the inferior federal courts.[341]

For treating defendants and their counsel in a hostile and blatantly partisan manner, Chase was impeached by the House of Representatives in 1804. He became the only Supreme Court Justice in United States history to be impeached and face trial in the Senate, despite the fact that the Constitution granted Congress the power to impeach and remove all civil officers convicted of high crimes and misdemeanors.[342] The Senate failed to convict Chase of the charges in 1805, however. The acquittal disturbed Jefferson greatly, and convinced the president that the impeachment process was faulty and inefficient. If Chase couldn't be forcibly removed from office, he feared that no unruly federal official ever would be.

In contrast nationalist disposition of Chase and his political associates, Jefferson's view of the Constitution acknowledged the separation of powers doctrine, and concluded that unconstitutional collusion between branches of government was a dangerous portent. He wholeheartedly believed that the branches working in unison would operate together to swallow the authority of the states, and such partisan behavior was not to be tolerated from a sitting judge. In Jefferson's mind, republican virtue depended on the earnest independence of all civil officers, and the manifest acceptance of partisan causes would fashion federal judges into petty tyrants.

Holding this position throughout his life, in 1820 Jefferson referred to the federal judiciary as an entity that trampled upon the sovereign rights of the states. Jefferson wrote that "the judiciary of the United States is the subtle corps of sappers and miners constantly working under ground to undermine the foundations of our confederated fabric. They are construing our constitution from co-ordination of a general and special government to a general and supreme one alone."[343]

Today, it is extremely rare for presidents and presidential candidates to criticize rulings of the federal judiciary or sitting judges on the Supreme Court. For instance, in the aftermath of the 2012 Supreme Court opinion in *National Federal of Independence Business v. Sebelius*, presidential candidate Mitt Romney accepted the court's finding that the Affordable Care Act of 2010 imposed a tax, and was thus constitutional. Even though the opinion seemed to contradict Romney's campaign platform, he refused to criticize the judges in question. "The Supreme Court has spoken," he said, "there's no way around that."[344] The Supreme Court came to such a conclusion despite the lack of enumerated authority in Article I, Section 8, and regardless of the lack of any provision to involve the federal government in health care. The judgement also incorrectly assumed that the document allows Congress to tax citizens to support unconstitutional purposes. On the contrary, the Constitution was widely promoted under the postulation that general government would only hold the powers delegated to it, and could only tax for specific purposes.

We can see from this instance alone that contemporary judges on the Supreme Court are broadly considered independent and infallible, as if an aura of constitutional cleanliness and judicial purity surrounds them. The court is not treated as the "despotic branch" that Jefferson warned about, despite the significant increase in the power of the federal judiciary. In the contemporary, the Supreme Court has effectively become a small oligarchy that makes binding decisions that are purported to "settle" issues for all time. This phenomenon cannot be attributed to a single particular political party, but has become a consensus between both major political parties and a large part of the public. Jefferson, to his great credit, was not one to believed that the federal courts could solve all constitutional issues.

DEVOTEES OF JEFFERSON

After Jefferson's death, his political philosophy was carried on by those who valued the axioms he paved the way for. These Jeffersonian devotees recognized that the foundation of the union was not premised upon unlimited submission to the federal government. To their great chagrin, figures hoping for a national consolidation of power rematerialized even after the Federalist Party died. These conditions made clear that Jefferson's ideas had to be revisited again by those who proudly considered themselves "Jeffersonian."

John Tyler, also a Virginian, grew up fondly remembering Jefferson dining at his own table. At the age of 19, the son of a wealthy plantation owner served Jefferson when the former president paid a visit to his family's Virginia home after completing his second term in office. Tyler considered Jefferson a marvelous conversationalist and was impressed with his tales from the past and his views on politics. That day, Jefferson seemed to make a significant and lasting impression on the boy. It was accordingly foreseeable that shortly after becoming president and taking the oath of office, Tyler proudly announced: "I shall act upon the principles which I have all along espoused…derived from the teachings of Jefferson and Madison...my reliance will be placed on the virtue and intelligence of the people."[345]

During his term in office, Tyler defined Jeffersonian. The Virginian carried out his political life in a constitutional fashion, and arguably remained even more faithful to this ideological doctrine than Jefferson himself. While he was attacked ferociously and lost numerous political friends, Tyler understood that the Constitution was an agreement between the states that produced a restrained government. Refusing to ignore this fact to placate the zeal of those who contested him, he maintained strict constitutional beliefs. Historian Oliver Chitwood called Tyler "an ideal of political consistency in an era of change." He "was not a man to regard himself as the custodian of a tradition, but he was a man to adhere with singular tenacity to that tradition."[346]

Like Jefferson, Tyler recognized that the nature of the United States Constitution was a compact, and understood the state governments had not yielded to the federal government power over all matters. As such, he explicitly rejected unconstitutional legislation that was placed before him. A man who consistently ranks at the bottom of "best president" polls, Tyler did much to perpetuate the cause of his fellow Virginian. A strict adherent to the Constitution, he was continually mocked and ridiculed by Whig forces that controlled Congress.

Early in his political career, Tyler helped create a coalition of opposition to the Second National Bank, and rejected the internal improvements platform the American Whigs championed during the late 1810s. As a senator, he condemned Andrew Jackson's threat of force during the Nullification Crisis and became the only senator to vote against the Force Bill in 1833. In doing so, he made a famous speech in support of South Carolina's position and attacked Jackson's policy. Adamantly opposed to the projection of military power against a state, Tyler viewed the Force Bill as an abominable dictum that would undermine the process by which the states had entered into the union in the first place. "I will not join in the denunciations which have been so loudly thundered against" South Carolina, he said, "nor will I deny she has much cause of complaint." Tyler thought Jackson's proclamation had "swept away the barriers of the Constitution and given us in place of the federal government, under which we had fondly believed we were living, a consolidated military despotism." As a firm believer in states' rights, the Jeffersonian's stance enunciated his constitutional views.[347]

Tyler was loathed by his political adversaries, especially during his presidency. Philip Hone, Former Mayor of New York, wrote in 1842 of his contempt toward the president:

One year of the rule of imbecility, arrogance, and prejudice has taught them the folly of selecting for Vice-President a man of whose fitness for the office of President they had no reasonable assurance.[348]

In an era where Whigs were the driving political force in Washington, Tyler openly defied his own party and maintained his disposition despite being the target of continual political attacks.

Tyler became president through obscure circumstances. As a Whig, he was elected as William Henry Harrison's vice president in 1840. When Harrison died of pneumonia a month after his inaugural address, Tyler immediately assumed the presidency and took the presidential oath of office.

Tyler's presidential oath was considered controversial at the time, because no consensus had been established in regard to who would become president if the sitting president died. However, it can be surmised that the assertions against his claim to the presidency were based on political grounds rather than on constitutional premises, as the Constitution notes that in the case of death, a president's powers "shall devolve on the Vice President."[349] Since the same powers and duties would be inherited by the vice president, including the "executive power" that would be granted to the president, it appears that Tyler's Whig opponents were acting opportunistically in their rejection of his claim. Nonetheless, his political adversaries contended that the he was merely something of an "acting" president, and soon responded to the new president's actions with considerable scorn.

In his first meeting of Harrison's former cabinet, Tyler was urged to continue the former president's policy of making decisions based on cabinet majority vote. The new president soundly rejected such a suggestion:

I beg your pardon, gentlemen; I am very glad to have in my Cabinet such able statesmen as you have proved yourselves to be. And I shall be pleased to avail myself of your counsel and advice. But I can never consent to being dictated to as to what I shall or shall not do. I, as President, shall be responsible for my administration. I hope to have your hearty co-operation in carrying out its measures. So long as you see fit to do this, I shall be glad to have you with me. When you think otherwise, your resignations will be accepted.[350]

Secretary of State Daniel Webster was particularly disturbed by Tyler's rejoinder, and resigned two years later. Indeed, Webster's renowned nationalist proclivities were incompatible with the Virginian's promise to uphold constitutional constraints.

From early in his presidency, Tyler made his rigid constitutional views unmistakable. In his first presidential address, he urged that those in the general government should "carefully abstain from all attempts to enlarge the range of powers thus granted to the several departments of the Government other than by an appeal to the people for additional grants." Doing otherwise, Tyler said, would "disturb that balance which the patriots and statesmen who framed the Constitution designed to establish between the Federal Government and the States composing the Union."[351]

Unsurprisingly, not all agreed with the president's unyielding constitutional vision. Under the leadership of Henry Clay, The Whigs tried to resurrect the idea of a new national bank several times, and each attempt was met with a presidential veto from Tyler. The party was bolstered in their efforts by the supposition that the Panic of 1837 would have been prevented if there had still been a national bank. In reality, British demand for cotton fell drastically while a new desire for hard currency emerged, causing a stagnation of capital flow from England to the United States.[352]

Tyler dreaded the idea of a national bank, just as Thomas Jefferson and Andrew Jackson had before him. He believed that such an institution would endeavor to shackle and subjugate future generations, and contended it would steal property from the current one. In the archetypal Jeffersonian tradition, he considered national banks wholly unconstitutional. Whig overseer Clay made two attempts to institute a new national bank nonetheless, using the Panic of 1837 as political capital. Tyler's opponents explained that the bank was "approved by some of the most competent financiers of this country and of England, and pronounced to be adequate to all our wants, safe in its operations, and calculated to furnish the most perfect currency that could be devised." Still, the president vetoed both of Clay's efforts. Naturally, his primary reason for vetoing each attempt was that it violated his states' rights conscience.[353] In so doing, Tyler waged a political war over the bank, realizing that the federal government lacked the enumerated authority to create such an establishment.

As chief executive, Tyler also rejected other bills that were unconstitu-tional. Despite political pressures to increase government revenue, he ve-toed a temporary protective tariff despite widespread popular appeal. After the veto, an attempt was made to pass a similar permanent tariff. Tyler again vetoed the second offering, which promised to raise the tariff rate above the prior decade's traditional rate of 20 percent. In contrast to the Whig leaders, the president wished to preserve the rate established by the Tariff of 1833 – the plan of compromise that provided resolution to the Nullification Crisis. Tyler recognized the need for nominal government revenue, but would not falter in his aim to moderate the tariff's function:

> While the Treasury is in a state of extreme embarrassment, requiring every dollar which it can make available, and when the government has not only to lay additional taxes, but to borrow money to meet pressing demands, the bill proposes to give away a fruitful source of revenue…a proceeding which I must regard as highly impolitic, if not unconstitu-tional.[354]

Tyler's veto was premised upon sound financial policy. According to bi-ographer Oliver Chitwood, it would have proven nearly impossible to bal-ance the federal budget while at the same time raising the tariff rates and continuing the distribution of land sale proceeds to the states. Undoubt-edly, the president's stance created additional friction between the execu-tive and legislative branches of the government. It also widened the rift between himself and the Whig Party, which the president was still a part of.[355] Nevertheless, any view that the president could be guided by the whims of unconstitutional compromise was mistaken.

Tyler's decisions burned any remaining bridges with his own party, and the Whigs in Congress officially expelled him. To use a term coined by Clay, he became "a president without a party."[356] Even in his own time, he was called "His Accidency," an insult used to mock the way he obtained the office. The Whigs in Congress even made an earnest effort to impeach Tyler, in the first attempt to do so in American history. Standing defiant, the president sent a letter of protest to the House of Representatives:

I am charged with violating pledges which I never gave...usurping powers not conferred by the law, and above all, with using the powers conferred upon the President by the Constitution from corrupt motivates and for unwarrantable ends.[357]

Ironically, Tyler usurped no powers, and it was actually Congress that persistently encouraged him to pass unconstitutional laws. If anything, the Whigs in Congress attempted to usurp powers not delegated by the Constitution. If not for the man in the executive office, they may have had their way.

Tyler could never be what his opponents wanted him to be, and his convictions were too strong to be shaped by crafty politicians. Rather than expect him to be swayed by political experience, the president demanded that his adversaries take him for what he was. Tyler's resolute deference to the constitutional compact that birthed the federal government unmistakably armed him with a strong grasp of constitutional limitations. Using that framework as a guide, he implemented its greatest ideals into his administration regardless of the powerful detractors that tried to hinder him. For his insistence and stubborn principles, he should be considered a heroic president rather than a forgotten one.

Beyond his own decision, Tyler placed men into his cabinet that shared his conception of the union. One of the most overlooked was brilliant statesmen Abel Upshur, whose definitive works have completely disappeared from the historical awareness of Americans. Nonetheless, through his own scholarship he countered the odious narrative of the nationalists and carried the Jeffersonian banner by his earnest defense of the constitutional compact.

Upshur, a Virginian who served as Tyler's secretary of state and secretary of the navy, published his thoughts on the federal Constitution in 1840. In an articulate manner, he defended the compact theory of the union in his work, *A Brief Enquiry Into the True Nature and Character of Our Federal Government: Being a Review of Judge Story's Commentaries On the Constitution of the United States*. Upshur's account contends that Joseph Story was mistaken, and that the United States was not created by an aggregation of "one people." He supported this view by pointing to the striking distinctions between the colonies that later became states and acted as parties to the Constitution:

> These colonial governments were clothed with the sovereign power of making laws, and of enforcing obedience to them, from their own people. The people of one colony owed no allegiance to the government of any other colony, and were not bound by its laws. The colonies had no common legislature, no common treasury, no common military power, no common judicatory. The people of one colony were not liable to pay taxes to any other colony, nor to bear arms in its defence; they had no right to vote in its elections; no influence nor control in its municipal government; no interest in its municipal institutions. There was no prescribed form by which the colonies could act together, for any purpose whatever; they were not known as "one people" in any one function of government.[358]

Upshur rightly recognized that the colonial charters, which gave the colonies legal right to exist, were granted to individuals that were not associated with people from the other states. His argument can be associated directly with those of Jefferson in *A Summary View of the Rights of British America* from decades earlier – both men cited this fact.

The only similarity between the colonies, as Upshur noted, was their common allegiance to the crown. Under Story's estimation that a singular group of American people ratified the Constitution, the inhabitants of Canada, Jamaica, and The Bahamas would also have to be included in such a group, since those locations were also British colonies in North America. He remarked that the states that actually ratified the Constitution acted autonomously, maintained different forms of government, held different legal interests, and enacted policy through different legislatures. Simply put, they grew to construct individual societies. Upshur recognized that "the English language affords no terms stronger than those which are here used to convey the idea of separateness, distinctness, and independence, among the colonies."[359] His persuasive refutation contradicted Story's claim that the Constitution was created in a cohesive act of the American people as a whole.

Upshur also noted that the states were so dissimilar that they deliberately refrained from creating a centralized authority to support each other in armed conflict. This argument is supported by the failure of Benjamin Franklin's Albany Plan, an unsuccessful attempt to create a unified government of the colonies. Even by 1775, the colonies were initially hesitant about lending support to Massachusetts, at first perceiving the Battles of Lexington and Concord as a regional affair.

Although Upshur wrote that *The Federalist* was "decidedly the best" commentary on the federal Constitution, he did not believe it should be taken as gospel. In defense of this position, he commented that "new questions have arisen, not then anticipated" in relation to the states and the federal government. Additionally, the state delegates to the Philadelphia Convention acted as ambassadors representing the governments of their respective states. Since the states had to ratify independently, the explanations given in the state conventions produced a more definitive understanding of the Constitution than any series of essays. As Upshur wrote, "*The Federalist* cannot be relied on, as full and safe authority in all cases."[360]

To refute the notion that the Declaration of Independence bound the colonies into a single homogenous society, Upshur explained:

But, as they were separate and distinct as colonies, the sovereignty over one could not vest, either in whole or in part, in any other. Each took to itself that sovereignty which applied to itself, and for which alone it had contended with the British Crown, to wit: the sovereignty over itself. Thus each colony became a free and sovereign State.[361]

Rather than Story, it was Upshur who understood that the famous American exposition recognized the states as independent entities, and was adopted only in common cause.

In support of the contention that state sovereignty was a crucial ingredient of the federal system, Upshur pointed to Article II of the Articles of Confederation – which guaranteed that "each state retains its sovereignty, freedom and independence." The primacy of the states, he recognized, was also acknowledged by the original preamble to the Constitution, which listed the separate states as the original creators of the union. Upshur countered the arguments of those who claimed that the Supremacy Clause made the states subordinate to the general government, noting that the Confederation government "was also "supreme," within its prescribed sphere of action."[362] To Upshur, this fact indicated that there were subjects over which the general government has no authority.

Upshur defended nullification as a principle that "contends only for the right of a State to prevent the Constitution from being violated by the general government, and not for the right either to repeal, abrogate or suspend it." He professed the Tenth Amendment's importance, writing that "the powers thus reserved, are not only reserved against the Federal Government in whole, but against each and every department thereof." Upshur suggested that "the judiciary is no more excepted out of the reservation than is the legislature or the executive."[363]

Perhaps Upshur's most compelling argument was made by his defense of the Virginia Resolution of 1798, which were adopted to resist the Sedition Act:

I confess that it seems to me exceedingly clear, that our Constitution is most worthless and tyrannical, if the usurpations of those who administer it, cannot be resisted by any means short of revolution. I have always considered the reserved powers of the Federal Government; and I have always considered it, not only the right, but the imperious duty of the States, so to apply that check, as not to dissolve the Union.[364]

Deeming nullification an "imperious duty" to ensure a state's presence in the union, Upshur refuted the allegation that asserting such a strategy was merely an attempt to "dissolve" it. In doing so, he echoed Madison's original contention that the states were "duty bound" to interpose in order to arrest "the progress of evil."

On every point, Upshur convincingly tore apart the arguments of a sitting judge on the Supreme Court, though he is rarely given any credit for doing so. While history proves that his studies were more factually accurate than Story's, but the nationalist narrative has prevailed. Modern academia and constitutional law curriculum give Story's commentaries and Marshall's opinions heightened emphasis, while Upshur is almost completely forgotten. Despite his accurate observations of the union's genesis, some still believe that the Jeffersonian view died or was "settled" as a result of the Federalists taking power in government, the South Carolina Nullification Crisis, or the rise of the Whigs. Upshur's commentaries, made after all of these events, should stand today as evidence to the contrary of such myths.

The Jeffersonian tradition was not only propagated by southerners. Franklin Pierce, another underappreciated president, was also an unwavering defender of the Constitution. Like Jefferson, he also considered the document the offspring of a compact between sovereign states. Like Tyler, Pierce is generally held in low regard, and is considered a low-ranking president by most contemporary accounts. Even in his own term, he was criticized for his strict constitutional outlook. From New Hampshire, Pierce was characterized as a "doughface" by his political rivals, a derogatory term for a northerner with southern sympathies.

Based on the perceived shortcomings of his presidency, academia has largely propagated a negative assessment of Pierce. In the *Wall Street Journal*, historian David Holzel wrote that he was "a complete failure as president," smugly adding that "the only important thing that happened during his administration was the first perforated postage stamps were made." A 2013 *New York Times* poll of historians ranked Pierce as the 42nd best president in United States history, placing him third from the bottom of the list. Furthermore, a compilation of twelve other surveys also graded him 42nd.[365] Considering Pierce's adherence to the original understanding of the Constitution, these modern perceptions could not be more unfair.

In 1854, the president famously vetoed an act to grant public lands for use as insane asylums. To defend his reasoning, Pierce wrote a note to the Senate:

> With this aim and to this end the fathers of the Republic framed the Constitution, in and by which the independent and sovereign States united themselves for certain specified objects and purposes, and for those only, leaving all powers not therein set forth as conferred on one or another of the three great departments — the legislative, the executive, and the judicial — indubitably with the States.[366]

Furthermore, Pierce referred to *The Federalist* No. 45, which noted that the powers delegated to the proposed Constitution are few and defined. Quoting Jefferson's famous manifesto on federalism, he added that "the support of the State governments in all their rights" was "the most competent administrations for our domestic concerns and the surest bulwark against anti-republican tendencies."[367]

Pierce referred to the importance of the states in the American political system. "The federal compact offers the best, if not the only, security for the preservation of our blessed inheritance of representative liberty," he wrote.[368] By extension of this guideline, he admitted that the Constitution requires that an executive act against his own personal inclinations when considering to sign bills into law:

In the performance of this duty, prescribed by the Constitution, I have been compelled to resist the deep sympathies of my own heart in favor of the humane purpose sought to be accomplished and to overcome the reluctance with which I dissent from the conclusions of the two Houses of Congress, and present my own opinions in opposition to the action of a coordinate branch of the Government which possesses so fully my confidence and respect.[369]

Referring to the general government as the "creature of the States," Pierce recognized that the colonists were "the inhabitants of colonies distinct in local government one from the other before the Revolution." By that Revolution," he wrote, "the colonies each became an independent State."[370] This perception mirrored the Declaration of Independence, which noted that the free and independent states all had the power to conduct war, levy peace, and do all things which states were known to do.

To the idea that the General Welfare Clause granted Congress the power to do all things of perceived benefit to the people, Pierce took umbrage:

It is not a substantive general power to provide for the welfare of the United States, but is a limitation on the grant of power to raise money by taxes, duties, and imposts. If it were otherwise, all the rest of the Constitution, consisting of carefully enumerated and cautiously guarded grants of specific powers, would have been useless, if not delusive.[371]

Things have changed very little since Pierce's time. To this day, the General Welfare Clause is constantly cited as justification for the federal government to enact any policy, pass any legislation, or make any statute that makes an appeal to the "general welfare of the people." However, this understanding of the clause has been thoroughly debunked by assurances made by Federalists during the ratification struggle. As a vigilant protector of the Constitution, Pierce realized this at a time in which many did not. He also understood that a list of enumerated powers would be inconsequential had the General Welfare Clause meant what his opponents alleged. This interpretation would grant the general government all powers to do anything regardless of all limitations, making the list superfluous. In basic terms, a Constitution of enumerated powers would be redundant and unnecessary if it also allowed the government to do anything and everything.

In the Veto Message of 1854 – which rejected legislation to fund unconstitutional public works projects – Pierce repeated the same constitutional mantra that Jefferson, Madison, Tyler, and Upshur had explained in detail. As a discipline of the Jeffersonian creed, the president referred to the Constitution as a "sacred instrument," using the document as a guide for his own executive decisions.

Like Jefferson, Pierce was a vocal opponent of perpetual debt and excessive spending. His administration confronted the debt debacle by paying off treasury bonds. While the United States national debt was at $63 million in 1848, his fiscal restraint brought the debt back down to $28 million.[372] At a time when his political opponents pushed for additional expenditures on internal improvements, Pierce knew that prolonged debt did nothing but force citizens into a condition of governmental servitude.

Long after his administration, Pierce sacrificed his reputation to defend civil liberties and speak out against the President Abraham Lincoln's constitutional transgressions. He was especially disdainful of the president's decision to punish political dissidents and suspend the writ of habeas corpus in Maryland. Such a dreadful precedent, he thought, would end in political calamity and despotic rule. Pierce biographer Peter Wallner likened the president as a martyr for his vision of the union and the Constitution.[373]

Pierce's stance was predicated upon the Baltimore Riots of 1861, and Lincoln's unwillingness to allow Maryland's legislature to convene. Lincoln refused to accept this because he feared Maryland would secede from the union, and Washington, D.C. would be geographically positioned between two Confederate states. In response to Lincoln's invasion of Maryland's republican government, the United States Supreme Court reprimanded the president. Through the case of *Ex parte Merryman*, the high court decided that Lincoln's actions were entirely unconstitutional.

Lincoln's refused to heed the opinion of Chief Justice Roger Taney, and the arbitrary scheme of imprisonment continued. Taney argued that the history of the American experience proved that the founders would not have given an American president "more regal and absolute power" over the personal liberties of the citizens than any king of England ever enjoyed. Lincoln scholar Thomas DiLorenzo cited three corroborating sources claiming that Lincoln issued an order for the arrest of Taney as a result of his viewpoint, a breathtaking act of despotism.[374]

During the Civil War, Pierce lamented that a "reign of terror" had overtaken the government. This condition, he declared, was "ruinous to the victors as well as the vanquished." Basing his principles upon the Constitution, the former president also chastised the Lincoln administration for suspending the writ of habeas corpus – a power confined only to the scope of Congressional power. Conversely, Lincoln had argued that secession was an illegitimate action, and as such, the Congressional prerequisite for the writ's suspension – where "Cases of Rebellion or Invasion the public safety may require it." – as annulled.[375] If there was no rebellion, there could be no suspension of the writ of habeas corpus. Maryland had not seceded, and the southern states that left the union wished to depart in peace, not to overthrow the federal government or engage in a rebellion.

A second cause for Pierce's dejection came on August 8, 1862, when Secretary of War Edwin Stanton declared martial law. In response, the former president apprehended that the general authority had devolved into an overt tyranny:

Our people have bowed so tamely to the march of glaring usurpation, that I suppose they will scarcely murmur at the late order of Mr. Stanton, placing the rights of the citizens, freedom of opinion, freedom of speech, personal liberty, primarily in the keeping of the Marshalls, superintendents or chiefs of police of any town, City or District and then turning them over to the tender mercies of a military commission. Is not this the worst form of despotism? Martial Law declared throughout the land, with the additional appendage of a band of prejudiced, passionate, irresponsible, abolition office holders, constituted as a special corps of accusers! What ideas must this Secretary have of the unlimited and unrestrained Central power when he assumes thus to impose duties upon and give instructions to "Superintendents or chiefs of police of any town City or district"? Let there be no more talk of Sovereign States, of Constitutional Rights—of trial by Jury—of legal protection for persons & property.[376]

On the same day, Stanton also issued a proclamation that specifically forbade anyone eligible for draft into the militia from leaving the United States.[377] Pierce's letter expressed extreme bitterness toward the policies, which trampled upon the sovereignty of the states that formed the constitutional compact. In so doing, he directly condemned the "central power" as an unrestrained entity that willfully violated the Constitution.

Despite the Lincoln administration's penchant for arbitrary arrests and indefinite detainment, admonition against the crown for extending martial law was also a common refrain of the British constitutional system. This concept was affirmed in the 1628 English Petition of Right, mentioned earlier as an important constitutional antecedent. Diverting from this lesson, however, Stanton's declaration had eradicated individual liberty, and Pierce would not remain silent in the face of it.

Pierce believed in the benefits of a federal union, but also recognized that the general government had gone far beyond the bounds of the Constitution through the centralization of power and enactment of oppressive policies. The distraught former president confessed he had "never desired to survive the wreck of the Union," but refused to tolerate the unbearable consolidation of power that had "nullified the Constitution." Ultimately, the circumstances led Pierce to acknowledge the natural right of secession.

"If we cannot live together in peace, then in peace and on just terms," he wrote, "let us separate."[378]

Prior to the war, Pierce favored diplomatic resolutions to the conflict, including the Crittenden Compromise, which had been proposed by Senator John Crittenden of Kentucky. The plan introduced a series of six potential constitutional amendments that were designed to bring a halt to the impending struggle. After the effort became futile, Pierce did not think his continued presence in Washington could help to bring an end the looming bloodshed. In despair, Pierce then mourned that he saw "no point for effective interposition."[379]

Pierce's political philosophy is not highly studied, and his reputation is usually maligned by modern detractors. Critics note Pierce's inability to control the formation of bitter factions during a trying time, or suggest he was overly sympathetic of the South. However, Wallner fittingly recognized Pierce as a "true Jeffersonian."[380] Rigorously abiding by his oath to the Constitution during a time when it was often abridged, ignored, and twisted by the federal government, Pierce believed that the document was the ultimate protector of the people's liberty. As a mechanism to defend against the arbitrary impulses of government, he thought, the framework provided perpetual value. "Doughface" or not, Pierce deserves adulation for his stubborn defense of the Constitution and the Jeffersonian political heritage.

JEFFERSON AND SECESSION

The result of the United States Civil War is commonly cited as an event that "resolved" the question of secession completely. The war's conclusion has also been described as a precedent concerning whether force should apply in response to seceding states. Nevertheless, the founding generation assured us the union was a voluntary arrangement, that departure from the general government was constitutionally permissible, and that the general government could never legitimately enforce the compact through force. The latter axiom was reached after years of exploitation by autocratic kings, which had ruled by the sword to force localities into their own political arrangements.

While it may seem surprising today, the idea that war would automatically befall entities that renounced membership in the union was once considered preposterous. In 1788, Melancton Smith of New York articulated such a view:

> The idea of a civil war among the states is abhorrent to the principles and feelings of almost every man of every rank in the union. It is so obvious to every one of the least reflection, that in such an event we should hazard the loss of all things, without the hope of gaining anything, that the man who should entertain a thought of this kind, would be justly deemed more fit to be shut up in Bedlam, than to be reasoned with. But the idea of one or more states attacking another, for insisting upon alterations upon the system, before it is adopted, is more extravagant still; it is contradicting every principle of liberty which has been entertained by the states, violating the most solemn compact, and taking from the state the right of deliberation.[381]

Smith's mindset was not alien to the founding generation. As described earlier, North Carolina and Rhode Island did not even ratify the Constitution until long after the First Congress met. However, hostilities were never raised toward these states as a result of their reluctance, and the federal government did not try to coerce them into the union. Smith suggested that such force would be repulsive to the principles of liberty. Smith inquired: "Can it, I say, be imagined, that in such a case, they would make war on a sister state?" He wrote that such an idea was "preposterous and chimerical."[382]

George Mason also rejected the idea that war would result from disassociation with the union. Concerning military enforcement of governmental policy, Mason asked whether the government would "use military force to compel the observance of a social compact." Scoffing at such a prospect, the renowned Virginian declared that doing so would be "destructive to the rights of the people."[383] Mason's words proved ironic and prophetic when his forecast came to be realized during the Lincoln administration.

In the run-up to war, Lincoln maintained erroneous impressions about the origins of the union, including his suggestion, in a famous oratory, that the union itself was a perpetual arrangement:

> I hold that in contemplation of universal law and of the Constitution the Union of these States is perpetual. Perpetuity is implied, if not expressed, in the fundamental law of all national governments. It is safe to assert that no government proper ever had a provision in its organic law for its own termination. Continue to execute all the express provisions of our National Constitution, and the Union will endure forever, it being impossible to destroy it except by some action not provided for in the instrument itself.[384]

Despite the widespread veneration of Lincoln's popular oratory, such an understanding directly controverted the acknowledged perspective of the founders that played roles in the formation of the union.

The American states first became independent upon their secession from the British government, articulating their reasoning for doing so in the Declaration of Independence and other local proclamations.[385] Seeking to associate with each other for specific purposes, the states ratified the Articles of Confederation in 1781. When many came to believe that the Articles of Confederation had shortcomings, a new framework was proposed. When the Constitution was adopted, the states ratified the new model voluntarily and without retribution, and the states departed from the existing Confederation government in peace.

Despite Lincoln's extrapolation that perpetuity of the union was implied by Constitution, this was never considered to be the ratified understanding. In fact, this notion was explicitly dispelled by several states. Contrary to Lincoln's reasoning, the "resumption clauses" that Virginia, New York, and Rhode Island inserted into their official ratification texts affirmed that the states could take back their own sovereign power following abuses by the government. Other states acknowledged these principles but did not explicitly write them into their respective texts, believing such powers to be inherent to any sovereign body as an extension of Lockean political doctrine. Ratification was secured, in many cases, by emphasizing that the states had the voluntary power to enter the union as sovereign entity on the same footing with the other states. On that basis, they could leave at will in the same manner.

In his first inaugural address, Jefferson commented that many had wished to "dissolve this Union" or "change its republican form" in the years prior to his election to the presidency. While he denied supporting such a drastic measure, he declined to portray such a decision as impermissible, and suggested instead that calls for secession were legitimate and acceptable. "If there be any among us who would wish to dissolve this Union or to change its republican form," he declared, "let them stand undisturbed as monuments of the safety with which error of opinion may be tolerated where reason is left free to combat it."[386] Wishing to preside over a free country of both Federalists and Republicans, Jefferson hoped that both political factions could avoid secession campaigns by appealing to reason rather than through the application of force.

Regardless, Jefferson maintained that secession was the free right of every sovereignty. When several New England states threatened to leave the union several years later, Jefferson wrote, "if any State in the Union will declare that it prefers separation....to a continuance in union...I have no hesitation in saying, 'let us separate.'"[387] In his seminal work *Democracy in America*, Alexis de Tocqueville, the most famous foreign observer of the early American republic, echoed the same understanding:

> The Union was formed by the voluntary agreement of the States; and, in uniting together, they have not forfeited their nationality, nor have they been reduced to the condition of one and the same people. If one of the States chose to withdraw its name from the contract, it would be difficult to disprove its right of doing so; and the Federal Government would have no means of maintaining its claims directly, either by force or by right.[388]

By the same strain of Jeffersonian philosophy, in 1824, famous Virginian statesman John Randolph of Roanoke recalled the genesis of the government as the "offspring of the States," and declared that the states had the power "to extinguish this Government at a blow."[389]

Without question, the founding fathers were a generation of secessionists. Before leaving the Confederation government under the Articles of

Confederation, their states had first seceded from a government they felt had overstepped its authority – that of Great Britain. They did so through passage of the Richard Henry Lee Resolution, which precipitated the Declaration of Independence. An honest reader needs to go no further than the document's preamble to realize that a separation from Britain was the common cause of the states.

Despite its short-term standing in American history, some have opined that the full title of the Articles of Confederation, "The Articles of Confederation and Perpetual Union," indicated that the union was meant to be perpetual. However, this supposition has been muddled by ignorance of legal context. As an 18th century legal term, "perpetual" did not mean "everlasting." Instead, the word indicated the lack of a native sunset provision that would terminate the original contract.[390] The same principle is affirmed by the 1783 Treaty of Paris, which ended hostilities in the War of Independence and called for "perpetual Peace and Harmony" between Britain and the American states. Despite this, the two countries went to war with each other less than two decades later. Moreover, both the dissolution of the Confederation government and the ratification of a new Constitution demonstrated that the founding generation did not deem the Articles to be cemented in stone for eternity.

The nationalist stranglehold on the union came not from the voluntary acquiescence of the states, but through the assertion of force and the establishment of precedents by the general government. In these cases, Congress, the president, and the federal courts have routinely substituted their own preferences in place of the Constitution's original intent. According to historian Nathan Coleman, history demonstrates that the triumph of nationalism over decentralized constitutionalism "came via the bayonet and continues now…through the federal treasury and appropriations."[391]

The honest pursuit of Jefferson's principles lasted far beyond his own age. Regardless of adversity, his conceptions were carried on by ideological disciples who sought to impede the constitutional desecrations of an ever-expanding federal government. While Jefferson has long since left the world, his ideas remain a timeless part of the American political tradition. They recognized the true genesis of the republic – a compact between sovereign and independent states.

Part II
How the Compact Has Been Dismantled

Chapter 6

An Exceptional War of Independence

In the 1760s and 1770s, the general dissatisfaction of the American colonies gradually led to an open revolt against Great Britain. Throughout the turmoil, colonists endeavored to reclaim their sovereign power through local governance, no longer wishing to be controlled by the commands of Parliament. Most historians refer to the American struggle against Britain as the "American Revolution," implying a national, unitary conflict between the states as a whole and Britain. This tendency is an unfortunate misconception that fails to accurately contextualize the cause of the American states.

The American campaign for independence bore no resemblance to the various revolutions that broke out in other nations. The American patriots did not supplant their customs, enact a reign of terror, or displace traditional institutions. The American patriots were hardly social levelers, and no dictator emerged in the aftermath of the scuffle – a Lenin, Mao, Robespierre, or Cromwell was nowhere to be seen. The American patriots sought not to uproot their culture, but to maintain it. To most historians, the American Revolution has therefore seemed downright conservative, if it could even be deemed a revolution at all.

Undoubtedly, the struggle for the independence of the American states was predicated upon a strenuous constitutional defense of American rights against British encroachment, to preserve the very form of government the colonies recognized and cherished.[392] This framework, patriots averred, had been threatened – and without a rightful exertion of resistance it would be lost forever. Rather than a revolution, but Americans witnessed a war of independence. Instead of seeking to remake or revolutionize society, Americans aspired to reclaim their own authority. Far from seeking to overthrow their central government, they hoped to prevent the British from interfering with the legislative process of their colonial assemblies. Most importantly, they wished to stifle the elevation of tyrannical central government.

The American quest for sovereignty stands in stark contrast to the experience of the French. The French Revolution, which transpired a decade later, was a murderous, bloody endeavor that completely recreated every aspect of French society. In the end, the revolutionary government that grew out of the catastrophe would change the country's federal structure, its calendar, and even its national religion. In contrast, the American War of Independence shifted the governing authority from Parliament to the states, while retaining the cultural characteristics and institutions of the respective localities.

While the post-royal French assembly formed a centralized bastion of power, the American states claimed authority as their own through state-based sovereigns. Unquestionably, the notable dissimilarity between the French Revolution and the American War of Independence plainly reveals the uniqueness of the American political system under the Constitution. The French revolutionaries aimed to change society in virtually every way, but the American states proudly kept their own religious identities, governments, and cultural traditions.

It is often asserted that the United States is an "exceptional" nation that holds unique characteristics that do not exist in any other corner of the world. Though far from a unitary nation, the United States has distinguishing features, though not in the ways that are often purported. Rather than possessing the unique responsibility to police the world against global infractions, the United States is distinctive because its central government was birthed by autonomous political sovereigns. In the advent of nearly all other political arrangements throughout world history, one ruler is simply exchanged for another and power always resides in a central body. The United States, then, is a union defined for its exceptional system of decentralized authority.

After Louis XVI was executed in 1793, the revolutionaries that took control of the country hoped to erase traditional institutions and transform the entire system of state administration. Remaking society, the new authorities believed, would rid France of the corruptibility of the crown and the appalling ramifications of the divine right of kings. However, to the most radical of the country's firebrands, the death of the king was not enough. With royalism still a popular cause in Europe and much of the world, the prospect of a coup to restore a king to power in France – much like England had witnessed by the Restoration of 1660 – was a threat that convinced some of the most ardent revolutionaries to drastic political action.

One of the ways to impede local uprisings and centralize power under the new republic came through a systematic plan of regional restructuring. After the king had been deposed, the government in Paris established its unitary administrative structure by redrawing the provinces within France to suit the convenience of the central government. The new French "departments," established in 1790 by the National Constituent Assembly, replaced representative regions with "political arithmetic." The new array of 83 French partitions drove wedges between French subcultures, disconnected peoples from natural resources and topography, and vanquished local centers of political authority.[393] The renovation was analogous to taking a proverbial eraser to ancient French borders that had been recognized for centuries. The change marked an obvious civic shift, the ascension of a strong central state that retained all political control over its subordinate regions.

Through the new redistricting scheme, France became a unified, single state rather than an aggregate of localities. Conversely, the American municipalities created the general authority and retained their own political boundaries and governments. Even when the states ceded land to the general authority – such as in the case of Virginia's 1781 cession of its northwestern lands – they did strictly by the state governments. Neither the

Articles of Confederation nor the Constitution that replaced it gave the general authority no power to redraw state borders for its own convenience.

During much of the French Revolution, the Committee of Public Safety acted as the executive authority of the country. As a council of oligarchs that wielded immense political power, this body exerted authority unlike any government even the Bourbon monarchs oversaw. Serving as the country's de-facto legislature, executive, and judiciary, the council assumed power with the rationalization that wartime conditions called for drastic measures to uproot counter-revolutionary activity. In comparison, during the American War of Independence the states functioned as distinctly separate entities, all of which had autonomous, relatively powerful governments. The Continental Congress existed to enact resolutions in the common cause of the states, but it did not have the power to pass law. The delegates served only as state ambassadors, representing their state's government in the body. Each of the state legislatures, state governors, and state courts held actual political power throughout the war.

During the French Revolution, the central authority in Paris embarked upon a rigorous de-Christianization effort. Many of the revolutionary forces associated the churches with the Bourbon monarchs, who stood to symbolize tyranny and decadence. Furthermore, some viewed the presence of churches in French society as a hazard to the new French government, which purported to offer a competing brand of egalitarian utopia. One revolutionary leader, Pierre Chaumette, proclaimed that "religious sophistry" had torn France apart for too long, and declared that "the superstition and hypocrisy" of Christianity was to be opposed at all costs. Chaumette ordered crucifixes destroyed, church property confiscated, and denounced clerical celibacy. His anti-Christian fervor also instigated a campaign to compel priests to marry, and forced the resignation of a prominent religious leader, the Bishop of Allier.[394] Eventually, all churches within Paris were forced to close under the revolutionary government.

The movement to eradicate Christianity from France started in Paris and swept through the other provinces. Christian symbols and statues were removed from streets, squares, and public areas. A revolutionary decree forced all religious emblems on the roads to be destroyed, burials to be conducted without any religious connotation, and cemetery signs to be built with the inscription "death is but an eternal sleep." Even towns and villages were required to change their names to accommodate this cultural upheaval. The town of St. Tropez, for example, was forced to change its name to Heraclee. Religious ceremonies, holidays, and celebrations were banned or replaced with secular alternatives. Through organized plunder, the French authorities seized gold and silver from the churches in order to finance the continuing French war effort.[395]

The French government forced clergy to take oaths to a national church, which would be paid for and defined by the government. Bishops who refused to swear such oaths were considered "nonjuring" or "refractory" priests. Not only were such individuals banned from conducting religious services, they were often subject to humiliating punishments such as public assault or verbal humiliation. In 1793, Committee of Public Safety passed one pernicious law to make all nonjuring priests and the persons harboring them susceptible to the penalty of death on sight. The revolutionary government hoped such measures would finally remove any oppositional influence held by the rebellious priests. Demonstrated by its vicious campaign against Christianity, the French Revolution was truly one of the most anti-Christian world events in history.

In 1794, after the French revolutionaries systematically dismantled all remaining aspects of Christianity in France, the government methodically replaced them with deistic equivalents. As the country's legislative body, The French National Convention then implemented the Cult of the Supreme Being, a new state religion based on deism. Principally inspired by revolutionary leader and member of the Committee on Public Safety, Maximilien de Robespierre, the Cult of the Supreme Being was ordained as the official religion of the French Republic. To inaugurate the country's abandonment of Christianity, Robespierre initiated a commemorative event in Paris to introduce the new state religion to the masses. The decadent ceremony to ordain the new religion transpired on June 8, 1794.

This elaborate pageant was deemed the "Festival of the Supreme Being." By its execution, Robespierre hoped to wipe Christianity from the French consciousness for good, and replace it with a theism based on his own conception of scientific enlightenment. As part of the spectacle, a large procession took place at a man-made mountain at a large public area of Paris known as the Champ de Mars. Atop the mountain was an "Altar of the Nation" and "Tree of Liberty" which stood as deistic symbols of revolution and longevity. A calculated affair, Robespierre deliberately swapped symbols of religious reverence with those of the French nation-state.

During the ceremony, Robespierre condemned the Bourbon kings for their religious practices, and blamed France's woes on Christianity:

> The monster which the genius of kings had vomited over France has gone back into nothingness. May all the crimes and all the misfortunes of the world disappear with it! Armed in turn with the daggers of fanaticism and the poisons of atheism, kings have always conspired to assassinate humanity. If they are able no longer to disfigure Divinity by superstition, to associate it with their crimes, they try to banish it from the earth, so that they may reign there alone with crime.[396]

Beyond this assault, Robespierre likened Christian religious practices to "sacrilegious plots" against the new French religious system.[397] Alternatively, he championed a return to the values of virtue and nature, condemning the religious establishments of pre-revolutionary France. The revolutionaries associated Christianity with the political exploitation of the Bourbon monarchs, the latest of which was executed by the state.

France also intentionally abolished its Gregorian calendar in order to remove all references to Christianity, and its replacement intended to highlight the republic's axioms of nature and reason rather than the tenets of traditional Christianity.[398] Likewise, the new system scrapped its traditional numeral system and created a new scheme based on key events from the French Revolution. For instance, since the French monarchy was abolished in 1792, that year became the first year of the new calendar. To follow suit, names of the French months were changed to reflect these tendencies as well.

Instead of punishing religious worship, erasing religious imagery, and embracing national deism, the American states retained separate religious identities and practices. Some states had varying official state religions, such as Congregational Church and the Church of England, while others never had any sort of connection to an official religion, such as Pennsylvania and New Jersey. In some states, such as Virginia, the legal religious establishment was abolished shortly after the war. Unlike the French government, no national power sought to criminalize the religious practices of individuals or eliminate state religious establishments. Similarly, no authority endeavored to change important cultural features, such as the Gregorian calendar the states observed.

When Napoleon Bonaparte came to power by overthrowing the French Directory in 1799, he announced that "the chaos and uncertainty of the revolution is going to be over." Betraying this declaration, Bonaparte soon implemented his own revolutionary schemes for the country. Soon afterward, he outmaneuvered the other oligarchs of the French Consulate and wrote his own Constitution for France. Known as the Constitution of the Year VIII, the instrument effectively gave Napoleon immense authority as First Consul, the most powerful figure in the country. This framework was later amended by the Constitution of the Year X, which legally permitted Napoleon to hold dictatorial power for life. Another addendum, the Constitution of the Year XII, established the Bonaparte family as a hereditary dynasty, a classic regal feature that was abolished in the aftermath of the revolution.

In due time, Napoleon replaced France's civil law with the Napoleonic Code, a civil legal system that survives in France and many French-speaking parts of the world. Emboldened by his coronation as Emperor of the French in 1804, he also made himself the nation's unrivaled civil and military ruler. In contrast, the legal systems of the American states were influenced by the common law system of the British. Even after forming a union, the states refrained from reinventing their own legal structures, seeing no reason to abandon the systems many scolded the British authorities for undermining. In their struggle with Britain, Americans were more concerned about legal transgressions than revolutionary conceptions.

None of these constitutional novelties were introduced at the behest of the people's representatives – they were instituted by the sole will of the emperor himself. Napoleon's constitution did not limit the Consulate to an enumerated list of powers. On the contrary, it assured that all authority could be held by the same body. Rather than to delineate and distribute powers, it simply affirmed Napoleon's unrivaled power. After the adoption of the new constitution, the emperor plunged Europe into war for another decade and a half, even as most nations on the continent formed allied coalitions against him. Without any constitutional limitation to his rule, Napoleon's edicts were legally binding upon all.

In the American states, no standing military leader usurped power from the states or ascended as a national political leader. In fact, a famous case to the contrary materialized after the War of Independence concluded. In 1783, George Washington famously resigned his military commission, dissolved the Continental Army, and retired to his homestead at Mount Vernon. Shocked by this development, even King George III of Britain called Washington "the greatest character of the age."[399] Additionally, when the British ministry sent peace delegations to negotiate with Washington during the war, the commander routinely deferred the diplomats to the Continental Congress. In an era where the triumph of an army usually meant the forcible ascension of its leading general to political power, Washington's actions stunned the world.

The French revolutionary experience was drastically different from the American states in its approach to religion, culture, and the war. As we can see, the French revolutionaries went beyond severing the cultural ties of their past – they systematically replaced their society with revolutionary alternatives. In France, it wasn't enough to reject the old – it was necessary to supplant the new. Refusing to make such sweeping changes, the American states took the alternative approach by preserving their own cultural traditions, civic institutions, and political boundaries.

The resolution to the American conflict also serves to illustrate the stark contrast between the origins of the modern French and American states. The 1783 Treaty of Paris, which formally ended the American War of Independence, reveals the American states secured peace and international standing as autonomous entities. In opposition to the mantra that the United States was a singular entity built by "one people," and confirming that the sovereignty of the states pre-dated the general government, the kingdom of Great Britain signed the agreement with the states separately:

His Brittanic Majesty acknowledges the said United States, viz., New Hampshire, Massachusetts Bay, Rhode Island and Providence Plantations, Connecticut, New York, New Jersey, Pennsylvania, Maryland, Virginia, North Carolina, South Carolina and Georgia, to be free sovereign and independent states, that he treats with them as such, and for

himself, his heirs, and successors, relinquishes all claims to the government, propriety, and territorial rights of the same and every part
thereof.[400]

The British government recognized the American states as individual, sovereign bodies that were independent of a national political arrangement.
This understanding was also verbalized in the Articles of Confederation,
which emphasized in Article II that each state retained its "sovereignty,
freedom, and independence." Surely, the states could not retain such characteristics if they did not first exist in a decentralized political configura-
tion.

Reinforcing this case, the treaty explicitly guaranteed peace between
Great Britain and the American polities as individuals. "There shall be a
firm and perpetual Peace between his Britannic Majesty and the said
States," it read.[401] Acting as representatives of the several states, the settlement was signed and sealed by John Adams, Benjamin Franklin, and
John Jay – all acting as ambassadors of states through the Confederation
government.

Only the distinctive American experience of the 1770s and 1780s could
produce the American constitutional compact. Foreign to this were all
other notable systems in human history, which did not respect the sovereignty of their localities to such a degree. While other nations were defined
by a strong central authority that used coercion to subdue its municipalities, the American constitutional apparatus maintained a unique orientation. Rather than a rule, the unconventional experiences of the American
states, in forming their constitutional compact, was a historical exception.

Refuting the notion that the states merged into a unitary entity in 1776,
the same polities maintained distrustful and often adversarial relations
with each other throughout the course of the war. Some collaboration occurred through the Continental Congress, but the individuality of the states
remained evident during the struggle for independence. John Adams, a
man with a unique perspective of these developments, explained the phenomenon:

The colonies had grown up under constitutions of government so different, there was so great a variety of religions, they were composed of

so many different nations, their customs, manners, and habits had so little resemblance, and their intercourse had been so rare, and their knowledge of each other so imperfect, that to unite them in the same principles in theory and the same system of action, was certainly a very difficult enterprise. The complete accomplishment of it in so short a time and by such simple means was perhaps a singular example in the history of mankind. Thirteen clocks were made to strike together – a perfection of mechanism which no artist had ever before effected.[402]

These "thirteen clocks," which to Adams recognized as having "so little resemblance," became the building blocks of the republic. Each fledgling state, acting in its own interests, waged war with Britain to preserve its political sovereignty.

Chapter 7

The Legacy of Alexander Hamilton and John Marshall

In parallel with the gradual erosion of state authority, the federal government has steadily grown into the national, supreme government of America. Over time, this transition has substantially altered the original structure and function of government the states created. Though the founding generation openly criticized and eventually revolted against the British crown, they eventually witnessed the same behavior under a domestic government.

The most disheartening aspect that underscores this process is the realization that liberty often wanes slowly over time. As Thomas Jefferson wrote, "the natural progress of things is for liberty to yield, and government to gain ground."[403] Such was the case in the United States, where the genuine compact of the republic was dismantled over time. No single act or event is responsible for this loss of state proprietorship, but several significant precedents set the United States upon this path.

During the ratification struggle, even those that hoped for a powerful federal government stressed the importance of the states and assured skeptics of their eminence in the federal system. For instance, Federalist James Wilson noted in Philadelphia that "the state governments ought to be preserved-the freedom of the people and their internal good police depends on their existence in full vigor."[404] Without the states to give life to the Constitution, the document lacked binding legal potency. Furthermore, states maintained all powers not delegated to the general authority. In sum, the Constitution was created for the convenience of the states, not for the suitability of a central government.

Shortly after the ratification campaign, the relative power of the states was threatened most substantially in the early republic through the supposition that the Constitution allowed the government to utilize powers other than those specifically listed in the document. The "implied powers doctrine," as it sometimes called, has acted to ignore constitutional boundaries and homogenize the states into a uniform nation. In the early republic, two individuals were most responsible for championing such an undertaking. As the ink was still drying on the federal compact, the precedents left by Alexander Hamilton and John Marshall reinvented the federal union.

As the first secretary of the treasury in the cabinet of George Washington, Hamilton aspired to combat the zealous advocates of a decentralized union through the executive office. With grandiose dreams of replicating the mercantile system of the British Empire, he quickly began work on a new economic plan for the United States. Tellingly, Hamilton had routinely asserted that the British form of government was the most perfect model on earth. An alien perspective to many republicans that apprehended the "living constitution" model of Britain, the view was consistent with the opinions the New Yorker had expressed during the Philadelphia Convention.

The plan Hamilton unveiled to Congress called for a national bank, protectionist tariffs, subsidies for domestic industry, and the creation of an enduring national debt. Though these proposals were constitutionally dubious from the outset, Hamilton's economic vision found favor with many northern delegates and their industrialist allies. More importantly, President Washington had the deepest respect for his treasury secretary, who had served him as an aide-de-camp during the war. Though Jeffersonians continually warned the new executive that Hamilton was an ambitious, ill-designing man, his opinions nearly always won the favor of the president.

Before ratification was considered by the several states, notes recorded at the Philadelphia Convention by James Madison and Robert Yates reveal that Hamilton favored a particularly kingly executive for the new government. Believing that the lack of executive force was a chief defect of the Articles of Confederation, he hoped the president's authority would be grand and imposing. Of course, this preference contrasted greatly with the subdued, limited executive office that resulted from the ratified Constitution.

In his tireless crusade to curtail the authority of the states and establish an imposing central government, Hamilton remarked in Philadelphia that the "national government ought to be able to support itself without the aid or interference of the state governments, and that therefore it was necessary to have full sovereignty." The powers of the states, he continued, were "dangerous to the national government, and ought to be extinguished, new modified, or reduced to a smaller scale."[405] Inclined to transform the states into the subordinate political unions of the central state, Hamilton's plan for government was remarkably unpopular in Philadelphia, and virtually ignored.

While admitting his ideas for government had been discarded, Hamilton supported the new Constitution under the belief that is was superior to the Articles of Confederation. As he did so, he admitted the model preserved the sovereignty of the American states. After declaring to the New York ratification convention that the states held supreme power over the federal government in their own sphere of authority, he reiterated the same position in *The Federalist* No. 81:

It is inherent in the nature of sovereignty not to be amenable to the suit of an individual without its consent. This is the general sense and general practice of mankind; and the exemption, as one of the attributes of sovereignty, is now enjoyed by the government of every State in the Union.[406]

In another essay, Hamilton wrote that "the States will retain all pre-existing authorities which may not be exclusively delegated to the federal head."[407] When explaining the framework to the states, then, Hamilton assured skeptics that the Constitution represented a federal model.

Shortly after ratification was secured, Hamilton quickly changed his tune. Rather than a meager list of enumerated power, Hamilton now alleged that Congress possessed the same type of general legislative authority that the Philadelphia Convention rejected. By extension of such authority, the United States could proactively guide the economic affairs of the union as a whole from the central government. Only by the sanction of Congress, a robust enforcement mechanism, and his new theory of constitutional interpretation, could his economic plans come to fruition.

Some modern scholars have cited Hamilton as a preeminent example of an early American capitalist. For instance, renowned historian Sean Wilentz has classified the New Yorker as "the visionary architect of the modern liberal capitalist economy."[408] On the contrary, a huge proponent of mercantilism, the 18th century anthesis of capitalism. Mercantile economic theory called for protectionist policies such as tariffs and trade privileges to restrict trade, a monopoly on banking, and government subsidies. Capitalism, on the hand, called for a series of voluntary exchanges by willing participants, the lack of impediments to trade such as taxes, and an emphasis on private property. Always finding favor with the former over the latter, Hamilton repeatedly criticized the disposition of his capitalist contemporary, Adam Smith, whose book *The Wealth of Nations* shaped the capitalist vision.

In his 1791 *Report on the Subject of Manufactures*, Hamilton described his economic objectives:

> To cherish and stimulate the activity of the human mind, by multiplying the objects of enterprise, is not among the least considerable of the expedients, by which the wealth of a nation may be promoted. Even things in themselves not positively advantageous, sometimes become so, by their tendency to provoke exertion. Every new scene, which is opened to the busy nature of man to rouse and exert itself, is the addition of a new energy to the general stock of effort. The spirit of enterprise, useful and prolific as it is, must necessarily be contracted or expanded in proportion to the simplicity or variety of the occupations and productions, which are to be found in a Society.[409]

Under his approach, government should pass legislation to promote the "wealth of a nation." In contrast to capitalist economic theory, Hamilton suggested that individuals would not be spurred to productive action unless they were encouraged to do so by government. The "general stock of effort," he wrote, must be continually widened or lessened by a central authority to protect industry and establish economic stability.

As part of his economic model, Hamilton proposed a system of government-issued "bounties" – or trade privileges to prop up domestic industry. In contradiction to this affinity, many ratifying states had rejected such a power and even recommended constitutional amendments to prohibit such behavior. For instance, Massachusetts, New Hampshire, and Rhode Island each drafted an amendment to ensure that Congress "erect no Company of Merchants with exclusive advantages of commerce." In addition, Hamilton's home state of New York went so far as to advise that "Congress do not impose any Excise on any Article (except Ardent Spirits) of the Growth, Production, or Manufacture of the United States."[410] Regardless of the explicit economic interests of the states, Hamilton sought his own course.

In alignment with mercantilist partialities, Hamilton expounded upon his theory of economic nationalism and professed a suspicion of free trade:

> For the purpose of this vent, a domestic market is greatly to be preferred to a foreign one; because it is in the nature of things, far more to be relied upon. It is a primary object of the policy of nations, to be able to supply themselves with subsistence from their own soils; and manufacturing nations, as far as circumstances permit, endeavor to procure, from the same source, the raw materials necessary for their own fabrics.[411]

By arguing that domestic goods are invariably superior to foreign goods, Hamilton neglected that foreign goods – procured through free trade – are often more desirable to consumers because of their lower cost or higher quality. Despite Hamilton's viewpoint that government spurred economic transaction, one of the true objectives of the new Constitution was to dismantle the network of trade barriers that developed between states during the 1780s.

In terms of his economic aspirations, Hamilton wrote that "there is no other expedient, than to promote manufacturing establishments." The treasury secretary claimed that American markets should be "calculated not only to increase the general stock of useful and productive labour; but even to improve the state of Agriculture in particular." Desiring for Congress "to advance the interests of those who are engaged in it," Hamilton assumed that the general government had the primary role in the growth of domestic manufacturing.[412] While Hamilton believed market promotion could only be achieved through increased government intervention, real markets are only promoted free exchanges without protective obstacles. Beyond this, the Constitution gave Congress no such authority to subsidize domestic industry.

Advancing penchant for economic protectionism, Hamilton specifically attacked the prospect of widespread free trade with other nations:

> A constant and increasing necessity, on their part, for the commodities of Europe, and only a partial and occasional demand for their own, in return, could not but expose them to a state of impoverishment, compared with the opulence to which their political and natural advantages authorize them to aspire.[413]

Hamilton assumed that a consumer desire to procure cheaper goods from Europe would induce invariable "impoverishment," despite the obvious benefits of foreign goods. Even if the cost of domestic goods were higher or their substance was inferior, Hamilton thought consumers should be encouraged to buy such products because of his penchant for economic nationalism. Of course, like all trade, foreign commerce would never take place at all if it were not beneficial to both the seller and the consumer, or if it impoverished either party.

To prop up domestic industry, Hamilton proclaimed his support for "bounties" – an 18th century term for corporate welfare:

> Bounties are in various instances proposed as one species of encouragement. It is a familiar objection to them, that they are difficult to be managed and liable to frauds. But neither that difficulty nor this danger seems sufficiently great to countervail the advantages of which they are productive, when rightly applied. And it is presumed to have been shewn, that they are in some cases, particular in the infancy of new enterprise indispensible.[414]

To determine the particulars of the bounties and the industries to which they should be applied, Hamilton insisted on the creation of government boards of arts, agriculture, manufacturing, and commerce. Under his plan, Congress would then "constitute a fund for paying the bounties which shall have been decreed." Once the fund was established, the commissioners of each department would arbitrarily "apply the fund confided to them" industries within the sphere of their control.[415] By granting broad power to apply the bounties, Hamilton's plan would make the new bureaucrats unelected overseers of the domestic economy. After a flurry of criticism, the First Congress rejected the treasury secretary's bounty program in 1791.

Beyond the constitutional hurdles that impeded his economic agenda, Hamilton never understood the truism that politicians and civil officials are not as shrewd as the markets. As such, they cannot adequately predict market demand, anticipate shortages, or objectively choose recipients of subsidies. Their judgments, however well informed, cannot replace market circumstances that emerge from a series of free exchanges. Hamilton's bounty system, then, gave central economic planners enormous power of the domestic economy.

In contrast to Hamilton, Thomas Jefferson was adamantly opposed to legal monopolies and a strong supporter of free trade. Jefferson condemned King George III for cutting off colonial trade "with all parts of the world," and championed "freedom of commerce against monopolies."[416] To coincide with the secretary of state's outlook, Adam Smith formative economic treatise noted a country's economic system was able to regulate itself, so long as individuals were left with substantial freedom to conduct exchanges. In such a way, rational self-interest established prosperity through voluntary cooperation. In this way, Smith's advocacy of capitalism and free trade was the system that Jefferson and his followers embraced, not Hamilton's.[417]

The failure of Hamilton's bounty program did not deter him from pushing forward with his quest to transform the United States into a bastion of mercantilism. The most conspicuous way he sought to do this was through the establishment of his British-oriented national bank. The Bank of England, which Hamilton's model would be based upon, encouraged avarice, greed, and self-interest. Bankers with the support of government on their side stood to profit greatly from interest on bonds, and those that saved money stood to lose purchasing power through the central manipulation of the interest rates. Under the modern system of centralized banking, we often find the same pervasive woes, and the contemporary Federal Reserve has become the institutional offspring of Hamilton's national bank.[418]

Even before Hamilton's campaign for a bank, the power to create such an establishment was rejected by the states. The ability to create a national bank was not listed among the federal government's enumerated powers, and several states adopted resolutions in their ratification ordinances indicating that Congress could not grant monopolies or erect any company with exclusive advantages over commerce. Despite the lack of constitutional authority, Hamilton ignored these inconveniences.

Hamilton's plans for a bank were largely influenced by Robert Morris, a Pennsylvanian financier who helped establish an institutional predecessor, the Bank of North America. During the 1780s, the issuance of paper money known as "Continentals" depreciated in value so badly that they were all but worthless by 1781. Responding to this crisis, Congress granted a monopoly to the new bank that allowed its notes to be receivable as tax payments to the states and Congress. Since the bank agreed to lend most of its new money to the Confederation, all taxpayers would be forced to pay the principal and interest. While the inflated currency caused economic ruin, Morris provided cheap credit to his political allies. The bank's currency severely depreciated in value by 1783, and the bank was privatized.[419]

Hamilton pitched his bank to the First Congress, which contained many Federalists that shared the New Yorker's proclivity for British banking. Even though an adversarial coalition – led by James Madison – fiercely challenged the utility and constitutionality of such an effort, the bank bill was passed by Congress in 1791. At this point, however, the bank had not cleared its final impasse, as President George Washington wavered on signing the bill. When the esteemed Virginian asked Hamilton to prepare an argument regarding the constitutionality of a national bank, the treasury secretary produced a lengthy report to convey his position. The new champion of American mercantilism defended the constitutionality of his proposed national bank in ways which would confound even the most impartial observers of the ratification campaign. In a stunning reversal from his documented positions in *The Federalist* and New York's ratification convention, Hamilton argued that the presence of "implied powers" within the Constitution allowed for the creation of an institution.

Through the Necessary and Proper Clause, Hamilton alleged, the Constitution permitted "implied, as well as express powers" and therefore "the former are effectually delegated as the latter." This meant, in contradiction to his earlier musings, that there were certain unspecified powers that the general government can make use of, even if they were not enumerated in the Constitution. Despite the antithetical nature of this conclusion in comparison to the ratified understanding, he proceeded to claim that these "implied" powers could be used as "an instrument or means of carrying into the execution any of the specified powers."[420]

In contrast to Hamilton's new position, the Necessary and Proper Clause was widely understood as a provision that allowed incidental actions to be taken in order to bring about the specific "foregoing" powers listed in the document. Regardless, Hamilton's new view purported that "the word necessary in the general clause can have no restrictive operation." In other words, Hamilton admitted that the power to charter corporations was not explicitly listed in the Constitution, but implied that Congress could do so in order to properly bring about other powers that were spelled out. As an extension of this reasoning, he averred, Congress could license a bank despite the lack of written affirmation of such an authority. Refuting his own words during the ratification struggle, Hamilton claimed that "the principle in question does not extend the power of the government beyond the prescribed limits, because it only affirms a power to incorporate for purposes within the sphere of the specified powers."[421]

While he produced a list of purposes that a bank could fulfill, all of such functions could be achieved in the absence of such a national bank. For example, Hamilton argued that foreign commerce could not be regulated without the existence of a national bank, even though Congress was empowered to do such a thing independently. Before the United States reestablished trade relations with Great Britain through the 1794 Jay Treaty, trade with the country was regulated to an extreme degree. Additionally, the Tariff Act of 1789 instituted supplementary means of regulating foreign trade by placing taxes on foreign goods. The law had been in effect for over a year before Hamilton wrote his opinion on the national bank, and the treasury secretary himself had been instrumental in crafting the policy.

Hamilton also attempted to justify the creation of a national bank on the basis the precedent of similar banks that existed in other parts of the world:

> They possess a general authority to regulate trade with foreign countries. This is a mean which has been practiced to that end by all the principal commercial nations; who have trading companies to this day which have subsisted for centuries. Why may not the United States constitutionally employ the means usual in other countries for attaining the ends entrusted to them?[422]

The mere existence of such a bank in other parts of the world, then, was a strong enough reason to consider it in the United States. Ironically, Hamilton's inquiry here was answered by himself and other supporters of the Constitution during the ratification campaign. Because the United States adopted a constitutional framework that confines the general government to a specific array of powers, Congress could not implement a bank.

In their own written opinions, both Secretary of State Thomas Jefferson and Attorney General Edmund Randolph denied that the establishment of the bank was constitutional. In response to Washington's inquiry, Jefferson contended that the power to charter a bank was nowhere to be found in the Constitution, that the document was widely promoted as one that would confer only the powers expressly delegated, that the bank was unnecessary, and that its existence would allow for too much central control over the economy. The "foundation" of the Constitution, wrote Jefferson, was rooted in the Tenth Amendment, which plainly admitted that all powers not delegated to the general government, nor prohibited to it, were reserved for the states or to the people. Departing from this aphorism, Jefferson wrote, was "to take possession of a boundless field of power, no longer susceptible of any definition."[423]

Ultimately, Washington sided with Hamilton and signed the bank bill, and the First National Bank was established. This precedent, as well as those set by the subsequent national banks in American history, have adversely affected the citizenry in several significant ways. Through the excessive printing of federal currency, the centralized authority enacts un-legislated taxes on individual wealth holdings. In addition, contemporary monetary woes are largely the result of Hamilton's creation. When the monetary supply is expanded by central banks, especially at an extraordi-nary rate, price inflation is the inevitable result. With national banks con-trolled by panels of unelected officials, individuals have little political re-course and few means to protect their wealth.

As another pillar of his economic vision, Hamilton argued that the gen-eral government should assume all of the outstanding debts of the states. Accruing during the course of the War of Independence, such fiscal obli-gations contributed greatly to the financial turmoil of the 1780s. The cre-ation of a national debt, Hamilton believed, would make the state entities subordinate to the central authority, provide the United States economic standing in the rest of the world, and allow the general government to exert more control over economic policy. Controversy followed Hamilton's idea, as many of the states, including Virginia, had already paid back much of its wartime debt. Consequently, several representatives argued that it would be immoral to tax such states pay back the debts of others.

As part of his objective, Hamilton recommended paying the remaining wartime debt from the Confederation government by issuing new securi-ties that could be purchased by investors. Aided by the existence of the new national bank, the scheme led to financial malfeasance. The institu-tion's financial overseers stood to profit enormously by both the resulting debt and through the possession of war bonds, which greatly depreciated during the time of the War of Independence. Hamilton's management of the treasury subjected him to personal accusations of financial corruption and misappropriation.[424]

In the end, a compromise was eventually struck between supporters of Hamilton's vision for state debt assumption, and those who sided with Jef-ferson. Congress would pass a bill to homogenize the state debts into a single national debt, and in return, Federalists agreed to move the federal capitol from Philadelphia to Washington, D.C. after a period of 10 years. In regret, Jefferson admitted years later that "of all the errors of my polit-ical life, this has occasioned me the deepest regret." Having taken part in a great political miscalculation, Jefferson wrote that Hamilton's system "flowed from principles adverse to liberty, and was calculated to undermine and demolish the republic." Perpetual debt was the tragic result of the arrangement, he lamented. Virginia's General Assembly also fiercely condemned the debt assumption plan as an unconstitutional encroachment upon state authority.[425]

In 1791, Hamilton also called for the creation of an excise tax on distilled spirits. "The whiskey tax," as it was soon called, made these beverages the first profitable goods to be taxed by the federal government. The treasury secretary came to believe that the new tax would prove largely uncontroversial, as it applied only to non-essential merchandise. However, because whiskey was the most popular distilled spirit in the country, and many entrepreneurs ventured westward to start whiskey enterprises, the policy soon provoked immense anger and oppositional to the new government.

As income taxes on certain classes of revenue, excise taxes disproportionately affect those who profit from sale or consumption of the product they apply to. Complaining that the policy would hinder their entrepreneurial pursuits and create widespread insolvency, the distillers portrayed their industry as one that could not possibly endure in light of the tax. In addition, because whiskey served as currency on the frontier due to the scarcity of hard money, the tax acted indirectly to penalize those that were not distillers.

Among those protesting the tax were settlers that had taken significant personal risks and endured substantial economic hardships to engage in whiskey enterprises. As the new government made clear its intention to enforce the tax, pockets of resistance developed on the frontier, and unrest grew to a breaking point. Rather than rural Pennsylvania alone, the core of opposition encompassed most of the western frontier.[426] After being sent to enforce the policy, tax inspector John Neville's home was attacked by 500 armed men. The failure of Washington's attempts at mediation proved frivolous, and many predicted the government would soon send in military forces to produce imminent bloodshed.

Jefferson and Randolph understood the public outcry and called for reconciliation with the distillers, while Hamilton proposed the imposition of military force to administer the excise. When Washington at first resisted Hamilton's recommendation, the treasury secretary began publishing essays under the pseudonym of "Tully" that called for a swift military conclusion. "If you presume to dispute the point by force," Hamilton wrote, "we are ready to measure swords with you." The potential for bloodshed, he continued, was "incomparably a less evil than the destruction of government." While Hamilton sought to define the rebellion as a small movement of ruffians with revolutionary aims, this was not the case. Resistance toward the tax was widespread, and the adversaries of the tax sought not to overthrow the general government.[427]

After first responding cautiously, Washington eventually decided to summon the militia of the several states to suppress the Whiskey Rebellion in 1794. While many arrests were made, hostilities subsided in large part after the commissioners made assurances that the tax would eventually be repealed.[428] Despite the ultimate response of the Washington administration, the general government found the policy to be incredibly challenging to enforce. Resistance against the policy continued in the frontiers, and the Republican Congress eventually repealed the whiskey tax in 1801. Believing that the law violated his free trade conscious and merely encouraged resentment toward the general government, Jefferson wholeheartedly supported the repeal.

Though his economic plans were highly controversial, some historians have claimed that Hamilton's reputation has suffered mostly because of several personal shortcomings. While it is true that Hamilton was involved himself in some personal mischief that would be considered condemnable even among his political allies – such as an adulterous liaison and political feuds that became personal – this is hardly the reason he is attacked by those who appreciate the Constitution's original intent. Truthfully, it was his historical dedication to mercantilism and his promotion to the implied powers doctrine that made Hamilton an objectionable figure. More than any other figure, his actions made him be the clear foe of the Constitution's originally ratified intent.

Once Hamilton was thrust into the limelight of power, he overstepped his authority to the detriment of America's constitutional system. By siding with his own proclivities over the intention of the sovereign states, he bypassed the overt restraints of the Constitution – many of which were designed specifically to constrain the very tendencies he favored. In so doing, Hamilton successfully convinced the most trusted man in the states that the Constitution did exactly what he and the other advocates of the document said it didn't. Tragically, Washington sided with his treasury secretary over Jefferson on almost every matter of substance.

Arguing that Hamilton's political victories created a disaster for the early republic, historian Thomas DiLorenzo wrote that "the political legacy of Alexander Hamilton reads like a catalog of the ills of modern government." Scholar Warren McFerran concurred with this outlook, adding that Hamilton worked to "convert the republic into a plutocracy in which the affairs of government would be conducted for the primary benefit of an aristocracy of wealth." Even to this day, the precedents Hamilton left are routinely cited by politicians aspiring to back their own unconstitutional schemes. "Because Hamilton won," DiLorenzo wrote, "the American people have lost."[429]

Though Hamilton resigned from the treasury in 1795 and lost political power on the federal stage, his nationalist machinations were quickly adopted by John Marshall. A prominent figure from Virginia that would soon become the Chief Justice of the United States Supreme Court, Marshall used his judicial authority to usurp the reserved powers of the states and transform the Constitution into a model that reflected Hamilton's outlook. In the early 19th century, Marshall's Supreme Court became the ultimate embodiment of what many of the Constitution's opponents feared most – a judiciary that overstepped its inherent authority and meddled unnecessarily in state law. Through sweeping court decisions, the Marshall Court made the federal court system into an anti-federal oligarchy that sided with federal expansion on almost every matter.

After John Jay had first declined the appointment, Marshall was elevated to his position of judicial prominence at the end of John Adams' presidency. Shortly thereafter, the Federalist Congress passed the Judiciary Act of 1801, a controversial law that radically transformed the federal court system through the creation of new courts and judges. The "Midnight Judges Act," as its opponents branded it, imposed upon the president an obligation to sign commissioners and have them delivered to his new judicial appointments in the last days of his presidency. By such a strategy, the president was able to methodically extend the power of the Federalists by shifting the party's presence from the legislative and executive branches to the judiciary. In the wake of Thomas Jefferson's political victory in the "Revolution of 1800," Adams' critics of the act reasoned that the policy was merely a cunning method to override the electoral will of the people.

One the president's commissions drafted for William Marbury, an avowed Federalist who Adams wished to make Justice of the Peace for the District of Columbia. The Senate confirmed the appointment of Marbury and many of the other judges, but Secretary of State John Marshall failed to deliver the commission to its intended recipient. When Jefferson assumed the presidency, he instructed new Secretary of State James Madison not to provide the undelivered commissions to the remaining "midnight judges." Indeed, the Constitution did not require the president to grant commissions to the previous administration's judicial appointees. On the contrary, Jefferson viewed the elections of 1800 as a referendum on the merits of Federalist rule. When his Republican Party secured the presidency and a majority in Congress, he understood the result of the elections as a denunciation of the Federalist order.

In response to the administrative inaction, Marbury brought forth a suit against Madison. The native of Maryland claimed that he was entitled to the commission and the position it granted, and hoped that judicial arbitration would force the Jefferson administration to honor the appointment. Per Marbury's suit, the federal courts should issue a writ of mandamus – a legal order to force Madison to comply with the delivery of the commission.

In the famous 1803 case of *Marbury v. Madison*, Marshall reprimanded the stance of the Jefferson administration and insisted that Marbury was indeed entitled to his commission. Withholding the commission, in his view, was "an act deemed by the Court not warranted by law, but violative of a vested legal right." Continuing his tirade, the chief justice likened the actions of Jefferson and Madison to that of a "mere political act."[430] Even though Jefferson acted in accordance with his own constitutional views concerning a function confined to his own branch of government, it did not stop Marshall from interjecting his own personal opinions on the matter. However, the high court stopped short of obliging Madison to deliver the commission, and Marbury never became a federal judge.

Through the pivotal opinion, Marshall determined that part of the Judiciary Act of 1789 – which set the baseline for the entire federal court system – was unconstitutional. For the first time, a federal court overturned a statute for its unconstitutionality. Marshall justified the court's behavior so:

> It is empathically the province and duty of the Judicial Department to say what the law is. Those who apply the rule to particular cases must, of necessity, expound and interpret that rule. If two laws conflict with each other, the Courts must decide on the operation of each.[431]

In deciding that part of the 1789 law contravened the Constitution, the court opined that Congress had expanded the court's authority beyond its constitutional limits by granting the Supreme Court original jurisdiction over mandamus suits. In doing so, Marbury lost his legal ability to bring forth the suit because it invalidated the chief premise upon which his case was built.

Several controversies erupted in the opinion's immediate aftermath. First, Marshall's condemnation of the Jefferson administration seemed to many an odious deflection of accountability. This was because, as Adam's secretary of state, Marshall was responsible for delivering the commission to Marbury. While Marshall lectured Jefferson and Madison for withholding the document, his own negligence arguably ignited the dispute in the first place. Because this meant a conflict of interest, some alleged, Marshall should have recused himself from the case.

In addition, some argued that Marshall ventured beyond his constitutional duties to adjudicate the case in the first place. According to this train of logic, the court's judgment that Marbury lacked standing in the court meant that the case should have been dismissed. Instead, Marshall produced a long, written opinion that considered issues far beyond the context of the case. To Republican adversaries of the partisan judge, Marshall deliberately exceeded his authority to chastise the Jefferson administration for political purposes. This arrogant propensity, thought Jefferson, undermined the checks and balances of the Constitution by allowing the judiciary to prescribe rules to the other branches of government.

With the passage of time, Marbury's commission became a relatively unimportant facet of the case. The Chief reason that *Marbury v. Madison* remains relevant is that the opinion set a precedent for the mythical doctrine of judicial supremacy. Without Marshall, the court's authority may never have been asserted so directly over the other branches, and the actors in the legislative and executive branch may have been more painstaking in their efforts to adopt their own constitutional narratives. As the next years proved, Marshall would only build on the power he carved out for the Supreme Court.

Before *Marbury v. Madison*, judicial review had only been exercised a handful of times in the history of the world. However, the power was not completely alien to the founding generation, as several states used the power in their own state courts prior to the Constitution's ratification.[432] Moreover, in the 1796 case of *Hylton v. United States*, it was widely acknowledged that the Supreme Court practiced judicial review merely by considering the constitutionality of the carriage tax, even though it declined to void the law in question.

During the ratification struggle, prominent figures championed judicial review as an essential mechanism to inhibit the legislature's ability to pass despotic laws. However, this opinion presumed that the judiciary would act independently from the other branches, and that the judges would avoid the allure of partisan politics. With the power to strike down egregious laws, skeptics of central power argued that judges could protect the Constitution from governmental infringement.

Another class of founders thought more cynically that the power of judicial review would tempt the judges to interject their own opinions into cases by negating laws they personally disliked. Those in this camp believed that laws should be cautiously made in the interests of the Constitution, and then left alone once passed. This group included figures such as John Mercer, John Dickinson, and William Richardson Davie.[433] Despite the debate on the advantage of judicial review, records from the ratification debates assure us that promoters of the Constitution intended the judiciary to possess such a power, and even promoted its usage. At Pennsylvania's ratification convention, for instance, James Wilson promised that federal judges would declare such unconstitutional acts "null and void."[434]

Despite the inclusion of judicial review in the constitutional framework, none of the document's proponents alleged that the federal courts would possess a monopoly on binding the other branches to its own constitutional perspectives. With the revelation that his own understanding of the Constitution differed so drastically from his peers in the federal courts, Jefferson explained that each branch held impetus to make their own constitutional judgments:

> Whether the judges are invested with exclusive authority to decide on the constitutionality of law has been heretofore a subject of consideration with me in the exercise of official duties. Certainly there is not a word in the constitution which has given that power to them more than to the executive or legislative branches.[435]

Undoubtedly, the Constitution directs the federal courts to uphold constitutional acts as the supreme law of the land under the presumption that the law is "made in Pursuance" to the bounds of the framework.[436] Nonetheless, as Jefferson pointed out, the document did not give the federal judiciary a monopoly on interpreting the constitutionality of laws. Indeed, the president would have to wield such a power to veto a bill, and representatives to vote against such a bill for its unconstitutionality.

Marshall's judicial philosophy continued to shape the early direction of the federal courts. In 1810, the case of *Fletcher v. Peck* came to the federal courts as a result of the Yazoo Land Scandal of 1794-1795, where Georgian legislators were bribed to sell huge plots of land at very low rates. When the corruption was discovered, the land grants were repealed by the Georgia legislature and the implicated legislators were ousted in the next state election cycle. This reversal was accomplished under a candid effort to restore public faith in the state government, and in accordance with Georgian law. Nevertheless, Marshall's opinion held that Georgia was forced to abide by the original fraudulent sale, despite the dishonesty involved in such a nefarious transaction.

The Marshall Court argued that the Contract Clause made the original sale, coated in bribery and corruption, a "mutually binding contract." The chief justice remained unwavering in his decision, despite the universally held legal notion that fraud negates contracts. This concept was acknowledged in the 1787 Northwest Ordinance, a legal precursor:

> In the just preservation of rights and property, it is understood, and declared, that no law ought ever to be made or have force in said territory,

that shall, in any manner whatever, interfere with or affect private contracts, or engagements, bona fide, and without fraud previously
formed.[437]

Under widely accepted federal precedent, the obligation of contracts was
only deemed relevant if the contracts in quest were absent of fraud. By
extension of this principle, a fraudulent contract was no contract at all. In
addition, Georgia had its own contract laws and stood perfectly capable of
settling this matter on its own, having handled all contract disputes prior
to the intervention of the federal courts. As in *Marbury v. Madison*, Marshall's impartiality also came into question in this case. This was because
the chief justice and his brother were substantial investors in unsettled
lands. As a result, many believed him to been predisposed to decide in the
favor of those who purchased land from the state.[438]

Regardless of Georgia's attempt to set things right, Marshall denied
that the state had such authority:

As to the idea that the grants of a legislature may be void because the
legislature are corrupt, it appears to me to be subject to insuperable difficulties. The acts of the supreme power of a country must be considered pure for the same reason that all sovereign acts must be considered
just – because there is no power that can declare them otherwise. The
absurdity in this case would have been strikingly perceived could the
party who passed the act of cession have got again into power and declared themselves pure and the intermediate legislature corrupt.[439]

According to the Virginian nationalist, the Supreme Court could force
states to uphold corrupt bargains, even if they were wholly devoid of good
faith. In concurrence, Judge William Johnson wrote that "a State does not
possess the power of revoking its own grants."[440] When corrupt state legislators engaged in perfidious acts, then, the citizens of the states were
obliged to endure the consequences. In the Marshall Court's estimation,
the people of Georgia was forced to accept the will of its corrupt former
representatives, even after the corruption was discovered, after the deals
were overturned by the state, and after the duplicitous legislators were
voted out of office.

According to Marshall, the original sale was a binding contract between parties whether or not the legislature making the sale was corrupted by bribery. "When a law is in the nature of a contract," Marshall wrote, "a repeal of that law cannot devest those rights." If a state endeavored to "pronounce its own deed invalid" in order to subvert corruption, it would violate the "absolute rights" of the parties agreeing to the contract. "A law annulling conveyances," he concluded, "is unconstitutional because it is a law impairing the obligation of contracts within the meaning of the Constitution of the United States."[441] According to Marshall, the reversal of the land sales meant that Georgia had violated the Contract Clause.[442]

If Marshall's supposition is to be honored, it is necessary to believe that corruption is not only a routine part of government, but one that is sanctioned by the federal courts. In his estimation, the government of Georgia could not adequately determine whether the original grant or the repeal were consistent with Georgian law. Marshall argued instead that the federal courts should intercede and hold authority over the state governments, extending judicial power above constitutional limitations. Namely, the same thing the patriots accused the British government of doing in the run-up to the War of Independence.

In this decision, Marshall showed astounding ignorance toward the history of the American union by likening the states to the mere municipalities of a larger nation:

> The validity of this rescinding act, then, might well be doubted, were Georgia a single sovereign power. But Georgia cannot be viewed as a single, unconnected, sovereign power, on whose legislature no other restrictions are imposed than may be found in its own Constitution. She is a part of a large empire; she is a member of the American Union; and that Union has a Constitution the supremacy of which all acknowledge, and which imposes limits to the legislatures of the several States which none claim a right to pass.[443]

According to Marshall, Georgia relinquished its sovereignty upon assent to the Constitution, and willingly entered into a "large empire." This allegation, of course, betrayed the common assurance by the document's supporters that ratification preserved the inherent sovereignty of each of the states.

For its far-reaching ramifications, *Fletcher v. Peck* was one of the most abominable federal court opinions in United States history. By overruling a state law for the first time, the Marshall Court transformed the federal judiciary into a meddlesome council that sought to police the internal affairs of the states. While judicial review was promoted as a tool to curtail the power of the general government, it had now been used to pervert local governance and amplify the authority of the federal judiciary. Surely, the Supreme Court's opinion in *Fletcher v. Peck* confirmed the suspicions of those who predicted the federal courts would inevitably encroach upon the reserved powers of the states.

The 1810 opinion also seemed to negate one of the most striking results of the Philadelphia Convention. It was there, after all, that delegates refused to adopt James Madison's proposal to give the general government a veto power over state law. By striking down Georgia's reversal of the land grants, the federal courts had done exactly that. Furthermore, during the ratification struggle, many Federalists assured opponents of the Constitution that the state courts would retain full prerogative to adjudicate matters of state law. Such a scenario even transpired in Marshall's state of Virginia, where the young lawyer insisted the same to an incredulous George Mason. After complaining that the Constitution would necessarily lead to the federal courts overwhelming the state counterparts, Marshall responded that such misgivings were completely without merit, and went so far as to mock the elder statesman.[444] After bearing witness to the enemies of the Constitution, Marshall reneged on his word after ascending to the high court.

The same penchant for nationalism followed Marshall to the 1819 case of *McCulloch v. Maryland*, which relegated the states to an even more denigrated position. The dispute began when the state of Maryland levied a tax upon out of bank notes that originated out-of-state, a deliberate attempt to impede the operations of the Second Bank of the United States. In 1818, Maryland's legislature made the proper constitutional argument that the general government assumed powers well beyond its enumerated scope to establish such a bank. By extension, the state alleged that such infringements could be impeded – as Federalists contended during the ratification debates – by state-based remedies. In its strategy of opposition to the bank, Maryland rightly maintained that the states had not delegated the power to create such an institution to the general government.

Notwithstanding Maryland's effort to preserve the ratified understanding of the Constitution, the Marshall Court opined that "there is nothing in the Constitution of the United States similar to the Articles of Confederation, which exclude incidental or implied powers."[445] Paradoxically, this declaration came just years after supporters of the Constitution vehemently asserted that the document provided no powers to Congress except those expressly listed. Marshall's opinion blatantly ignored the Tenth Amendment, which Jefferson considered the bedrock of the federal constitution. The chief justice's constitutional narrative, as incongruent as it was, prolonged Alexander Hamilton's theory of implied powers in a new era.

Marshall's contention that Maryland lacked the authority to tax federal notes was especially ironic in that because Luther Martin argued on behalf of the state's case. Martin, one of the most talented lawyers of his time, had been at the Philadelphia Convention as a delegate of Maryland, while Marshall was not in attendance at all. While Martin insisted rightly that the Constitution had been created by the states, Marshall wrote that it "would be difficult to sustain" such a proposition, and claimed that the Constitution had been established by one homogenous group of people.[446] Though the Federalists had long lost Congress and the presidency – never again to return to political prominence – Marshall insisted on using the federal bench to preserve the party's brand of nationalism.

Alarmingly, the Supreme Court opinion in *McCulloch v. Maryland* also purported that it was lawful for the general government to establish a corporation. In so doing, the judiciary sided with Hamilton's reprehensible interpretation of the Necessary and Proper Clause, which postulated that the federal government could assume a variety of powers that were not enumerated – including the ability to charter a national bank. In repudiation of the Constitution's original intent, the high court also held that the word "necessary" in the clause did not mean "absolutely necessary." In Marshall's estimation, the provision lacked any limiting function.

Having opposed the constitutional legitimacy of national banks since his disputes with Hamilton in 1791, Thomas Jefferson found the decision incredibly disturbing. The Virginia statesmen wrote that the Marshall Court had evolved into a "reprobated system" that had been driving the states into consolidation "on every occasion." Jefferson warned that under the Marshall Court, the Constitution had become a "mere thing of wax in the hands of the judiciary, which they may twist, and shape into any form they please."[447]

Before the Marshall Court, the states successfully curtailed the power of the federal judiciary after an early attempt to expand the court's authority. In the famous 1793 case of *Chisholm v. Georgia*, the court arbitrated a dispute over payments owed by Georgia for supplies that were loaned to the state during the War of Independence. Nevertheless, Georgia did not appear in federal court, and argued that as a state with sovereign immunity, its consent was necessary for the matter to be taken up by the Supreme Court. In a 4-1 opinion, the court determined that sovereign power was not retained by states, and a decision was made in favor of the plaintiff. The lone dissenter, Justice James Iredell, objected to the decision because the Constitution did not grant federal courts the power to hear the case without Georgia's consent.

Almost immediately after this outcome, the states came to believe that the Jay Court had assumed too much power for the federal judiciary. Congress responded by crafting a proposed 11th Amendment, which clarified that states hold sovereign immunity against suits made by citizens of other states in federal court. Though Jay maintained control over the court, fellow Federalist Caleb Strong of Massachusetts drafted the amendment, further illustrating the popularity of this addendum. The states quickly ratified the amendment, directly overriding the court's decision. While the maxim of sovereign immunity was implicit prior to the constitutional amendment, the verbiage reiterated the principle.[448] With broad support from Federalists as well as their ideological adversaries, the bipartisan nature of the amendment's acceptance was noteworthy. The episode also proved that prior to Marshall, the Supreme Court's expansionary tendencies were once effectively held in check by the states.

In the contemporary, it is much more likely for the federal courts to find state laws unconstitutional compared to their federal counterparts. By comparison, federal laws are almost never invalidated, a phenomenon which allows both branches to grow in power. After the case of *Marbury v. Madison*, the Supreme Court did not overturn another federal law until the 1857 case of *Dred Scott v. Sandford*, a period of over 50 years. Apparently, the court's position during this timeframe was that every law passed by the federal government was fully constitutional.

The loss of local autonomy and the development of nationalist-oriented governments has been a worldwide phenomenon, a trend that can be observed in all corners of the world. Despite obvious evidence to the contrary, this transition is often considered and promoted as a beneficial societal trend. Additionally, some of the most infamous tyrants in the world have encouraged such a consolidation of power, and in turn viewed federal systems as barriers to their autocratic inclinations.

Even Adolf Hitler recognized this in *Mein Kampf*. In a chapter called "Federalism as a Mask," the infamous leader of the Third Reich described his utter indignation toward federalism. According to Hitler, it would be "impossible to preach a federalistic form for the Reich, at the same time depreciating, reviling, and befouling the most essential section of such a state structure." He stressed that Germany "cannot grant to any individual state within the nation and the state representing it state sovereignty and sovereignty in point of political power."[449] It remains quite obvious that Hitler regarded a federated league of nations as an impediment to his ability to amass power.

Hitler also argued that the political structure of Germany was much unlike the United States. "The great difference between the German states, from a purely territorial standpoint," he explained, "permits no comparison with the formation of the American Union."[450] Indeed, it was easier for foreign observers to realize the uniqueness present in the decentralized American republic because of its sharp contrast with rest of the world. Certainly, such a framework made it more difficult for those wishing to nationalize political authority under a single umbrella.

The same trend toward nationalism emerged in modern Asia. The Kangxi Emperor, the longest reigning emperor in Chinese History, brutally suppressed several regional uprisings during the Qing Dynasty. It was during that time that Wu Sangui, a former Chinese military general, instigated a plot to establish decentralized rule in the country. After the Kangxi Emperor attempted to relocate Wu to Manchuria, the latter declared himself Emperor of the "Great Zhou Dynasty," hoping to dissolve ties with the Qing entirely. In response, an enraged Emperor Kangxi decided to strike militarily against Wu and his supporters. Despite the violent reprisal, several other provinces followed suit by attempting to sever relations with the Qing and establish their own sovereignties. When Wu died of disease, the separation effort failed, and the Kangxi Emperor had his corpse scattered across the provinces of China.[451]

Several centuries later, another attempt at establishing localized government in China failed. Hong Xiuquan established the Kingdom of Heavenly Peace in Nanjing, China in the mid-19th century, after attracting a mass group of followers. Hong experienced several revelations that led him to believe that he was the Chinese brother of Jesus Christ, and his epiphany sparked political aspirations. Hong formed his own kingdom in southeastern China, and liberalized society by banning the practice of footbinding and by repealing edicts that prevented certain classes from being educated. Viewing Hong's acts as a concerted rebellion, the Qing Dynasty set out to destroy his new government. The Taiping Rebellion, as it became to be called, was a conflict of enormous proportions. By the rampant spread of disease and immense bloodshed, the catastrophe claimed the lives of approximately 20 million Chinese.[452] In its triumph over Hong's forces, the Qing Dynasty once again suppressed local autonomy in China by force.

A similar situation unfolded in 19th century Japan, when the provinces of Choshu and Satsuma attempted to secede from the Meiji government for fear that the country's modernization efforts would lead to the subjugation of the samurai class. The severance produced a conflict known as the Satsuma Rebellion ensued, and the samurai were overwhelmed by the central government's superior weaponry and training. As a result of the unsuccessful attempt to federalize Japan, the unruly provinces were forcibly occupied, the country abandoned its gold standard in an embrace of paper money, and the samurai class was systematically eradicated. Without the diffusion of political authority, the Meiji government established absolute rule over all of Japan.

While geographically and culturally dissimilar, these examples are certainly reminiscent of the natural inclination for central authorities to grow more and more powerful over time, especially when government restrictions are not valued or reasserted. In similar fashion, the American union has trended toward a centralized, consolidated state, where local acts of defiance have often been suppressed through the imposition of legal precedents and the exertion of military might. The main consequence of this, contrary to Jefferson's ideal, is that Americans now reside in a United States of Hamilton and Marshall's design.

Chapter 8

The "Sweeping Clauses" – What Do They Really Mean?

During the contentious ratification debates in the states, many objected to the Constitution on the basis that several clauses found within the document would provide the general government with boundless power. These provisions, cynics suggested, were but founts of despotism that would ensure the establishment of a general government with unlimited authority and supreme control over the states. Among the "sweeping clauses," as the eminent Patrick Henry called them, were the General Welfare Clause, the Commerce Clause, the Necessary and Proper Clause, and the Supremacy Clause. According to the ardent foes of the Constitution, the existence of these provisions would cause federal officials to read every possibly ambiguity into the Constitution's text to empower the government further.[453]

Nevertheless, the supporters of the Constitution told Henry and other disbelievers that their apprehensions were without merit. In Virginia, Edmund Randolph insisted that the general government only possessed the powers it was "expressly" delegated. To refute efforts "to pervert and destroy the new plan," James Wilson made the same arguments in his State House Yard Speech in Pennsylvania. Alexander Hamilton, John Jay, and James Madison repeated the same assurances in *The Federalist* and in their own respective ratification conventions. Taking the lead role in their own states, Charles Pinckney, James Iredell, and Rufus King also portrayed the Constitution as an instrument of limited powers.

While these matters were discussed during the ratification struggle, many of the broad, expansive definitions attributed to the controversial clauses did not surface until many years after the Constitution's inception. Most of these reinterpretations seem to have been formed to support the implementation of certain government policies, or to justify other government arrangements. Today, these clauses are used as rationalization to justify all sorts of deplorable policies, from government mandates to deprivation of due process. They have been reinterpreted by the courts and used by the legislature to justify the creation of law on any subject.

Part of this tendency has materialized through a complete misunderstanding of how the Constitution was to be understood. The writers of the Constitution specified powers under the notion that all powers unlisted could not be exercised by the general government. Despite this demonstrable truth, some suggest that the general government has the power to legislate on any matter as long as no textual prohibition exists. Under that scenario, the Constitution reads as superfluous and absurd. If a written constitution authorizes limitless power, there is no point in having a written constitution at all. If a constitution doesn't limit authority in some way, it has no purpose.

THE GENERAL WELFARE CLAUSE

In modern times, one source of modern federal overreach has been derived from the notion that the Constitution granted a vast array of authority not expressly listed. By extension, this theory purports that anything the federal government does to promote the "general welfare" of the people is constitutionally permissible. By the same line of reasoning, Congress has assumed the power to legislate on a host of matters that were intended to be confined to the states and localities.

Under the preamble of the Constitution, "We the People" intended the Constitution, among other aims, "to promote the general welfare." This verbiage is sometimes cited as evidence that the general government was founded with a general authority to provide such ends, no matter the means. Despite this, the presence of the text "general welfare," as it appears in the preamble of the document, does not delegate any authority to the government. Instead, it is a summative statement which explains the reasons for which the rest of the document was constructed.

According to James Madison, the "general terms used in the introductory propositions" of the preamble were intended to reflect the common interests of the states that formed the union. On the contrary of those alleging that the preamble granted an unrestricted ability to legislate, he insisted that the term was "never meant to be inserted" into "the text of the Constitution." To expound upon this, historian Brion McClanahan clarified that "a preamble is a declaration of intent." Its function, then, was merely to describe "the proposed document in broad strokes, but has no legal value and is not a declaration of rights or liberties."[454]

In addition to the reference in the preamble, the General Welfare Clause, as it appears in Article I, Section 8, is often perceived as a source of a boundless, unspecified reservoir of authority. In stark contrast to this propensity, Madison described the same provision as one that actually affirmed – rather than denied – that the document was one of limited authority. As "a restraint on the exercise of a power expressly delegated to Congress," the clause restricted the power of "of regulating commerce with foreign nations" to specific parameters.[455] As a figure deeply involved in the writing and ratification of the Constitution, it would be difficult to reject Madison's perspective in favor of contemporary theories of interpretation.

Also disposing of the expansive interpretation of the General Welfare Clause is the fact that every callous dictator, king, and autocrat who ever lived has appealed to the general welfare of his people. Historically, the same reasoning has often been used to justify the seizure of property, violation of civil rights, and even genocide. If a pledge of good intentions thwarted tyrannical impulses, there would be no need for a written constitution of enumerated powers. As history has revealed, though, the assurances of despotic kings and Parliaments have not been enough to secure the liberty of the people.

The debates from the ratification struggle confirm that the General Welfare Clause limited Congress' power to tax and held the general government to fixed purposes. For instance, David Ramsey told South

Carolinians that Congressional power was "confined to provide for the common defense and the general welfare of the United States," such that only "the general concerns of the union ought to be managed by the general government." To the contrary of the idea that the clause granted broad power, Madison pointed to the structure of the Constitution. Why would the document include enumerated powers, Madison asked in *The Federalist* No. 41, "if these and all others were meant to be included in the preceding general power?"[456]

Despite those who spread falsehoods, Madison defended the original meaning of the clause throughout his life. This was aptly demonstrated during a 1792 debate on the Cod Fishery Bill, where the Congress mulled granting subsidies to cod fisheries. Like most modern legislation, proponents appealed to the general interests of the people and assured opponents that the bill would protect the local economy. The bill's sponsor, Samuel Livermore, insisted it was necessary to "give encouragement to our fishermen, and, by that encouragement, to increase their numbers." Providing economic protection to the fisheries, he declared, was of "great importance to such persons as choose to employ their capitals in the fishery business."[457] Livermore justified the bill by stating that it was imperative for the entirety of the United States:

> I believe it will not be disputed that the business itself is of considerable importance to the United States, insomuch as it affords a certain proportion of remittance or exportation to foreign countries, and does not impoverish the country, but enriches it by the addition of so much wealth drawn from the sea.[458]

Madison interjected, warning that this type of legislation was not constitutionally permissible. "Those who proposed the Constitution conceived," he professed, "that this is not an indefinite Government, deriving its power from the general terms prefixed to the specified powers, but a limited Government tied down to the specified powers which explain and define the general terms." Those who pointed to the General Welfare Clause to rationalize the Cod Fishery Bill, then, must "either admit" the fallacy "or give up their doctrine."[459]

As one of his last acts as president, Madison vetoed the Bonus Bill of 1817, an effort to build a series of roads, bridges, and canals on the basis of the General Welfare Clause. There too, the Virginian rejected the idea that the provision such an expansion of power:

> If a general power to construct roads and canals, and to improve the navigation of water courses, with the train of powers incident thereto, be not possessed by Congress, the assent of the States in the mode provided in the bill can not confer the power. The only cases in which the consent and cession of particular States can extend the power of Congress are those specified and provided for in the Constitution.[460]

Despite favoring the bill in question, Madison categorically denied that the clause authorized the act. In his message to Congress, the president asserted that a constitutional amendment would be necessary to grant the authority.

In addition to these circumstances, the Tenth Amendment made clear that all powers that are neither specifically delegated to the general government, nor prohibited from being exercised by the states, are reserved to the states or to the people. Even before the Bill of Rights was added, Alexander Hamilton wrote that the principle was inherent to the original Constitution:

> An entire consolidation of the States into one complete national sovereignty would imply an entire subordination of the parts; and whatever powers might remain in them, would be altogether dependent on the general will. But the plan of the convention aims only at a partial union or consolidation, the State governments would clearly retain all rights of sovereignty which they before had, and which were not, by that act, exclusively delegated to the United States.[461]

Although Hamilton favored a legal framework that featured an "entire subordination of the parts," that wasn't the product of the Philadelphia Convention, and the proponents of the Constitution were forced to admit so during the ratification campaign.

During the ratification struggle, Hamilton worked diligently to convince skeptics that the controversial clauses should not imply the all-en-
compassing authority they feared. His position at this time should not be
confused with his later actions after ratification, which seemed to refute
his original explanations. Indeed, after insisting that the General Welfare
Clause did not grant the government unenumerated power, Hamilton later
cited the clause to justify his own plans for the national economy.[462] In a
stroke of deceit, he changed his tune only after the Constitution was ratified.

Governor Edmund Randolph of Virginia responded to naysayers in his
own state who feared the "indefinite power of providing for the general
welfare." Contradicting these detractors, he declared that "no such power
is given...Were not this the case, the following part of the clause would
be absurd. It would have been treason against common language."[463] After
correcting the wrongly held claims about the General Welfare Clause,
Randolph also indicated that such a mutation of the clause would render
the entire document incongruous.

Randolph's opinion on this matter is particularly compelling, as he
championed the Virginia Plan, which called for a general legislative authority. Given that the final Constitution represented a drastic deviation
from the Virginia Plan, he expressed his reservations by refusing to sign
the document.[464] In addition to this, Randolph published a pamphlet justifying his rejection and outlining his concerns. By the time of Virginia's
state ratification in Richmond, he turned into an influential proponent of
the document, despite the document's lack of nationalist characteristics.
Randolph's stance adds weight to this interpretation of the clause, since
his explanation for the phrase satisfied the opponents and helped convince
Virginia to ratify.

Oliver Ellsworth of Connecticut also argued that the General Welfare
Clause did not allow for taxes to be raised for the execution of all powers,
stating that "it does not say that congress shall have all these sources of
revenue, and the states none...they do not take away that which is necessary for the states." Like many of his peers, Ellsworth reiterated that "this
constitution defines the extent of the powers of the general government. If
they make a law which the constitution does not authorize, it is void."[465]
Echoing these sentiments, Thomas Jefferson wrote the following:

They are not to lay taxes *ad libitum, for any purpose they please*; but only to pay the debts, to provide for the welfare of the Union. In like manner, they are not to do any thing they please, to provide for the general welfare, but only to lay taxes for that purpose. To consider the latter phrase, not as describing the purpose of the first, but as giving a distinct and individual power to do any act they please which might be for the good of the Union, would render all the preceding and subsequent enumerations of power completely useless. It would reduce the whole instrument to a single phrase – that of insinuating a Congress with the power to do whatever would be for the good of the United States; and, as they would be the sole judges of the good or evil, it would be also a power to do whatever evil they please.[466]

Contending that the General Welfare Clause had such an expansive function, thought Jefferson, would absurdly diminish the Constitution to a single phrase. To do so, he thought, would negate the basis for the document and empower the Congress to a nonsensical degree.

The radical reinterpretation of the General Welfare Cause is a relatively recent phenomenon. For many years after the ratification, its true meaning was widely understood. Senator Levi Woodbury of New Hampshire realized this several decades later, writing in 1830 that "many powers are not ceded to the general government, but are expressly withheld to the states and people; and right is, in my opinion, given to promote the "general welfare" by granting money or lands, but in the exercise of specific powers granted, in the modes prescribed, by the Constitution."[467]

Roger Sherman, who moved to insert the "general welfare" terminology added to the Constitution in the Philadelphia Convention, is perhaps the best source of clarification in regard to the oft-misunderstood passage. Sherman moved to insert the clause to ensure the term would be connected with the clause for laying taxes and duties. In other words, he wanted to make it explicit that taxes could only be collected for the specified powers. Sherman made the observation that the "objects of the Union" were "few." Sherman listed "defence against foreign danger," defense "against internal disputes & a resort to force," and "regulating foreign commerce & drawing revenue from it" as the powers of the general government. Brion McClanahan wrote that the initial proposal to insert the clause was rejected because it was considered to be redundant and unnecessary, passing only after Sherman's persistence. Moreover, the verbiage "general welfare" also existed in a similar form in the Articles of Confederation, where it was never purported to have the function of granting Congress unlimited authority.[468]

Madison prophetically warned of the horrors that would result from a broad interpretation of the General Welfare Clause. Having an excellent understanding of world history and ancient governments, Madison understood consolidation of power would inevitably come to pass if the federal government could behave in a completely arbitrary fashion:

> If Congress can employ money indefinitely to the general welfare, and are the sole and supreme judges of the general welfare, they may take the care of religion into their own hands; they may appoint teachers in every state, county, and parish, and pay them out of their public treasury; they may take into their own hands the education of children, establishing in like manner schools throughout the Union; they may assume the provision for the poor; they may undertake the regulation of all roads other than post-roads; in short, every thing, from the highest object of state legislation down to the most minute object of police, would be thrown under the power of Congress; for every object I have mentioned would admit the application of money, and might be called, if Congress pleased, provisions for the general welfare.[469]

In retrospect, Madison's words have proven decidedly clairvoyant. While all of the functions he listed were considered unimaginable at the time, they have all since come to fruition in some form. After continual reinterpretation of the same clause, the enlargement of the general government has gradually come to pass.

Until the 20th century, the federal courts actually imposed a narrow interpretation of the General Welfare Clause. However, several cases demonstrate the extent to which federal judges have stretched the ratified meaning. In the 1936 case of *United States v. Butler*, for example, the Supreme Court ruled that the ability to tax and spend was an independent power that did not have to be connected to the constitutional purposes explained by the Constitution's proponents. The Supreme Court took this assertion to an extreme in 1937, deciding through *Helvering v. Davis* that

Congress had a plenary power to tax and spend for any purpose – and that this authority was limited only by Congress' voluntary discretion. Through *South Dakota v. Dole* in 1987, the same body determined that the federal government had the general power to force the states to national standards of Congress's choice. In the contemporary, the federal courts have maintained a "blank check" view of the clause, transforming it entirely from a plainly understood term to an unrestrained grant of power.

THE COMMERCE CLAUSE

The Commerce Clause has also become one of the most misconstrued portions of the Constitution, evident from its continual misapplication by the general government. The originally ratified meaning provided Congress the power to "regulate Commerce with foreign Nations, and among the several States, and with the Indian Tribes." Far from the original understanding of this text, the federal government has incrementally used its language to justify various forms of trade suppression. In a departure from its original purpose, Congress has used the clause to constrain and eliminate both interstate and intrastate commerce.

The first reason to dispute the modern version of the Commerce Clause is based on historical semantics. In todays' age, the term "regulate" often means to control or restrain. However, the term carried a drastically different meaning to those who wrote and ratified the Constitution. Samuel Johnson's 1785 *Dictionary of the English Language* defined "regulate" as "to adjust by rule or method" and "to direct." Therefore, regulating trade was to establish a foundation for its continuance. Even today, the word carries the definition "to adjust so as to ensure accuracy of operation," and "to put in good order."[470]

When the Articles of Confederation were put into effect, a series of economic hardships convinced the representatives of the clause's necessity. Under the Confederation system, the inflationary Continental currency and state bills of credit led to economic depravity. Madison wrote in 1786 that a "general rage for paper money" caused an economic calamity in states that legally permitted debtors to pay their creditors in paper money. By doing so, lenders "paid the expense of the farce." In regard to Rhode Island's experiment with bills of credit, George Washington wrote that paper money "has had the effect in your state that it will ever have, to ruin commerce, oppress the honest, and open the door to every species of fraud and injustice." Similarly, Thomas Jefferson proclaimed that paper money "is liable to be abused, has been, is, and forever will be abused, in every country in which it is permitted."[471] The widespread trepidations on the dangers of paper money undoubtedly inspired the delegates to take measures to ensure commercial tranquility.

In the 1780s, the states also passed individual debt forgiveness measures, which compounded the economic problems and extended the financial misfortunes of the states. Various laws – often called "private relief" acts – were implemented that legally absolved specific persons of their debts, even in cases where the debt was held by individuals in another state. To many, the approach was an abominable and repulsive affront to debt holders, and undermined the financial obligations of individuals. The reason for the addition of the Contract Clause was to prevent debts from being purged in such arbitrary fashion, and without the consent of the debt holders.[472] Considering this intention alongside the Commerce Clause, the founders intended to prevent trade discrimination.

The writers of the Constitution feared that states with substantial cultural or ideological differences would continue to act in a manner which would legally protect citizens in their own states at expense of debt holders in other regions. They responded to this prospect through the Commerce Clause, which was explained as text that would prevent venal legislative behavior and encouraging commercial sincerity between states.

Another reason for the clause's formulation was the rigid network of protectionism that developed during the Critical Period. Soon after the states became independent from Britain, they enacted various barriers to trade – including tariffs and internal trade privileges – that hindered commerce with other states. As the trade schism between states widened, Madison described the phenomenon in a 1786 letter:

The States are every day giving proofs that separate regulations are more likely to set them by the ears than to attain the common object. When Massachusetts set on foot a retaliation of the policy of Great Britain, Connecticut declared her ports free. New Jersey served New York in the same way. And Delaware I am told has lately followed the example in [sic] oppostion to the commercial plans of Pennsylvania. A miscarriage of this attempt to unite the States in some effectual plan will have another effect of a serious nature. It will dissipate every prospect of drawing a steady revenue from our imposts…Another unhappy effect of a continuance of the present anarchy of our commerce will be a continuance of the unfavorable balance on it, which, by draining us of our metals, furnishes pretexts for the pernicious substitution of paper money, for indulgences to debtors, for postponement of taxes. In fact most of our political evils may be traced up to our commercial ones, as most of our moral may to our political.[473]

Though understanding the difficulty in convincing the states to align on a free commercial policy, he urged the adoption of amendments to the Articles of the Confederation to invent one. Though the Annapolis Convention of 1786 had failed to bring such a plan to fruition, the issue was certainly on the minds of delegates as they arrived to the Philadelphia Convention of 1787.

In addition to the trade barriers between states, foreign trade faced various difficulties as well. While the Confederation could enact treaties with other nations, it had no power over external commerce. In addition, the lack of naval protection hindered maritime trade. As the Confederation Congress brought about policy in the common interests of the states, many believed a uniform system of foreign trade could be handled in a similar way.

Despite the campaign for free trade, in an era where each of the states maintained their own import taxes, British-oriented mercantilists argued that whatever benefit such a condition would bring to consumers would be negated by the elimination of domestic markets within the individual states. Even so, by the time the Constitution was drafted, the campaign to decommission the protectionist system was a popular cause. With the primary purpose of eliminating trade between states through the establishment of a free trade zone within the states, the Commerce Clause was designed to encourage trade rather than restrict it.

In the state ratification conventions, the Commerce Clause was described in the same way. In Massachusetts, for instance, Thomas Dawes opined that the Commerce Clause would encourage New England's shipping:

> If we wish to encourage our own manufactures – to preserve our own commerce – to raise the value of our own lands, we must give Congress the powers in question.[474]

Nathaniel Gorham agreed with Dawes, and explained that the provision would allow for additional trade opportunities between the states and foreign nations. Gorham lamented trade restrictions, protective taxes, and monopolies, and cited the clause as functioning to abolish such policies:

> They prohibit our oil, fish, lumber, pot and pearl ashes, from being imported into their territories in order to favor Nova Scotia, for they know we cannot make general retaliating laws. They have a design in Nova Scotia, to rival us in the fishery and our situation at present favors their design. From the abundance of our markets, we could supply them with beef, butter, pork...but they lay what restrictions on them they please; they dare not do, was there an adequate power lodged in the general government to regulate commerce.[475]

Rather than allowing the general government to suppress or restrict trade, Gorham thought the clause would actually boost commerce. Former governor and delegate James Bowdoin elaborated upon this principle:

> But if we attend our trade, as it is at present, we shall find that the miserable state of it is owing to a like want of power in congress. Other nations prohibit our vessels from entering their ports, or lay heavy duties on our exports carried thither; and we have no retaliating or regulating power over their vessels and exports to prevent it...If it be asked, how are these evils, and others that might be mentioned, to be remedied? The answer is short, by giving congress adequate and proper power.[476]

Far from a mandate to stifle trade, Massachusetts clearly understood the Commerce Clause as a mechanism to encourage commerce and remove the policies at the root of the economic crisis of the 1780s.

In Pennsylvania, this sentiment was echoed by Thomas McKean, who wrote that the clause would "invigorate your commerce, and encourage ship-building." In Virginia, Edmund Randolph stated his understanding of the power meant that "commerce will flourish; the impost will therefore be more sure and productive." The governor made the supplementary argument that the Commerce Clause made it possible to "defend our commerce" from unneeded restriction. Madison referred to this power as a "superintending authority over the reciprocal trade of confederate States."[477]

Even Alexander Hamilton, who held mercantilism in high regard, adopted such a position in *The Federalist* No. 11:

> An unrestrained intercourse between the states themselves will advance the trade of each, by an interchange of their respective productions, not only for the supply of reciprocal wants at home, but for exportation to foreign markets.[478]

Notwithstanding these detailed clarifications in the assemblies that considered and ratified the Constitution, the federal courts of the modern age fail to characterize the clause as a supervisory power that preserved "unrestrained" trade. While the Commerce Clause intended to remove obstructions and irregularities of trade, it is now invoked to impede or eliminate any possibility of commerce.

Using the Commerce Clause as justification, President Franklin Roosevelt was determined to establish a federal minimum wage in hopes it would lead to greater prosperity in the midst of economic hardship. Although this notion was based upon faulty economic premises, such legislation was upheld by the Supreme Court in the 1937 case of *West Coast Hotel Co. v. Parrish*. The court rationalized its judgment by citing the Commerce Clause, despite the clear evidence that its interpretation was based on an unintended expansion of the clause's power. Similarly, the court held that Congress could impose price controls on dairy products in 1942 through its opinion in *United States v. Wrightwood Dairy Co.* The Supreme Court even went as far to declare the Tenth Amendment functionally irrelevant in the 1941 case of *United States v. Darby Lumber Co.*, where it made the following absurd claim:

The amendment states but a truism that all is retained which has not been surrendered. There is nothing in the history of its adoption to suggest that it was more than declaratory of the relationship between the national and state governments as it had been established by the Constitution before the amendment, or that its purpose was other than to allay fears that the new national government might seek to exercise powers not granted, and that the states might not be able to exercise fully their reserved powers.[479]

With such an allegation, the Supreme Court purported that the Tenth Amendment was introduced simply to quell apprehensions rather than to do what it said. In truth, it explicitly confined all powers not enumerated to the states or the people. Time and time again, the federal judiciary has authorized virtually every attempt of Congress to meddle in the economic behavior of individuals. In so doing, the federal courts have effectively colluded with the legislature to allow for any kind of commercial regulation imaginable.

The most preposterous example of jurisprudential distortion of the Commerce Clause was made in the 1942 case of *Wickard v. Filburn*. The dispute came after the Great Depression, where the federal government instituted various policies to limit the production of crops in the hope that prices would rise and benefit farmers. Roscoe Filburn, a private farmer, grew wheat in excess of the amount permitted by the federal government. Filburn's legal team realized that the Constitution placed no limitation upon the cultivation and consumption of his crops, and by attempting to do so, the federal government was violating his rights. They argued that "such activities are…beyond the reach of congressional power under the Commerce Clause, since they are local in character, and their effect upon interstate commerce are at most indirect."[480] Since the wheat he produced was never sold or distributed in any way, in state or out of state, he could never be subject to regulation under the Commerce Clause by the original understanding of the Constitution. Regardless, the Supreme Court issued a 9-0 decision against Filburn:

The decline in the export trade has left a large surplus in production which, in connection with an abnormally large supply of wheat and other grains in recent years, caused congestion in a number of markets; tied up railroad cars, and caused elevators in some instances to turn away grains, and railroads to institute embargoes to prevent further congestion.[481]

The opinion held that growing a surplus of wheat was a violation of the Commerce Clause, because Filburn's actions served as an alternative to purchasing wheat on the market. Therefore, the federal government claimed the right to regulate the private crop yields that were grown and consumed within a state.

The natural extension of ridiculous explanation, of course, is that the federal government can regulate the production commodity grown or created, even if it was consumed on one's own property. To the Supreme Court, the poor condition of the wheat market – the result of federal policies price controls and production quotas – was justification enough to reprimand a man attempting to grow wheat for his own use. Ever since the opinion, the courts have relied upon the *Wickard v. Filburn* precedent to regulate economic behavior and prosecute individuals for growing commodities it does not approve of.

In the more recent 2005 case of *Gonzales v. Raich*, the Supreme Court ruled that Congress can criminalize the production of home-grown cannabis, even if state law allows the growth of such a plant. The 6-3 opinion also determined that such a restriction would be rigorously enforced, even if the plant was consumed in someone's backyard. Operating against the original spirit of the Commerce Clause, the judiciary decided once again that it could impede and regulate intrastate commerce. In his dissent, Supreme Court Justice Clarence Thomas strongly disagreed with the majority opinion:

Certainly no evidence from the founding suggests that "commerce" included the mere possession of a good or some personal activity that did not involve trade or exchange for value. In the early days of the Republic, it would have been unthinkable that Congress could prohibit the local cultivation, possession, and consumption of marijuana.[482]

Confirming this sentiment was the fact that no commerce had taken place "among the several states." Thomas wrote that if the court could levy such inflexible prohibitions, it could also regulate "quilting bees," "clothes drives," and "potluck suppers" throughout the states.[483] In humorous fashion, Thomas illustrated that the Congress would have no boundaries whatsoever under such an interpretation. The contemporary Supreme Court, however, has often made clear that it overwhelmingly favors jurisprudence through stare decisis – conclusions based on precedent – over the original intent of the controversial clauses. The last century especially has revealed that the personal opinions of federal judges have often triumphed over constitutional boundaries.

THE NECESSARY AND PROPER CLAUSE

The Necessary and Proper Clause has also had a long history of reinterpretation, beginning in the early years of the republic. A key source of dispute between Federalists and Jefferson's Republicans, the clause caused a notable rift in George Washington's administration. As explained earlier, the Necessary and Proper Clause was first transformed by Alexander Hamilton to justify the creation of his national bank. Today, the same clause is similarly cited to conjure a broad array of powers for Congress, much like the General Welfare Clause.

In many instances during the ratification conventions, it was made perfectly clear that the Necessary and Proper Clause did not create any new powers, but merely allowed incidental acts to be made to carry out the "foregoing powers." The text of Article I, Section 8 of the Constitution is quite clear in this regard, and none of the Federalist advocates of the document pointed to the clause as the source of unlisted authority.

In Pennsylvania's 1787 ratification convention, a controversy over the clause illustrated this fact. James Wilson, who had played a key role at the Philadelphia Convention, adamantly dispelled the notion that the provision gave Congress a boundless authority:

It is said, that Congress shall have power to make all laws which shall be necessary and proper, those words are limited, and defined by the following, "for carrying into the execution the foregoing powers." It is saying no more than that the powers we have already particularly given, shall be effectually carried into execution.[484]

Wilson elaborated that the Necessary and Proper Clause "is not meant to give congress merely an illusive show of authority, to deceive themselves or constituents any longer." It meant instead that the assembly "shall have the power of carrying into effect the laws, which they shall make under the powers vested in them by this constitution."[485]

The chief promoter of the Constitution in his state, Wilson added the context that same clause, "with which so much fault has been found, gives no more, or others powers; nor does it in any degree go beyond the particular enumeration."[486] His reply was made in direct response to widespread Anti-Federalist allegations to the contrary, and fell in line entirely with what he had said in his State Yard Speech. Seeing this refutation soundly put down by a great friend of the Constitution, how can we believe that this argument still remains and is considered quite compelling today? The truth is that political ambitions and federal court rulings have gradually morphed this clause into a substantive, commanding clause that grants unforeseen power.

In New York's ratification convention in Poughkeepsie, John Williams expressed similar concern over the Necessary and Proper Clause. The provision "would tend to annihilate the state governments," he feared. By way of such "indefinite" power, he alleged that "the legislature under this constitution may pass any law they may think proper." Chancellor Robert Livingston, overseer of the highest court in the state, countered that "the gentleman's argument falls to the ground."[487] Alexander Hamilton explained that this was because the clause simply allowed Congress to pass laws necessary to carry out the enumerated authority, not undermine the reserved powers of the states:

> I insist, that it never can be the interest of the national legislature, to destroy the state government. It can derive no advantage from such an event; but, on the contrary, would lose an indispensible support, a necessary aid in executing the laws, and conveying the influence of government to the doors of the people.[488]

As we can see, Hamilton's original stance on the clause was the one accepted by his state. Though he later betrayed this perception of the clause in pursuit of his own political aspirations, it was not the latter version that convinced his state to ratify the Constitution.

In Virginia, Edmund Randolph responded to Patrick Henry persuasive ridicule of the clause by denying that "complete and unlimited legislation is vested in the United States." Instead, he claimed, "this supposition is founded on false reasoning...in the general Constitution, the powers are enumerated."[489] As we can see, time and time again were such assertions of overarching power countered in the state ratification conventions. Undeniably, the expansive version of the Necessary and Proper Clause was completely dismissed in favor of the explanation provided by Federalists.

James Madison's consistent view of the Necessary and Proper Clause, like the General Welfare Clause, was apparent in his decision to veto the Bonus Bill of 1817 – a plan that called for the federal construction of various roads, bridges, and canals throughout the country. While explaining that he personally favored the construction of the infrastructure in his veto message, he denied the policy's constitutionality on a federal level. Instead of embracing his own personal proclivities through a disregard of the Constitution, he maintained that the document barred such an act. "The legislative powers vested in Congress are specified and enumerated in the eighth section of the first article of the Constitution," he said, "and it does not appear that the power proposed to be exercised by the bill is among the enumerated powers."[490]

According to Madison, using the controversial clause as justification for the law "would be contrary to the established and consistent rules of interpretation, as rendering the special and careful enumeration of powers which follow the clause nugatory and improper." Signing the law in question, he continued, "would have the effect of giving to Congress a general power of legislation instead of the defined and limited one hitherto understood to belong to them." The power to build domestic infrastructure, therefore, could "not be deduced from any part of it without an inadmissible latitude of construction and reliance on insufficient precedents." Madison insisted that the endeavor would necessitate the addition of a constitutional amendment that allowed for the authority. "I have no option but to withhold my signature from it" until such a time, he wrote.[491]

According to Madison, the constitutional system of the United States "depends on a definite partition of powers between the General and the State Governments."[492] This was the basis of the framework was created from the outset, he claimed, and the most inviolable principle of constitutional construction. In the contemporary, however, the Necessary and Proper Clause is regularly used – to the detriment of the states – as a rubber stamp for the federal government. In a process that has defined the federal court system for over a century, new powers never yet discovered are routinely considered constitutional. In the 1896 case of *United States v. Gettysburg Electric Ry. Co.*, for instance, the court determined that the Necessary and Proper Clause allowed the federal government to seize private railroad property in the interest of historical preservation. In a similar metamorphosis of the clause's plain meaning, the court determined that the federal government could restrict the medicinal use of alcohol based on its interpretation of the provision in the 1926 case of *Lambert v. Yellowley*.

Through a controversial decision in the 2010 case of *United States v. Comstock*, the Supreme Court even upheld a federal law that allowed indefinite federal detainment of criminal defendants on the same basis. In his majority opinion, Justice Stephen Breyer alleged that the clause granted the same expansive set of powers that the founders rejected:

> First, the Necessary and Proper Clause grants Congress broad authority to enact federal legislation… Accordingly, the Necessary and Proper Clause makes clear that the Constitution's grants of specific federal legislative authority are accompanied by broad power to enact laws that are "convenient or useful" or "conducive" to the authority's "beneficial exercise."[493]

Breyer also cited John Marshall's opinion in *McCulloch v. Maryland* to reiterate that "necessary" does not mean "absolutely necessary," despite the true explanation that was offered during the state ratification conventions.[494] Certainly, the provision has often been misconstrued by the legal community in an earnest effort to endorse federal supremacy.

Through a series of expansionary legal precedents, the Commerce Clause's original meaning has been distorted beyond imagination. As an absolute inversion of the clause's original purpose, the federal courts have

successfully transformed the provision from one which intended to encourage free trade into an unlimited license for the federal government to
meddle with every aspect of trade. Under the new theory of interpretation,
foreign trade, trade between states, trade within a state, and independent
consumption is now subject to plenary control by the general government.

THE SUPREMACY CLAUSE

During the ratification debates, supporters of the Constitution described
that the Supremacy Clause would function to ensure that unconstitutional
law was not supreme or binding. Ironically, in great contrast to this conception, the federal courts now suggest that the clause has the opposite
function. The Supremacy Clause, the orthodox narrative suggests, invariably negates the contradictory laws of the states and makes all Congressional laws supreme. Indeed, the official website of the United States Senate supposes that the Supremacy Clause "assures that the Constitution and
federal laws and treaties take precedence over state law and binds all
judges to adhere to that principle in their courts."[495] However, the prose
was intended to do no such thing. The Supremacy Clause declares only
that laws passed in "pursuance" of the Constitution are to be considered
the supreme law of the land. The concept is simple – if the law enacted is
not constitutional, it is no law at all.

Avowing history and educated in the natural development of governments, the founders realized that the general government would eventually
attempt to enact unconstitutional law. The past had only proven that at
some point, calculating and deceitful politicians would pursue such aims
to achieve their political desires or expand their own authority. America's
cultural history was filled with examples in which the "living document"
model of the British constitution led kings to violate and interfere with the
rights of the people, and the government justified such actions by claiming
inherent right of nobility or regal fortitude. The Supremacy Clause, they
hoped, would therefore invalidate such a destructive tendency.

As one of the first to articulate the original meaning of the Supremacy
Clause, Thomas McKean told Pennsylvania's ratification convention that
the clause gave Congress purview only over matters within the enumerated
scope of legislative authority:

The meaning which appears to be plain and well expressed is simply this, that Congress have the power of making laws upon any subject over which the proposed plan gives them a jurisdiction, and that those laws, thus made in pursuance of the Constitution, shall be binding upon the states.[496]

In other words, the clause applied a strict prerequisite for law to be legally supreme – it had to be constitutional.

Alexander Hamilton, who recommended the most supreme, powerful general government of all at the Philadelphia Convention, also argued to the contrary of modern interpretations of the clause. After echoing McKean's clarification at New York's ratification convention in Poughkeepsie, Hamilton added that the states would remain supreme in the execution of their own reserved powers:

I maintain that the word supreme imports no more than this — that the Constitution, and laws made in pursuance thereof, cannot be controlled or defeated by any other law. The acts of the United States, therefore, will be absolutely obligatory as to all the proper objects and powers of the general government...but the laws of Congress are restricted to a certain sphere, and when they depart from this sphere, they are no longer supreme or binding. In the same manner the States have certain independent powers, in which their laws are supreme; for example, in making and executing laws concerning the punishment of certain crimes, such as murder, theft, etc., the States cannot be controlled.[497]

In *The Federalist* No. 33, Hamilton repeated the same explanation he provided in the convention. "It will not, I presume, have escaped observation," he wrote, that the Supremacy Clause "expressly confines this supremacy to laws made pursuant to the Constitution."[498] According to Hamilton, if a law was unconstitutional, it was not supreme. In *The Federalist* No. 78, he regurgitated the same meaning for a third time:

There is no position which depends on clearer principles, than that every act of a delegated authority contrary to the tenor of the commission under which it is exercised, is void. No legislative act, therefore, contrary to the constitution, can be valid.[499]

In overt fashion, Hamilton insisted that the general government only commanded supremacy of that which was confined to its own sphere of constitutional authority. At the same time, other spheres of governance, held by and reserved to the states, would stand undisturbed.

Nationalist-oriented government proposals were consciously rejected in Philadelphia in favor of a federal league of states, and the Supremacy Clause was an aftereffect of this result. Clear from the notes of the Philadelphia Convention of was that pitches for a "supreme" legislature, executive, and court system were patently overruled. Such a dismissal was indicative of the conscious effort to erect a system of limited power, where laws that violated the Constitution were to be disregarded by way of the Supremacy Clause.

The Supremacy Clause was based on Article XIII of the Articles of Confederation, which noted that "every State shall abide by the determination of the United States in Congress assembled, on all questions which by this Confederation is submitted to them." This suggested that there were some matters the Confederation government would not have authority over, issues that would only be handled by state authorities. Furthermore, this provision postulated that "the Articles of this Confederation shall be inviolably observed by every State." In addition, it was Luther Martin of Maryland that introduced the protype of the clause at the Philadelphia Convention. A fanatic of decentralized government, Martin had moved to include the clause to restrict Congress' lawmaking power to acts "made by virtue & in pursuance of the articles of the Union."[500]

Law that is passed by the general government faces extremely strict criteria – that it is "pursuant" to the Constitution. As an unambiguous precondition, the existence of the Supremacy Clause is another indication that the constitution was a compact. By building the general government, provision makes clear that the states ceded only a subset of powers while keeping the remainder. Rather than pledge allegiance to the notion of federal supremacy, elected federal officials therefore swear to support and defend the Constitution of the United States. An important distinction, the ritual implies that the Constitution is binding above unconstitutional acts that would not qualify as the "supreme law of the land."

Even John Marshall, a man who contributed more to the growth of the federal judiciary than any other figure, realized the potential for unconstitutional law to be passed by the general government. "It is…not entirely unworthy of observation," he wrote, "that in declaring what shall be the supreme law of the land, the constitution itself is first mentioned." It was "not the laws of the United States generally" that were supreme, "but those only which shall be made in pursuance of the constitution, have that rank."[501]

FEDERALISTS VS. ANTI-FEDERALISTS

Throughout the ratification campaign, the supporters of the Constitution assured disbelievers that provocative clauses would give the government no additional, unspecified power. However, the enemies of the framework suggested that no matter what the motives, the federal government would seize power regardless, and cite these clauses as justification. With such obvious disagreement, which side was correct?

The Federalists were correct in asserting that the product of the Philadelphia convention would be a document that gives limited power to a general government, contrary to the original model for the Virginia Plan and Hamiltonian vision. On the other hand, the Anti-Federalists were precise in their diagnosis of the problems that would transpire in the new government under the Constitution. As we've seen, modern constitutional violations bear astounding resemblance to the horrors suggested by George Mason, Patrick Henry, Robert Yates, William Paca, John Lansing, Willie Jones, Rawlins Lowndes, and others.

Much of the growth in federal power has come as the direct result of the government using these clauses as excuses to assume more authority, despite the spirit of the Constitution and its original understanding. Today, the federal courts continually cite these clauses as the basis for wide expansions of central power. Undoubtedly, the modern reinterpretation of these clauses has invariably worked to dismantle the original characteristics of the compact among states. Departing from these original principles has led to the capricious government and the continual growth of centralized authority.

By the end of the state ratification conventions, the now-maligned clauses were not considered ambiguous or unclear – they were described at length and to the satisfaction of the most skeptical regions of the United States. Nevertheless, the original intent of the clauses have largely fallen out of the American political psyche. If the states remain unable to overturn these annexations of power, the federal government will continue to make them with impunity until the states are reduced to a feeble condition. This phenomenon, of course, is a contemporary American trend.

As we can see, the modern legal perspective concerning these clauses does not meet the scrutiny of the historical record, and the original debates and writings of the ratification struggle are rarely cited. Many of these omissions are purposeful – if they were referenced, they would serve to refute every conflicting claim regarding these clauses, and act to dismantle the distortion created by the federal courts. To impede these modern trends, the Constitution needs to be rightly viewed as a foundational baseline, not an elastic mold that can be stretched indefinitely by all who would want to. The ultimate argument against the "living document" myth that floods society was made long before our current generation. As Edmund Randolph put it: "For if its powers were to be general, an enumeration would be needless."[502]

Chapter 9

The Problem and
the Proper Recourse

With the rampant expansion of the general government, what is the proper recourse for the states? Thomas Jefferson opined that the states could preserve their own sovereignty only by determining the constitutionality of laws themselves, and by applying nullification as the "rightful remedy" against federal usurpation. Despite the logical and historical support for his recommendation, the process can seem like a painstaking task. With a contemporary populace that is largely unaware of the merits of nullification, how can the states react to the continual violations? Even if state representatives are properly educated on these principles, how can they be adapted to the modern age?

Today's federal government acknowledges few limitations on its own power, despite the legal standing of the Constitution. When George Washington declared that the document is "sacredly obligatory upon all," he did not make exceptions for politicians.[503] The founding generation realized that elected officials would be the first to abridge the maxims of the Constitution. As he urged Virginians to "guard with jealous attention the public liberty," Patrick Henry declared it was necessary to "suspect everyone who approaches that jewel." No measure would preserve the rights of the people, he asserted, "but downright force."[504] Instead of blindly following political leaders, the citizenry was advised to resist the authorities. We should be moved by Washington and Henry's words, and follow their example. However, it should also be understood that words are not enough to impart a steadfast impression on the world. In actuality, constitutional idealism can only go so far. Where idealism fails, concerted acts of resistance can carry an idea the rest of the way.

If despotism is to be properly counteracted, one should not wait for the federal courts to weigh in on controversial laws, or for Congress to repeal the same. As the American War of Independence proved, it was not enough to rely on federal courts to halt expansionary tendencies or to "vote the bums out." Undoubtedly, Jefferson's ideals can still triumph through strategies of resistance against unconstitutional edicts and compelling educational campaigns. A learned citizenry equipped with the knowledge of the Constitution, its antecedents, and its greatest axioms, is the most powerful force that can lead a society to liberty.

Various political factions regularly condemn politicians for violating the Constitution. Nevertheless, partisan behavior often impedes individuals from doing the same to member of their own political affiliation. While the Constitution is sometimes used as a refuge for political minorities, seldom will a majority party acknowledge their own programs as unconstitutional. This spectacle is entirely consistent with the experiences of the founding generation, which ruefully witnessed Parliament's affirmations that its actions were constitutional. This transpired even as factions of patriot Whigs objected and organized to obstruct the enforcement of the egregious laws. The British government continued to implement tyrannical policy nonetheless, and its power was constrained only when challenged directly through the conscious rejection of the controversial acts. When the people were vigilant, they effectively thwarted the government and reasserted their rights.

Citizens and politicians of any political party are wise to remain consistent on constitutional adherence, whether or not the president happens to be a member of their own party, or whether their party has control of the current Congress. As American history has shown, all parties are responsible for constitutional violations. When politicians are allowed to remain more loyal to their own party than to the Constitution, the most severe problem in constitutional government is exemplified.

One of the primary reasons the republic has drifted from its founding principles is through the enlargement of executive authority. From a subdued figure with limited prerogative, the American president has become a transcendent character with immense power. Although this phenomenon has happened gradually throughout United States history, the transition has been especially apparent in the 20th century.

Since the 17th Amendment eradicated state representation in the federal government, legislators have generally deferred much of their own authority to the president. For example, Congress has permitted the executive to initiate his own wars and military strikes, despite the fact that the Constitution provides Congress with the sole power to declare war. After unilaterally ordering such strikes, presidents have consistently employed their own Justice Department to rationalize their behavior. In so doing, they often cite the precedents of their predecessors or make drastic legal stretches to validate their actions.

In the last century, the state governors have also been reduced to relative weakness while the president has gained more and more power. Today, people think of the President of the United States as the "Leader of the Free World," and consider him as the most powerful person on the planet. This was not always the case, and the office was never designed to receive such reverence. In fact, the state governors once held more power than the United States president, and the Constitution was designed to prevent the accumulation of too much power in the executive office.

Despite the modern trajectory of the executive office, there are only a few powers documented in Article II of the Constitution, and the legislature has considerable ability to check the president in virtually all of his roles. Regardless, the American president has often received undue veneration as a political mastermind, and he is often expected to drive policy unilaterally without the sanction of Congress. Today, a passive executive is almost always considered inept, indecisive, or inattentive. On the contrary of this perception, those who wrote and ratified the Constitution did not desire for an imposing, kingly executive to occupy the presidential office. Instead, they intended the office to hold minimal authority, with the main purpose of carrying out the will of the legislature. In light of England's most nefarious kings, the reasons for this should be obvious.

In addition to the rise of the imperial presidency, state and local authority has also suffered at the hands of religious intrusion. Indeed, federal attempts to standardize society and craft uniform policies has been used to impede religious practice, a process that is often justified on the basis of historical misconceptions. For instance, the common claim that Thomas Jefferson opposed religious influence in government – by his pronouncement of "separation of church and state" – has often been used to inhibit religious exercise, remove religious symbolism, or to intervene in churches or individual religious practice.

While the founders were not concerned about religious influence in society, they certainly dreaded the propensity for government to intervene in the churches and meddle with the individual religious practices of its citizens. While religious minorities often faced campaigns of persecution and barriers to civil office at the state level, records prove that the writers of the Constitution did not aim to suppress religious practices at the federal level. This philosophical inclination was undoubtedly a reaction to the treacherous deeds of English kings, who regularly interfered in the religious practices of British subjects. From King John's unpopular attempt to confirm John de Gray as Archduke of Canterbury, to Charles I's infamous ambition to persecute Puritans, to James II's obligatory readings of royal proclamations from the pulpit, religious intervention was always apprehended. All of these antecedents lead the founders to believe that religious interference hindered liberty.

The phrase "separation of church and state," now used to justify any governmental attempt to vanquish religion from the public realm, originated in an 1802 letter from Jefferson to the Danbury Baptists. Prior to Jefferson's response, the congregation wrote to the president to ask whether he intended to abide by his commitment to religious liberty and protection of religious minorities. As a small sect in many states, Baptists were surely concerned about possible religious favoritism, which had prevented them from obtaining political office in many regions. Such was the case in Connecticut, which maintained an established Congregationalist church omitted and explicit guarantee of free religious exercise. By his response, Jefferson encouraged the Baptists by promising not to use the power of the general government to restrict or hinder their religious practices.

To the contrary of the claim that the founders opposed all forms of religious expression in government, the United States Capitol building was made into a church on Sundays. Several representatives and presidents, including Jefferson and Madison, attended services there. At the Philadelphia Convention, Benjamin Franklin suggested that the body adopt a resolution calling for prayers to be made each morning. John Locke's *Two Treatises of Government*, which was held in high esteem by many delegates, called for an appeal to heaven when all other attempts of exacting justice fail. The phrase "An Appeal to Heaven" was thus incorporated into a popular flag that was often used to represent patriot causes. Each session of Congress began with a prayer. During the War of Independence, the British outlawed Bibles from being printed in the United States, so the Continental Congress authorized Robert Aitken to print and distribute the first American Bible. The Philadelphia Convention was heavily dominated by Protestants, but also included members of minority denominations. These individuals undoubtedly carried their religious identities with them in their civic duties.[505]

There are countless examples disproving the claim that the founding generation shunned religious influence in government. While the founders disagreed on many things, one thing they were inclined to agree upon was that it would be tyrannical for the state to intervene into religious matters. By the First Amendment and the prohibition on religious oaths, the Constitution restricted the federal government from endorsing religious favoritism or establishing a national religion. Most importantly, it guaranteed that Congress could not interfere in the religious exercise of Americans.

Rather than discourage religious practice, Jefferson's "wall of separation" prevented the government from interfering with the religious practices of individuals. The First Amendment to the Constitution, Jefferson wrote, prohibited the general government from discriminating against Baptists. The same principle, however, did not mean that the federal government could remove religious symbols from the public realm. Anytime it endeavors to do so, it necessarily contradicts the First Amendment and Jefferson's famous letter. Rather than a guarantee of religious secularism, religious nonintervention is what created a true "wall of separation" between church and state.

Notwithstanding this context, the comprehensive transformation of this proverb has led the federal government to remove religious imagery from the public arena, even in the states where it has no jurisdiction. Through such policies, the federal government has acted to erode the "free exercise" spirit of the First Amendment. These policies give the federal government excuse to interject their will on the states, and override local statutes and court decisions. This is especially ironic considering that the states carried various deep-rooted religious identities, and many had official state churches long into the 19th century. At that point, there was no consensus on which type of religious establishment, imagery, and practices were to be allowed, but each state assumed the right to decide these matters within their own sovereignties.

Beyond suppressing religious expression, the federal courts have expanded their authority to the detriment of states in many other ways. One of the ways this shift has come to fruition is through the enlargement of the federal court system itself. Even though the early courts did much to widen the extent of their own power, but the contemporary federal court system has taken hold of more power than John Marshall ever imagined. Today's federal judges, especially those on the Supreme Court, are treated as if they have a certain unworldly understanding of the Constitution that is far superior to that of other elected officials and citizens of the states. Their own constitutional positions are also considered more substantial than what the founders said about the text they now reinterpret. In the wake of a significant Supreme Court opinion, modern politicians are often led to accept such judgments as gospel, as if an aura of unaltered truth follows the justices. Realizing this, Justice Robert Jackson once declared that Supreme Court judges are "infallible only because we are final."[506] As we know, the assertion that federal judges were "infallible" was challenged directly from the beginning of the republic.

The chief purpose of the federal courts was to resolve conflicts by applying federal laws to the few cases which were to be heard by a central judiciary. Those who lived under the Articles of Confederation, after all, saw good reason to establish a court, mostly to handle disputes between states. Under Article III, the federal court system was given original jurisdiction in only three types of cases. Additionally, Congress holds the power to limit the appellate jurisdiction of the courts, allowing it to effectively strip federal jurisdiction entirely in many cases. Nevertheless, Congress almost never invokes this authority, and elected officials almost never acknowledge its existence. Reciprocating Congressional refusal to check the federal courts, the same judicial system rarely sides against the federal government. Far from acting as a legitimate check upon unconstitutional action, the federal courts have almost never struck down federal actions or laws that were clearly unconstitutional. When the federal courts take action against a law in the contemporary, it is almost always a state law.

By refusing to hear any appeals to convictions under the Sedition Act, the early Federalists adopted the stance that such a horrendous act was fully constitutional. Judicial expansion was propelled even further by precedents set in motion by the Marshall Court, which habitually ruled against the states when they dared to challenge the absolutism of the federal government. Many decades later, the Melville Fuller Court denied that New York could set its own labor rules, an absurd invasion of state authority and an abnegation of federalism. When Franklin Roosevelt threatened to pack the Supreme Court with as many new judges as it took to approve his New Deal policies, the justices responded by magically finding favor with his unconstitutional penchants. Even from the first presidential administrations, the federal judiciary has mostly served to legitimize the growth of the federal government.

The 17th Amendment to the Constitution has also led to an acute erosion of state sovereignty. Prior to this amendment, United States Senators were appointed by their respective state legislatures rather than selected by the electorate. In such a role, their chief duty was to act as the sovereign representative of the state which appointed them, and to accept the instructions from their state legislatures in regard to voting. In the Massachusetts ratification convention, for instance, Fisher Ames called the senators "ambassadors of the states."[507] In the same convention, Rufus King made the same case for their purpose:

> The state legislatures, if they find their delegates erring, can and will instruct them. Will this not be a check? When they hear the voice of the people solemnly dictating to them their duty, they will be bold men indeed to act contrary to it.[508]

Embroiled in a bitter fight over the Constitution in New York, John Jay spoke of the same concept. "There will be a constant correspondence between senators and the state executives," he professed, "who will be able, from time to time, to afford them all that particular information which particular circumstances may require."[509] By the time of the First Congress, the states used the power of legislative instruction to influence federal policy, exercising this power in earnest.

When schisms between senators and their respective state governments created conflicts of interest, some senators even resigned from their seats rather than to heed the instructions of their local assemblies. In 1809, for instance, Senator John Quincy Adams of Massachusetts broke from the Federalists and resigned his seat rather than to follow the anti-embargo instructions he received from the Massachusetts General Court. In another case, Senator Peleg Sprague resigned his seat in 1835 when his advocacy for a national bank was at odds with that of the Maine legislature.

Because the founders intended for the states to directly influence the Senate, the 17th Amendment largely eviscerated the original purpose of the body. Before the amendment, senators were always held accountable to their home states, and could be forced out of office if they were not performing the wishes of their respective state legislatures. This served as a de-facto recall process, which embodied the legislative constraints the writers of the Constitution intended.

At New York's ratification convention, Alexander Hamilton conceded that the senators would be completely dependent upon the authority of the states. "The senators will constantly be attended with a reflection, that their future existence is absolutely in the power of the states," he remarked."[510] The language and spirit of the Constitution confirmed that the states had control over its own senators, thereby allowing the states a high degree of command over the general government's legislative acts, treaties, and civil appointments.

This original system, which recognized the state legislatures as vital aspects of the American republic, offered several advantages. Today, constituents must wait a period of no less than six years to replace their senators. This gives politicians an ample amount of time to "correct" their voting behavior to compensate. This cyclical process could be considered inconsistent with the needs of the state, exercising an effective reversal and allowing the state populations to forget their earlier actions. The 17th Amendment has allowed senators to become true politicians that vote to their inclinations rather than the necessity of their home states, changing only when it becomes politically expedient or for electoral considerations. In this way, states are "stuck" for six years with a powerful official who may be acting in a contradictory manner.

Unlike in the early republic, the modern United States Congress convenes periodically throughout the entire year, and the output of legislation far surpasses that of the antebellum period. Whether the Constitution permits it or not, today's Congress passes law on virtually every matter without the input of the states. Under the pre-17th Amendment Constitution, this type of situation was absolutely impossible, as the state-oriented senators ensured that each region of the United States had representation over matters of pressing importance, such as treaties, civil appointments, declarations of war, and all legislation.

In the Philadelphia Convention, James Wilson was the only delegate who recommended choosing senators through popular elections. Highlighting the unpopularity of this suggestion, his proposal was defeated 10-1.[511] Outside of Wilson, the delegates feared that senators would grow too powerful and the states would lose all influence in the federal government. In observation of modern political trends, this forecast has clearly come to pass. Through the 17th Amendment, the federal government has become more nationalist, less representative, and more out of touch with the citizens of the states. In turn, senators have become the creatures of national lobbying groups rather than the representatives of their home governments.

With the arrival of the Progressive Era came the rallying cry of democracy and a new brand of American nationalism. In several ways, this shift did much to terminate the federal orientation of the union. President Woodrow Wilson's drive to make the world "safe for democracy" led him to involve the United States in a senseless European war of unprecedented bloodshed. Those who dared to criticize or obstruct the effort were then targeted by the Espionage Act of 1917, a villainous law that officially criminalized military insubordination, interference with military recruitment, and war dissent. Acts of opposition to the overall war effort were furiously suppressed by the federal government. In every way, the policy was the 20th century version of the 1798 Sedition Act, a quest to vanquish those who rejected an expansive general government.

Through the passage of the Espionage Act, the federal government hoped to eliminate all types of anti-war activities. Violation of the law was punishable by a fine of $10,000 and/or imprisonment for up to twenty years. Not only was the law blatantly unconstitutional, its enforcement was highly oppressive. For instance, outspoken politician from Wisconsin, Victor Berger, was sentenced to 20 years in federal prison for publishing anti-war newspaper editorials. Despite this, the people of his state elected him to three successive terms in the House of Representatives. Congress, acting in resentment toward his successful election, refused to seat him until his sentence was overturned years after the war. For criticizing the management of the American Red Cross during the war, Louis Nagler was charged under the Espionage Act and sentenced to 20 in prison. A man named Morris Zucker from Brooklyn was also sentenced to 15 years in prison for seditious comments.[512] In 2013, the federal government resurrected the abhorrent law again, using it to charge Edward Snowden for the dissemination of classified intelligence documents.

Regardless of the assurances made during ratification of the Constitution, the federal courts have generally accepted that virtually all laws are constitutional by virtue of their passage through Congress. Realizing this, politicians in high office continually invoke federal court opinions to justify their own political aims, whether or not such precedents conform to the Constitution's originally ratified meaning. Unconstitutional actions are frequently rationalized by citing former ones, and the federal courts have frequently endeavored to interject and shape policy, subverting the state authorities in the process.

One way this has been done is through misinterpretation and application of the 14th Amendment to the Constitution. This amendment, which was originally written and ratified to guarantee basic rights to freedmen the wake of the Civil War, is now used by the federal courts to police the states and dispose of local laws the federal judges are personally opposed to. The argument used to justify this misapplication is predicated on what has become known as the "incorporation doctrine." Under this theory of constitutional interpretation, the ratification of the 14th Amendment incorporated the first eight amendments in the Bill of Rights – originally intended only as barriers against federal authority – against the state authorities in the same manner.

The Bill of Rights, as it was ratified in 1791, never did such a thing, a fact made clear by the document's preamble:

> The Conventions of a number of the States, having at the time of their adopting the Constitution, expressed a desire, in order to prevent misconstruction or abuse of its powers, that further declaratory and restrictive clauses should be added: And as extending the ground of public confidence in the Government, will best ensure the beneficent ends of its institution.[513]

Noticeably, the Bill of Rights imposed a series of limitations upon the general government, brought about by petition during the ratification struggle and accepted by the states during the First Congress. Due to the widespread trepidation that the general government would violate the most basic rights of the people, many delegates refused to ratify the Constitution until such an addendum was made. Those who shared this popular viewpoint included Luther Martin, George Mason, and Elbridge Gerry – all prominent figures that objected to the omission of a bill of rights.

After the shared anxieties of these individuals spurred a popular movement to modify the Constitution, many of the states drafted prospective amendments and placed them into their ratification texts. Instead of suggesting means to curtail the power of the state authorities, the amendments expressed various aspirations to limit federal power. The state of Massachusetts even spelled this out explicitly in its 1788 ratification ordinance:

> It is the opinion of this convention, that certain amendments and alterations in the said constitution would remove the fears, and quiet the apprehensions of many of the good people of this commonwealth, and more effectually guard against an undue administration **of the federal government**.[emphasis added][514]

Similarly, New Hampshire's ratification document echoed this sentiment verbatim. The ratification instrument of New York listed several proposals, all of which designated only Congress as the body to be inhibited by each measure.[515] A cursory examination of the ratification texts from all states demonstrates the same phenomenon, and no state proposed limitations upon its own sovereign power. The states intended the amendments to inhibit the general government, not the states. Such became the case when the Bill of Rights was ratified on December 15, 1791, giving legal standing to the first ten amendments.

At the exact time the Bill of Rights was ratified, many of the states had official established churches, restrictions on certain types of speech, and minor restrictions on bearing arms in certain locations. At no point were any of these policies deemed constitutionally impermissible under the federal Bill of Rights. In addition, the First Amendment stated that "Congress shall make no law" respecting an establishment of religion, making clear the body it intended to restrain. Even by the time of the famous 1833 Supreme Court case of *Barron v. Baltimore*, where a suit alleged that the Fifth Amendment extended to the state of Maryland, this concept was acknowledged by the Supreme Court:

> Had the framers of [the Bill of Rights] intended them to be limitations on the powers of the State governments, they would have imitated the framers of the original Constitution, and have expressed that intention. Had Congress engaged in the extraordinary occupation of improving the Constitutions of the several States by affording the people additional protection from the exercise of power by their own governments in matters which concerned themselves alone, they would have declared this purpose in plain and intelligible language.[516]

Though John Barron's counsel justified their suit on the basis that the Bill of Rights limited the state governments, it is instead clear that the states used the first eight amendments to restrict the general government alone. Indeed, the relatively modern view that the Bill of Rights created state restrictions did not even emerge until the 20th century.

Decades after the 14th Amendment was ratified, federal lawyers began to build cases around the idea that the same amendment had incorporated the Bill of Rights limitations against the state governments. In the contemporary, the federal courts have regularly justified their attempts to meddle in the internal affairs of the states upon the same premise. Despite the widespread acceptance of this mantra among the legal community and academia, no such purpose was suggested by the 14th Amendment's chief architects and advocates. Moreover, the Congressional debates refute the mere suggestion that the clause carried such a function.

Rather than a device to restrain the states from exercising reserved powers, the 14th Amendment's chief purpose was to affirm that freedmen held the same basic process rights as their white counterparts. With the fear that states would curtail the basic liberties of former slaves after they had been emancipated via the 13th Amendment, Congress believed the amendment necessary to constitutionalize the Civil Rights Act of 1866. Under the law, freedmen would be legally empowered "to make and enforce contracts, to sue, be parties, and give evidence, to inherit, purchase, lease, sell, hold, and convey real and personal property," and would be entitled to all other rights as were "enjoyed by white citizens."

According to West Virginian George Latham, a key proponent of the amendment in the House of Representatives, the Civil Rights Act "covers exactly the same ground as the amendment." Senator Lyman Trumbull, who made painstaking strides to ensure the bill's passage, recognized the function of the act to be "a reiteration of the rights as set forth in the Civil Rights Bill." On several occasions, Trumbull added that the law had no application whatsoever except when states that discriminated against freedmen by withholding the traditional rights articulated therein. In the same fashion, Senator John Sherman of Ohio remarked that "the first section [of the amendment] was an embodiment of the [Civil Rights] Act."[517] Clearly, the function of the 14th Amendment was intimately connected to the aims of the Civil Rights Act.

In regard to 14th Amendment guarantee to "equal protection under the law," the intention was that all rights afford to white citizens in 1866 were to be applied to all individuals. Rather than create a new set of rights for certain classes of individuals, it was expected that the enumerated rights would be enjoyed by all. This meant that the if the right was not afforded to a white citizen in 1866, it wasn't expected to be extended to anyone.[518] For example, the law did not empower the federal courts to overturn state laws that prevented individuals under the age of 18 from voting.

Alternative applications of the 14th Amendment – including the supposed incorporation of the Bill of Rights – were never revealed by the Congressional debates. In his groundbreaking work on the subject, *Government by Judiciary: The Transformation of the Fourteenth Amendment*, historian and constitutional scholar Raoul Berger summed this up in the following way:

> If there was a concealed intention to go beyond the Civil Rights Act, it was not ratified because, first, ratification requires disclosure of material facts, whereas there was no disclosure that the Amendment was meant to uproot, for example, traditional State judicial procedures and practices; and, second, a surrender of recognized rights may not be presumed but must be proved.[519]

In cases that followed on the heels of the 14th Amendment, the federal courts continued to hold that the Bill of Rights did not apply to the state governments. As Berger wrote, "no such purpose was entertained" by advocates of the amendment.[520] It was not interpreted otherwise for over 55 years after its ratification, when the federal judiciary carved out new authority for themselves in the 1920s and 1930s. Only at this point, many decades after the amendment's ratification and a series of legal precedents that denied the same, did the federal courts opine that the 14th Amendment incorporated the Bill of Rights restrictions against the states.

Another historical instance which refutes the incorporation doctrine can be found in a failed attempt by James Blaine to apply several specific Bill of Rights limitations to the states in 1875. At that point, the senator championed a new constitutional amendment to impose the First Amendment against the states. The proposal died in the House of Representatives, failing to achieve the two-thirds vote necessary to be sent to the states for consideration. If the 14th Amendment did what the federal courts now say it did, Blaine's proposal would have been redundant and unnecessary.

Even by 1922, the federal courts maintained that the 14th Amendment did not have the effect of incorporation. This was validated in the case of *Prudential Insurance Company of America v. Cheek*, which concerned New York's ability to restrict freedom of speech. The Supreme Court opinion stated categorically that the amendment did not apply to the states:

> But, as we have stated, neither the Fourteenth Amendment nor any other provision of the Constitution of the United States imposes upon the states any restrictions about 'freedom of speech' or the 'liberty of silence'; nor, we may add, does it confer any right of privacy upon either persons or corporations.[521]

This result indicates that the incorporation doctrine was not even acknowledged by the courts until many decades after the amendment's ratification. As such, the allegation that it had such a function was the conjuration of scheming lawyers.

The extent to which the incorporation doctrine has influenced modern jurisprudence cannot be overstated. Reinterpretation of the 14th Amendment has given the federal government license to overturn states laws and conform local governments to a national code. As a result of this practice, federal courts now serve as a police force against state laws it does not like, rather than function as a branch that settles federal disputes. Rather than apply the amendments against the states in the same way the founders expected them to restrict the general government, the incorporation doctrine is most often used instead to negate state laws federal judges personally dislike. Without regard to the sentiments of the local electorate, judges are now able to interject their own opinions into local matters and redefine rights in a way they were never meant to. It has made the federal judiciary into a nationalist, untouchable branch of government.

Perhaps the most litigated element of the Constitution, the misconstrued 14th Amendment has allowed the judiciary to intervene with the admission policies of state institutions, obliged the states to pay welfare benefits to arbitrary classes of residents, prohibited the states from curbing their own welfare programs, and even force state schools to conduct federally-oriented hearings prior to subjecting students to suspension. Incorporation has also been used as the foundation for various unconstitutional schemes. For instance, during the 1970s, the Warren Court came very close to finding a mandatory minimum income rate based upon 14th Amendment grounds. Had it not been for a strenuous effort of opposition, scholar David Bernstein explained that the Supreme Court "might very well have entrenched the American welfare state in the morass of modern constitutional law." By this transformation, the federal courts have gone far beyond the confines of the Bill of Rights to craft a plethora of costly privileges undreamed of by the founders.[522]

Originally meant to obviate state laws that hindered former slaves, the 14th Amendment was intended to ensure that aggrieved peoples would be treated no differently from whites. In modern implementation, however, the prose has been used to justify a whole host of new "rights" that are usually privileges paid for by one class that are distributed to another by government force. The advent of these new rights has also usurped legislative authority, and allowed the judiciary to become unelected policymakers.

The wording of the Fifth Amendment and 14th Amendment featured terminology that was widely understood at the time of each amendment's ratification, and the guarantee of due process rights found within both amendments related unambiguously to court proceedings. "The words "due process" have a precise technical import," Alexander Hamilton explained in 1787, "and are only applicable to the process and proceedings of the courts of justice."[523] In spite of recent trends to stretch "due process" to include the grant of substantive rights, historical records leave no indicative that the amendment was meant to justify the endless creation of new federal rights that require state funding or the conscription of labor to provide.

Far from respecting due process as a guarantee to procedural safeguards, the federal courts have used the text to overturn state legislation and the opinions of local courts. For instance, when Nebraska decided to change its school curriculum to alter its foreign language programs, the court stepped in and ruled in *Meyer v. Nebraska* that such restrictions violated the Due Process Clause of the 14th Amendment. Apparently, by 1923 all Americans miraculously had the "constitutional right" to learn German, and the power to force states to adopt particular methods of instruction or curriculum was suddenly a federal duty.

In a deviation from the norm, some modern federal judges have expressed doubt as to the validity of the incorporation doctrine, but such opinions are often glossed over or ignored entirely. For instance, former federal judge and Supreme Court nominee Robert Bork denied the legitimacy of the creed. According to Bork, the incorporation doctrine inappropriately expanded the Supreme Court's power and threatened federalism.

Tellingly, he also decried the extent to which the federal courts had overridden judicial interpretations of the states. Doing so "meant making its interpretations of the various amendments the uniform law throughout the nation, which had never occurred before," Bork wrote.[524]

Outside the scope of judicial overreach, many of the most egregious offenses against the Constitution have occurred under the administrations of popular American presidents. For instance, in 1942 President Franklin Roosevelt ventured far from intended constitutional boundaries in order to detain people of Italian and Japanese ancestry into internment camps. Following the entry of the United States into World War II, the president justified his groundbreaking policy through the claim that the continued presence of both groups would inspire seditious and rebellious behavior. Roosevelt introduced his internment program through the issuance of an unlegislated edict, Executive Order 9066:

> Now, therefore, by virtue of the authority vested in me as President of the United States, and Commander in Chief of the Army and Navy, I hereby authorize and direct the Secretary of War, and the Military Commanders whom he may from time to time designate, whenever he or any designated Commander deems such action necessary or desirable, to prescribe military areas in such places and of such extent as he or the appropriate Military Commander may determine, from which any or all persons may be excluded, and with respect to which, the right of any person to enter, remain in, or leave shall be subject to whatever restrictions the Secretary of War or the appropriate Military Commander may impose in his discretion.[525]

Cruelly reminiscent of anti-Jewish programs enacted by the Third Reich in Germany, Roosevelt's decree was a clear-cut violation of the Fifth Amendment guarantee to life, liberty, and property. The order was also imposed by executive decree, bypassing Congress and appearing as the command of an all-powerful monarch.

President Roosevelt engaged in efforts to relocate citizens by issuing a secondary decree, Executive Order 9102, which specifically established the War Relocation Authority. The new federal institution was bestowed the power to forcibly seize and relocate individuals into the camps.

Refusing to reverse this heartless transgression, the federal courts gave the policy legal credence. Demonstrating the complicity of the federal judiciary in the exploit, the court ruled that Roosevelt's actions were wholly constitutional in the 1944 case of *Korematsu v. United States*.

The majority opinion, written by Justice Hugo Black, stated that the court was unable to conclude that it was beyond the war powers of Congress and the president to confine people of Japanese ancestry to the designated "war areas." This assertion was made despite the fact that the Constitution confers no such power to either branch. Nevertheless, Black wrote that the president's new agency could not be reprimanded despite its loose criteria for determining whether individuals were "disloyal," and thus subject to such exclusion, relocation, and confinement. In the judge's estimation, internment was necessary to protect against means of unproven espionage. In considering the actions to intern citizens, Black wrote that "we cannot – by availing ourselves of the calm perspective of hindsight – now say that, at the time, these actions were unjustified."[526]

Justice Frank Murphy vehemently dissented to the opinion of the majority, and condemned "the abhorrent and despicable treatment of minority groups by the dictatorial tyrannies which this nation is now pledged to destroy."[527] Murphy correctly added that the exclusion policy went "over the very brink of constitutional power."[528] Individuals must not be deprived of their constitutional rights, he wrote, despite the government's concerns for security.[529] Murphy recognized the reason for the Fifth Amendment's existence and understood that a despotic condition would arise if the government ignored it. Without regard to Murphy's warning, the Supreme Court ruled in favor of the federal program by a margin of six to three – giving a judicial seal of approval for Roosevelt's treacherous internment program.

Additionally, in the *Ex parte Endo* case of 1944, the court ruled that loyal citizens of the United States, no matter their background, could be systematically singled out and detained indefinitely without cause or respect to due process. In the unanimous opinion, Justice William Douglas wrote that Roosevelt merely desired "the protection of the war effort against espionage and sabotage." The "powers conferred by the orders," he continued, must be considered in such a light.[530] Devoid of any constitutional justification, Douglas' opinion was based upon impulsive deference toward the president and his command of the relocation plan.

In the 1943 case of *Hirabayashi v. the United States*, the Supreme Court also ruled that the federal government could make mandated curfews binding upon minority groups when the United States was at war. The opinion noted that it was "within the constitutional authority of Congress and the Executive, acting together, to prescribe this curfew order as an emergency wartime measure." On the contrary, of course, the Constitution permitted no authority of this kind. While the court found that the curfew "did not unconstitutionally discriminate against citizens of Japanese ancestry," the exact opposite was true, as Japanese Americans on the West coast were the only group targeted by the measure.[531]

According to the court's perplexing reasoning, the Fifth Amendment only restricts Congress from enacting discriminatory legislation, not the president. Constitutionally, this justification was unconvincing and irrelevant, as the Bill of Rights protects individuals from any federal attempt to suppress due process. Moreover, the president doesn't have the constitutional prerogative to make policy at all. If one is to take the opinion in earnest, Congress can violate any protections affirmed by the Bill of Rights as long as it doesn't "discriminate" against arbitrary groups.

The Constitution does not grant the executive the power to detain innocent citizens, though various occupants have gradually assumed the ability to do so through legal precedent. As was the case in the 1940s, the presence of war has often given ill-designing oppressors license to enact pernicious schemes. Roosevelt's system of forced relocation, internment, and curfew mandates serve only to demonstrate that extent to which the citizenry has deferred political power to federal judges, and policymaking authority to devious presidents.

Like all actors in the federal government, federal judges hold political opinions, embrace political ideologies, and serve political agendas. Contrary to the convention narrative, they do not invariably understand the Constitution better than inquisitive scholars, and their legal training is often obfuscated by studies of case law rather than the writings of the ratification struggle. By asserting so much control over local matters, the Supreme Court has undoubtedly become the oligarchy the Anti-Federalists alleged it would, and the central fiefdom the Federalists assured it wouldn't.

By providing the president the power to enforce the laws of Congress, the writers of the Constitution empowered the executive to provide his subordinates instructions or make incidental changes that applied only to the executive branch. In the modern age, however, presidents of all political stripes have used executive orders unconstitutionally to supplant the legislative process entirely. Under the originally ratified Constitution, the president cannot unilaterally impose policy, or usurp the powers of Congress. "The magistrate in whom the whole executive power resides cannot of himself make a law," James Madison wrote.[532] Despite the clear confines of executive power, modern presidents often violate these boundaries with impunity. The frequency at which the legislative process has been subverted by presidents has even led the populace to accept executive edicts as a genuine function of the executive branch.

The first presidents issued very few executive instructions, none of which bypassed Congress to initiate policy. George Washington, for instance, made a request for the Confederation government to prepare a list of reports which would help him and his cabinet perform their duties. He wrote that these reports would "impress me with a full, precise, and distinct general idea of the affairs of the United States."[533] Additionally, he proclaimed a specific day in 1789 as a day of thanksgiving, which was strictly voluntary and non-binding on individuals. John Quincy Adams issued a general order in 1826 to honor the life of Thomas Jefferson, who at that time was recently deceased. In 1837, Martin Van Buren wrote an order to provide then-former President Andrew Jackson with medical care. None of these examples subjected Americans to the policy whims of the executive, or exercised powers not prescribed by the Constitution. On the contrary, the executive acts of this era were the legitimate enactments of the president's command over the executive office.

This restrained, passive version of executive authority continued into the early 20th century. By the mid-19th century, however, the term "executive order" was born, and the Abraham Lincoln administration brought forth a new form of application. Deviating from the Constitution's original intent, executive orders were only then used to legislate – often on controversial matters – from the executive office. In the early 20th century,

Presidents Theodore Roosevelt took executive orders to a new level, making 1,081 orders after a term in which William McKinley had made 185. Serving as a model for an imperial presidency, Roosevelt's administration stretched executive power far beyond the bounds of constitutional authority.

Roosevelt saw himself and the presidential office as the unique representative of America as a whole. By the natural consequence of this view, he thought that the president should impose law himself, regardless of the Constitution's restrictions:

> In theory the Executive has nothing to do with legislation. In practice as things now are, the Executive is or ought to be peculiarly representative of the people as a whole. As often as not the action of the Executive offers the only means by which the people can get the legislation they demand and ought to have. Therefore a good executive under the present conditions of American political life must take a very active interest in getting the right kind of legislation, in addition to performing his executive duties with an eye single to the public welfare.[534]

With a haughty and overstated view of the presidency, Roosevelt applied this theory to his own presidency. For instance, he used executive power to make an "executive agreement" with another world power, the Dominican Republic, without the advice and consent of the Senate – a Constitutionally-mandated requirement for treaties with foreign powers. Engaging in these diplomatic undertakings unilaterally, he hoped to avoid involving the Senate at all.

Through his executive orders, Roosevelt placed executive authority upon a new, inflated trajectory that would never be stopped. From his presidency onward, the president would often be viewed as the originator of policy rather than the approver and enforcer. Historian Thomas Woods wrote that Roosevelt's legacy is today "cherished by neoconservatives and other nationalists but deplored by Americans who still possess a lingering attachment to the republic the framers established."[535]

A few decades later, Franklin Roosevelt issued thousands of executive orders, most of which assumed the same function the former Roosevelt laid the groundwork for. Many of the latter Roosevelt's orders, such as the

infamous Executive Order 9066, transformed the executive into an imperial superintendent. Far from a president of the founders' design, the occupant of the oval office cited executive precedent to disregard the will of
the states and inflict tyrannical and oppressive policies. In virtually all
cases, the orders were left unchallenged by the federal judiciary, and Congress often endorsed the unconstitutional schemes of 20th century presidents. This abstraction of executive orders has never changed. Over the
course of 150 years, constitutional management of the executive branch
had mutated into a source of power that even the kings of Europe did not
possess.

The inclination for an executive to unilaterally impose policy on the
behalf of the country at large was apprehended from the early days of the
republic. For instance, George Washington's 1793 Neutrality Proclamation – which articulated that the United States would assume a neutral posture in regard to the wars of the French Revolution – ignited concerns in
regard to executive authority. The first president's gesture aggravated tensions with the new French republic, which had sought wartime support
from its ally and fellow rival of Great Britain. In deciding that the republic
detach itself from such affairs, Washington argued that the alliance created
with the French monarchy was rendered null when Louis XVI was beheaded. Even though Congress later endorsed the measure, Washington's
pronouncement was still thought by some to be a controversial deed. Alexander Hamilton supported the proclamation as a means to appease Britain, and contended the president was imbued with the power to direct foreign policy by virtue of his office. James Madison argued against this authority, writing under the pseudonym "Helvidius" that the policy had been
designed by "foreigners and degenerate citizens among us, who hate our
republican government and the French Revolution."[536]

In opposition, Madison perceived that the Constitution only granted the
executive, as well as the other branches, powers that were incidental to
their respective departments. The executive office, he claimed, was largely
confined to appointing, instructing, and supervising those who execute the
laws. The powers explicitly delegated to the president did not include the
ability to put the country on a footing of neutrality, Madison wrote, in the
same way they did not permit him to declare war. Conversely, Madison
wrote that legislative powers were "expressly vested" in Congress alone

and could not be exercised by any other branch except in situations where the Constitution has qualified otherwise – as in the case of veto power. The supposition that the president had a monopoly on the interpretation of treaties – which had to be endorsed by the Senate – was also a mistaken assumption, he added.[537]

Confirming Madison's assertions were the records of the state ratification debates, which revealed that many delegates apprehended the tendency to blend the legislative duties with the functions of the other branches. William Davie of North Carolina, for instance, wrote that such a prospect would be a "dangerous" affront to republicanism – one which the Constitution guarded against. "Such accumulated powers were inadmissible," he averred. In a similar incident, James Iredell stated that "the President is of a very different nature from a monarch." Therefore, the American executive could not act in an "arbitrary, haughty manner" to impose his will. Iredell noted that Constitution's unmilkable embrace of the separation of powers doctrine would serve no purpose if "each power had no means to defend itself against the encroachment of the others."[538]

Even while in Washington's cabinet, Secretary of State Thomas Jefferson criticized the Neutrality Proclamation on the same grounds. The Constitution, he contended, left most decision-making power over foreign affairs in the hands of Congress. "All legislative Powers herein granted shall be vested in a Congress of the United States," the document reads. If the founding generation would have intended for the president to be able to pass super-legislative decrees, such as those made by the kings of Europe, they would have adopted the governmental model of the kingly executive under the design of Alexander Hamilton. Instead, they decided that the president cannot act as a chief legislator or enact any lawmaking power whatsoever. As mild as Washington's decision seems today, the debate over the Neutrality Proclamation illustrated the degree to which the founding generation was serious about inhibiting the power of the executive.

The remarkable evolution of war powers has also gradually contributed to the loss of state and local authority. Especially in the last century, presidents are almost never challenged in a serious way when they choose to deploy military forces throughout the world. Emboldened by the conduct of their predecessors, presidents routinely order military strikes against foreign powers. In the process, the Congress rarely asserts it plenary authority under the Constitution to do the same, allowing the president to exploit the confines of the executive office. This inclination has become as prominent as sweeping executive authority, and is equally destructive to liberty.

While exploitation of war powers took place prior to the 20th century exploited war powers, it was not until the 1950s that these current trends started to take root. At that point, President Harry Truman's aspired to send forces to Korea to stop the Soviet-Chinese invasion. Despite the lack of Congressional authorization, Truman committed thousands of troops to the conflict. The president was fiercely attacked for his actions in the Senate, notably by prominent Senator Robert Taft:

> In the case of Korea, where a war was already under way, we had no right to send troops to a nation, with whom we had no treaty, to defend it against attack by another action, no matter how unprincipled that aggression might be, unless the whole matter was submitted to Congress and a declaration of war or some other direct authority obtained.[539]

In response to Taft's admonishment, Truman devoted his attention to providing legal validity for his actions. Consequently, he employed a host of government spokesmen to argue that his deed was not an unusual departure from Constitution standards. Like those who defended the absolute prerogative of the English kings, the president's lawyers cited the past acts of Truman's predecessors to validate his actions. Despite the volley of persuasive attacks against the president, it has been Truman's position that most Americans accept today. Setting aside the clear constitutional requirement, Congress has never declared a war since World War II.

Presidents have energetically cited the War Powers Act, which fundamentally rewrote portions of Article I, Section 8 of the Constitution, to justify their military strikes and foreign invasions. Passed in 1973, the law authorized the president to send troops into harm's way for up to 60 days, for whatever reason, without the consent of Congress. Although traditional historical accounts claim that the War Powers Act intended to restrict the president's war-making authority in the wake of the Vietnam War, it has instead given sanction and legal force to the endless streak of modern militarism.

The judicial and executive branches are not the only entities that have violated the Constitution. Paralleling the constitutional abnegations of the federal courts and the president is Congress, which has accentuated its own control over the states by its fondness for violating the 10th Amendment. Ignoring the reserved powers of the states, Congress creates and endorses law pertaining to health care, education, transportation, airport security, welfare, energy, agriculture, housing, disaster recovery, and a host of other subjects it has no delegated power over.

In the process of legislating on virtually all subjects of note, Congress has also destroyed the financial standing of Americans through runaway spending. The multitude of costly acts and government offices has created a preponderance of federal debt, which has subjugated individuals to a condition of subservience and left the states powerless to respond to the financial calamity. Thomas Jefferson, the great architect of American federalism, wrote of a potential cure to this problem in 1798. A constitutional amendment to prohibit the federal government from outspending the treasury's holdings would do much to mollify these woes, he thought:

> I wish it were possible to obtain a single amendment to our Constitution. I would be willing to depend on that alone for the reduction of the administration of our government; I mean an additional article taking from the Federal Government the power of borrowing.[540]

Today known as "a balanced budget amendment," the eminent Virginian understood that frugality was key to liberating individuals from the chains of federal debt. With the potential of forcibly removing from federal politicians the ability to spend on earmarks, pet projects, and other expenditures that are unconstitutional, the prospect has failed to attract the support of the same individuals it intends to restrict.

Even though Americans are guaranteed the liberty to petition and air grievances against the federal government, urging federal politicians to adopt one's ideological goals almost always fails to achieve significant results in the contemporary epoch. The most significant reason for this is that contemporary Americans lack representation in the federal government. The House of Representatives was originally tied by the Constitution to a ratio of one representative for every 30,000 inhabitants, but as of

2015 there is only one representative in the assembly for every 738,000.[541] In addition, individuals have little sway with the Senate, which is populated by figures that are often more beholden to national lobbying groups than home constituencies. With letter writing campaigns as exercises in futility, many citizens find themselves disgruntled over their own lack of influence in the federal government. Surely, there must be other ways that individuals can defy the unconstitutional and immoral acts of the federal government.

Nullification, the approach Thomas Jefferson considered "the rightful remedy" against constitutional usurpation, is the most effective strategy that can be taken to preserve liberty. As a method that can be employed quickly, it has proven to be the most constitutionally sound way to assert the states' countervailing force against the federal government. Since individuals are much more connected with their local representatives than their federal counterparts, they can make momentous strides to obstruct federal policy on a state level. Carrying forward the Jeffersonian mantra, nullification has successfully counteracted the enforcement of unconstitutional federal acts, and restored the proper balance of power between the states and federal government.

The axiom started with Thomas Jefferson and James Madison's 1798 crusade against the Sedition Act, and terminated only in its expiration. In 1854, same strategy was utilized by Sherman Booth, who courageously led a group of citizens to rescue fugitive slave Joshua Glover and thwart the 1850 Fugitive Slave Act. In 1955, Rosa Parks embraced the same spirit of defiance when she refused to give up her seat on the bus in Montgomery, Alabama. On many occasions, the indignation of individuals has delivered the tangible rollback of unconstitutional policies – more successfully than any electoral victory has given.

The same umbrage against tyranny persuaded the rebel barons to curtail the ruthlessness of King John in 1215. In 1649, the same spirit inspired English Parliament to execute a malevolent king for violating his country's constitutional framework. Identical precepts swept a oppressor from the same throne, and reasserted the people's rights in 1688-1689. Treading the same path, the American states severed all ties with Great Britain, bringing redemption to local government in the process. Indeed, many of the world's most momentous struggles for liberty have ended in considerable losses of life and treasure. Even though modern nullification campaigns require immense diligence, they can often produce palpable results without such losses.

As of this writing, state legislatures are using nullification to combat the invasive use of federal drones, federal firearm restrictions, indefinite detention mandates, federal restrictions on illicit substances, the enactment of national education standards, and other unconstitutional offences. By way of single issue-based coalitions, resistance against federal overreach has even crossed party lines. With the ultimate aim of protecting individual rights and safeguarding the Constitution, nullification can be applied in the modern age.

In one such campaign, Governor Steve Bullock of Montana made clear that his state rejected the validity of the federal REAL ID Act. In a fiery letter to the federal department, Bullock contended that his state's ability to maintain its own identification standards has been sufficient, "independent of federal mandate." Under the constitutional doctrine of anti-commandeering that even the Supreme Court has acknowledged, Montana is pushing back at coercive attempts to force the state to adopt federal identification standards.[542]

Several states are currently considering bills that not only reject federal restrictions on firearms, but anticipate and nullify future ones as well. A recent bill in Missouri contained the following resolution:

> All federal acts, laws, executive orders, administrative orders, court orders, rules, and regulations, whether past, present, or future, which infringe on the people's right to keep and bear arms as guaranteed by the Second Amendment to the United States Constitution and Article I, Section 23 of the Missouri Constitution shall be invalid in this state, shall not be recognized by this state, shall be specifically rejected by this state, and shall be considered **null and void and of no effect** in this state.[emphasis added][543]

The bill also emphasizes that Missouri is "duty bound to oppose every infraction of those principles which constitute the basis of the Union of the States."[544] Passed by the House and Senate, the measure was met with the veto of Governor Jay Nixon. Nevertheless, the governor's veto was overridden by the House. Despite the ultimate demise of Missouri's attempt, Idaho passed a similar firearm nullification bill that was signed into law the same year.[545]

By way of the same strategy used by Jefferson and Madison in 1798, states are standing up to attempts to deprive individuals of liberty. In the most radical of these applications, Tennessee, Utah, and Maryland have entertained bills that would stifle the supply of water and power to National Security Agency facilities within their respective borders.[546] With the rise of the department's pervasive warrantless surveillance program, these states have made a strong statements on behalf of those who seek to eviscerate unconstitutional behavior and protect privacy rights.

Understanding privacy to be a recognized liberty and affirmed by the Fourth Amendment, Maryland's bill would even cut resources to National Security Agency Headquarters in Fort Meade. In defense of his bill, state delegate and bill sponsor Michael Smigiel articulated that the plan would protect citizens of his state from federal intrusion. "I want Maryland standing with its back to its people holding a shield," he declared, "not facing them holding a sword."[547] The earnest pursuit of such a solution, no doubt, illustrates the stark contrast between state representatives and their federal counterparts.

Modern nullification efforts have long transcended the days when the strategy was considered only as a means to reject federal marijuana restrictions. Today, nullification is used to counter all kinds of pernicious federal policies, with expediency in mind. Without requiring constitutional amendments, federal court opinions, particular electoral outcomes, or federal lawmakers, nullification preserves liberty and suffocates the federal government's perpetual thirst for power.

Most problems in government are not the result of a single political movement, party, or individual. Present-day hardships, though now woven into the fabric of our society, have emerged only after many decades of wrongdoing. It is sometimes easy to be cynical about the continuance of our ailments, but there is always recourse. Nullification, local activism, and education campaigns are all effective approaches that can be used to restore the American republic to the vision of the founders. No matter how dire the situation or how futile patriotic efforts may sometimes seem, the "Principles of '98" can be invoked once more.

Despite the political turmoil in his own life, Thomas Jefferson never believed that the situation was too dire to set right if republican principles were re-embraced. In the midst of the Sedition Act Crisis, Jefferson hinged his own hope on the fortitude of the American people:

> The spirit of 1776 is not dead. It has only been slumbering. The body of the American people is substantially republican. But their virtuous feelings have been played on by some fact with more fiction; they have been the dupes of artful maneuvers, and made for a moment to be willing instruments in forging chains for themselves. But times and truth dissipated the delusion, and opened their eyes.[548]

It is only through true understanding of our republic's compact that we can retune our efforts and persevere through the obstacles before us. Similarly, the "artful maneuvers" attempted by our own oppressors must always be anticipated and rejected. By heeding Jefferson's advice, we would all do much to sow the seeds of liberty in every pasture.

Documents

Magna Carta (1215)

Preamble:

John, by the grace of God, king of England, lord of Ireland, duke of Normandy and Aquitaine, and count of Anjou, to the archbishop, bishops, abbots, earls, barons, justiciaries, foresters, sheriffs, stewards, servants, and to all his bailiffs and liege subjects, greetings. Know that, having regard to God and for the salvation of our soul, and those of all our ancestors and heirs, and unto the honor of God and the advancement of his holy Church and for the rectifying of our realm, we have granted as underwritten by advice of our venerable fathers, Stephen, archbishop of Canterbury, primate of all England and cardinal of the holy Roman Church, Henry, archbishop of Dublin, William of London, Peter of Winchester, Jocelyn of Bath and Glastonbury, Hugh of Lincoln, Walter of Worcester, William of Coventry, Benedict of Rochester, bishops; of Master Pandulf, subdeacon and member of the household of our lord the Pope, of brother Aymeric (master of the Knights of the Temple in England), and of the illustrious men William Marshal, earl of Pembroke, William, earl of Salisbury, William, earl of Warenne, William, earl of Arundel, Alan of Galloway (constable of Scotland), Waren Fitz Gerold, Peter Fitz Herbert, Hubert De Burgh (seneschal of Poitou), Hugh de Neville, Matthew Fitz Herbert, Thomas Basset, Alan Basset, Philip d'Aubigny, Robert of Roppesley, John Marshal, John Fitz Hugh, and others, our liegemen.

1. In the first place we have granted to God, and by this our present charter confirmed for us and our heirs forever that the English Church shall be free, and shall have her rights entire, and her liberties inviolate; and we will that it be thus observed; which is apparent from this that the freedom of elections, which is reckoned most important and very essential to the English Church, we, of our pure and unconstrained will, did grant, and did by our charter confirm and did obtain the ratification of the same from our lord, Pope Innocent III, before the quarrel arose between us and our barons: and this we will observe, and our will is that it be observed in good faith by our heirs forever. We have also granted to all freemen of our kingdom, for us and our heirs forever, all the underwritten liberties, to be had and held by them and their heirs, of us and our heirs forever.

2. If any of our earls or barons, or others holding of us in chief by military service shall have died, and at the time of his death his heir shall be full of age and owe "relief", he shall have his inheritance by the old relief, to wit, the heir or heirs of an earl, for the whole baroncy of an earl by L100; the heir or heirs of a baron, L100 for a whole barony; the heir or heirs of a knight, 100s, at most, and whoever owes less let him give less, according to the ancient custom of fees.

3. If, however, the heir of any one of the aforesaid has been under age and in wardship, let him have his inheritance without relief and without fine when he comes of age.

4. The guardian of the land of an heir who is thus under age, shall take from the land of the heir nothing but reasonable produce, reasonable customs, and reasonable services, and that without destruction or waste of men or goods; and if we have committed the wardship of the lands of any such minor to the sheriff, or to any other who is responsible to us for its issues, and he has made destruction or waster of what he holds in wardship, we will take of him amends, and the land shall be committed to two lawful and discreet men of that fee, who shall be responsible for the issues to us or to him to whom we shall assign them; and if we have given or sold the wardship of any such land to anyone and he has therein made destruction or waste, he shall lose that wardship, and it shall be transferred to two lawful and discreet men of that fief, who shall be responsible to us in like manner as aforesaid.

5. The guardian, moreover, so long as he has the wardship of the land, shall keep up the houses, parks, fishponds, stanks, mills, and other things pertaining to the land, out of the issues of the same land; and he shall restore to the heir, when he has come to full age, all his land, stocked with ploughs and wainage, according as the season of husbandry shall require, and the issues of the land can reasonable bear.

6. Heirs shall be married without disparagement, yet so that before the marriage takes place the nearest in blood to that heir shall have notice.

7. A widow, after the death of her husband, shall forthwith and without difficulty have her marriage portion and inheritance; nor shall she give anything for her dower, or for her marriage portion, or for the inheritance which her husband and she held on the day of the death of that husband; and she may remain in the house of her husband for forty days after his death, within which time her dower shall be assigned to her.

8. No widow shall be compelled to marry, so long as she prefers to live without a husband; provided always that she gives security not to marry without our consent, if she holds of us, or without the consent of the lord of whom she holds, if she holds of another.

9. Neither we nor our bailiffs will seize any land or rent for any debt, as long as the chattels of the debtor are sufficient to repay the debt; nor shall the sureties of the debtor be distrained so long as the principal debtor is able to satisfy the debt; and if the principal debtor shall fail to pay the debt, having nothing wherewith to pay it, then the sureties shall answer for the debt; and let them have the lands and rents of the debtor, if they desire them, until they are indemnified for the debt which they have paid for him, unless the principal debtor can show proof that he is discharged thereof as against the said sureties.

10. If one who has borrowed from the Jews any sum, great or small, die before that loan be repaid, the debt shall not bear interest while the heir is under age, of whomsoever he may hold; and if the debt fall into our hands, we will not take anything except the principal sum contained in the bond.

11. And if anyone die indebted to the Jews, his wife shall have her dower and pay nothing of that debt; and if any children of the deceased are left under age, necessaries shall be provided for them in keeping with the holding of the deceased; and out of the residue the debt shall be paid, reserving, however, service due to feudal lords; in like manner let it be done touching debts due to others than Jews.

12. No scutage not aid shall be imposed on our kingdom, unless by common counsel of our kingdom, except for ransoming our person, for making our eldest son a knight, and for once marrying our eldest daughter; and for these there shall not be levied more than a reasonable aid. In like manner it shall be done concerning aids from the city of London.

13. And the city of London shall have all it ancient liberties and free customs, as well by land as by water; furthermore, we decree and grant that all other cities, boroughs, towns, and ports shall have all their liberties and free customs.

14. And for obtaining the common counsel of the kingdom anent the assessing of an aid (except in the three cases aforesaid) or of a scutage, we will cause to be summoned the archbishops, bishops, abbots, earls, and greater barons, severally by our letters; and we will moveover cause to be summoned generally, through our sheriffs and bailiffs, and others who hold of us in chief, for a fixed date, namely, after the expiry of at least forty days, and at a fixed place; and in all letters of such summons we will specify the reason of the summons. And when the summons has thus been made, the business shall proceed on the day appointed, according to the counsel of such as are present, although not all who were summoned have come.

15. We will not for the future grant to anyone license to take an aid from his own free tenants, except to ransom his person, to make his eldest son a knight, and once to marry his eldest daughter; and on each of these occasions there shall be levied only a reasonable aid.

16. No one shall be distrained for performance of greater service for a knight's fee, or for any other free tenement, than is due therefrom.

17. Common pleas shall not follow our court, but shall be held in some fixed place.

18. Inquests of novel disseisin, of mort d'ancestor, and of darrein presentment shall not be held elsewhere than in their own county courts, and that in manner following; We, or, if we should be out of the realm, our chief justiciar, will send two justiciaries through every county four times a year, who shall alone with four knights of the county chosen by the county, hold the said assizes in the county court, on the day and in the place of meeting of that court.

19. And if any of the said assizes cannot be taken on the day of the county court, let there remain of the knights and freeholders, who were present at the county court on that day, as many as may be required for the efficient making of judgments, according as the business be more or less.

20. A freeman shall not be amerced for a slight offense, except in accordance with the degree of the offense; and for a grave offense he shall be amerced in accordance with the gravity of the offense, yet saving always his "contentment"; and a merchant in the same way, saving his "merchandise"; and a villein shall be amerced in the same way, saving his "wainage" if they have fallen into our mercy: and none of the aforesaid amercements shall be imposed except by the oath of honest men of the neighborhood.

21. Earls and barons shall not be amerced except through their peers, and only in accordance with the degree of the offense.

22. A clerk shall not be amerced in respect of his lay holding except after the manner of the others aforesaid; further, he shall not be amerced in accordance with the extent of his ecclesiastical benefice.

23. No village or individual shall be compelled to make bridges at river banks, except those who from of old were legally bound to do so.

24. No sheriff, constable, coroners, or others of our bailiffs, shall hold pleas of our Crown.

25. All counties, hundred, wapentakes, and trithings (except our demesne manors) shall remain at the old rents, and without any additional payment.

26. If anyone holding of us a lay fief shall die, and our sheriff or bailiff shall exhibit our letters patent of summons for a debt which the deceased owed us, it shall be lawful for our sheriff or bailiff to attach and enroll the chattels of the deceased, found upon the lay fief, to the value of that debt, at the sight of law worthy men, provided always that nothing whatever be thence removed until the debt which is evident shall be fully paid to us; and the residue shall be left to the executors to fulfill the will of the deceased; and if there be nothing due from him to us, all the chattels shall go to the deceased, saving to his wife and children their reasonable shares.

27. If any freeman shall die intestate, his chattels shall be distributed by the hands of his nearest kinsfolk and friends, under supervision of the Church, saving to every one the debts which the deceased owed to him.

28. No constable or other bailiff of ours shall take corn or other provisions from anyone without immediately tendering money therefor, unless he can have postponement thereof by permission of the seller.

29. No constable shall compel any knight to give money in lieu of castle-guard, when he is willing to perform it in his own person, or (if he himself cannot do it from any reasonable cause) then by another responsible man. Further, if we have led or sent him upon military service, he shall be relieved from guard in proportion to the time during which he has been on service because of us.

30. No sheriff or bailiff of ours, or other person, shall take the horses or carts of any freeman for transport duty, against the will of the said freeman.

31. Neither we nor our bailiffs shall take, for our castles or for any other work of ours, wood which is not ours, against the will of the owner of that wood.

32. We will not retain beyond one year and one day, the lands those who have been convicted of felony, and the lands shall thereafter be handed over to the lords of the fiefs.

33. All kydells for the future shall be removed altogether from Thames and Medway, and throughout all England, except upon the seashore.

34. The writ which is called praecipe shall not for the future be issued to anyone, regarding any tenement whereby a freeman may lose his court.

35. Let there be one measure of wine throughout our whole realm; and one measure of ale; and one measure of corn, to wit, "the London quarter"; and one width of cloth (whether dyed, or russet, or "halberget"), to wit, two ells within the selvedges; of weights also let it be as of measures.

36. Nothing in future shall be given or taken for a writ of inquisition of life or limbs, but freely it shall be granted, and never denied.

37. If anyone holds of us by fee-farm, either by socage or by burage, or of any other land by knight's service, we will not (by reason of that fee-farm, socage, or burgage), have the wardship of the heir, or of such land of his as if of the fief of that other; nor shall we have wardship of that fee-farm, socage, or burgage, unless such fee-farm owes knight's service. We will not by reason of any small serjeancy which anyone may hold of us by the service of rendering to us knives, arrows, or the like, have wardship of his heir or of the land which he holds of another lord by knight's service.

38. No bailiff for the future shall, upon his own unsupported complaint, put anyone to his "law", without credible witnesses brought for this purposes.

39. No freemen shall be taken or imprisoned or disseised or exiled or in any way destroyed, nor will we go upon him nor send upon him, except by the lawful judgment of his peers or by the law of the land.

40. To no one will we sell, to no one will we refuse or delay, right or justice.

41. All merchants shall have safe and secure exit from England, and entry to England, with the right to tarry there and to move about as well by land as by water, for buying and selling by the ancient and right customs, quit from all evil tolls, except (in time of war) such merchants as are of the land at war with us. And if such are found in our land at the beginning of the war, they shall be detained, without injury to their bodies or goods, until information be received by us, or by our chief justiciar, how the merchants of our land found in the land at war with us are treated; and if our men are safe there, the others shall be safe in our land.

42. It shall be lawful in future for anyone (excepting always those imprisoned or outlawed in accordance with the law of the kingdom, and natives of any country at war with us, and merchants, who shall be treated as if above provided) to leave our kingdom and to return, safe and secure by land and water, except for a short period in time of war, on grounds of public policy- reserving always the allegiance due to us.

43. If anyone holding of some escheat (such as the honor of Wallingford, Nottingham, Boulogne, Lancaster, or of other escheats which are in our hands and are baronies) shall die, his heir shall give no other relief, and perform no other service to us than he would have done to the baron if that barony had been in the baron's hand; and we shall hold it in the same manner in which the baron held it.

44. Men who dwell without the forest need not henceforth come before our justiciaries of the forest upon a general summons, unless they are in plea, or sureties of one or more, who are attached for the forest.

45. We will appoint as justices, constables, sheriffs, or bailiffs only such as know the law of the realm and mean to observe it well.

46. All barons who have founded abbeys, concerning which they hold charters from the kings of England, or of which they have long continued possession, shall have the wardship of them, when vacant, as they ought to have.

47. All forests that have been made such in our time shall forthwith be disafforsted; and a similar course shall be followed with regard to river banks that have been placed "in defense" by us in our time.

48. All evil customs connected with forests and warrens, foresters and warreners, sheriffs and their officers, river banks and their wardens, shall immediately by inquired into in each county by twelve sworn knights of the same county chosen by the honest men of the same county, and shall, within forty days of the said inquest, be utterly abolished, so as never to be restored, provided always that we previously have intimation thereof, or our justiciar, if we should not be in England.

49. We will immediately restore all hostages and charters delivered to us by Englishmen, as sureties of the peace of faithful service.

50. We will entirely remove from their bailiwicks, the relations of Gerard of Athee (so that in future they shall have no bailiwick in England); namely, Engelard of Cigogne, Peter, Guy, and Andrew of Chanceaux, Guy of Cigogne, Geoffrey of Martigny with his brothers, Philip Mark with his brothers and his nephew Geoffrey, and the whole brood of the same.

51. As soon as peace is restored, we will banish from the kingdom all foreign born knights, crossbowmen, serjeants, and mercenary soldiers who have come with horses and arms to the kingdom's hurt.

52. If anyone has been dispossessed or removed by us, without the legal judgment of his peers, from his lands, castles, franchises, or from his right, we will immediately restore them to him; and if a dispute arise over this, then let it be decided by the five and twenty barons of whom mention is made below in the clause for securing the peace. Moreover, for all those possessions, from which anyone has, without the lawful judgment of his peers, been disseised or removed, by our father, King Henry, or by our brother, King Richard, and which we retain in our hand (or which as possessed by others, to whom we are bound to warrant them) we shall have respite until the usual term of crusaders; excepting those things about which a plea has been raised, or an inquest made by our order, before our taking of the cross; but as soon as we return from the expedition, we will immediately grant full justice therein.

53. We shall have, moreover, the same respite and in the same manner in rendering justice concerning the disafforestation or retention of those forests which Henry our father and Richard our brother afforested, and concerning the wardship of lands which are of the fief of another (namely, such wardships as we have hitherto had by reason of a fief which anyone held of us by knight's service), and concerning abbeys founded on other fiefs than our own, in which the lord of the fee claims to have right; and when we have returned, or if we desist from our expedition, we will immediately grant full justice to all who complain of such things.

54. No one shall be arrested or imprisoned upon the appeal of a woman, for the death of any other than her husband.

55. All fines made with us unjustly and against the law of the land, and all amercements, imposed unjustly and against the law of the land, shall be entirely remitted, or else it shall be done concerning them according to the decision of the five and twenty barons whom mention is made below in the clause for securing the pease, or according to the judgment of the majority of the same, along with the aforesaid Stephen, archbishop of Canterbury, if he can be present, and such others as he may wish to bring with him for this purpose, and if he cannot be present the business shall nevertheless proceed without him, provided always that if any one or more of the aforesaid five and twenty barons are in a similar suit, they shall be removed as far as concerns this particular judgment, others being substituted in their places after having been selected by the rest of the same five and twenty for this purpose only, and after having been sworn.

56. If we have disseised or removed Welshmen from lands or liberties, or other things, without the legal judgment of their peers in England or in Wales, they shall be immediately restored to them; and if a dispute arise over this, then let it be decided in the marches by the judgment of their peers; for the tenements in England according to the law of England, for tenements in Wales according to the law of Wales, and for tenements in the marches according to the law of the marches. Welshmen shall do the same to us and ours.

57. Further, for all those possessions from which any Welshman has, without the lawful judgment of his peers, been disseised or removed by King Henry our father, or King Richard our brother, and which we retain in our hand (or which are possessed by others, and which we ought to warrant), we will have respite until the usual term of crusaders; excepting those things about which a plea has been raised or an inquest made by our order before we took the cross; but as soon as we return (or if perchance we desist from our expedition), we will immediately grant full justice in accordance with the laws of the Welsh and in relation to the foresaid regions.

58. We will immediately give up the son of Llywelyn and all the hostages of Wales, and the charters delivered to us as security for the peace.

59. We will do towards Alexander, king of Scots, concerning the return of his sisters and his hostages, and concerning his franchises, and his right, in the same manner as we shall do towards our owher barons of England, unless it ought to be otherwise according to the charters which we hold from William his father, formerly king of Scots; and this shall be according to the judgment of his peers in our court.

60. Moreover, all these aforesaid customs and liberties, the observances of which we have granted in our kingdom as far as pertains to us towards our men, shall be observed by all of our kingdom, as well clergy as laymen, as far as pertains to them towards their men.

61. Since, moveover, for God and the amendment of our kingdom and for the better allaying of the quarrel that has arisen between us and our barons, we have granted all these concessions, desirous that they should enjoy them in complete and firm endurance forever, we give and grant to them the underwritten security, namely, that the barons choose five and twenty barons of the kingdom, whomsoever they will, who shall be bound with all their might, to observe and hold, and cause to be observed, the peace and liberties we have granted and confirmed to them by this our present Charter, so that if we, or our justiciar, or our bailiffs or any one of our officers, shall in anything be at fault towards anyone, or shall have broken any one of the articles of this peace or of this security, and the offense be notified to four barons of the foresaid five and twenty, the said four barons shall repair to us (or our justiciar, if we are out of the realm) and, laying the transgression before us, petition to have that transgression redressed without delay. And if we shall not have corrected the transgression (or, in the event of our being out of the realm, if our justiciar shall not have corrected it) within forty days, reckoning from the time it has been intimated to us (or to our justiciar, if we should be out of the realm), the four barons aforesaid shall refer that matter to the rest of the five and twenty barons, and those five and twenty barons shall, together with the community of the whole realm, distrain and distress us in all possible ways, namely, by seizing our castles, lands, possessions, and in any other way they can, until redress has been obtained as they deem fit, saving harmless our own person, and the persons of our queen and children; and when redress has been obtained, they shall resume their old relations towards us. And let whoever in the country desires it, swear to obey the orders of the said five and twenty barons for the execution of all the aforesaid matters, and along with them, to molest us to the utmost of his power; and we publicly and freely grant leave to everyone who wishes to swear, and we shall never forbid anyone to swear. All those, moreover, in the land who of themselves and of their own accord are unwilling to swear to the twenty five to help them in constraining and molesting us, we shall by our command compel the same to swear to the effect foresaid. And if any one of the five and twenty barons shall have died or departed from the land, or be incapacitated in any other manner which would prevent the foresaid provisions being carried out, those of the said twenty five barons who are left shall choose another in his place according to their own judgment, and he shall be sworn in the same way as the others. Further, in all matters, the execution of which is entrusted, to these twenty five barons, if perchance these twenty five are present and disagree about anything, or if some of them, after being summoned, are unwilling or unable to be present, that which the majority of those present ordain or command shall be held as fixed and established, exactly as if the whole twenty five had concurred in this; and the said twenty five shall swear that they will faithfully observe all that is aforesaid, and cause it to be observed with all their might. And we shall procure nothing from anyone, directly or indirectly, whereby any part of these concessions and liberties might be revoked or diminished; and if any such things has been procured, let it be void and null, and we shall never use it personally or by another.

62. And all the will, hatreds, and bitterness that have arisen between us and our men, clergy and lay, from the date of the quarrel, we have completely remitted and pardoned to everyone. Moreover, all trespasses occasioned by the said quarrel, from Easter in the sixteenth year of our reign till the restoration of peace, we have fully remitted to all, both clergy and laymen, and completely forgiven, as far as pertains to us. And on this head, we have caused to be made for them letters testimonial patent of the lord Stephen, archbishop of Canterbury, of the lord Henry, archbishop of Dublin, of the bishops aforesaid, and of Master Pandulf as touching this security and the concessions aforesaid.

63. Wherefore we will and firmly order that the English Church be free, and that the men in our kingdom have and hold all the aforesaid liberties, rights, and concessions, well and peaceably, freely and quietly, fully and wholly, for themselves and their heirs, of us and our heirs, in all respects and in all places forever, as is aforesaid. An oath, moreover, has been taken, as well on our part as on the part of the barons, that all these conditions aforesaid shall be kept in good faith and without evil intent. Given under our hand - the above named and many others being witnesses - in the meadow which is called Runnymede, between Windsor and Staines, on the fifteenth day of June, in the seventeenth year of our reign.

The Petition of Right (1628)

The Petition exhibited to his Majesty by the Lords Spiritual and Temporal, and Commons, in this present Parliament assembled, concerning divers Rights and Liberties of the Subjects, with the King's Majesty's royal answer thereunto in full Parliament.

To the King's Most Excellent Majesty,

Humbly show unto our Sovereign Lord the King, the Lords Spiritual and Temporal, and Commons in Parliament assembles, that whereas it is declared and enacted by a statute made in the time of the reign of King Edward I, commonly called Stratutum de Tellagio non Concedendo, that no tallage or aid shall be laid or levied by the king or his heirs in this realm, without the good will and assent of the archbishops, bishops, earls, barons, knights, burgesses, and other the freemen of the commonalty of this realm; and by authority of parliament holden in the five-and-twentieth year of the reign of King Edward III, it is declared and enacted, that from thenceforth no person should be compelled to make any loans to the king against his will, because such loans were against reason and the franchise of the land; and by other laws of this realm it is provided, that none should be charged by any charge or imposition called a benevolence, nor by such like charge; by which statutes before mentioned, and other the good laws and statutes of this realm, your subjects have inherited this freedom, that they should not be compelled to contribute to any tax, tallage, aid, or other like charge not set by common consent, in parliament.

II. Yet nevertheless of late divers commissions directed to sundry commissioners in several counties, with instructions, have issued; by means whereof your people have been in divers places assembled, and required to lend certain sums of money unto your Majesty, and many of them, upon their refusal so to do, have had an oath administered unto them not warrantable by the laws or statutes of this realm, and have been constrained to become bound and make appearance and give utterance before your Privy Council and in other places, and others of them have been therefore imprisoned, confined, and sundry other ways molested and disquieted; and divers other charges have been laid and levied upon your people in several counties by lord lieutenants, deputy lieutenants, commissioners for musters, justices of peace and others, by command or direction from your Majesty, or your Privy Council, against the laws and free custom of the realm.

III. And whereas also by the statute called 'The Great Charter of the Liberties of England,' it is declared and enacted, that no freeman may be taken or imprisoned or be disseized of his freehold or liberties, or his free customs, or be outlawed or exiled, or in any manner destroyed, but by the lawful judgment of his peers, or by the law of the land.

IV. And in the eight-and-twentieth year of the reign of King Edward III, it was declared and enacted by authority of parliament, that no man, of what estate or condition that he be, should be put out of his land or tenements, nor taken, nor imprisoned, nor disinherited nor put to death without being brought to answer by due process of law.

V. Nevertheless, against the tenor of the said statutes, and other the good laws and statutes of your realm to that end provided, divers of your subjects have of late been imprisoned without any cause showed; and when for their deliverance they were brought before your justices by your Majesty's writs of habeas corpus, there to undergo and receive as the court should order, and their keepers commanded to certify the causes of their detainer, no cause was certified, but that they were detained by your Majesty's special command, signified by the lords of your Privy Council, and yet were returned back to several prisons, without being charged with anything to which they might make answer according to the law.

VI. And whereas of late great companies of soldiers and mariners have been dispersed into divers counties of the realm, and the inhabitants against their wills have been compelled to receive them into their houses, and there to suffer them to sojourn against the laws and customs of this realm, and to the great grievance and vexation of the people.

VII. And whereas also by authority of parliament, in the five-and-twentieth year of the reign of King Edward III, it is declared and enacted, that no man shall be forejudged of life or limb against the form of the Great

Charter and the law of the land; and by the said Great Charter and other the laws and statutes of this your realm, no man ought to be adjudged to death but by the laws established in this your realm, either by the customs of the same realm, or by acts of parliament: and whereas no offender of what kind soever is exempted from the proceedings to be used, and punishments to be inflicted by the laws and statutes of this your realm; nevertheless of late time divers commissions under your Majesty's great seal have issued forth, by which certain persons have been assigned and appointed commissioners with power and authority to proceed within the land, according to the justice of martial law, against such soldiers or mariners, or other dissolute persons joining with them, as should commit any murder, robbery, felony, mutiny, or other outrage or misdemeanor whatsoever, and by such summary course and order as is agreeable to martial law, and is used in armies in time of war, to proceed to the trial and condemnation of such offenders, and them to cause to be executed and put to death according to the law martial.

VIII. By pretext whereof some of your Majesty's subjects have been by some of the said commissioners put to death, when and where, if by the laws and statutes of the land they had deserved death, by the same laws and statutes also they might, and by no other ought to have been judged and executed.

IX. And also sundry grievous offenders, by color thereof claiming an exemption, have escaped the punishments due to them by the laws and statutes of this your realm, by reason that divers of your officers and ministers of justice have unjustly refused or forborne to proceed against such offenders according to the same laws and statutes, upon pretense that the said offenders were punishable only by martial law, and by authority of such commissions as aforesaid; which commissions, and all other of like nature, are wholly and directly contrary to the said laws and statutes of this your realm.

X. They do therefore humbly pray your most excellent Majesty, that no man hereafter be compelled to make or yield any gift, loan, benevolence, tax, or such like charge, without common consent by act of parliament; and that none be called to make answer, or take such oath, or to give attendance, or be confined, or otherwise molested or disquieted concerning the same or for refusal thereof; and that no freeman, in any such manner as is before mentioned, be imprisoned or detained; and that your Majesty would be pleased to remove the said soldiers and mariners, and that your people may not be so burdened in time to come; and that the aforesaid commissions, for proceeding by martial law, may be revoked and annulled; and that hereafter no commissions of like nature may issue forth to any person or persons whatsoever to be executed as aforesaid, lest by color of them any of your Majesty's subjects be destroyed or put to death contrary to the laws and franchise of the land.

XI. All which they most humbly pray of your most excellent Majesty as their rights and liberties, according to the laws and statutes of this realm; and that your Majesty would also vouchsafe to declare, that the awards, doings, and proceedings, to the prejudice of your people in any of the premises, shall not be drawn hereafter into consequence or example; and that your Majesty would be also graciously pleased, for the further comfort and safety of your people, to declare your royal will and pleasure, that in the things aforesaid all your officers and ministers shall serve you according to the laws and statutes of this realm, as they tender the honor of your Majesty, and the prosperity of this kingdom.

English Bill of Rights (1689)

An Act Declaring the Rights and Liberties of the Subject and Settling the Succession of the Crown

Whereas the Lords Spiritual and Temporal and Commons assembled at Westminster, lawfully, fully and freely representing all the estates of the people of this realm, did upon the thirteenth day of February in the year of our Lord one thousand six hundred eighty-eight [old style date] present unto their Majesties, then called and known by the names and style of William and Mary, prince and princess of Orange, being present in their proper persons, a certain declaration in writing made by the said Lords and Commons in the words following, viz.:

Whereas the late King James the Second, by the assistance of divers evil counsellors, judges and ministers employed by him, did endeavour to subvert and extirpate the Protestant religion and the laws and liberties of this kingdom;

By assuming and exercising a power of dispensing with and suspending of laws and the execution of laws without consent of Parliament;

By committing and prosecuting divers worthy prelates for humbly petitioning to be excused from concurring to the said assumed power;

By issuing and causing to be executed a commission under the great seal for erecting a court called the Court of Commissioners for Ecclesiastical Causes;

By levying money for and to the use of the Crown by pretence of prerogative for other time and in other manner than the same was granted by Parliament;

By raising and keeping a standing army within this kingdom in time of peace without consent of Parliament, and quartering soldiers contrary to law;

By causing several good subjects being Protestants to be disarmed at the same time when papists were both armed and employed contrary to law;

By violating the freedom of election of members to serve in Parliament;

By prosecutions in the Court of King's Bench for matters and causes cognizable only in Parliament, and by divers other arbitrary and illegal courses;

And whereas of late years partial corrupt and unqualified persons have been returned and served on juries in trials, and particularly divers jurors in trials for high treason which were not freeholders;

And excessive bail hath been required of persons committed in criminal cases to elude the benefit of the laws made for the liberty of the subjects;

And excessive fines have been imposed;

And illegal and cruel punishments inflicted;

And several grants and promises made of fines and forfeitures before any conviction or judgment against the persons upon whom the same were to be levied;

All which are utterly and directly contrary to the known laws and statutes and freedom of this realm;

And whereas the said late King James the Second having abdicated the government and the throne being thereby vacant, his Highness the prince of Orange (whom it hath pleased Almighty God to make the glorious instrument of delivering this kingdom from popery and arbitrary power) did (by the advice of the Lords Spiritual and Temporal and divers principal persons of the Commons) cause letters to be written to the Lords Spiritual and Temporal being Protestants, and other letters to the several counties, cities, universities, boroughs and cinque ports, for the choosing of such persons to represent them as were of right to be sent to Parliament, to meet and sit at Westminster upon the two and twentieth day of January in this year one thousand six hundred eighty and eight [old style date], in order to such an establishment as that their religion, laws and liberties might no again be in danger of being subverted, upon which letters elections having been accordingly made;

And thereupon the said Lords Spiritual and Temporal and Commons, pursuant to their respective letters and elections, being now assembled in a full and free representative of this nation, taking into their most serious consideration the best means for attaining the ends aforesaid, do in the first place (as their ancestors in like case have usually done) for the vindicating and asserting their ancient rights and liberties declare

That the pretended power of suspending the laws or the execution of laws by regal authority without consent of Parliament is illegal;

That the pretended power of dispensing with laws or the execution of laws by regal authority, as it hath been assumed and exercised of late, is illegal;

That the commission for erecting the late Court of Commissioners for Ecclesiastical Causes, and all other commissions and courts of like nature, are illegal and pernicious;

That levying money for or to the use of the Crown by pretence of prerogative, without grant of Parliament, for longer time, or in other manner than the same is or shall be granted, is illegal;

That it is the right of the subjects to petition the king, and all commitments and prosecutions for such petitioning are illegal;

That the raising or keeping a standing army within the kingdom in time of peace, unless it be with consent of Parliament, is against law;

That the subjects which are Protestants may have arms for their defence suitable to their conditions and as allowed by law;

That election of members of Parliament ought to be free;

That the freedom of speech and debates or proceedings in Parliament ought not to be impeached or questioned in any court or place out of Parliament;

That excessive bail ought not to be required, nor excessive fines imposed, nor cruel and unusual punishments inflicted;

That jurors ought to be duly impanelled and returned, and jurors which pass upon men in trials for high treason ought to be freeholders;

That all grants and promises of fines and forfeitures of particular persons before conviction are illegal and void;

And that for redress of all grievances, and for the amending, strengthening and preserving of the laws, Parliaments ought to be held frequently.

And they do claim, demand and insist upon all and singular the premises as their undoubted rights and liberties, and that no declarations, judgments, doings or proceedings to the prejudice of the people in any of the said premises ought in any wise to be drawn hereafter into consequence or example; to which demand of their rights they are particularly encouraged by the declaration of his Highness the prince of Orange as being the only means for obtaining a full redress and remedy therein. Having therefore an entire confidence that his said Highness the prince of Orange will perfect the deliverance so far advanced by him, and will still preserve them from the violation of their rights which they have here asserted, and from all other attempts upon their religion, rights and liberties, the said Lords Spiritual and Temporal and Commons assembled at Westminster do resolve that William and Mary, prince and princess of Orange, be and be declared king and queen of England, France and Ireland and the dominions thereunto belonging, to hold the crown and royal dignity of the said kingdoms and dominions to them, the said prince and princess, during their lives and the life of the survivor to them, and that the sole and full exercise of the regal power be only in and executed by the said prince of Orange in the names of the said prince and princess during their joint lives, and after their deceases the said crown and royal dignity of the same kingdoms and dominions to be to the heirs of the body of the said princess, and for default of such issue to the Princess Anne of Denmark and the heirs of her body, and for default of such issue to the heirs of the body of the said prince of Orange. And the Lords Spiritual and Temporal and Commons do pray the said prince and princess to accept the same accordingly.

And that the oaths hereafter mentioned be taken by all persons of whom the oaths have allegiance and supremacy might be required by law, instead of them; and that the said oaths of allegiance and supremacy be abrogated.

I, A.B., do sincerely promise and swear that I will be faithful and bear true allegiance to their Majesties King William and Queen Mary. So help me God.

I, A.B., do swear that I do from my heart abhor, detest and abjure as impious and heretical this damnable doctrine and position, that princes excommunicated or deprived by the Pope or any authority of the see of Rome may be deposed or murdered by their subjects or any other whatsoever. And I do declare that no foreign prince, person, prelate, state or potentate hath or ought to have any jurisdiction, power, superiority, pre-eminence or authority, ecclesiastical or spiritual, within this realm. So help me God.

Upon which their said Majesties did accept the crown and royal dignity of the kingdoms of England, France and Ireland, and the dominions thereunto belonging, according to the resolution and desire of the said Lords and Commons contained in the said declaration. And thereupon their Majesties were pleased that the said Lords Spiritual and Temporal and Commons, being the two Houses of Parliament, should continue to sit, and with their Majesties' royal concurrence make effectual provision for the settlement of the religion, laws and liberties of this kingdom, so that the same for the future might not be in danger again of being subverted, to which the said Lords Spiritual and Temporal and Commons did agree, and proceed to act accordingly. Now in pursuance of the premises the said Lords Spiritual and Temporal and Commons in Parliament assembled, for the ratifying, confirming and establishing the said declaration and the articles, clauses, matters and things therein contained by the force of law made in due form by authority of Parliament, do pray that it may be declared and enacted that all and singular the rights and liberties asserted and claimed in the said declaration are the true, ancient and indubitable rights and liberties of the people of this kingdom, and so shall be esteemed, allowed, adjudged, deemed and taken to be; and that all and every the particulars aforesaid shall be firmly and strictly holden and observed as they are expressed in the said declaration, and all officers and ministers whatsoever shall serve their Majesties and their successors according to the same in all time to come. And the said Lords Spiritual and Temporal and Commons, seriously considering how it hath pleased Almighty God in his marvellous providence and merciful goodness to this nation to provide and preserve their said Majesties' royal persons most happily to reign over us upon the throne of their ancestors, for which they render unto him from the bottom of their hearts their humblest thanks and praises, do truly, firmly, assuredly and in the sincerity of their hearts think, and do hereby recognize, acknowledge and declare, that King James the Second having abdicated the government, and their Majesties having accepted the crown and royal dignity as aforesaid, their said Majesties did become, were, are and of right ought to be by the laws of this realm our sovereign liege lord and lady, king and queen of England, France and Ireland and the dominions thereunto belonging, in and to whose princely persons the royal state, crown and dignity of the said realms with all honours, styles, titles, regalities, prerogatives, powers, jurisdictions and authorities to the same belonging and appertaining are most fully, rightfully and entirely invested and incorporated, united and annexed. And for preventing all questions and divisions in this realm by reason of any pretended titles to the crown, and for preserving a certainty in the succession thereof, in and upon which the unity, peace, tranquility and safety of this nation doth under God wholly consist and depend, the said Lords Spiritual and Temporal and Commons do beseech their Majesties that it may be enacted, established and declared, that the crown and regal government of the said kingdoms and dominions, with all and singular the premises thereunto belonging and appertaining, shall be and continue to their said Majesties and the survivor of them during their lives and the life of the survivor of them, and that the entire, perfect and full exercise of the regal power and government be only in and executed by his Majesty in the names of both their Majesties during their joint lives; and after their deceases the said crown and premises shall be and remain to the heirs of the body of her Majesty, and for default of such issue to her Royal Highness the Princess Anne of Denmark and the heirs of the body of his said Majesty; and thereunto the said Lords Spiritual and Temporal and Commons do in the name of all the people aforesaid most humbly and faithfully submit themselves, their heirs and posterities for ever, and do faithfully promise that they will stand to, maintain and defend their said Majesties and also the limitation and succession of the crown herein specified and contained, to the utmost of their powers with their lives and estates against all persons whatsoever that shall attempt anything to the contrary. And whereas it hath been found by experience that it is inconsistent with the safety and welfare of this Protestant kingdom to be governed by a popish prince, or by any king or queen marrying a papist, the said Lords Spiritual and Temporal and Commons do further pray that it may be enacted, that all and every person and persons that is, are or shall be reconciled to or shall hold communion with the see or Church of Rome, or shall profess the popish religion, or shall marry a papist, shall be excluded and be for ever incapable to inherit, possess or enjoy the crown and government of this realm and Ireland and the dominions thereunto belonging or any part of the same, or to have, use or exercise any regal power, authority or jurisdiction within the same; and in all and every such case or cases the people of these realms shall be and are hereby absolved of their allegiance; and the said crown and government shall from time to time descend to and be enjoyed by such person or persons being Protestants as should have inherited and enjoyed the same in case the said person or persons so reconciled, holding communion or professing or marrying as aforesaid were naturally dead; and that every king and queen of this realm who at any time hereafter shall come to and succeed in the imperial crown of this kingdom shall on the first day of the meeting of the first Parliament next after his or her coming to the crown, sitting in his or her throne in the House of Peers in the presence of the Lords and Commons therein assembled, or at his or her coronation before such person or persons who shall administer the coronation oath to him or her at the time of his or her taking the said oath (which shall first happen), make, subscribe and audibly repeat the declaration mentioned in the statute made in the thirtieth year of the reign of King Charles the Second entitled, An Act for the more effectual preserving the king's person and government by disabling papists from sitting in either House of Parliament. But if it shall happen that such king or queen upon his or her succession to the crown of this realm shall be under the age of twelve years, then every such king or queen shall make, subscribe and audibly repeat the same declaration at his or her coronation or the first day of the meeting of the first Parliament as aforesaid which shall first happen after such king or queen shall have attained the said age of twelve years. All which their Majesties are contented and pleased shall be declared, enacted and established by authority of this present Parliament, and shall stand, remain and be the law of this realm for ever; and the same are by their said Majesties, by and with the advice and consent of the Lords Spiritual and Temporal and Commons in Parliament assembled and by the authority of the same, declared, enacted and established accordingly.

II. And be it further declared and enacted by the authority aforesaid, that from and after this present session of Parliament no dispensation by non obstante of or to any statute or any part thereof shall be allowed, but that the same shall be held void and of no effect, except a dispensation be allowed of in such statute, and except in such cases as shall be specially provided for by one or more bill or bills to be passed during this present session of Parliament.

III. Provided that no charter or grant or pardon granted before the three and twentieth day of October in the year of our Lord one thousand six hundred eighty-nine shall be any ways impeached or invalidated by this Act, but that the same shall be and remain of the same force and effect in law and no other than as if this Act had never been made.

The Declaration of Independence (1776)

IN CONGRESS, July 4, 1776.

The unanimous Declaration of the thirteen united States of America,

When in the Course of human events, it becomes necessary for one people to dissolve the political bands which have connected them with another, and to assume among the powers of the earth, the separate and equal station to which the Laws of Nature and of Nature's God entitle them, a decent respect to the opinions of mankind requires that they should declare the causes which impel them to the separation.

We hold these truths to be self-evident, that all men are created equal, that they are endowed by their Creator with certain unalienable Rights, that among these are Life, Liberty and the pursuit of Happiness.--That to secure these rights, Governments are instituted among Men, deriving their just powers from the consent of the governed, --That whenever any Form of Government becomes destructive of these ends, it is the Right of the People to alter or to abolish it, and to institute new Government, laying its foundation on such principles and organizing its powers in such form, as to them shall seem most likely to effect their Safety and Happiness. Prudence, indeed, will dictate that Governments long established should not be changed for light and transient causes; and accordingly all experience hath shewn, that mankind are more disposed to suffer, while evils are sufferable, than to right themselves by abolishing the forms to which they are accustomed. But when a long train of abuses and usurpations, pursuing invariably the same Object evinces a design to reduce them under absolute Despotism, it is their right, it is their duty, to throw off such Government, and to provide new Guards for their future security.--Such has been the patient sufferance of these Colonies; and such is now the necessity which constrains them to alter their former Systems of Government. The history of the present King of Great Britain is a history of repeated injuries and usurpations, all having in direct object the establishment of an absolute

Tyranny over these States. To prove this, let Facts be submitted to a candid world.

He has refused his Assent to Laws, the most wholesome and necessary for the public good.

He has forbidden his Governors to pass Laws of immediate and pressing importance, unless suspended in their operation till his Assent should be obtained; and when so suspended, he has utterly neglected to attend to them.

He has refused to pass other Laws for the accommodation of large districts of people, unless those people would relinquish the right of Representation in the Legislature, a right inestimable to them and formidable to tyrants only.

He has called together legislative bodies at places unusual, uncomfortable, and distant from the depository of their public Records, for the sole purpose of fatiguing them into compliance with his measures.

He has dissolved Representative Houses repeatedly, for opposing with manly firmness his invasions on the rights of the people.

He has refused for a long time, after such dissolutions, to cause others to be elected; whereby the Legislative powers, incapable of Annihilation, have returned to the People at large for their exercise; the State remaining in the mean time exposed to all the dangers of invasion from without, and convulsions within.

He has endeavoured to prevent the population of these States; for that purpose obstructing the Laws for Naturalization of Foreigners; refusing to pass others to encourage their migrations hither, and raising the conditions of new Appropriations of Lands.

He has obstructed the Administration of Justice, by refusing his Assent to Laws for establishing Judiciary powers.

He has made Judges dependent on his Will alone, for the tenure of their offices, and the amount and payment of their salaries.

He has erected a multitude of New Offices, and sent hither swarms of Officers to harrass our people, and eat out their substance.

He has kept among us, in times of peace, Standing Armies without the Consent of our legislatures.

He has affected to render the Military independent of and superior to the Civil power.

He has combined with others to subject us to a jurisdiction foreign to our constitution, and unacknowledged by our laws; giving his Assent to their Acts of pretended Legislation:

For Quartering large bodies of armed troops among us:

For protecting them, by a mock Trial, from punishment for any Murders which they should commit on the Inhabitants of these States:

For cutting off our Trade with all parts of the world:

For imposing Taxes on us without our Consent:

For depriving us in many cases, of the benefits of Trial by Jury:

For transporting us beyond Seas to be tried for pretended offences

For abolishing the free System of English Laws in a neighbouring Province, establishing therein an Arbitrary government, and enlarging its Boundaries so as to render it at once an example and fit instrument for introducing the same absolute rule into these Colonies:

For taking away our Charters, abolishing our most valuable Laws, and altering fundamentally the Forms of our Governments:

For suspending our own Legislatures, and declaring themselves invested with power to legislate for us in all cases whatsoever.

He has abdicated Government here, by declaring us out of his Protection and waging War against us.

He has plundered our seas, ravaged our Coasts, burnt our towns, and destroyed the lives of our people.

He is at this time transporting large Armies of foreign Mercenaries to compleat the works of death, desolation and tyranny, already begun with circumstances of Cruelty & perfidy scarcely paralleled in the most barbarous ages, and totally unworthy the Head of a civilized nation.

He has constrained our fellow Citizens taken Captive on the high Seas to bear Arms against their Country, to become the executioners of their friends and Brethren, or to fall themselves by their Hands.

He has excited domestic insurrections amongst us, and has endeavoured to bring on the inhabitants of our frontiers, the merciless Indian Savages, whose known rule of warfare, is an undistinguished destruction of all ages, sexes and conditions.

In every stage of these Oppressions We have Petitioned for Redress in the most humble terms: Our repeated Petitions have been answered only by repeated injury. A Prince whose character is thus marked by every act which may define a Tyrant, is unfit to be the ruler of a free people.

Nor have We been wanting in attentions to our Brittish brethren. We have warned them from time to time of attempts by their legislature to extend an unwarrantable jurisdiction over us. We have reminded them of the circumstances of our emigration and settlement here. We have appealed to their native justice and magnanimity, and we have conjured them by the ties of our common kindred to disavow these usurpations, which, would inevitably interrupt our connections and correspondence. They too have been deaf to the voice of justice and of consanguinity. We must, therefore, acquiesce in the necessity, which denounces our Separation, and hold them, as we hold the rest of mankind, Enemies in War, in Peace Friends.

We, therefore, the Representatives of the united States of America, in General Congress, Assembled, appealing to the Supreme Judge of the world for the rectitude of our intentions, do, in the Name, and by Authority of the good People of these Colonies, solemnly publish and declare, That these United Colonies are, and of Right ought to be Free and Independen

States; that they are Absolved from all Allegiance to the British Crown, and that all political connection between them and the State of Great Britain, is and ought to be totally dissolved; and that as Free and Independent States, they have full Power to levy War, conclude Peace, contract Alliances, establish Commerce, and to do all other Acts and Things which Independent States may of right do. And for the support of this Declaration, with a firm reliance on the protection of divine Providence, we mutually pledge to each other our Lives, our Fortunes and our sacred Honor.

The Constitution of the United States (1787)

We the People of the United States, in Order to form a more perfect Union, establish Justice, insure domestic Tranquility, provide for the common defence, promote the general Welfare, and secure the Blessings of Liberty to ourselves and our Posterity, do ordain and establish this Constitution for the United States of America.

Article. I.

Section. 1.

All legislative Powers herein granted shall be vested in a Congress of the United States, which shall consist of a Senate and House of Representatives.

Section. 2.

The House of Representatives shall be composed of Members chosen every second Year by the People of the several States, and the Electors in each State shall have the Qualifications requisite for Electors of the most numerous Branch of the State Legislature.

No Person shall be a Representative who shall not have attained to the Age of twenty five Years, and been seven Years a Citizen of the United States, and who shall not, when elected, be an Inhabitant of that State in which he shall be chosen.

Representatives and direct Taxes shall be apportioned among the several States which may be included within this Union, according to their respective Numbers, which shall be determined by adding to the whole Number of free Persons, including those bound to Service for a Term of Years, and excluding Indians not taxed, three fifths of all other Persons. The actual Enumeration shall be made within three Years after the first Meeting of the Congress of the United States, and within every subsequent Term of ten Years, in such Manner as they shall by Law direct. The Number of Representatives shall not exceed one for every thirty Thousand, but each State shall have at Least one Representative; and until such enumeration shall be made, the State of New Hampshire shall be entitled to chuse three, Massachusetts eight, Rhode-Island and Providence Plantations one, Connecticut five, New-York six, New Jersey four, Pennsylvania eight, Delaware one, Maryland six, Virginia ten, North Carolina five, South Carolina five, and Georgia three.

When vacancies happen in the Representation from any State, the Executive Authority thereof shall issue Writs of Election to fill such Vacancies.

The House of Representatives shall chuse their Speaker and other Officers; and shall have the sole Power of Impeachment.

Section. 3.

The Senate of the United States shall be composed of two Senators from each State, chosen by the Legislature thereof for six Years; and each Senator shall have one Vote.

Immediately after they shall be assembled in Consequence of the first Election, they shall be divided as equally as may be into three Classes. The Seats of the Senators of the first Class shall be vacated at the Expiration of the second Year, of the second Class at the Expiration of the fourth Year, and of the third Class at the Expiration of the sixth Year, so that one third may be chosen every second Year; and if Vacancies happen by Resignation, or otherwise, during the Recess of the Legislature of any State, the Executive thereof may make temporary Appointments until the next Meeting of the Legislature, which shall then fill such Vacancies.

No Person shall be a Senator who shall not have attained to the Age of thirty Years, and been nine Years a Citizen of the United States, and who shall not, when elected, be an Inhabitant of that State for which he shall be chosen.

The Vice President of the United States shall be President of the Senate, but shall have no Vote, unless they be equally divided.

The Senate shall chuse their other Officers, and also a President pro tempore, in the Absence of the Vice President, or when he shall exercise the Office of President of the United States.

The Senate shall have the sole Power to try all Impeachments. When sitting for that Purpose, they shall be on Oath or Affirmation. When the President of the United States is tried, the Chief Justice shall preside: And no Person shall be convicted without the Concurrence of two thirds of the Members present.

Judgment in Cases of Impeachment shall not extend further than to removal from Office, and disqualification to hold and enjoy any Office of honor, Trust or Profit under the United States: but the Party convicted shall nevertheless be liable and subject to Indictment, Trial, Judgment and Punishment, according to Law.

Section. 4.

The Times, Places and Manner of holding Elections for Senators and Representatives, shall be prescribed in each State by the Legislature thereof; but the Congress may at any time by Law make or alter such Regulations, except as to the Places of chusing Senators.

The Congress shall assemble at least once in every Year, and such Meeting shall be on the first Monday in December, unless they shall by Law appoint a different Day.

Section. 5.

Each House shall be the Judge of the Elections, Returns and Qualifications of its own Members, and a Majority of each shall constitute a Quorum to do Business; but a smaller Number may adjourn from day to day, and may be authorized to compel the Attendance of absent Members, in such Manner, and under such Penalties as each House may provide.

Each House may determine the Rules of its Proceedings, punish its Members for disorderly Behaviour, and, with the Concurrence of two thirds expel a Member.

Each House shall keep a Journal of its Proceedings, and from time to time publish the same, excepting such Parts as may in their Judgment require Secrecy; and the Yeas and Nays of the Members of either House on any question shall, at the Desire of one fifth of those Present, be entered on the Journal.

Neither House, during the Session of Congress, shall, without the Consent of the other, adjourn for more than three days, nor to any other Place than that in which the two Houses shall be sitting.

Section. 6.

The Senators and Representatives shall receive a Compensation for their Services, to be ascertained by Law, and paid out of the Treasury of the United States. They shall in all Cases, except Treason, Felony and Breach of the Peace, be privileged from Arrest during their Attendance at the Session of their respective Houses, and in going to and returning from the same; and for any Speech or Debate in either House, they shall not be questioned in any other Place.

No Senator or Representative shall, during the Time for which he was elected, be appointed to any civil Office under the Authority of the United States, which shall have been created, or the Emoluments whereof shall have been encreased during such time; and no Person holding any Office under the United States, shall be a Member of either House during his Continuance in Office.

Section. 7.

All Bills for raising Revenue shall originate in the House of Representatives; but the Senate may propose or concur with Amendments as on other Bills.

Every Bill which shall have passed the House of Representatives and the Senate, shall, before it become a Law, be presented to the President of the United States: If he approve he shall sign it, but if not he shall return it, with his Objections to that House in which it shall have originated, who shall enter the Objections at large on their Journal, and proceed to reconsider it. If after such Reconsideration two thirds of that House shall agree to pass the Bill, it shall be sent, together with the Objections, to the other House, by which it shall likewise be reconsidered, and if approved by two thirds of that House, it shall become a Law. But in all such Cases the Votes of both Houses shall be determined by yeas and Nays, and the Names of the Persons voting for and against the Bill shall be entered on the Journal of each House respectively. If any Bill shall not be returned by the President within ten Days (Sundays excepted) after it shall have been presented to him, the Same shall be a Law, in like Manner as if he had signed it, unless the Congress by their Adjournment prevent its Return, in which Case it shall not be a Law.

Every Order, Resolution, or Vote to which the Concurrence of the Senate and House of Representatives may be necessary (except on a question of Adjournment) shall be presented to the President of the United States; and before the Same shall take Effect, shall be approved by him, or being disapproved by him, shall be repassed by two thirds of the Senate and House of Representatives, according to the Rules and Limitations prescribed in the Case of a Bill.

Section. 8.

The Congress shall have Power To lay and collect Taxes, Duties, Imposts and Excises, to pay the Debts and provide for the common Defence and general Welfare of the United States; but all Duties, Imposts and Excises shall be uniform throughout the United States;

To borrow Money on the credit of the United States;

To regulate Commerce with foreign Nations, and among the several States, and with the Indian Tribes;

To establish an uniform Rule of Naturalization, and uniform Laws on the subject of Bankruptcies throughout the United States;

To coin Money, regulate the Value thereof, and of foreign Coin, and fix the Standard of Weights and Measures;

To provide for the Punishment of counterfeiting the Securities and current Coin of the United States;

To establish Post Offices and post Roads;

To promote the Progress of Science and useful Arts, by securing for limited Times to Authors and Inventors the exclusive Right to their respective Writings and Discoveries;

To constitute Tribunals inferior to the supreme Court;

To define and punish Piracies and Felonies committed on the high Seas, and Offences against the Law of Nations;

To declare War, grant Letters of Marque and Reprisal, and make Rules concerning Captures on Land and Water;

To raise and support Armies, but no Appropriation of Money to that Use shall be for a longer Term than two Years;

To provide and maintain a Navy;

To make Rules for the Government and Regulation of the land and naval Forces;

To provide for calling forth the Militia to execute the Laws of the Union, suppress Insurrections and repel Invasions;

To provide for organizing, arming, and disciplining, the Militia, and for governing such Part of them as may be employed in the Service of the United States, reserving to the States respectively, the Appointment of the Officers, and the Authority of training the Militia according to the discipline prescribed by Congress;

To exercise exclusive Legislation in all Cases whatsoever, over such District (not exceeding ten Miles square) as may, by Cession of particular States, and the Acceptance of Congress, become the Seat of the Government of the United States, and to exercise like Authority over all Places purchased by the Consent of the Legislature of the State in which the Same shall be, for the Erection of Forts, Magazines, Arsenals, dock-Yards, and other needful Buildings;--And

To make all Laws which shall be necessary and proper for carrying into Execution the foregoing Powers, and all other Powers vested by this Constitution in the Government of the United States, or in any Department or Officer thereof.

Section. 9.

The Migration or Importation of such Persons as any of the States now existing shall think proper to admit, shall not be prohibited by the Congress prior to the Year one thousand eight hundred and eight, but a Tax or duty may be imposed on such Importation, not exceeding ten dollars for each Person.

The Privilege of the Writ of Habeas Corpus shall not be suspended, unless when in Cases of Rebellion or Invasion the public Safety may require it.

No Bill of Attainder or ex post facto Law shall be passed.

No Capitation, or other direct, Tax shall be laid, unless in Proportion to the Census or enumeration herein before directed to be taken.

No Tax or Duty shall be laid on Articles exported from any State.

No Preference shall be given by any Regulation of Commerce or Revenue to the Ports of one State over those of another; nor shall Vessels bound to, or from, one State, be obliged to enter, clear, or pay Duties in another.

No Money shall be drawn from the Treasury, but in Consequence of Appropriations made by Law; and a regular Statement and Account of the Receipts and Expenditures of all public Money shall be published from time to time.

No Title of Nobility shall be granted by the United States: And no Person holding any Office of Profit or Trust under them, shall, without the Consent of the Congress, accept of any present, Emolument, Office, or Title of any kind whatever, from any King, Prince, or foreign State.

Section. 10.

No State shall enter into any Treaty, Alliance, or Confederation; grant Letters of Marque and Reprisal; coin Money; emit Bills of Credit; make any Thing but gold and silver Coin a Tender in Payment of Debts; pass any Bill of Attainder, ex post facto Law, or Law impairing the Obligation of Contracts, or grant any Title of Nobility.

No State shall, without the Consent of the Congress, lay any Imposts or Duties on Imports or Exports, except what may be absolutely necessary for executing it's inspection Laws: and the net Produce of all Duties and Imposts, laid by any State on Imports or Exports, shall be for the Use of the Treasury of the United States; and all such Laws shall be subject to the Revision and Controul of the Congress.

No State shall, without the Consent of Congress, lay any Duty of Tonnage, keep Troops, or Ships of War in time of Peace, enter into any Agreement or Compact with another State, or with a foreign Power, or engage in War, unless actually invaded, or in such imminent Danger as will not admit of delay.

Article. II.

Section. 1.

The executive Power shall be vested in a President of the United States of America. He shall hold his Office during the Term of four Years, and, together with the Vice President, chosen for the same Term, be elected, as follows:

Each State shall appoint, in such Manner as the Legislature thereof may direct, a Number of Electors, equal to the whole Number of Senators and Representatives to which the State may be entitled in the Congress: but no Senator or Representative, or Person holding an Office of Trust or Profit under the United States, shall be appointed an Elector.

The Electors shall meet in their respective States, and vote by Ballot for two Persons, of whom one at least shall not be an Inhabitant of the same State with themselves. And they shall make a List of all the Persons voted for, and of the Number of Votes for each; which List they shall sign and certify, and transmit sealed to the Seat of the Government of the United States, directed to the President of the Senate. The President of the Senate shall, in the Presence of the Senate and House of Representatives, open all the Certificates, and the Votes shall then be counted. The Person having the greatest Number of Votes shall be the President, if such Number be a Majority of the whole Number of Electors appointed; and if there be more than one who have such Majority, and have an equal Number of Votes, then the House of Representatives shall immediately chuse by Ballot one of them for President; and if no Person have a Majority, then from the five highest on the List the said House shall in like Manner chuse the President. But in chusing the President, the Votes shall be taken by States, the Representation from each State having one Vote; A quorum for this purpose shall consist of a Member or Members from two thirds of the States, and a Majority of all the States shall be necessary to a Choice. In every Case, after the Choice of the President, the Person having the greatest Number of Votes of the Electors shall be the Vice President. But if there should remain two or more who have equal Votes, the Senate shall chuse from them by Ballot the Vice President.

The Congress may determine the Time of chusing the Electors, and the Day on which they shall give their Votes; which Day shall be the same throughout the United States.

No Person except a natural born Citizen, or a Citizen of the United States, at the time of the Adoption of this Constitution, shall be eligible to the Office of President; neither shall any Person be eligible to that Office who shall not have attained to the Age of thirty five Years, and been fourteen Years a Resident within the United States.

In Case of the Removal of the President from Office, or of his Death, Resignation, or Inability to discharge the Powers and Duties of the said Office the Same shall devolve on the Vice President, and the Congress may by Law provide for the Case of Removal, Death, Resignation or Inability both of the President and Vice President, declaring what Officer shall then act as President, and such Officer shall act accordingly, until the Disability be removed, or a President shall be elected.

The President shall, at stated Times, receive for his Services, a Compensation, which shall neither be increased nor diminished during the Period for which he shall have been elected, and he shall not receive within that Period any other Emolument from the United States, or any of them.

Before he enter on the Execution of his Office, he shall take the following Oath or Affirmation:--"I do solemnly swear (or affirm) that I will faithfully execute the Office of President of the United States, and will to the best of my Ability, preserve, protect and defend the Constitution of the United States."

Section. 2.

The President shall be Commander in Chief of the Army and Navy of the United States, and of the Militia of the several States, when called into the actual Service of the United States; he may require the Opinion, in writing, of the principal Officer in each of the executive Departments, upon any Subject relating to the Duties of their respective Offices, and he shall have Power to grant Reprieves and Pardons for Offences against the United States, except in Cases of Impeachment.

He shall have Power, by and with the Advice and Consent of the Senate, to make Treaties, provided two thirds of the Senators present concur; and he shall nominate, and by and with the Advice and Consent of the Senate, shall appoint Ambassadors, other public Ministers and Consuls, Judges of the supreme Court, and all other Officers of the United States, whose Appointments are not herein otherwise provided for, and which shall be established by Law: but the Congress may by Law vest the Appointment of such inferior Officers, as they think proper, in the President alone, in the Courts of Law, or in the Heads of Departments.

The President shall have Power to fill up all Vacancies that may happen during the Recess of the Senate, by granting Commissions which shall expire at the End of their next Session.

Section. 3.

He shall from time to time give to the Congress Information of the State of the Union, and recommend to their Consideration such Measures as he shall judge necessary and expedient; he may, on extraordinary Occasions, convene both Houses, or either of them, and in Case of Disagreement between them, with Respect to the Time of Adjournment, he may adjourn them to such Time as he shall think proper; he shall receive Ambassadors and other public Ministers; he shall take Care that the Laws be faithfully executed, and shall Commission all the Officers of the United States.

Section. 4.

The President, Vice President and all civil Officers of the United States, shall be removed from Office on Impeachment for, and Conviction of, Treason, Bribery, or other high Crimes and Misdemeanors.

Article III.

Section. 1.

The judicial Power of the United States shall be vested in one supreme Court, and in such inferior Courts as the Congress may from time to time ordain and establish. The Judges, both of the supreme and inferior Courts, shall hold their Offices during good Behaviour, and shall, at stated Times, receive for their Services a Compensation, which shall not be diminished during their Continuance in Office.

Section. 2.

The judicial Power shall extend to all Cases, in Law and Equity, arising under this Constitution, the Laws of the United States, and Treaties made, or which shall be made, under their Authority;--to all Cases affecting Ambassadors, other public Ministers and Consuls;--to all Cases of admiralty and maritime Jurisdiction;--to Controversies to which the United States shall be a Party;--to Controversies between two or more States;-- between a State and Citizens of another State,--between Citizens of different

States,--between Citizens of the same State claiming Lands under Grants of different States, and between a State, or the Citizens thereof, and foreign States, Citizens or Subjects.

In all Cases affecting Ambassadors, other public Ministers and Consuls, and those in which a State shall be Party, the supreme Court shall have original Jurisdiction. In all the other Cases before mentioned, the supreme Court shall have appellate Jurisdiction, both as to Law and Fact, with such Exceptions, and under such Regulations as the Congress shall make.

The Trial of all Crimes, except in Cases of Impeachment, shall be by Jury; and such Trial shall be held in the State where the said Crimes shall have been committed; but when not committed within any State, the Trial shall be at such Place or Places as the Congress may by Law have directed.

Section. 3.

Treason against the United States, shall consist only in levying War against them, or in adhering to their Enemies, giving them Aid and Comfort. No Person shall be convicted of Treason unless on the Testimony of two Witnesses to the same overt Act, or on Confession in open Court.

The Congress shall have Power to declare the Punishment of Treason, but no Attainder of Treason shall work Corruption of Blood, or Forfeiture except during the Life of the Person attainted.

Article. IV.

Section. 1.

Full Faith and Credit shall be given in each State to the public Acts, Records, and judicial Proceedings of every other State. And the Congress may by general Laws prescribe the Manner in which such Acts, Records and Proceedings shall be proved, and the Effect thereof.

Section. 2.

The Citizens of each State shall be entitled to all Privileges and Immunities of Citizens in the several States.

A Person charged in any State with Treason, Felony, or other Crime, who shall flee from Justice, and be found in another State, shall on Demand of the executive Authority of the State from which he fled, be delivered up, to be removed to the State having Jurisdiction of the Crime.

No Person held to Service or Labour in one State, under the Laws thereof, escaping into another, shall, in Consequence of any Law or Regulation therein, be discharged from such Service or Labour, but shall be delivered up on Claim of the Party to whom such Service or Labour may be due.

Section. 3.

New States may be admitted by the Congress into this Union; but no new State shall be formed or erected within the Jurisdiction of any other State; nor any State be formed by the Junction of two or more States, or Parts of States, without the Consent of the Legislatures of the States concerned as well as of the Congress.

The Congress shall have Power to dispose of and make all needful Rules and Regulations respecting the Territory or other Property belonging to the United States; and nothing in this Constitution shall be so construed as to Prejudice any Claims of the United States, or of any particular State.

Section. 4.

The United States shall guarantee to every State in this Union a Republican Form of Government, and shall protect each of them against Invasion; and on Application of the Legislature, or of the Executive (when the Legislature cannot be convened), against domestic Violence.

Article. V.

The Congress, whenever two thirds of both Houses shall deem it necessary, shall propose Amendments to this Constitution, or, on the

Application of the Legislatures of two thirds of the several States, shall call a Convention for proposing Amendments, which, in either Case, shall be valid to all Intents and Purposes, as Part of this Constitution, when ratified by the Legislatures of three fourths of the several States, or by Conventions in three fourths thereof, as the one or the other Mode of Ratification may be proposed by the Congress; Provided that no Amendment which may be made prior to the Year One thousand eight hundred and eight shall in any Manner affect the first and fourth Clauses in the Ninth Section of the first Article; and that no State, without its Consent, shall be deprived of its equal Suffrage in the Senate.

Article. VI.

All Debts contracted and Engagements entered into, before the Adoption of this Constitution, shall be as valid against the United States under this Constitution, as under the Confederation.

This Constitution, and the Laws of the United States which shall be made in Pursuance thereof; and all Treaties made, or which shall be made, under the Authority of the United States, shall be the supreme Law of the Land; and the Judges in every State shall be bound thereby, any Thing in the Constitution or Laws of any State to the Contrary notwithstanding.

The Senators and Representatives before mentioned, and the Members of the several State Legislatures, and all executive and judicial Officers, both of the United States and of the several States, shall be bound by Oath or Affirmation, to support this Constitution; but no religious Test shall ever be required as a Qualification to any Office or public Trust under the United States.

Article. VII.

The Ratification of the Conventions of nine States, shall be sufficient for the Establishment of this Constitution between the States so ratifying the Same.

The Word, "the," being interlined between the seventh and eighth Lines of the first Page, the Word "Thirty" being partly written on an Erazure in the fifteenth Line of the first Page, The Words "is tried" being interlined between the thirty second and thirty third Lines of the first Page and the Word "the" being interlined between the forty third and forty fourth Lines of the second Page.

Attest William Jackson Secretary

done in Convention by the Unanimous Consent of the States present the Seventeenth Day of September in the Year of our Lord one thousand seven hundred and Eighty seven and of the Independance of the United States of America the Twelfth In witness whereof We have hereunto subscribed our Names,

G°. Washington
Presidt and deputy from Virginia

Delaware
Geo: Read
Gunning Bedford jun
John Dickinson
Richard Bassett
Jaco: Broom

Maryland
James McHenry
Dan of St Thos. Jenifer
Danl. Carroll

Virginia
John Blair
James Madison Jr.

North Carolina
Wm. Blount
Richd. Dobbs Spaight

Hu Williamson

South Carolina
J. Rutledge
Charles Cotesworth Pinckney
Charles Pinckney
Pierce Butler

Georgia
William Few
Abr Baldwin

New Hampshire
John Langdon
Nicholas Gilman

Massachusetts
Nathaniel Gorham
Rufus King

Connecticut
Wm. Saml. Johnson
Roger Sherman

New York
Alexander Hamilton

New Jersey
Wil: Livingston
David Brearley
Wm. Paterson
Jona: Dayton

Pennsylvania
B Franklin
Thomas Mifflin

Robt. Morris
Geo. Clymer
Thos. FitzSimons
Jared Ingersoll
James Wilson
Gouv Morris

Draft of the Kentucky Resolutions of 1798

1. *Resolved*, That the several States composing the United States of America, are not united on the principle of unlimited submission to their General Government; but that, by a compact under the style and title of a Constitution for the United States, and of amendments thereto, they constituted a General Government for special purposes, -- delegated to that government certain definite powers, reserving, each State to itself, the residuary mass of right to their own self-government; and that whensoever the General Government assumes undelegated powers, its acts are unauthoritative, void, and of no force; that to this compact each State acceded as a State, and is an integral party, its co-States forming, as to itself, the other party: that the government created by this compact was not made the exclusive or final judge of the extent of the powers delegated to itself; since that would have made its discretion, and not the Constitution, the measure of its powers; but that, as in all other cases of compact among powers having no common judge, each party has an equal right to judge for itself, as well of infractions as of the mode and measure of redress.

2. *Resolved*, That the Constitution of the United States, having delegated to Congress a power to punish treason, counterfeiting the securities and current coin of the United States, piracies, and felonies committed on the high seas, and offences against the law of nations, and no other crimes whatsoever; and it being true as a general principle, and one of the amendments to the Constitution having also declared, that "the powers not delegated to the United States by the Constitution, nor prohibited by it to the States, are reserved to the States respectively, or to the people," therefore the act of Congress, passed on the 14th day of July, 1798, and intituled "An Act in addition to the act intituled An Act for the punishment of certain crimes against the United States," as also the act passed by them on the -- day of June, 1798, intituled "An Act to punish frauds committed on the bank of the United States," (and all their other acts which assume to create, define, or punish crimes, other than those so enumerated in the Constitution,) are altogether void, and of no force; and that the power to create, define, and punish such other crimes is reserved, and, of right,

appertains solely and exclusively to the respective States, each within its own territory.

3. *Resolved*, That it is true as a general principle, and is also expressly declared by one of the amendments to the Constitution, that "the powers not delegated to the United States by the Constitution, nor prohibited by it to the States, are reserved to the States respectively, or to the people;" and that no power over the freedom of religion, freedom of speech, or freedom of the press being delegated to the United States by the Constitution, nor prohibited by it to the States, all lawful powers respecting the same did of right remain, and were reserved to the States or the people: that thus was manifested their determination to retain to themselves the right of judging how far the licentiousness of speech and of the press may be abridged without lessening their useful freedom, and how far those abuses which cannot be separated from their use should be tolerated, rather than the use be destroyed. And thus also they guarded against all abridgment by the United States of the freedom of religious opinions and exercises, and retained to themselves the right of protecting the same, as this State, by a law passed on the general demand of its citizens, had already protected them from all human restraint or interference. And that in addition to this general principle and express declaration, another and more special provision has been made by one of the amendments to the Constitution, which expressly declares, that "Congress shall make no law respecting an establishment of religion, or prohibiting the free exercise thereof, or abridging the freedom of speech or of the press:" thereby guarding in the same sentence, and under the same words, the freedom of religion, of speech, and of the press: insomuch, that whatever violated either, throws down the sanctuary which covers the others, and that libels, falsehood, and defamation, equally with heresy and false religion, are withheld from the cognizance of federal tribunals. That, therefore, the act of Congress of the United States, passed on the 14th day of July, 1798, intituled "An Act in addition to the act intituled An Act for the punishment of certain crimes against the United States," which does abridge the freedom of the press, is not law, but is altogether void, and of no force.

4. *Resolved*, That alien friends are under the jurisdiction and protection of the laws of the State wherein they are: that no power over them has been

delegated to the United States, nor prohibited to the individual States, distinct from their power over citizens. And it being true as a general principle, and one of the amendments to the Constitution having also declared, that "the powers not delegated to the United States by the Constitution, nor prohibited by it to the States, are reserved to the States respectively, or to the people," the act of the Congress of the United States, passed on the -- day of July, 1798, intituled "An Act concerning aliens," which assumes powers over alien friends, not delegated by the Constitution, is not law, but is altogether void, and of no force.

5. *Resolved*, That in addition to the general principle, as well as the express declaration, that powers not delegated are reserved, another and more special provision, inserted in the Constitution from abundant caution, has declared that "the migration or importation of such persons as any of the States now existing shall think proper to admit, shall not be prohibited by the Congress prior to the year 1808;" that this commonwealth does admit the migration of alien friends, described as the subject of the said act concerning aliens: that a provision against prohibiting their migration, is a provision against all acts equivalent thereto, or it would be nugatory: that to remove them when migrated, is equivalent to a prohibition of their migration, and is, therefore, contrary to the said provision of the Constitution, and void.

6. *Resolved*, That the imprisonment of a person under the protection of the laws of this commonwealth, on his failure to obey the simple order of the President to depart out of the United States, as is undertaken by said act intituled "An Act concerning aliens," is contrary to the Constitution, one amendment to which has provided that "no person shall be deprived of liberty without due process of law;" and that another having provided that "in all criminal prosecutions the accused shall enjoy the right to public trial by an impartial jury, to be informed of the nature and cause of the accusation, to be confronted with the witnesses against him, to have compulsory process for obtaining witnesses in his favor, and to have the assistance of counsel for his defence," the same act, undertaking to authorize the President to remove a person out of the United States, who is under the protection of the law, on his own suspicion, without accusation, without jury, without public trial, without confrontation of the witnesses against him,

without hearing witnesses in his favor, without defence, without counsel, is contrary to the provision also of the Constitution, is therefore not law, but utterly void, and of no force: that transferring the power of judging any person, who is under the protection of the laws, from the courts to the President of the United States, as is undertaken by the same act concerning aliens, is against the article of the Constitution which provides that "the judicial power of the United States shall be vested in courts, the judges of which shall hold their offices during good behavior;" and that the said act is void for that reason also. And it is further to be noted, that this transfer of judiciary power is to that magistrate of the General Government who already possesses all the Executive, and a negative on all legislative powers.

7. *Resolved*, That the construction applied by the General Government (as is evidenced by sundry of their proceedings) to those parts of the Constitution of the United States which delegate to Congress a power "to lay and collect taxes, duties, imports, and excises, to pay the debts, and provide for the common defence and general welfare of the United States," and "to make all laws which shall be necessary and proper for carrying into execution the powers vested by the Constitution in the government of the United States, or in any department or officer thereof," goes to the destruction of all limits prescribed to their power by the Constitution: that words meant by the instrument to be subsidiary only to the execution of limited powers, ought not to be so construed as themselves to give unlimited powers, nor a part to be so taken as to destroy the whole residue of that instrument: that the proceedings of the General Government under color of these articles, will be a fit and necessary subject of revisal and correction, at a time of greater tranquillity, while those specified in the preceding resolutions call for immediate redress.

8th. *Resolved*, That a committee of conference and correspondence be appointed, who shall have in charge to communicate the preceding resolutions to the legislatures of the several States; to assure them that this commonwealth continues in the same esteem of their friendship and union which it has manifested from that moment at which a common danger first suggested a common union: that it considers union, for specified national purposes, and particularly to those specified in their late federal compact to be friendly to the peace, happiness and prosperity of all the States: that faithful to that compact, according to the plain intent and meaning in which it was understood and acceded to by the several parties, it is sincerely anxious for its preservation: that it does also believe, that to take from the States all the powers of self-government and transfer them to a general and consolidated government, without regard to the special delegations and reservations solemnly agreed to in that compact, is not for the peace, happiness or prosperity of these States; and that therefore this commonwealth is determined, as it doubts not its co-States are, to submit to undelegated, and consequently unlimited powers in no man, or body of men on earth: that in cases of an abuse of the delegated powers, the members of the General Government, being chosen by the people, a change by the people would be the constitutional remedy; but, where powers are assumed which have not been delegated, a nullification of the act is the rightful remedy: that every State has a natural right in cases not within the compact, (casus non foederis,) to nullify of their own authority all assumptions of power by others within their limits: that without this right, they would be under the dominion, absolute and unlimited, of whosoever might exercise this right of judgment for them: that nevertheless, this commonwealth, from motives of regard and respect for its co-States, has wished to communicate with them on the subject: that with them alone it is proper to communicate, they alone being parties to the compact, and solely authorized to judge in the last resort of the powers exercised under it, Congress being not a party, but merely the creature of the compact, and subject as to its assumptions of power to the final judgment of those by whom, and for whose use itself and its powers were all created and modified: that if the acts before specified should stand, these conclusions would flow from them; that the General Government may place any act they think proper on the list of crimes, and punish it themselves whether enumerated or not enumerated by the Constitution as cognizable by them: that they may transfer its cognizance to the President, or any other person, who may himself be the accuser, counsel, judge and jury, whose suspicions may be the evidence, his order the sentence, his officer the executioner, and his breast the sole record of the transaction: that a very numerous and valuable description of the inhabitants of these States being, by this precedent, reduced, as outlaws, to the absolute dominion of one man, and the barrier of the Constitution thus swept away from us all, no rampart now remains against the passions and the powers of a majority in Congress to protect from a like exportation, or other more grievous punishment, the minority of the same body, the legislatures, judges, governors, and counsellors of the States, nor their other peaceable inhabitants, who may venture to reclaim the constitutional rights and liberties of the States and people, or who for other causes, good or bad, may be obnoxious to the views, or marked by the suspicions of the President, or be thought dangerous to his or their election, or other interests, public or personal: that the friendless alien has indeed been selected as the safest subject of a first experiment; but the citizen will soon follow, or rather, has already followed, for already has a sedition act marked him as its prey: that these and successive acts of the same character, unless arrested at the threshold, necessarily drive these States into revolution and blood, and will furnish new calumnies against republican government, and new pretexts for those who wish it to be believed that man cannot be governed but by a rod of iron: that it would be a dangerous delusion were a confidence in the men of our choice to silence our fears for the safety of our rights: that confidence is everywhere the parent of despotism -- free government is founded in jealousy, and not in confidence; it is jealousy and not confidence which prescribes limited constitutions, to bind down those whom we are obliged to trust with power: that our Constitution has accordingly fixed the limits to which, and no further, our confidence may go; and let the honest advocate of confidence read the alien and sedition acts, and say if the Constitution has not been wise in fixing limits to the government it created, and whether we should be wise in destroying those limits. Let him say what the government is, if it be not a tyranny, which the men of our choice have conferred on our President, and the President of our choice has assented to, and accepted over the friendly strangers to whom the mild spirit of our country and its laws have pledged hospitality and protection: that the men of our choice have more respected the bare suspicions of the President, than the solid right of innocence, the claims of justification, the sacred force of truth, and the forms and substance of law and justice. In questions of power, then, let no more be heard of confidence in man, but bind him down from mischief by the chains of the Constitution. That this commonwealth does therefore call on its co-States for an expression of their sentiments on the act concerning aliens, and for the punishment of certain crimes herein before specified, plainly declaring whether these acts are or are not authorized by the federal compact. And it doubts not that their sense will be so announced as to prove their attachment unaltered to limited government, whether general or particular. And that the rights and liberties of their co-States will be exposed to no dangers by remaining embarked in a common bottom with their own. That they will concur with this commonwealth in considering the said acts as so palpably against the Constitution as to amount to an undisguised declaration that that compact is not meant to be the measure of the powers of the General Government, but that it will proceed in the exercise over these States, of all powers whatsoever: that they will view this as seizing the rights of the States, and consolidating them in the hands of the General Government, with a power assumed to bind the States, not merely as the cases made federal, (casus foederis,) but in all cases whatsoever, by laws made, not with their consent, but by others against their consent: that this would be to surrender the form of government we have chosen, and live under one deriving its powers from its own will, and not from our authority; and that the co-States, recurring to their natural right in cases not made federal, will concur in declaring these acts void, and of no force, and will each take measures of its own for providing that neither these acts, nor any others of the General Government not plainly and intentionally authorized by the Constitution, shall be exercised within their respective territories.

9th. *Resolved*, That the said committee be authorized to communicate by writing or personal conferences, at any times or places whatever, with any person or person who may be appointed by any one or more co-States to correspond or confer with them; and that they lay their proceedings before the next session of Assembly.

Virginia Resolutions of 1798

RESOLVED, That the General Assembly of Virginia, doth unequivocably express a firm resolution to maintain and defend the Constitution of the United States, and the Constitution of this State, against every aggression either foreign or domestic, and that they will support the government of the United States in all measures warranted by the former.

That this assembly most solemnly declares a warm attachment to the Union of the States, to maintain which it pledges all its powers; and that for this end, it is their duty to watch over and oppose every infraction of those principles which constitute the only basis of that Union, because a faithful observance of them, can alone secure it's existence and the public happiness.

That this Assembly doth explicitly and peremptorily declare, that it views the powers of the federal government, as resulting from the compact, to which the states are parties; as limited by the plain sense and intention of the instrument constituting the compact; as no further valid that they are authorized by the grants enumerated in that compact; and that in case of a deliberate, palpable, and dangerous exercise of other powers, not granted by the said compact, the states who are parties thereto, have the right, and are in duty bound, to interpose for arresting the progress of the evil, and for maintaining within their respective limits, the authorities, rights and liberties appertaining to them.

That the General Assembly doth also express its deep regret, that a spirit has in sundry instances, been manifested by the federal government, to enlarge its powers by forced constructions of the constitutional charter which defines them; and that implications have appeared of a design to expound certain general phrases (which having been copied from the very limited grant of power, in the former articles of confederation were the less liable to be misconstrued) so as to destroy the meaning and effect, of the particular enumeration which necessarily explains and limits the general phrases; and so as to consolidate the states by degrees, into one sovereignty, the obvious tendency and inevitable consequence of which would be, to transform the present republican system of the United States, into an absolute, or at best a mixed monarchy.

That the General Assembly doth particularly protest against the palpable and alarming infractions of the Constitution, in the two late cases of the "Alien and Sedition Acts" passed at the last session of Congress; the first of which exercises a power no where delegated to the federal government, and which by uniting legislative and judicial powers to those of executive, subverts the general principles of free government; as well as the particular organization, and positive provisions of the federal constitution; and the other of which acts, exercises in like manner, a power not delegated by the constitution, but on the contrary, expressly and positively forbidden by one of the amendments thererto; a power, which more than any other, ought to produce universal alarm, because it is levelled against that right of freely examining public characters and measures, and of free communication among the people thereon, which has ever been justly deemed, the only effectual guardian of every other right.

That this state having by its Convention, which ratified the federal Constitution, expressly declared, that among other essential rights, "the Liberty of Conscience and of the Press cannot be cancelled, abridged, restrained, or modified by any authority of the United States," and from its extreme anxiety to guard these rights from every possible attack of sophistry or ambition, having with other states, recommended an amendment for that purpose, which amendment was, in due time, annexed to the Constitution; it would mark a reproachable inconsistency, and criminal degeneracy, if an indifference were now shewn, to the most palpable violation of one of the Rights, thus declared and secured; and to the establishment of a precedent which may be fatal to the other.

That the good people of this commonwealth, having ever felt, and continuing to feel, the most sincere affection for their brethren of the other states the truest anxiety for establishing and perpetuating the union of all; and the most scrupulous fidelity to that constitution, which is the pledge of mutual friendship, and the instrument of mutual happiness; the General Assembly doth solemenly appeal to the like dispositions of the other states in confidence that they will concur with this commonwealth in declaring, as it does hereby declare, that the acts aforesaid, are unconstitutional; and that the necessary and proper measures will be taken by each, for co-operating with this state, in maintaining the Authorities, Rights, and Liberties, referred to the States respectively, or to the people.

That the Governor be desired, to transmit a copy of the foregoing Resolutions to the executive authority of each of the other states, with a request that the same may be communicated to the Legislature thereof; and that a copy be furnished to each of the Senators and Representatives representing this state in the Congress of the United States.

Agreed to by the Senate, December 24, 1798.

Acknowledgements

There are many people who have contributed greatly to the completion of this work. Some assisted indirectly, giving me moral support and providing encouragement. Others worked with me to perfect this work, correct errors, and provide suggestions. All who are listed here contributed significantly.

My father, for instilling within me an appreciation for history and keeping me on my toes. The rest of my family, for also being an invaluable source of support throughout my life. Jake Duesenberg, for being a friend throughout much of my life, and regularly encouraging me to continue down the path of writing and speaking. Jack Rogers, for reassurance and for providing me a regular platform to speak on topics related to the United States Constitution.

KrisAnne Hall, for setting brushfires of freedom in the minds of patriots throughout the United States, and for inspiring me by her "Roots of Liberty" seminar. Kevin Gutzman, for answering some specific questions I had and for encouraging my studies. Matt Wolf, Brandy Grove, Melessa Henderson, and Amanda Bowers, for helping me edit this work.

Tom Woods, Brion McClanahan, Tom DiLorenzo, Clyde Wilson, Raoul Berger, Ayn Rand, Murray Rothbard, Andrew Napolitano, Forrest McDonald, Jeffrey Rogers Hummel, Jack Greene, Gordon Wood, Bill Kauffman, Oliver Chitwood, Shelby Foote, and Edward Vallance for inspiring my reading interests over the years.

The Tenth Amendment Center, for disseminating constitutional ideas and instilling hope in patriots. Also, for providing me with a platform to spread the ideals of liberty through the power of the written word. The Ludwig von Mises Institute, for promoting the cause of human freedom more efficiently than the combined actions of all governments in human history.

The founding generation, for their vigilance and for purchasing liberty for generations beyond their own lives. To all other unnamed patriots that have supported my efforts. To those I never knew, but shed blood for the continuance of liberty. My heavenly father, who infused me with my life and liberty, both understood as maxims that existed long before governments of men. To all those who made great suggestions over the progression of this writing, gave positive feedback, and urged me to continue writing and researching even when I questioned myself.

About the Author

David Benner speaks regularly in Minnesota on topics related to the United States Constitution, founding principles, and United States history. He has spoken to audiences of 30 to 600, taught a diverse array of age groups, and is a frequent guest speaker on local television and radio shows. His areas of focus include the Philadelphia Convention of 1787, Nullification, State Ratification Conventions of 1787-1790, Constitutional Antecedents, and Modern Asia. David writes articles for The Tenth Amendment Center and Abbeville Institute on a variety of topics. He also contributes writings to several local publications.

David adheres to the compact view of the Constitution as espoused by Thomas Jefferson and James Madison. He recognizes that the Constitution was not ratified by "one people," but by several distinctly sovereign entities, which by state ratification gave the Constitution legally binding status. David actively denies and refutes modern understandings of the Constitution made long after the ratification conventions, which claim that the Constitution is a "living document" that grants the federal government a vast reservoir of "implied" powers.

David believes strongly that the Constitution was not written and implemented in a whimsical fashion, but instead through a particularly laborious and exhaustive understanding of the British experience that the founders lived under and observed. That generation recognized the usurpation of power by tyrannical kings through treacherous means, and understood the historical processes used to stop it and constrain a ruling authority. It is only through an avid understanding of approximately 800 years of the British and American experience that we can understand the framework of the United States Constitution.

David considers himself as Jeffersonian at heart and teaches about the dangers of an overreaching centralized authority, viewing the states as the "surest bulwarks against antirepublican tendencies." He is an opponent of perpetual debt, centralized banking, and fiat currency, and uses constitutional arguments in support of these positions.

David was born in Knoxville, Tennessee, and has lived most of his life in Minnesota and Wisconsin. He has a Bachelor's Degree in History Education from the University of Wisconsin, River Falls. He currently resides in Roseville, Minnesota.

Notes

CHAPTER 1
THE COMPACT: AN OUTLAWED PERSPECTIVE

¹ Speech of Patrick Henry, March 23, 1775, in *American Oratory, or Selections from the Speeches of Eminent Americans* (Philadelphia: Desilver, Thomas & Co, 1836), 14.

² *The Debates in the Several State Conventions on the Adoption of the Federal Constitution,* Edited by Jonathan Elliot (Washington: Taylor & Maury, 1861), Volume II, 107. Hereafter, Volumes I-V from the same collection will be frequently referenced.

³ *The Debates in the Several State Conventions on the Adoption of the Federal Constitution*, Volume II, 202; First Inaugural Address of Thomas Jefferson, March 4, 1801, The Avalon Project, January 4, 2014; available at http://avalon.law.yale.edu/19th_century/jefinau1.asp

⁴ The Federalist No. 39, in Alexander Hamilton, James Madison, and John Jay, *The Federalist*, Edited by Jacob E. Cooke (Middletown: Wesleyan University, 1961), 254. *The Federalist* essays were written under the pseudonym of Publius. All other references to *The Federalist* are from this version.

⁵ James Madison to Daniel Webster, March 15, 1833, in *Letters and Other Writings of James Madison* (Philadelphia: J.B. Lippincott & Co, 1865), Volume 4, 293.

⁵ Thomas Woods, *Nullification: How to Resist Federal Tyranny in the 21st Century* (Washington, DC: Regnery Publishing, 2010), 88.

⁷ "Remarks of the Honorable Edwin Meese III, Attorney General of the United States," June 11, 1986, United States Department of Justice, September 26, 2013; available at http://www.justice.gov/ag/aghistory/meese/1986/06-11-1986.pdf

⁸ David Walker, *Oxford Companion to Law* in *Dictionary of American Biography* (London: Macmillian Pub Co, 1981), Volume XI, 102-108.

⁹ Joseph Story, *Commentaries on the Constitution of the United States: With a Preliminary Review of the Constitutional History of the Colonies and States, Before the Adoption of the Constitution* (Boston: Hilliard, Gray, and Company, 1833), 117-121.

[10] Ibid, 146-147.

[11] Thomas Woods, *Nullification*, 101. To highlight the lack of controversy, the eventual alteration was made by the Committee on Style, without recorded objection or debate.

[12] *The Debates in the Several State Conventions on the Adoption of the Federal Constitution,* Volume III, 94.

[13] *The Debates in the Several State Conventions on the Adoption of the Federal Constitution*, Volume II, 199.

[14] Address by Melanchthon Smith, in *Pamphlets on the Constitution of the United States, Published During its Discussion by the People 1787-1788*, Edited by Paul Leicester Ford (Brooklyn: Paul Leicester Ford, 1888), 97; *The Debates in the Several State Conventions on the Adoption of the Federal Constitution*, Volume III, 625-626.

[15] Speech on Surveys for Roads and Canals, January 30, 1824, in Russell Kirk, *John Randolph of Roanoke: A Study in American Politics* (Chicago: University of Chicago, 1997), 419-420.

[16] The Federalist No. 15, in *The Federalist*, 94.

CHAPTER 2
THE WAR OF INDEPENDENCE
AS A CONSTITUTIONAL CRISIS

[17] Gordon Wood, *The Creation of the American Republic: 1776-1787* (Chapel Hill: University of North Carolina Press, 1998), 10-13; Charles Louise de Secondat, Baron de Montesquieu, *The Spirit of the Laws* (London: T. Evans, 1777), Volume I, 202, 212; Dissertation, in *The Works of John Adams, Second President of the United States* (Boston: Charles C. Little and James Brown, 1851), Volume III, 462; The Committee of Correspondence of Boston to the Committee of Correspondence of Littleton, in *The Writings of Samuel Adams*, Edited by Henry Alonzo Cushing (New York: G.P. Putnam's Sons, 1907), Volume III, 15.

[18] Speech in the Convention for the Province of Pennsylvania, Held at Philadelphia, in January, 1775, in *Collected Works of James Wilson*, Edited by Kermit Hall and Mark David Hall (Indianapolis: Liberty Fund, 2007), Volume I, 39; Ibid. 4; Gordon Wood, *The Creation of the American Republic: 1776-1787*, 10.

[19] Murray Rothbard, *Conceived in Liberty* (Auburn: Ludwig von Mises Institute, 1999), 801.

[20] Against Writs of Assistance, in *Classics of American Political and Constitutional Thought*, Edited by Scott Hammond, Kevin Hardwick, and Howard Luber (Indianapolis: Hackett Publishing Company, 2007), Volume 1, 151.

[21] Ibid, 153.

[22] James Otis, *Rights of the British Colonies Asserted and Proved* (Boston: 1764) 109.

[23] Against Writs of Assistance, in *Classics of American Political and Constitutional Thought*, Volume 1, 152.

[24] Ibid, 153.

[25] Letter IX, in John Dickinson, *Letters from a Farmer in Pennsylvania: To the Inhabitants of the British Colonies* (New York: The Outlook Company, 1903), 93.

[26] William Tudor, *The Life of James Otis, of Massachusetts: Containing Also, Notices of Some Contemporary Characters and Events, from the Year 1760 to 1775* (Charleston: Nabu, 2010), 60-61; John Ridpath, *James Otis, the Pre-Revolutionist* (Milwaukee: H.G. Campbell, 1903), 57-58; John Morse, *John Adams* (New York: Houghton, 1924), 23.

[27] Murray Rothbard, *Conceived in Liberty*, 802.

[28] Mercy Otis Warren, *History of the Rise, Progress, and Termination of the American Revolution* (Boston: Manning and Loring, 1805), Volume I, 85.

[29] John Adams to Mercy Otis Warren, September 10, 1783, Quoted in *History of the Rise, Progress, and Termination of the American Revolution,* Volume 1, 89.

[30] Resolves of the House of Burgesses in Virginia, in Moses Coit Tyler, *Patrick Henry* (Boston: Houghton, Mifflin and Company, 1887), 62-63.

[31] Ibid, 63; Murray Rothbard, *Conceived in Liberty*, 865.

[32] Ibid, 866-870.

[33] Ibid, 882, 886-888.

[34] Ibid, 874-888.

[35] Edmund Morgan and Helen Morgan, *The Stamp Act Crisis: Prologue to Revolution* (Chapel Hill: University of North Carolina Press, 1995), 188; Murray Rothbard, *Conceived in Liberty*, 894.

[36] Ibid, 914-915.

[37] The American Crisis III, in Thomas Paine, *Political Writings,* 112.

[38] To the Inhabitants of Great Britain, in *Life and Correspondence of James Iredell,* Edited by Griffith McRee (New York: D. Appleton and Company, 1857), Volume I, 207.

[39] Ibid, 209.

[40] Ibid, 217.

[41] Ibid, 216-217.

[42] Ibid, 219.

[43] Letter I, in John Dickinson, *Letters from a Farmer in Pennsylvania: To the Inhabitants of the British Colonies*, 10.

[44] James Otis, *Rights of the British Colonies Asserted and Proved* (Boston: 1764), 50-53.

[45] Samuel Adams, *The Rights of the Colonists* (Boston: Directors of the Old South Work, 1906), 419-422.

[46] Fairfax County Resolves, in *The Writings of Georgia Washington*, Edited by Jared Sparks (Boston: Russel, Odiorne, and Metcalf, 1883), Volume II, 488-490.

[47] Murray Rothbard, *Conceived in Liberty*, 1024-1032.

[48] Ibid, 1036-1039.

[49] Mercy Otis Warren, *History of the Rise, Progress, and Termination of the American Revolution* (Indianapolis: Liberty Fund, 1989), Volume 1, 76.

[50] Ibid, 45-48.

[51] Ibid, 42-43.

[52] Ibid, 43.

[53] This passage comes from the 1689 English Bill of Rights, which is included in the "Documents" section.

[54] Mercy Otis Warren, *History of the Rise, Progress, and Termination of the American Revolution,* Volume 1, 43.

[55] Ibid, 136-139.

[56] "Historian of the American Revolution (Memory): American Treasures of the Library of Congress," Library of Congress, September 30, 2013; available at http://www.loc.gov/exhibits/treasures/trm089.html; Nancy Rubin Stuart, *The Muse of the Revolution: The Secret Pen of Mercy Otis Warren and the Founding of a Nation* (Boston: Beacon Press, 2008), 5.

[57] The Rights of the Colonies Examined, in *Records of the Colony of Rhode Island and Providence Plantations, in New England,* Edited by John Russell Bartlett (Providence: Knowlees, Anthony & Co., 1861), Volume VI, 420; Bernard Bailyn, *The Ideological Origins of the American Revolution* (Cambridge: Belknap Press, 1992), 213-216.

[58] Fairfax County Resolves, in *The Writings of Georgia Washington*, Volume II, 490.

[59] Ibid; Pennsylvania Resolves, 21 September 1765, in *A Collection of Interesting, Authentic Papers, Relative to the Dispute Between Great Britain and America; Shewing the Causes and Progress of that Misunderstanding, from 1764 to 1775* (London: J. Almon, 1777), 21. See third resolution; Resolutions of the House of Representatives, October 25, 1765, in *Speeches of the Governors of Massachusetts, from 1765 to 1775* (Boston: Russell and Gardner, 1818), 50. See third resolution.

[60] Moses Coit Tyler, *Patrick Henry*, 62-63; George Washington to Robert Cary & Company, September 20, 1765, in *George Washington: Writings*, Edited by John Rhodehamel (New York: Library of America, 1997), 116; Braintree, December 18, 1765, in *The Adams Papers: Diary and Autobiography of John Adams*, vol. 1, *1755–1770*, Edited by L. H. Butterfield. (Cambridge: Harvard University Press, 1961), Volume 1, 263–265.

[61] A Summary View of the Rights of British America, in *Thomas Jefferson:* Writings, Edited by Merrill D. Peterson (New York: Viking Press, 1984), 108-109.

[62] Ibid.

[63] Ibid.

[64] Ibid, 110.

[65] Ibid.

[66] Common Sense, in *The Writings of Thomas Paine*, Edited by Moncure Daniel Conway (4 Vols., New York: G.P. Putnam's Sons, 1894), I:94.

[67] Ibid, 87.

[68] Ibid, 72.

[69] James Madison to Thomas Jefferson, October 24, 1787, in *James Madison Writings 1772-1836* (New York, Library of America, 1999), 147.

[70] The Rights of Man, in *Common Sense, Rights of Man, and other Essential Writings of Thomas Paine* (New York: New American Library, 2003), xxii.

[71] Ibid, 172.

[72] Ibid, 175.

[73] Speech of Patrick Henry, March 23, 1775, in *American Oratory, or Selections from the Speeches of Eminent Americans*, 15.

[74] Ibid.

[75] Harlow Unger, *Lion of Liberty: Patrick Henry and the Call to a New Nation*, 281.

[76] Benjamin Franklin, William Temple Franklin, and William Duane, *Memoirs of Benjamin Franklin* (New York: Derby & Jackson, 1869), Volume I, 114.

[77] By the King, A Proclamation for Suppressing Rebellion and Sedition, in Thomas Pownall, *The Remembrancer, Or Impartial Repository of Public Events* (London: J. Almon, 1775), Volume I, 148.

[78] For a transcription of the speech, see "King George III's Address to Parliament, October 27, 1775," Library of Congress, November 2, 2013; available at https://www.loc.gov/resource/rbpe.10803800/?st=text

[79] Ibid.

[80] These charges against George III were listed in the Declaration of Independence, written to justify the severance from Great Britain.

[81] Ibid.

CHAPTER 3
ESSENTIAL CONSTITUTIONAL ANTECEDENTS

[82] Letter I, in John Dickinson, *Letters from a Farmer in Pennsylvania: To the Inhabitants of the British Colonies*, 88.

[83] Ibid; The Federalist No. 84, in *The Federalist*, 578.

[84] John Richard Green, *A Short History of the English People* (London: Macmillan and Co, 1874), 114.

[85] Ralph Turner, *King John* (New York: Longman, 1994), 13; W.L. Warren, *King John* (Los Angeles: University of California, 1978), 259.

[86] John Lawler and Gail Lawler, *A Short Historical Introduction to the Law of Real Property* (Washington, DC: Beard Books, 2000), 6; Ralph Turner, *King John*, 114; Frank McLynn, *Lionheart and Lackland: King Richard, King John and the Wars of Conquest* (London: Vintage, 2007), 288.

[87] Benjamin Franklin, *Poor Richard Improved, 1758*, in *Benjamin Franklin: Writings* (New York: Literary Classics, 1987), 1296.

[88] Ralph Turner, *King John*, 13, 90.

[89] Magna Carta, in *Introduction to Contemporary Civilization in the West* (New York: Columbia University, 1960), Volume I, 55, 417.

[90] Ralph Turner, *King John*, 158-159.

[91] Various clauses within Article I of the Constitution require that both indirect and direct taxes must be levied by Congress; Magna Carta, in *Introduction to Contemporary Civilization in the West:* Volume I, 419.

[92] Magna Carta, in *Introduction to Contemporary Civilization in the West:* Volume I, 421.

[93] Ibid, 423.

368 Notes

[94] This comes from one of the enumerated powers of Congress in Article I, Section 8.

[95] Thomas Jefferson to David Humphreys, March 18, 1789, in *Jefferson: Political Writings*, Edited by Joyce Appleby and Terence Ball (Cambridge: Cambridge University, 1999), 113.

[96] August 27, 1789, in *The Congressional Register: History of the Proceedings and Debates of the First House of Representatives of the United States* (New York: Hodge, Allen, and Campbell, 1790), 220. This was spoken during floor debate over the Second Amendment to the United States Constitution; James Madison, *Notes of Debates in the Federal Convention of 1787*, 214-215; *The Debates in the Several State Conventions on the Adoption of the Federal Constitution,* Volume II, 97.

[97] Magna Carta, in *Introduction to Contemporary Civilization in the West:* Volume I, 421.

[98] This clause resides in Article I, Section 9.

[99] Federal Farmer VI, in *The Complete Anti-Federalist*, Edited by Herbert Storing (Chicago: The University of Chicago Press, 1981), Volume I, 260.

[100] This limitation on the president's appointment power is explained in Article II, Section 2 of the Constitution.

[101] A Summary View of the Rights of British America, in *Thomas Jefferson: Writings*, 105-106.

[102] Ibid, 106.

[103] A Summary View of the Rights of British America, in *Thomas Jefferson: Writings, 108.*

[104] *Magna Charta, the Bill of Rights; with The Petition of Right, Presented to Charles I by the Lords and Commons, Together with His Majesty's Answer, and the Coronation Oath*, Printed by E. Thomas (London: Law-Booksellers, 1817), 23; The Eighth Amendment to the United States Constitution protects individuals from excessive bail and fines, and from cruel and unusual punishments.

[105] *Magna Charta, the Bill of Rights; with The Petition of Right, Presented to Charles I by the Lords and Commons, Together with His Majesty's Answer, and the Coronation Oath*, 21.

[106] Ibid, 22.

[107] Ibid, 22-24.

[108] Christopher Hibbert, *Charles I: A Life of Religion, War, and Treason* (New York: Palgrave Macmillan, 2007), 102.

[109] Samuel Rawson Gardiner and Great Britain Parliament, *The Constitutional Documents of the Puritan Revolution, 1628-1660* (Oxford: Clarendon Press, 1889), 130-131.

[110] Ibid, 135-137.

[111] Ibid 135.

[112] Ibid, 134.

[113] Christopher Hibbert, *Charles I: A Life of Religion, War, and Treason*, 160.

[114] Ibid, 177-180.

[115] Charles Carlton, *Going to the Wars: The Experience of the British Civil War 1638-1651* (London: Routledge, 1995), 213.

[116] Thomas Corns, *The Royal Image: Representations of Charles I* (Cambridge University Press, 199), 88; Christopher Hibbert, *Charles I: A Life of Religion, War, and Treason*, 251.

[117] Ibid, 256-274.

[118] Federal Farmer XI, in *The American Revolution: Writings from the Pamphlet Debate: 1764-1772*, Edited by Gordon Wood (New York: Library of America, 2015), 474-475.

[119] Antonio Fraser, *Oliver Cromwell: The Lord Protector* (New York: Alfred A. Knopf, 1973), 420.

[120] Ibid, 421.

[121] For Mason's self-description as a "man of 1688," see Kevin Gutzman, *The Politically Incorrect Guide To the Constitution* (Washington, DC: Regnery Publishing, 2007), 30.

[122] John Miller, *The Glorious Revolution*, Second Edition (New York: Longman, 1997), 7.

[123] Ibid, 7, 103-104.

[124] Ibid, 9.

[125] Ibid, 8; Edward Vallance, *The Glorious Revolution: 1688 – Britain's Fight For Liberty* (New York: Pegasus Books, 2008), 96; John Miller, *The Glorious Revolution*, 6.

[126] Ibid, 7-8; Edward Vallance, *The Glorious Revolution: 1688 – Britain's Fight For Liberty*, 106.

[127] John Miller, *The Glorious Revolution*, 1-3.

[128] Ibid, 2.

[129] Edward Vallance, *The Glorious Revolution: 1688 – Britain's Fight For Liberty*, 109-110.

[130] John Lord Campbell, *The Lives of the Lord Chancellors and Keepers of the Great Seal of England: From the Earliest Times Till the Reign of King George IV* (Philadelphia: Lee and Blanchard, 1847), Volume III, 438.

[131] *The Debates in the Several State Conventions on the Adoption of the Federal Constitution,* Volume III, 316-317.

[132] John Miller, *The Glorious Revolution*, 47, 76; Gordon Wood, *The Radicalism of the American Revolution* (New York: Alfred A. Knopf, 1991), 13.

CHAPTER 4
THE PHILADELPHIA CONVENTION
AND STATE RATIFICATION CONVENTIONS

[33] Andrew Napolitano, *Constitutional Chaos: What Happens When the Government Breaks Its Own Laws* (Nashville: Thomas Nelson, 2004), 196.

[34] See Remark, February 9, 1789, in *The Papers of Benjamin Franklin*, Edited by Leonard W. Labaree (New Haven: Yale University Press, 1959), 417.

[35] Charles Louise de Secondat, Baron de Montesquieu, *The Spirit of the Laws*, Volume I, 199.

[36] James Madison, *Notes of Debates in the Federal Convention of 1787*, 311.

[137] Thomas Woods, *The Politically Incorrect Guide to American History* (Washington, DC: Regnery Publishing, 2004), 18.

[138] James Madison, *Notes of Debates in the Federal Convention of 1787*, 105.

[139] The Federalist No. 58, in *The Federalist*, 394.

[140] Ibid.

[141] *The Debates in the Several State Conventions on the Adoption of the Federal Constitution,* Volume II, 233.

[142] Ibid, 349.

[143] James Madison, *Notes of Debates in the Federal Convention of 1787*, 104-105.

[144] Ibid, 610.

[145] James Madison to Thomas Jefferson, October 24, 1787, in *James Madison: Writings 1772-1836*, 149.

[146] *The Debates in the Several State Conventions on the Adoption of the Federal Constitution,* Volume IV, 159; Report on a National Bank, in *Alexander Hamilton: Writings*, Edited by Joanne Freeman (New York: The Library of America, 2001), 591.

[147] *Pennsylvania and the Federal Constitution, 1787-1788*, Edited by John Bach McMaster and Frederick Dawson Stone (Lancaster: Inquirer, 1888), 279.

[148] James Madison, *Notes of Debates in the Federal Convention of 1787*, 541-542.

[149] Ibid, 7; Ibid, 544.

[150] Robert Yates, *Notes of the Secret Debates of the Federal Convention of 1787* (Hawthorne: Omni, 1986), 145-147.

[151] Warren McFerran, *Birth of the Republic: The Origin of the United States* (Gretna: Pelican, 2005), 233; James Madison, *Notes of Debates in the Federal Convention of 1787*, 140. The day after Hamilton made his lengthy case for a nationalist government, the delegates ignored it entirely and launched into discussions of the New Jersey Plan instead.

[152] For instance, under its 1776 constitution, South Carolina provided its governor with the power plenary power to make and execute war, unilaterally enter into treaties with foreign governments, and even dissolve the legislature.

[153] Robert Yates, *Notes of the Secret Debates of the Federal Convention of 1787*, 10-11, 114-116; James Madison, *Notes of Debates in the Federal Convention of 1787*, 88-92.

[154] Ibid, 305.

[155] James Madison to Thomas Jefferson, October 24, 1787, in *James Madison: Writings 1772-1836*, 149.

[156] Ibid, 136.

[157] Kevin Gutzman, *Madison and the Making of America* (New York: St. Martin's 2012), 138; James Madison, *Notes of Debates in the Federal Convention of 1787* 305.

[158] James Madison, *James Madison: Writings 1772-1836*, 144-147.

[159] Thomas Woods, "The Truth About James Madison," LewRockwell.com, September 22, 2013; available at http://www.lewrockwell.com/2012/02/thomas woods/the-truth-about-james-madison/

[160] Brutus I, in *The Debate on the Constitution Federalist and Antifederalist Speeches, Articles, and Letters During the Struggle over Ratification, Part One*

September 1787 to February 1788, Edited by Bernard Bailyn (New York: The Library of America, 1993), 166.

[161] Ibid, 165; An Old Whig IV, in *Federalists and Antifederalists: The Debate Over Ratification of the Constitution* (Lanham: Rowman & Littlefield, 1998), 18.

[162] Article VII, Section 1 of the Constitution specifies that nine states "shall be sufficient for the Establishment of this Constitution between the States so ratifying the Same."

[163] The Federalist No. 39, in *The Federalist*, 254; *The Debates in the Several State Conventions on the Adoption of the Federal Constitution*, Volume IV, 24.

[164] *The Debate on the Constitution Federalist and Antifederalist Speeches,* Part One, 65; The Federalist No. 84, in *The Federalist*, 578.

[165] Ibid, 579.

[166] *The Debate on the Constitution Federalist and Antifederalist Speeches,* Part One, 65.

[167] Ibid.

[168] Ibid, 63-64.

[169] Philadelphiensis IX, in *The Complete Anti-Federalist*, Volume III, 127-128.

[170] Ibid.

[171] *The Debate on the Constitution Federalist and Antifederalist Speeches,* Part One, 65-67.

[172] Old Whig Essay IV, October 1787, in *The Essential Antifederalist*, Edited by William Allen and Gordon Lloyd (Lanham: Rowman & Littlefield, 2002), 171.

[173] An Old Whig I, in *The Debate on the Constitution: Federalist and Antifederalist Speeches,* Part One, 124.

[174] Centinel II, in *The Debate on the Constitution: Federalist and Antifederalist Speeches,* Part One, 189.

[175] *The Debates in the Several State Conventions on the Adoption of the Federal Constitution*, Volume IV, 179.

[176] Ibid, 220.

[177] Brion McClanahan, *The Founding Fathers Guide to the Constitution* (Washington, DC: Regnery Publishing, 2013), 160; *The Debates in the Several State Conventions on the Adoption of the Federal Constitution*, Volume IV, 182.

[178] Ibid, 153.

[179] Joseph Habersham to John Habersham Augusta, December 29, 1787, "The Georgia Ratification Convention Meets", teachingamericanhistory.org, December 13, 2013; available at http://teachingamericanhistory.org/library/document/the-georgia-ratifying-convention-meets/

[180] *The Debates in the Several State Conventions on the Adoption of the Federal Constitution*, Volume II, 185-186.

[181] Ibid, 200-202.

[182] A Countryman II, in *The Debate on the Constitution Part One: Federalist and Antifederalist Speeches,* Part One, 412-414.

[183] *The Debates in the Several State Conventions on the Adoption of the Federal Constitution*, Volume II, 196, 199, 201-202.

[184] Sherman and Ellsworth's Letter, September 26, 1787, in *The Debates in the Several State Conventions on the Adoption of the Federal Constitution*, Volume I, 531.

[185] *The Debates in the Several State Conventions on the Adoption of the Federal Constitution*, Volume II, 45-46

[186] Ibid, 60, 66.

[187] Ibid, 80.

[188] Ibid, 87.

[189] *Luther Martin's Letter on the Federal Convention of 1787*, in *The Debates in the Several State Conventions on the Adoption of the Federal Constitution*, Volume I, 438.

[190] *The Debates in the Several State Conventions on the Adoption of the Federal Constitution*, Volume II, 548-549.

[191] Ibid, 555-556.

[192] Ibid.

[193] *The Debates in the Several State Conventions on the Adoption of the Federal Constitution*, Volume IV, 253-254.

[194] Ibid, 264.

[195] Ibid, 313-316, 337-338.

[196] *The Debates in the Several State Conventions on the Adoption of the Federal Constitution*, Volume I, 358.

[197] Kevin Gutzman, *Virginia's American Revolution: From Dominion to Republic, 1776-1840* (New York: Lexington Books, 2007), 86-92.

[198] Quoted in Henry Mayer, *A Son of Thunder* (New York: Grove Press, 1991), 370.

[199] *The Debates in the Several State Conventions on the Adoption of the Federal Constitution*, Volume III, 521.

[200] Ibid, 523, 552.

[201] Ibid, 554.

[202] Kevin Gutzman, *Virginia's American Revolution: From Dominion to Republic, 1776-1840*, 99; *The Debates in the Several State Conventions on the Adoption of the Federal Constitution*, Volume III, 467, 598.

[203] Kevin Gutzman, *Virginia's American Revolution: From Dominion to Republic, 1776-1840*, 87.

[204] *The Debates in the Several State Conventions on the Adoption of the Federal Constitution*, Volume II, 376.

[205] Cato V, in *The Debate on the Constitution: Federalist and Antifederalist Speeches*, Part One, 399-402.

[206] Ibid, 401-402; *The Debates in the Several State Conventions on the Adoption of the Federal Constitution*, Volume II, 403.

[207] Ibid, 362.

[208] Ibid.

[209] Ibid, 274.

[210] Forrest McDonald, *E Pluribus Unum: The Formation of the American Republic, 1776-1790* (Indianapolis: Liberty Fund, 1979), 362-363. Privately an

publicly, Alexander Hamilton suggested that New York City could withdraw from the state and join the union alone.

[211] See Albert Furtwangler, *The Authority of Publius* (London: Cornell University, 1984). Furtwangler made several arguments to support the contention that the series was not highly distributed or widely read, despite the contemporary prominence of the series.

[212] *The Debates in the Several State Conventions on the Adoption of the Federal Constitution*, Volume II, 411.

[213] Ibid, Volume I, 327.

[214] *The Debates in the Several State Conventions on the Adoption of the Federal Constitution*, Volume IV, 161-162.

[215] *The Debates in the Several State Conventions on the Adoption of the Federal Constitution*, Volume I, 360.

[216] *The Debates in the Several State Conventions on the Adoption of the Federal Constitution*, Volume III, 464, 626.

[217] Ibid, 588.

[218] *The Anti-Federalist Papers and the Constitution Conventions Debates: The Clashes and the Compromises that Gave Birth to our Form of Government*, Edited by Ralph Ketcham (New York: Signet Classic, 2003), 225.

[219] See Forrest McDonald, *E Pluribus Unum: The Formation of the American Republic, 1776-1790* (Indianapolis: Liberty Fund, 1979), 362-363. Privately and publicly, Alexander Hamilton suggested that New York City could withdraw from the state and join the union alone.

[220] Edmund Randolph most famously made this argument in Virginia's Ratification Convention, where he professed that "every exercise of a power not expressly delegated" was "a violation of the constitution." See *The Debates in the Several State Conventions on the Adoption of the Federal Constitution*, Volume III, 576. Prominent Federalists in several other states also made similar assurances.

[221] Thomas Jefferson to Elbridge Gerry, January 26, 1799, in *Thomas Jefferson: Writings,* 1056.

[222] The Federalist No. 39, in *The Federalist*, 254.

[223] Quoted in Thornton Anderson, *Creating the Constitution: The Convention of 1787 and the First Congress* (University Park: Pennsylvania State University, 1993), 180; *The Debates in the Several State Conventions on the Adoption of the Federal Constitution*, Volume IV, 194.

[224] See Thornton Anderson, *Creating the Constitution: The Convention of 1787 and the First Congress*, 180.

[225] Ibid.

[226] Ibid.

CHAPTER 5
THE JEFFERSONIAN TRADITION

[27] John Adams, *Adams on Adams*, Edited by Paul Zall (Lexington: University Press of Kentucky, 2004), 75-76.

[228] Thomas Jefferson, *Thomas Jefferson: Writings*, 19.

[229] Steven Dworetz, *The Unvarnished Doctrine: Locke, Liberalism, and the American Revolution* (Durham: Duke University, 1989), 135; James Otis, *A Vindication of the Conduct of the House of Representatives of the Province on the Massachusetts-Bay: Most Particularly in the Last Session of the General Assembly* (Boston: Edes & Gill, 1762), 20; Benjamin Franklin, *The Works of Benjamin Franklin*, Edited by Jared Sparks (Boston: Tappan & Whittemore, 1836), 131; Thomas Jefferson to James Madison, August 30, 1823, in *The Writings of Thomas Jefferson*, Edited by Andrew Lipscomb (Washington, DC: The Thomas Jefferson Memorial Association, 1904), 462; Thomas Jefferson to John Trumbull, February 15, 1789, in *Thomas Jefferson: Writings*, 939.

[230] Ibid, 24; See the Declaratory Act of 1766, a Parliamentary Act that followed the revocation of the Stamp Act of 1765. This law reasserted that Parliament's authority in America was that same as it was in Britain and reiterated that laws passed by Parliament are invariably binding upon the colonies.

[231] Declaration of Independence, in *Thomas Jefferson: Writings*, 24; See Thomas Woods, *Nullification*, 96.

[232] Thomas McKean favored independence, while George Read opposed it.

[233] John Taylor, *New Views of the Constitution of the United States* (Clark: The Lawbook Exchange, 2010), 6-7; Robert Yates, *Notes of the Secret Debates of the Federal Convention of 1787*, 151.

[234] Kevin Gutzman, *Madison and the Making of America*, 40-41.

[235] Ibid, 41.

[236] Ibid, 46.

[237] Merrill D. Peterson, *The Political Writings of Thomas Jefferson* (Annapolis: GraphTec, 1993), 42.

[238] Ibid.

[239] Ibid, 43.

[240] Thomas Jefferson to Elbridge Gerry, January 26, 1799, in *Thomas Jefferson: Writings*, 1057.

[241] Kevin Gutzman, *Madison and the Making of America*, 48.

[242] Merrill D. Peterson, *The Political Writings of Thomas Jefferson*, 43-44.

[243] Kevin Gutzman, *Madison and the Making of America*, 46-48.

[244] Kevin Gutzman, *Madison and the Making of America*, 271.

[245] John Taylor of Caroline, *New Views of the Constitution of the United States* (Washington, DC: Regnery Publishing, 2000), 232, 321.

[246] Thomas Jefferson to John Taylor, June 4, 1798, in *Thomas Jefferson: Writings* 1049.

[247] Ibid.

[248] Ibid, 1050.

[249] Ibid.

[250] For more information on the Whiskey Rebellion and the 1794 invasion of Pennsylvania, see Brion McClanahan, *9 Presidents Who Screwed Up America And Four Who Tried to Save Her* (Washington, DC: Regnery Publishing, 2016) 9-12.

[251] Thomas Jefferson, *The Kentucky Resolution of 1799*, in *The Debates in the Several State Conventions on the Adoption of the Federal Constitution,* Volume IV, 545.

[252] Madison's Report on the Virginia Resolutions, in *The Debates in the Several State Conventions on the Adoption of the Federal Constitution,* Volume IV, 549.

[253] Juhani Rudanko, *James Madison and Freedom of Speech: Major Debates in the Early Republic* (Lanham: University Press of America, 2004), 70.

[254] Susan Dunn, *Sister Revolutions: French Lighting, American Light* (New York: Faber and Faber, 1999), 148.

[255] Geoffrey Stone, *Perilous Times: Free Speech in Wartime from the Sedition Act of* 1798 (New York: W.W. Norton & Company, 2004), 64; Mike Farrel and Mary Carmen Cupito, *Newspapers: A Complete Guide to the Industry* (New York: Peter Lang, 2010), 55; Kevin Gutzman, *Madison and the Making of America*, 271. For inflation calculation for 1798's currency in 2015, see "CPI Inflation Calculator," OfficialData.org, January 6, 2015; available at https://www.officialdata.org/us/inflation/1798

[256] Geoffrey Stone, *Perilous Times: Free Speech in Wartime from the Sedition Act of* 1798, 65.

[257] Kevin Gutzman, *Madison and the Making of America*, 270.

[258] Marcel Bax and Daniel Kadar, *Understanding Historical (Im)Politeness: Relational Linguistic Practice Over Time and Across Cultures* (Philadlephia: John Benjamins, 2012), 85.

[259] John Miller, *Crisis in Freedom: The Alien and Sedition Acts* (Boston: Little Brown, 1951), 108.

[260] Kevin Gutzman, *Madison and the Making of America*, 273.

[261] Luigi Marco Bassani, *Liberty, State & Union: The Political Theory of Thomas Jefferson* (Macon: Mercer University, 2010), 175.

[262] Draft of the Kentucky Resolutions, in *Thomas Jefferson: Writings*, 449.

[263] Opinion on the Constitutionality of a National Bank, in *Thomas Jefferson: Writings*, 416.

[264] Draft of the Kentucky Resolutions, in *Thomas Jefferson: Writings*, 449.

[265] Ibid, 451.

[266] Ibid, 449.

[267] Ibid, 453-455.

[268] Ibid, 449.

[269] Ibid, 453-456.

[270] Dumas Malone, *Jefferson and His Time* (Boston: Little, Brown and Company, 1962), Volume III, 394.

[271] Thomas Woods, *Nullification*, 54.

[272] Virginia Resolutions Against the Alien and Sedition Acts, in *James Madison: Writings 1772-1836*, 589.

[273] Ibid.

[274] Ibid.

[275] Ibid, 589-590.

[276] Ibid, 590.

[277] Ibid.

[278] Ibid, 590-591.

[279] For instance, see Adrienne Koch and Harry Ammon, "The Virginia and Kentucky Resolutions: An Episode in Jefferson's and Madison's Defense of Civil Liberties," The William and Mary Quarterly Volume 5, No. 2 (1948): 147-176.

[280] Resolutions of Virginia and Kentucky, Penned by Madison and Jefferson, *in Relation to the Alien and Sedition Acts, and the Debates and Proceeds in the House of Delegates of Virginia, On the Same, in December 1798*, Edited by Robert I. Smith (Richmond: Samuel Shepherd, 1835), 75-80.

[281] Ibid, 81.

[282] Ibid, 92-93, 123, 161, 207-208.

[283] Kevin Gutzman, *Madison and the Making of America*, 275; Resolutions of Virginia and Kentucky, Penned by Madison and Jefferson, *in Relation to the Alien and Sedition Acts, and the Debates and Proceeds in the House of Delegates of Virginia, On the Same, in December 1798*, 203; Kevin Gutzman, "A Troublesome Legacy: James Madison and the Principles of '98," *Journal of the Early Republic* Volume 15, No. 4 (1995): 581.

[284] Thomas Jefferson to James Madison, August 3, 1799, in *The Republic of Letters: The Correspondence between Jefferson and Madison 1776-1826,* Edited by James Morton Smith (New York: W.W. Norton & Company, 1995), Volume 2, 1119.

[285] Ibid, 239-240.

[286] Ibid, 240.

[287] Ibid, 241.

[288] The Federalist No. 46, in *The Federalist*, 319-320.

[289] The Federalist No. 85, in *The Federalist*, 593.

[290] Report on the Alien and Sedition Acts, in *James Madison: Writings 1772-1836*, 609-610; Kevin Gutzman, *James Madison and the Making of America*, 276.

[291] Report on the Alien and Sedition Acts, in *James Madison: Writings 1772-1836*, 610-611.

[292] Ibid, 611.

[293] Ibid, 613.

[294] Ibid, 611; See The Federalist No. 46, in *The Federalist*, 319-320. In cases of unconstitutional or even unpopular law, Madison suggested that the states had "the advantage in the means of defeating such encroachments" through a concerted "refusal to co-operate with officers of the Union." He advised that doing so would lead to "very serious impediments" and "would present obstructions which the Federal Government would hardly be willing to encounter."

[295] Report on the Alien and Sedition Acts, in *James Madison: Writings 1772-1836* 613.

[296] Ibid.

[297] Ibid, 612.

[298] Ibid, 628.

[299] Ibid, 647-648.

[300] Ibid, 619.

[301] Ibid, 642.

[302] See Opinion on the Constitutionality of a National Bank, in *Alexander Hamilton: Writings*, 613-646.

[303] William Watkins, *Reclaiming the American Revolution: The Kentucky and Virginia Resolutions and Their Legacy* (New York: Palgrave Macmillan, 2004), 79; Kevin Gutzman, *James Madison and the Making of America*, 276.

[304] Wendell Bird, "Reassessing Responses to the Virginia and Kentucky Resolutions: New Evidence from the Tennessee and Georgia Resolutions and from Other States," *Journal of the Early Republic* Volume 35, No. 4 (Winter 2015): 530.

[305] Ibid, 535.

[306] Ibid, 528, 543-544.

[307] Adrienne Koch and Harry Ammon, "The Virginia and Kentucky Resolutions: An Episode in Jefferson's and Madison's Defense of Civil Liberties," *The William and Mary Quarterly* Volume 5, No. 2 (April, 1948): 147, 162-164.

[308] Kevin Gutzman, *Virginia's American Revolution: From Dominion to Republic, 1776-1840*, 118.

[309] Exposition and Protest, Reported by the Special Committee of the House of Representatives of South Carolina on the Tariff, in *The Statutes at Large of South Carolina: Containing Acts, Records, and Documents of a Constitutional Character*, Edited by Thomas Cooper (Columbia: A.S. Johnston, 1836), 248.

[310] Ibid.

[311] Ibid, 247-252.

[312] Ibid, 248.

[313] Ibid, 260, 266.

[314] Ibid, 263, 266-267, 273.

[315] F.W. Taussig, *The Tariff History of the United States* (New York: Augustus M. Kelley, 1967), 109-110.

[316] "South Carolina Ordinance of Nullification, November 24, 1832," The Avalon Project: Documents in Law, History, and Diplomacy, December 9, 2013; available at http://avalon.law.yale.edu/19th_century/ordnull.asp

[317] Exposition and Protest, Reported by the Special Committee of the House of Representatives of South Carolina on the Tariff, in *The Statutes at Large of South Carolina: Containing Acts, Records, and Documents of a Constitutional Character*, 271-273.

[318] Robert Remini, *The Life of Andrew Jackson* (New York: HarperCollins, 2010), 241.

[319] Quoted in Jon Meacham, *American Lion: Andrew Jackson in the White House* (New York: Random House, 2008), xviii.

[320] Robert Remini, *Andrew Jackson and the Course of American Democracy: 1833-1845* (New York: Harper & Roe, 1984), 29-36.

[321] Ibid, xviii (Introduction), 227; "Professor Robert Remini: The Jacksonian Era," ushistory.org, September 9, 2013; available at http://www.ushistory.org/us/historians/remini.asp

[22] Thomas Woods, *Nullification*, 60-65.

[23] Connecticut on the Conscription Bill, October Session, 1814, in *State Documents on Federal Relations: The States and the United States*, Edited by Herman Ames (Philadelphia: University of Pennsylvania, 1911), 76.

[324] Report of the Hartford Convention, in *The Book of the Constitution: Containing the Constitution of the United States, a Synopsis of The Several State Constitutions, with Various other Important Documents and Useful Information*, Edited by Edwin Williams (New York: Peter Hill, 1833), 100.

[325] Ibid, 101.

[326] Quoted in Richard Current, *Daniel Webster and the Rise of National Conservatism* (Boston: Little, Brown and Company, 1955), 16-18; Thomas Woods, *Nullification*, 66.

[327] The federal commissioners received ten dollars for returning a slave, and five dollars if the slave was released.

[328] Joint Resolution of the Legislature of Wisconsin, March 19, 1859, in Thomas Woods, *Nullification*, 262.

[329] *The General Statutes of the State of Vermont: Passed at the Annual Session of the General Assembly, Commencing October 9, 1862*, Second Edition (Cambridge: Riverside, 1870), Section 27, 350.

[330] Mike Maharrey, "Personal Liberty Laws: A Nullification History Lesson," Tenth Amendment Center, October 4, 2014; available at http://tenthamendmentcenter.com/2013/03/06/personal-liberty-laws-a-nullification-history-lesson/

[331] *Declaration of the Immediate Causes Which Induce and Justify the Secession of South Carolina from the Federal Union*, in Orville James Victor, *The History, Civil, Political and Military, of the Southern Rebellion* (New York: James D. Torrey, 1861), Volume I, 98.

[332] Farewell Speech to the Senate by Jefferson Davis, in *Great Debates in American History: From the Debates in the British Parliament on the Stamp Act (1764-1765) to the Debates in Congress at the Close of the Taft Administration (1912-1913)*, Edited by Marion Mills Miller (New York: Current Literature, 1913), Volume V, 440-441.

[333] Quoted in Henry Cleveland, *Alexander H. Stephens, in Public and Private, with Letters and Speeches, Before, During, and Since the War* (Philadelphia: National Publishing Company, 1866), 115. Stephens was involved in a debate regarding the legitimacy of South Carolina's nullification of the controversial federal tariffs.

[334] This is a reference to the types of cases the federal judiciary has the power to adjudicate according to Article III, Section 2 of the Constitution.

[335] Thomas Jefferson to Abigail Adams, June 13, 1804, in *Thomas Jefferson: Writings*, 1145-1146.

[336] Gordon Wood, *Empire of Liberty: A History of the Early Republic, 1789-1815* (New York: Oxford University Press, 2009), 293, 420-422.

[337] In the state ratification debates, many leading Federalists insisted that judges would have this power. For instance, see The Federalist No. 78, in *The Federalist* 524; *The Debates in the Several State Conventions on the Adoption of the Federal Constitution*, Volume II, 196; Ibid, III, 553; Ibid, IV, 71. In New York, Alexander Hamilton explained that federal judges would use judicial review to invalidate unconstitutional laws. In Connecticut, Oliver Ellsworth similarly iterated that if Congress "make a law which the constitution does not authorize," federal judges "will declare it to be void." In Virginia, John Marshall of Virginia insisted that

federal judges "would not consider such a law as coming under their jurisdiction," and therefore "declare it void." In North Carolina, John Steele noted that judicial review was "constructed as to be a check," such that "if the Congress make laws inconsistent with the Constitution, independent judges would not uphold them."

[338] Thomas Jefferson to William Jarvis, September 28, 1820, in *The Writings of Thomas Jefferson: Being His Autobiography, Correspondence, Reports, Messages, Addresses, and Other Writings, Official and Private,* Edited by Henry Augustine Washington (New York: Derby & Jackson, 1859), Volume VI, 178.

[339] Norman Risjord, *Thomas Jefferson* (Lanham: Madison House, 2002), 136.

[340] Thomas Jefferson to Abigail Adams, September 11, 1804, in John Robert Irelan, *History of the Life, Administration, and Times of Thomas Jefferson, Third President of the United States* (Chicago: Fairbanks and Palmer, 1886), 374.

[341] Norman Risjord, *Thomas Jefferson,* 137-138; *Trial of Samuel Chase, An Associate Justice of the Supreme Court of the United States, Impeached by the House of Representatives, for High Crimes and Misdemeanors, before the Senate of the United States,* Edited by Samuel Smith and Thomas Lloyd (Washington: Samuel Smith, 1805), Volume I, 95; Article I, Section 8 of the Constitution grants this power. In addition, Article III, Section 1 notes that Congress may ordain the inferior courts "from time to time."

[342] This comes from Article II, Section 4 of the Constitution.

[343] Thomas Jefferson to Thomas Ritchie Monticello, December 25, 1820, in *Thomas Jefferson: Writings,* 1446.

[344] Avik Roy, "Romney: 'The Supreme Court Has Spoken...It's a Tax,'" National Review Online, September 30, 2013; available at http://www.nationalreview.com/corner/304747/romney-supreme-court-has-spokenits-tax-avik-roy

[345] Gary May, *John Tyler: The American Presidents Series: The 10th President,* 1841-1845 (New York: Henry Holt and Company, 2008), 9; Robert Seager II, *And Tyler Too: A Biography of John and Julia Gardiner Tyler* (New York: McGraw-Hill Book Company, 1963), 149.

[346] Oliver Chitwood, *John Tyler: Champion of the Old South* (Newtown: American Political Biography, 2006), vii-viii (Forward).

[347] Ibid, 114-115.

[348] Philip Hone, *The Diary of Philip Hone 1828-1851* (New York: Cornell University, 1889), Volume One, 123.

[349] This comes from Article II, Section 1 of the Constitution.

[350] Oliver Chitwood, *John Tyler: Champion of the Old South,* 270.

[351] John Tyler, Address Upon Assuming the Office of the President of the United States, April 9, 1841, accessed September 10, 2013; available at http://www.presidency.ucsb.edu/ws/?pid=533

[352] Peter Temin, *The Jacksonian Economy* (New York: W.W. Norton, 1969), 88.

[353] Oliver Chitwood, *John Tyler: Champion of the Old South,* 267, 292.

[354] Ibid, 299.

[355] Ibid.

[356] Ibid, 317.

[357] Ibid, 301-302.

358 Abel Upshur, *A Brief Enquiry Into the True Nature and Character of our Federal Government: Being a Review of Judge Story's Commentaries on the Constitution of the United States* (Petersburg, VA: Edmund and Julian C. Ruffin, 1840), 14-15.

359 Ibid, 17.

360 Ibid, 5-6.

361 Ibid, 44.

362 Ibid, 67.

363 Ibid, 66, 84.

364 Nullification: An Exposition of the Virginia Resolutions of 1798, in Thomas Woods, *Nullification*, 222.

365 Cynthia Crossen, "Historians Struggle to Give Franklin Pierce a Spotlight," Wall Street Journal, September 14, 2013; available at http://online.wsj.com/article/0,,SB10449191961697237 03,00.html; Nate Silver, "Contemplating Obama's Place in History, Statistically," New York Times, September 14, 2013; available at http://fivethirtyeight.blogs.nytimes.com/2013/01/23/contemplating-obamas-place-in-history-statistically; Jamie Frater, "Top 10 Worst US Presidents," Listverse, September 14, 2013; available at http://listverse.com/2007/11/06/top-10-worst-us-presidents/

366 Veto Message, in *The Statesman's Manual: Containing the Addresses and Messages of the Presidents of the United States*, Edited by Edwin Williams (New York: Edward Walker, 1895), Volume III, 2046-2053.

367 Ibid.

368 Ibid.

369 Ibid.

370 Ibid.

371 Ibid.

372 Thomas DiLorenzo, *Hamilton's Curse* (New York: Crown Publishing Group, 2009), 52.

373 Peter Wallner, *Franklin Pierce: Martyr for the Union* (Concord: Plaidswede Publishing, 2007), 362.

374 Thomas DiLorenzo, *The Real Lincoln* (Roseville: Prima Publishing, 2002), 136; Thomas DiLorenzo, *Lincoln Unmasked: What You're Not Supposed to Know about Dishonest Abe* (New York: Three Rivers, 2006), 93-94.

375 Peter Wallner, *Franklin Pierce: Martyr for the Union*, 338; This comes from Article I, Section 9 of the Constitution. The power is associated with Congress (Article I), not the executive (Article II).

376 Franklin Pierce to John H. George, August 11, 1862, Pierce Papers, Library of Congress.

377 Stephen Neff, Justice in Blue and Gray: A Legal History of the Civil War (Cambridge: Harvard University Press, 2010), 43.

378 Peter Wallner, *Franklin Pierce: Martyr for the Union*, 332-334.

379 Ibid, 335.

380 Ibid, 375.

381 Address By Melanchthon Smith, *in Pamphlets on the Constitution of th United States, Published During its Discussion by the People 1787-1788*, 97.

[382] Ibid, 98.

[383] Robert Yates, *Secret Proceedings and Debates of the Federal Convention of 1787*, 154-155.

[384] First Inagural Address of Abraham Lincoln, March 4, 1861, The Avalon Project, January 4, 2014; available at http://avalon.law.yale.edu/19th_century/lincoln1.asp

[385] Several states declared independence prior to the adoption of the Declaration of Independence, including Rhode Island, Virginia, and North Carolina.

[386] First Inagural Address of Thomas Jefferson, March 4, 1801, The Avalon Project, January 4, 2014; available at http://avalon.law.yale.edu/19th_century/jefinau1.asp

[387] Thomas Jefferson to William H. Crawford, June 20, 1816, in *The Writings of Thomas Jefferson,* Volume XI, 1816.

[388] Alexis de Tocqueville, *Democracy in America*, Edited by Bruce Frohnen (Washington, DC: Regnery Publishing, 2002), 306.

[389] Speech on Surveys for Roads and Canals, January 30, 1824, in Russell Kirk, *John Randolph of Roanoke: A Study in American Politics*, 420.

[390] See Thomas Woods, Unimaginative Conservatives at the Imaginative Conservative, January 10, 2013, TomWoods.com, January 4, 2014; available at http://tomwoods.com/blog/unimaginative-conservatives-at-the-imaginative-conservative/

[391] Aaron Coleman, "Competing Conceptions of Union and Ordered Liberty," Law & Liberty, March 14, 2019; available at https://www.lawliberty.org/liberty-classic/competing-conceptions-of-union-and-ordered-liberty-in-the-webster-hayne-debate/

CHAPTER 6
AN EXCEPTIONAL WAR OF INDEPENDENCE

[392] Gordon Wood, *The Radicalism of the American Revolution*, 3-4; Gordon Wood, *The Creation of the American Republic: 1776-1787*, 10-13. Wood revealed that the American patriots revered the British constitution and sought to prevent it from being undermined by tyranny.

[393] Simon Schama, *Citizens: A Chronicle of the French Revolution* (New York: Random House, 1989), 475-477.

[394] Christopher Hibbert, *The Days of the French Revolution* (New York: Quill, 1999), 230.

[395] Peter Kropotkin, *The Great French Revolution, 1789-1793* (New York: G.P. Putnam's Sons, 1909), 521; Christopher Hibbert, *The Days of the French Revolution*, 232; Gwynne Lewis, *The French Revolution: Rethinking the Debate* (New York: Routledge, 1999), 45.

[396] The Festival of the Supreme Being, in *Modern Eloquence: Political Oratory*, Edited by Thomas Brackett Reed (Philadelphia: John D. Morris and Company, 1903), 1757.

[397] Ibid.

[398] Christopher Hibbert, *The Days of the French Revolution*, 231.

[399] Daniel Gedacht, *George Washington: Leader of a New Nation* (New York: Rosen, 2004), 99.

[400] "Transcript of Treaty of Paris (1783)," Our Documents, September 3, 2013; available at http://www.ourdocuments.gov/doc.php?doc=6&page=transcript

[401] Ibid.

[402] John Adams to Hezekiah Niles, February 13, 1818, in Charles Francis Adams, *The Works of John Adams* (Boston: Little, Brown and Company, 1856), Volume X, 283.

CHAPTER 7
THE LEGACY OF ALEXANDER HAMILTON
AND JOHN MARSHALL

[403] Thomas Jefferson to Edward Carrington, May 27, 1788, in *The Papers of Thomas Jefferson* (Princeton: Princeton University Press, 1956), Volume 13, 208-210.

[404] Robert Yates, *Notes of the Secret Debates of the Federal Convention of 1787*, 9.

[405] Ibid, 30.

[406] The Federalist No. 81, in *The Federalist*, 548-549.

[407] The Federalist No. 82, in *The Federalist*, 553.

[408] Sean Wilentz, Review of *Empire of Liberty: A History of the Early Republic, 1789-1815*, by Gordon Wood, *Journal of American History* Volume 97, No. 2 (2010): 476.

[409] *Report on Manufactures*, in *Alexander Hamilton: Writings*, 663-664.

[410] *The Debates in the Several State Conventions on the Adoption of the Federal Constitution*, Volume I, 354-373.

[411] *Report on Manufactures*, in *Alexander Hamilton: Writings*, 664.

[412] Ibid, 666.

[413] Ibid, 668-669.

[414] Ibid, 731.

[415] Ibid, 732-734.

[416] Thomas Jefferson to Alexander Donald, February 7, 1788, in *Thomas Jefferson: Writings*, 919.

[417] Thomas DiLorenzo, *Hamilton's Curse*, 101-102.

[418] Edward Vallance, *The Glorious Revolution: 1688 – Britain's Fight For Liberty*, 226. For information on the Federal Reserve Bank, see Murray Rothbard, *The Case Against the Fed* (Auburn: Ludwig von Mises Institute, 1994); G. Edward Griffin, *The Creature From Jekyll Island: A Second Look at the Federal Reserve* (Westlake Village: American Media, 1995).

[419] Murray Rothbard, *The Mystery of Banking* (Auburn: The Ludwig Von Mises Institute, 2008), 191-193.

[420] Opinion on the Constitutionality of a National Bank, in *Alexander Hamilton: Writings*, 615-616. Hamilton's claim converted his assertions in favor of th

Constitution in the ratification debates in New York, where he insisted categorically that the only powers to be legitimately exercised by the general government were those specifically delegated to it.

421 Ibid, 631.

422 Ibid, 642.

423 Opinion on the Constitutionality of a National Bank, in *Thomas Jefferson: Writings*, 416.

424 See James Callender, *A History of the United States for 1796* (Philadelphia: Snowden & M'Corkle, 1797).

425 Thomas Jefferson to George Washington, September 9, 1792, in *Thomas Jefferson: Writings*, 993-994; Kevin Gutzman, *Thomas Jefferson – Revolutionary: A Radical's Struggle to Remake America* (New York: St. Martin's Press, 2017), 37-38.

426 Thomas Woods, *33 Questions About American History You're Not Supposed to Ask* (New York: Crown, 2007), 160.

427 Tully No. II, in *Alexander Hamilton: The Works of Alexander Hamilton*, Edited by Henry Cabot Lodge (New York: G.P. Putnam's Sons, 1904), Volume IV, 416; See Thomas Woods, *Questions About American History You're Not Supposed to Ask*, 159-164.

428 Ibid.

429 Thomas DiLorenzo, *Hamilton's Curse*, 4; Warren McFerran, *Political Sovereignty: The Supreme Authority in the United States* (Gretna: Pelican, 2005), 109; Thomas DiLorenzo, *Hamilton's Curse*, 209.

430 Marbury v. Madison, 5 US 162-164 (1803).

431 Ibid, 5 US 177.

432 For instance, see the 1784 New York case of Rutgers v. Waddington, where the state's highest court negated an act that confiscated the property of Tories.

433 Brion McClanahan, *The Founding Fathers Guide to the Constitution*, 139-140.

434 *The Debates in the Several State Conventions on the Adoption of the Federal Constitution,* Volume II, 489.

435 Thomas Jefferson to W. H. Torrance, June 11, 1815, in The Founder's Constitution, November 29, 2013; available at http://press-pubs.uchicago.edu/founders/documents/a1_10_1s13.html

436 The precondition for law to be considered legitimate and supreme is found in Article VI, Section 2.

437 See Kevin Gutzman, *The Politically Incorrect Guide to the Constitution*, 82. Gutzman quoted from the Northwest Ordinance of 1787.

438 Ibid, 82-83.

439 Fletcher v. Peck, 10 US 144 (1810).

440 Ibid, 10 US 143.

441 Ibid, 10 US 87.

442 Ibid, 10 US 136.

443 Ibid, 10 US 136.

444 *The Debates in the Several State Conventions on the Adoption of the Federal Constitution*, Volume III, 552.

445 McCulloch v. Maryland, 17 US 136 (1819).

[446] Ibid, 17 US 402-405.

[447] Thomas Jefferson to Spencer Roane, September 6, 1819, in *Thomas Jefferson: Writings*, 1425-1426.

[448] See The Federalist No. 81, in *The Federalist*, 548-549. Alexander Hamilton insisted that "it is inherent in the nature of sovereignty, not to be amenable to the suit of an individual without its consent," and argued that forcing states into such federal suits would involve the "destruction of a pre-existing right of the State governments."

[449] Adolf Hitler, *Mein Kampf*, Translated by Ralph Manheim (New York: Houghton Mifflin Company, 1998), 559-560, 575.

[450] Ibid, 567.

[451] Jonathan Spence, *Emperor of China* (New York: Alfred A. Knopf, 1988), xvii, 31.

[452] Jonathan Spence, *Search for Modern China* (New York: W.W. Norton & Company, 2012), 805.

CHAPTER 8
THE "SWEEPING CLAUSES" –
WHAT DO THEY REALLY MEAN?

[453] Kevin Gutzman, *Madison and the Making of America*, 234.

[454] James Madison to Robert S. Garnett, February 11, 1824, in *Letters and Other Writings of James Madison* (Philadlephia: J.B. Lippincott, 1865), Volume 3, 367; Brion McClanahan, *The Founding Fathers Guide to the Constitution*, 8.

[455] *The Debates in the Several State Conventions on the Adoption of the Federal Constitution,* Volume III, 455.

[456] Address by David Ramsay, in *The Federalist And Other Contemporary Papers on the Constitution of the United States*, Edited by E.H. Scott (New York: Scott, Foresman and Company, 1894), 919; The Federalist No. 41, in *The Federalist*, 278.

[457] Debate on Cod Fisheries, in *Abridgement of the Debates of Congress, from 1789 to 1856,* Edited by Thomas Benton (New York: D. Appleton and Company, 1857), Volume I, 360.

[458] Ibid.

[459] United States Congress, *A Second Federalist: Congress Creates a Government*, Edited by Charles S. Hyneman and George W. Carey (New York: Meredith 1967), 114.

[460] Veto Message, in *The Writings of James Madison*, Edited by Gaillard Hun (New York: G.P. Putnam's Sons, 1908), Volume VIII, 388.

[461] The Federalist No. 32, in *The Federalist*, 199-200.

[462] Thomas DiLorenzo, *Hamilton's Curse*, 112-113.

[463] James Madison, *Notes of Debates in the Federal Convention of 1787*, 201; *The Debates in the Several State Conventions on the Adoption of the Federal Constitution,* Volume III, 466.

[464] Kevin Gutzman, *Virginia's American Revolution: From Dominion to Republic, 1776-1840*, 85.

[465] *The Debates in the Several State Conventions on the Adoption of the Federal Constitution,* Volume II, 196.

[466] Ideas of Mr. Jefferson on Banks, in *The Debates in the Several State Conventions on the Adoption of the Federal Constitution,* Volume IV, 610.

[467] Ibid, 522. Levi made this case in the Senate on the topic of public lands.

[468] James Madison, *Notes of Debates in the Federal Convention of 1787*, 74, 530; Brion McClanahan, *The Founding Fathers Guide to the Constitution*, 42-43; See Articles of Confederation, Article III.

[469] *The Debates in the Several State Conventions on the Adoption of the Federal Constitution,* Volume IV, 429.

[470] Samuel Johnson, *A Dictionary of the English Language*, Sixth Edition (London: J.F. Rivington, 1785), Volume II, 484; Randy Barnett, "The Original Meaning of the Commerce Clause," *University of Chicago Law Review* Volume 68 (Winter 2001): 115-125; Regulate. Dictionary.com. *The American Heritage Science Dictionary*. Houghton Mifflin Company. December 28, 2016, available at: http://www.dictionary.com/browse/regulate

[471] James Madison to Thomas Jefferson, August 12, 1786, in *James Madison: Writings 1772-1836*, 53; George Washington to Jabez Bowen, January 9, 1787, Quoted in George Bancroft, *A Plea for the Constitution of the U.S. of America: Wounded in the House of Its Guardians* (New York: Harper & Brothers, 1886), 88; Thomas Jefferson to John Wayles Eppes, November 6, 1813, in *The Writings of Thomas Jefferson: Correspondence*, Edited by Henry Augustine Washington (New York: Derby & Jackson, 1859), 246.

[472] The text that prohibits states from passing "Laws impairing the Obligation of Contracts" in Article I, Section 10 is often referred to as the Contract Clause.

[473] James Madison to Thomas Jefferson, March 18, 1786, in *Documentary History of the Constitution of the United States of America* (Washington: Department of State, 1905), 8.

[474] *The Debates in the Several State Conventions on the Adoption of the Federal Constitution,* Volume II, 59.

[475] Ibid, 106-107.

[476] Ibid, 83.

[477] Ibid, 542, Ibid, Volume III, 101; The Federalist No. 42, in *The Federalist*, 284.

[478] The Federalist No. 11, in *The Federalist*, 71.

[479] United States v. Darby, 312 US 124 (1941)

[480] Wickard v. Filburn, 317 US 111 (1942).

[481] Ibid.

[482] Donald Kommers, John Finn, and Gary Jacobson, *American Constitutional Law: Essays, Cases, and Comparative Notes* (Lanham: Bowman & Littlefield, 2010), Volume 1, 375

[483] Quoted in Henry Mark Holzer, *The Supreme Court Opinions of Clarence Thomas: 1991-2011*, Second Edition (Jefferson: McFarland & Company, 2012), 6.

[484] *The Debates in the Several State Conventions on the Adoption of the Federal Constitution,* Volume II, 468.

[485] Ibid, 448-449.

[486] Ibid, 468.

[487] Ibid, 330, 338, 385.

[488] Ibid, 353.

[489] *The Debates in the Several State Conventions on the Adoption of the Federal Constitution,* Volume III, 464.

[490] Veto Message, in *The Writings of James Madison*, Volume VIII, 386.

[491] Ibid, 387-388.

[492] Ibid.

[493] United States v. Comstock, 560 US 126 (2010)

[494] Ibid.

[495] "Constitution of the United States," United States Senate, September 23, 2013; available at http://www.senate.gov/civics/constitution_item/constitution.htm

[496] *Pennsylvania and the Federal Constitution, 1787-1788*, 277.

[497] *The Debates in the Several State Conventions on the Adoption of the Federal Constitution,* Volume II, 362.

[498] The Federalist No. 33, in *The Federalist*, 207.

[499] The Federalist No. 78, in *The Federalist*, 524.

[500] James Madison, *Notes of Debates in the Federal Convention of 1787*, 305-306.

[501] Marbury v. Madison, 5 US (1 Cranch) 137 (1803).

[502] *The Debates in the Several State Conventions on the Adoption of the Federal Constitution,* Volume III, 464.

CHAPTER 9
THE PROBLEM AND THE PROPER RECOURSE

[503] George Washington, Farewell Address (1796) in *George Washington: Writings*, 968.

[504] *The Debates in the Several State Conventions on the Adoption of the Federal Constitution,* Volume III, 45.

[505] See *Signers of the Constitution: Historic Places Commemorating the Signing of the Constitution*, Edited by Robert Ferris (Washington: United States Department of the Interior, 1976), 138. The delegates at the Philadelphia Convention were overwhelmingly Protestant. Only two, Daniel Carroll and Thomas Fitzsimons, were Roman Catholic.

[506] Brown v. Allen, 344 US 443 (1953).

[507] *The Debates in the Several State Conventions on the Adoption of the Federal Constitution,* Volume II, 46.

[508] Ibid, 47.

[509] Ibid, 283.

[510] Ibid, 317-318.

[511] James Madison, *Notes of Debates in the Federal Convention of 1787*, 82-83 87.

[512] Arthur Garrison, *Supreme Court Jurisprudence in Times of National Crisis, Terrorism, and War: A Historical Perspective* (Lanham: Rowman & Littlefield, 2011), 92; Andrew Napolitano, *Theodore and Woodrow: How Two American Presidents Destroyed Constitutional Freedoms* (Nashville, Thomas Nelson, 2012), 228-229; Roy Talbert, *Negative Intelligence: The Army and the American Left, 1917-1941* (Jackson: University Press of Mississippi, 1991), 141.

[513] This is the first portion of the preamble to the United States Bill of Rights. While it is rarely printed alongside most facsimiles, it serves as an important factor showing the intention of the first ten amendments to the Constitution and the limitations made toward the general government on behalf of the ratifying states.

[514] *The Debates in the Several State Conventions on the Adoption of the Federal Constitution,* Volume I, 354.

[515] Ibid, 358-363.

[516] Barron v. Baltimore, 32 US 250 (1833).

[517] Congressional Globe of the 39th Congress, 1st Session, 1866, 2883; Joseph James, *The Framing of the Fourteenth Amendment* (Chicago: University of Illinois Press, 1966), 161; Charles Fairman, "Does the Fourteenth Amendment Incorporate the Bill of Rights?" Stanford Law Review 2, No. 1 (1949): 77.

[518] Raoul Berger, *Government by Judiciary: The Transformation of the Fourteenth Amendment*, Second Edition (Indianapolis: Liberty Fund, 1997), 219.

[519] Raoul Berger, *Government by Judiciary: The Transformation of the Fourteenth Amendment*, 173.

[520] Ibid, 171.

[521] Prudential Ins. Co v. Cheek, 259 US 543 (1922).

[522] See David Bernstein, "Equal Protection for Economic Liberty: Is the Court Ready?" Cato Institute Policy Analysis, No. 181, October 5, 1992; available at http://object.cato.org/sites/cato.org/files/pubs/pdf/pa181.pdf; Raoul Berger, *Government by Judiciary*, 186.

[523] Quoted in Ibid, 222.

[524] Robert Bork, *The Tempting of America: The Political Seduction of the Law* (New York: Touchstone, 1990), 94.

[525] Leslie Hatamiya, *Righting a Wrong: Japanese Americans and the Passage of the Civil Liberties Act of 1988* (Stanford: Stanford University,1993), Appendix B.

[526] Korematsu v. United States, 323 US 217-218, 224 (1944).

[527] Ibid, 323 US 240.

[528] Ibid, 323 US 233.

[529] Ibid, 323 US 234.

[530] Ex parte Mitsuye Endo, 323 US 300 (1944).

[31] Hirabayashi v. United States, 320 US 92, 101 (1943).

[32] The Federalist No. 47, in *The Federalist*, 326.

[33] Harold C. Relyea, *Presidential Directives: Background and Overview, Congressional Research Service, CRS Report for Congress,* Number 98-611, July 16, 1998, 1.

[34] Theodore Roosevelt, *The Autobiography of Theodore Roosevelt*, Edited by Wayne Andrews (New York: Octagon, 1975), 282.

[535] Thomas Woods, "Theodore Roosevelt and the Modern Presidency," Ludwig von Mises Institute, October 19, 2013; available at https://mises.org/library/theodore-roosevelt-and-modern-presidency

[536] Ralph Ketcham, James Madison: A Biography (Charlottesville: University of Virginia, 1971), 436.

[537] Alexander Hamilton and James Madison, *The Pacificus-Helvidius Debates of 1793-1794*, Edited by Morton Frisch (Indianapolis: Liberty Fund, 2007), 60-64.

[538] *The Debates in the Several State Conventions on the Adoption of the Federal Constitution,* Volume IV, 74, 120-121, 356.

[539] Quoted in Thomas Woods, *33 Questions About American History You're Not Supposed to Ask*, 92.

[540] Thomas Jefferson to John Taylor, November 26, 1798, in Thomas Jefferson, *The Writings of Thomas Jefferson: Correspondence*, 260.

[541] This is based on a projected population of approximately 321 million residents in the United States. See "Annual Estimates of the Resident Population: April 1, 2010 to July 1, 2015," United States Census Bureau; September 5, 2015; available at https://www2.census.gov/programs-surveys/popest/tables/2010-2015/state/totals/PEPANNRES.pdf

[542] Dave Benner, "Montana: Staying the Course over REAL ID," Tenth Amendment Center, February 13, 2014; available at http://blog.tenthamendmentcenter.com/2014/01/montana-staying-the-course-over-real-id. The anti-commandeering doctrine asserts that even when the federal government exercises its constitutional authority, states are not obliged to cooperate by assisting with the implementation of federal law. When forced to rule on the issue, even the Supreme Court has recognized the legitimacy of this notion. See the opinions of *Prigg v. Pennsylvania* (1842), *New York v. United States* (1992), *Printz v. United States* (1997), and *Independence Business v. Sebelius* (2012) for additional information on this topic.

[543] "House Bill No. 1439, 97th General Assembly," Missouri House of Representatives, February 13, 2014; available at http://www.house.mo.gov/billtracking/bills141/biltxt/intro/HB1439I.htm

[544] Ibid.

[545] Marshall Griffin, "Missouri Senate Sends Gun Control Nullification to Mo. House; House Version Passes Committee," St. Louis Public Radio, Feb 21, 2014; available at https://news.stlpublicradio.org/post/missouri-senate-sends-gun-control-nullification-bill-mo-house-house-version-passes-committee; Debbie Bryce "Nullifying Federal Gun Laws in Idaho: Gov Butch Otter Signs Senate Bill 1332 Into Law," Idaho State Journal, March 25, 2014; available at https://www.idahostatejournal.com/members/nullifying-federal-gun-laws-in-idaho-gov-butch-otter-signs/article_97429e26-b3f0-11e3-8581-001a4bcf887a.html

[546] Jacob Kastrenakes, "Maryland Lawmakers Want to Cripple the NSA's Headquarters," The Verge, February 11, 2014; available at https://www.theverge.com/2014/2/11/5401398/nsa-hq-water-electricity-cut-off-maryland-bill

[547] Mike Maharrey, "New Maryland Legislation Targets Water, Electricity to NSA Headquarters," Tenth Amendment Center, February 13, 2014; available a

http://tenthamendmentcenter.com/2014/02/10/new-maryland-legislation-targets-water-electricity-to-nsa-hq

[548] Thomas Jefferson to Thomas Lomax, March 12, 1799, in *Thomas Jefferson: Writings*, 1062.

Made in United States
Troutdale, OR
01/09/2024

16822832R00217